NOTHING

LESS THAN

FULL

VICTORY

An Association of the U.S. Army Book

NOTHING LESS THAN FULL VICTORY

EDWARD G. MILLER

Americians at War in Europe, 1944–1945

Naval Institute Press
Annapolis, Maryland

Naval Institute Press
291 Wood Road
Annapolis, MD 21402

Library of Congress Cataloging-in-Publication Data

Miller, Edward G., 1958–
Nothing less than full victory : Americans at war in Europe 1944–1945 / by Edward G. Miller.
    p. cm.
Includes bibliographical references and index.
ISBN-13: 978-1-59114-494-6 (alk. paper)
ISBN-10: 1-59114-494-9 (alk. paper)
1. United States. Army—History—World War, 1939–1945. 2. World War, 1939–1945—Campaigns—Western Front. I. Title.
D769.M56 2007
940.54'1273—dc22

                                                              2006033529

Printed in the United States of America on acid-free paper ♾

14 13 12 11 10 09 08 07   9 8 7 6 5 4 3 2
First Printing

Frontispiece courtesy U.S. Coast Guard.

To the 135,576 soldiers
killed in combat in the
European Theater of Operations,
6 June 1944 – 8 May 1945

"And I heard the voice of the Lord saying, 'Whom shall I send? And who will go for us?' Then I said, 'Here I am. Send Me.'"

—Isaiah 6:8, RSV

CONTENTS

MAPS

PREFACE

THIS BOOK IS about development and change, or "transformation" of an Army at war. Specifically, it is about the triumph of American ground troops over great odds to defeat what was arguably one of the most proficient armies in history, and it is a first attempt to set the record straight regarding GI performance against the complete background of logistics, organization, training, and deployment—areas that even military professionals sometimes neglect to consider. The setting is the 1944–1945 campaign in Western Europe—the largest, and arguably the most important, ground campaign in American history. The focus, however, is not on the strategic picture. Rather, it is on the individual soldier and the small unit, where, as one veteran remarked to me, "they do the dying." The story that follows is not well known, yet it is vital to helping general audiences and professionals alike understand what this nation accomplished over six decades ago. Weapons and doctrine change, but war and soldiers do not. No weapon exists which eliminates fear and uncertainty from fighting a war. In the fundamental human respect, combat in the twenty-first century is remarkably similar to what it was generations ago. Goals and enabling technology change, but man does not.

When war came to Europe, the U.S. Army was a third-rate ground force with some senior generals who still believed in the relevance of horse cavalry. Four years later, it was engaged in a global war and using rudimentary electronic computers. Between 1940 and 1944, the Army grew from about 145,000 to over 8,000,000 soldiers. GIs in 1944 were using doctrine, organizations, and weapons that did not exist a few years before. A major in 1940 might be in command of a 15,000-soldier division four years later. Men in college when the war began might be in charge of eight-hundred-soldier battalions in 1945. Teenagers needing a good job in 1941 might be first sergeant of a 190-soldier rifle company by the time they were twenty-two years of age. Responsibility for lives came quickly. Recruiting, organizing, training, employing, and sustaining

the Army, while simultaneously developing new processes and procedures for its organization and operation, remain an impressive feat over
six decades later. From a handful of small posts scattered across the continental United States, the Army's real estate portfolio grew to one comparable to the size of the state of Michigan. Combat and logistical units
operated at the end of 100,000 miles of supply lines. An Army with little
more than promise at first took the lead in planning, launching, and supporting one of the most complex and important operations in the history
of warfare—the cross-Channel attack into France. The world had not
seen anything like it before, and it will likely not see it again.

It is unfortunate that scholars and the general public alike still look
at these events and assume that the Army's success was somehow preor-
dained. They see production statistics and believe that a flood of material
reached the foxholes in time to be employed against a worn-down, poorly
equipped, and beaten enemy. Lacking real-world experience in planning
and managing logistics, such observers fail to consider the vagaries of
weather and terrain or of synchronizing complex timetables for global
movements and resupply in their general conclusions about the relative
effectiveness of armies. In fact, the German soldier often had a technological edge, and the *relative* odds at the front were often close at least
through the beginning of 1945. Many observers have spent more time
excusing German performance than trying to determine why the
Americans did as well as they did under the circumstances. German generals often attributed their defeat to American technology and weight of
numbers rather than to their own inadequacies and a nearly obsessive
focus on tactical execution to the exclusion of those activities required for
generating combat power.

Americans on the eve of World War II heard from pundits that technology—for example, strategic bombers—would be the decisive factor in
a future war. Because wars have been and will continue to be decided by
physical contact and occupation of territory, technology cannot be decisive without the will to employ ground forces in close combat. It took
some time for the public and those in positions of responsibility in government and business to accept what thinking soldiers had always known:
there was only one path to victory over such an efficient and professionally led opponent as the German military. Because Germany was fundamentally a continental power, its army was the main target, and it was
possible to ensure its defeat only by a direct ground attack. High-tech
weapons would not by themselves decide the outcome; as appealing as
technology was, such weapons would not by themselves decide the

outcome of the war in any theater. Yet the decisive weapons, the GIs in the foxholes and in support, were not as well supplied and supported as people think. They often lacked tank and anti-tank support. Their clothing was inadequate for the worst winter in decades. Poor weather often negated the effectiveness of air and artillery support. Hasty training and replacement of combat casualties exposed men to needless risk. U.S. machine guns were substandard compared to those in German hands, and the Germans had many more of them to begin with. Troops also had to contend with instances of poor support on the home front. The Germans, as hard pressed as they were, had better combat vehicles, more automatic weapons in the infantry units, and the advantages inherent in fighting a defensive battle. Their artillery was often present in a comparable number to that supporting the Americans. The German military tradition and emphasis on small-unit leadership were superior to those of the United States, and the impact was sometimes telling indeed. It is true that American rearmament had a decisive and global impact on the outcome of World War II, but there is also a considerable gap between potential and performance. Hardware means little unless soldiers are trained and adequately supported in their effort to bring power to bear at the decisive place and time on the battlefield. America fought a capable, determined, and tough opponent on the ground.

Having lived with the bloodletting of World War I, the British did not believe early in World War II they had the resources to support a direct attack into Germany, and they pressed hard for years for a strategy of winning on the periphery of the continent. They did not put their full weight toward the invasion until 1943, when it was clear that America would start contributing the majority of resources. The Americans, on the other hand, pressed hard for a decisive campaign aimed directly at the war-making capacity of the enemy. There was a lot riding on the shoulders of the GI—there would be no second chance to defeat Germany. The U.S. Army did not do well at first. Its performance was so disturbing that senior British officers wondered if it could ever make a substantive contribution to the defeat of Germany. They doubted the wisdom of the American emphasis on the direct attack.

There is little wonder that they did so. On its own initiative after World War I, America had rendered its army less potent than Germany's under the Treaty of Versailles. Lack of money hampered or stopped much basic research and development, and conservatively thinking generals shut out many new concepts. Yet between 1940 and the end of the war, the Army successfully transformed itself from a constabulary to a global power.

It operated on a scale that dwarfed the forces of the other combatants—even the Soviet Union had shorter lines of supply. It modernized equipment and changed its approach to fighting. During the actions described in this book alone, Americans fought in deserts, cities, mountains, littorals, and farms. This is why industrial output alone cannot account for its success against the Germans. Will, spirit, character, and courage were key. Soldiers could not rely on material to do the hard work for them.

No book can be the last word on a historical topic. For example, specific research in the field of logistics is needed to lay to rest once and for all the issue of the "broad-front" and "narrow-front" strategy. Additional research will also continue to reveal not only *what* happened but also *why* events unfolded as they did. This book is only a start, as it describes small-unit combat as carried out in the 12th U.S. Army Group between D-Day and VE Day against the background of events that led up to the campaign in Western Europe. Telling this kind of story requires the study of thousands of documents, often prepared under stressful conditions. Staff officers themselves were sometimes confused about times, locations, and the identification and strength of enemy units. Fatigue and fear played a role in the accuracy with which events were reported. Even the combat historians assigned by the War Department to record events shortly after they happened faced a daunting task. Describing the German side is hard, of course, because of lack of detailed records. However, it is possible to gain a picture detailed enough to allow evenhanded comparisons.

I have been lucky over the last twenty years to be able to spend many days walking the ground where the events described in this book happened. I am responsible for any errors in the following pages. However, numerous people have made this work rewarding and enjoyable; they include soldier-historian colleagues like Roger Cirillo, Doug Nash, Mark Reardon, and Rob Rush. Civilian historians who have provided valuable counsel include Edward "Mac" Coffman, Chris Gabel, Steve Lofgren, and Larry Kaplan. In addition to veterans mentioned in the text, notes, and bibliography with whom I have corresponded or talked, others who have assisted me include the late Keith "Kit" Bonn; Calvin C. Boykin, Mary Ellison, William O. Hickok, Les Leggett, *Donald Marsh*, Edward J. Malouf, Tom MacKnight, and Steven L. Ossad. In Europe, there are William C.C. Cavanagh, Hubert Gees, Gevert Haslob, Andre Meurisse, Klaus Schulz, and Günter von der Weiden. I must also thank my wife, Connie, for suffering through visits to battlefields in all kinds of weather, and our daughter, Catherine, who at age six made her first trip to the Hürtgen Forest.

INTRODUCTION
NIGHT PATROL

H OVEN, GERMANY, MIDNIGHT, 30 December 1944: Lt. Everett E. Pruitt, a twenty-seven-year-old native of Texas, motioned the six men of his reconnaissance patrol to move out toward German lines. Wet snow covered the ground. What had been a lingering rain was turning to sleet. Pruitt's weary men stepped past other physically and mentally exhausted GIs hunkered in damp foxholes. They whispered to the patrol that they were glad someone else was going out that night.

Pruitt was leader of the 415th Infantry Regiment's Intelligence and Reconnaissance Platoon, then operating northeast of the city of Aachen, Germany. His orders were to cross the Roer River (it ran generally parallel to the regiment's front line), penetrate the enemy defenses without detection, and bring back a couple of prisoners for interrogation. The regiment's intelligence officer needed to know why vehicle traffic was increasing behind the enemy lines. His commander was concerned that the regiment would have a hard time holding off a major counterattack. A German offensive several miles to the south was in its second week, and the fighting was extremely heavy. There would be no reinforcements to speak of if the Germans attacked here, too, and the regiment's rifle companies were at no more than 60 percent of their authorized strength of 193 soldiers.

Col. John Cochran, commander of the 415th, had personally selected Pruitt to lead the I&R Platoon. It operated independently to gain information on the enemy and the terrain. The platoon leader had to be resourceful and act in the absence of orders. He also had to ensure that each of his sergeants was trained well enough to take charge of the platoon if he were wounded or killed. Cochran allowed Pruitt to select any man in the regiment that he wanted. Each of them had to have a superb military record and be in top physical condition. Ideally, they would have played varsity sports in high school or college. Pruitt's standards were high, and he demanded perfection. He permitted himself no luxury that his men did not also receive. "They made an unbeatable team," recalled a former staff officer.

A machine-gun position a few hundred yards to the front of the U.S. foxholes looked like a good place to get the prisoners. Three or four Germans armed with rifles and a submachine gun manned the position day and night. The GIs used an artillery telescope to identify positively the position, which they noticed was located in the median of the unfinished autobahn that ran through the area. After they confirmed the value of the objective, they used engineer survey equipment to calculate its distance. Pruitt conducted a rehearsal of the mission.

Twisted steel girders of a demolished bridge marked the Roer crossing site. It was well after midnight on 30 December before all the men had threaded their way through the structure and reached the opposite bank of the river. A few rounds of U.S. artillery thundered overhead and crashed into the river flats to mask the patrol's noise. Pruitt took a count of his men—all were present and ready to go on. No one knew they were in a German minefield.

Pvt. Duane Robey, a tall, heavyset twenty-one-year-old, brought up the rear of the column. His ultimate mission was to survive. If the Germans attacked the patrol, he was to return to American lines with whatever information about the enemy he knew at the time. He walked slowly, bent over to reduce his silhouette. While doing this, he spotted a nearly imperceptible lump in the snow. It was about 1:00 AM on 31 December.

"It was so quiet that the slightest movement by any of us could be heard. Even the snowflakes striking the ground seemed loud," recalled Robey.

His left leg suddenly jerked upward. A sledgehammer hit him in the head. His helmet and rifle flew into the darkness. When he came to, he knew that he had stepped on an anti-personnel mine. There was no feeling in the injured leg. Robey sat up and saw a mangled foot turned back on the shin.

Sgt. John Major crawled to Robey and helped him make a tourniquet from his equipment belt and a piece of the white sheet that he was wearing as camouflage. Lieutenant Pruitt and two others also crawled to Robey.

Pruitt whispered that the explosion had marked their exact location and alerted the enemy. There was no chance of getting through the rest of the minefield without losing more men. Pruitt decided to end the mission. He helped the other men pick Robey up.

"For God's sake," Robey pleaded, "don't anyone step on a mine."

Wham! Private Gaines screamed. Robey flew upward. A sharp pain hit him in the back.

Silence. Robey tried desperately to move his legs. He prayed harder than he had ever prayed before. "It was an awful big favor to ask [of God], but I began to crawl very fast with the lieutenant protecting me."

Gaines was sobbing softly. He had lost two fingers on his left hand, and his right foot was gone. The flash had burned Private Glick's hands, but he was otherwise uninjured.

Lieutenant Pruitt thought they were about fifty yards from the German machine-gun nest. Two of his six men were down, and one was injured. They were stuck in a minefield behind German lines on the wrong side of a river. There was a burst of machine-gun fire. Bullets suddenly zipped past them. Mortar rounds began to explode nearby. The Americans could see each other in the flashes. They could also see the forms of men with rifles heading toward them. It was time to get back to the Roer.

Sergeant Major followed Pruitt. Sgt. Charles Lynde covered Robey and Gaines, who were crawling. Glick and a soldier named Clark brought up the rear.

Explosion. Lynde flew back. Mine. He lost a foot and had a six-inch-long piece of jagged metal in his side. Major went to help. Pruitt told everyone else to keep moving toward the river. He and Clark now brought up the rear. They would cover the four wounded men and Sergeant Major.

Several German infantrymen, meanwhile, were working hard to get between the patrol and the river. They nearly succeeded. Seconds after the Americans reached the riverbank, the Germans opened fire. Pruitt and Clark were still a few yards behind the others. Pruitt felt a searing pain in an arm. Bullet. He kept moving anyway, and a few minutes later, he found Glick, who was in pain from the burns to his hands. Pruitt told him not to wait for the others but to get back to the regiment as fast as he could and have an observer call for mortar fire to cover the patrol. When Glick left, Pruitt waited for the others to crawl onto the remains of the bridge. As soon as he had accounted for them, he headed back to find and hold off the approaching enemy. He stopped every few seconds to fire his carbine. Perhaps the enemy would think there were several Americans nearby.

Pruitt thought he saw at least one German fall. He continued trying to draw the attention of the enemy away from his men. Robey by this time was well out on the damaged bridge. He turned to throw a couple of grenades toward sounds he thought might be Germans trying to cut them off. Dull explosions mixed with the clang of bullets hitting the metal girders and the popping sound of Pruitt's carbine from somewhere in the darkness. Sergeant Major also stopped and started firing his rifle.

It became quiet not long after that. Major hoped the fire had discouraged the enemy from following them across the river. It was only twenty yards wide at that point, but to the exhausted Americans, as long as the Germans stayed put it might as well be a thousand.

Clark then came up and whispered to Major that he could still see the Germans, silhouetted against the snow. Where was Pruitt? Major raised his rifle to fire at the approaching enemy and to signal the lieutenant that they were still waiting for him. Before he could get a shot off, though, American mortar fire began to explode on the German-held side of the river.

Private Robey, meanwhile, had limped to the base of the concrete bridge pier that he needed to cross. He could see no more damaged steel girders that he could use as a ladder. Robey summoned his last ounce of strength and climbed a heavy rope dangling from the pier. He paused at the top of the pier to catch his breath, but he was so exhausted that he simply rolled off of it and fell into the freezing water. He hit a piece of the old road surface that was only partially submerged. Robey was stunned, but he would not drown. Gaines and Lynde followed him to the pier and got across it without incident.

Pruitt, meanwhile, had reached the crossing point, but he was still on the enemy-held side of the river. After he learned that the wounded men were getting across, he went back toward the enemy to continue his one-man rear-guard battle. Major and Clark remained nearby to provide what cover to him they could under the limited visibility. They could not see much, but they heard more carbine fire.

Pruitt returned only when he was nearly out of ammunition. He whispered to Clark and Major that they should get across the Roer in order to save themselves. He unsheathed his bayonet, but before he could go back out the German infantry finally caught up. A savage, hand-to-hand fight lasted for a few minutes before the surviving Germans disappeared into the night. The Americans were not injured, and Clark left with Major for the crossing site. They took with them some documents they had found on a dead Landser. Pruitt stayed put to cover them.

German mortar rounds now began to hammer the ground around the crossing site. Snow on the rim of the craters melted, and the dirt was black with powder residue. Fragments peppered the steel debris. The injured men were so cold that their wounds no longer bled. Pruitt returned to the crossing only when he was out of bullets and grenades. Someone said that all were present except for Clark, and they headed for safety. Pruitt did not hesitate. He ran back toward the German-held side of the river to look for him. Clark, however, had half floated, half crawled, across the Roer. He yelled back that everyone was safe. Glick brought up some medics about that time (4:00 AM). Pruitt finally crossed, but he refused treatment for his own wound until the medics could look after all of his men. He helped keep Robey warm until the medics brought up a stretcher.

One of the medics who helped pick up Robey asked under his breath, "Why do we always get the big heavy ones?"

Pruitt did not have a prisoner, but he did have all his men.[1]

CHAPTER I

BEGINNINGS

AMERICA DID NOT have a modern Army when war flared in Europe in 1939. Congress did not provide even minimum funds for research and development. Weapons were obsolete, and many senior officers believed the horse still had an important place in modern combat. Future enemies had armies that numbered in the hundreds of thousands, if not millions. Except for World War I, the nation's only experience in mobilizing and moving large forces had been in the Civil War. Manuals covering common operating doctrine and the system of professional officer education were relatively new concepts.[1] Until the beginning of the twentieth century, however, the United States had no ground force responsibilities since it was only an emerging world power, and a frontier constabulary was about all the country needed. Reforms stemming from the chaos of Spanish-American War mobilization included the formation of a small general staff and efforts at centralized control of highly independent staff bureaus. A few officers gained combat experience in the Philippines (1899–1904).[2]

Congress in 1916 increased the size of the Regular Army, and National Guardsmen for the first time had to swear an oath to obey the president and defend the Constitution in addition to their traditional responsibilities to their states. The federal government would provide funds, trainers, and standard equipment. Guard units would be organized like regular units and would be the principal trained reserve force. This was important legislation, because the president could call Guardsmen to serve overseas.[3] Foreign observers remained unimpressed. A German officer reported that the enlisted men were nothing more than an amalgam of immigrants.[4] Even on the eve of entry into World War I, the Punitive Expedition into Mexico exposed significant organizational and logistic problems. The airplanes supporting the expedition were out of service within a few weeks.[5]

Not surprisingly, the new American Expeditionary Force (AEF) required considerable training upon its overseas deployment beginning

1

in mid-1917. Industrial mobilization was a problem, and foreign governments supplied much equipment (most training manuals were translations of French and British publications). French and British officers gave the AEF mixed reviews, though a French report of October 1918 said the troops performed "splendidly." A British report prepared the same month said the Army was not well organized, equipped, or trained. It was "ignorant" of modern war, and it would take a year to become "a serious fighting force."[6] Staff work was not bad, considering that no American had ever planned for the movement and supply of such large bodies of troops across thousands of miles of ocean. Well-documented logistic problems led to near paralysis at the front in the final weeks of the war.[7] Rapid expansion of the Regular Army and Guard led to critical shortages of experienced noncommissioned officers (NCOs) and junior officers. Communications from the front to the rear were usually poor, and adjacent units often lost contact with one another. An inadequate personnel replacement system forced the breakup of some divisions and use of their soldiers as replacements for combat losses. Yet no one claimed the individual soldier was anything but brave and dedicated.

As a result, the AEF was less prepared for what its commander termed "open warfare" than it was for "smothering German machine guns with American flesh."[8] Compounding the problems were conflicts over the relationship between the War Department and the AEF. General Pershing was answerable only to the secretary of war and the president, and he operated virtually independently of the War Department and the chief of staff, Gen. Peyton C. March, who had to think about raising and training an army to send Pershing in the first place. Unlike his relatively weak predecessors, March was tough and focused. He established the modern foundation of the chief of staff as the senior army officer, regardless of the position of the overseas theater commander. This served the nation well in its biggest test, during World War II and it is unfortunate that March's accomplishments have remained so obscure to many military historians.[9]

Complacency bred in victory, disillusionment with foreign affairs, the protection of two oceans, and unprecedented domestic changes led to public disinterest in external matters after the war. Congress in 1920 passed a defense bill that authorized the president to use the Guard only when Congress approved mobilization of soldiers in excess of the strength of the Regular Army, and it established a new organization based on geographic areas with assigned Regular, Organized Reserve, and Guard divisions. However, the bill also reflected intellectual discord and internal wrangling that effectively delayed the development of modern combat doctrine for two decades. The legislation also abolished the wartime tank corps and placed tank development in the hands of the infantry.[10] Without the threat of armed invasion, and with hundreds of millions of dollars' worth of leftover equipment, there was no incentive to spend money on a large standing army or on research and development. The world simply passed by the U.S. Army. Businessmen, whose votes counted for something in Washington, understood the need for a strong navy to guard shipping lanes, but they could see no reason to modernize ground forces. Too few people understood that modern equipment like tanks and electronic equipment had lengthened the time needed to build, train, and equip forces. The average lag time between design and provisioning grew from months to years.[11]

Congress went too far in cutting appropriations for the Army, and successive administrations failed to prove to the public the importance of retaining quality soldiers and modern equipment. It is said that soldiers at a post near Chicago were allowed only a single light bulb on their barracks floor, and reportedly the toilet-paper ration in one infantry regiment was limited to three sheets per soldier per day.[12] By 1926, the strength of the Regular Army was under 136,000 men, though it was authorized over 280,000.[13] Because Congress would not appropriate funds to support the manpower authorized under the law, the War Department had to inactivate ground units to man an expanding Air Corps.[14] The problem was that some ground units were already so far below strength that they could not even conduct their own training, much less that of the Guard and Reserve. Generals also shared the blame for the lack of readiness. They sometimes sent mixed signals to Capitol Hill, and congressmen complained that staff officers would not give them clear answers during budget hearings. Federal law prohibited executive branch officials (including military officers) from publicly stating disagreement with budget submissions from the White House, and while some generals complained privately about lack of funds and personnel, many also maintained an unrealistic, but all too public, "can do" attitude.[15]

Annual War Department reports give a good overview of the situation. During the Depression, for example, Congress directed the Army to organize and train the Civilian Conservation Corps (CCC). While officers assigned to the CCC got some experience in managing lower-level operations, their departure from Reserve Officer Training Corps and National Guard duty to do so ultimately led to the neglect of units that would be involved in a mobilization. Training came to a virtual standstill.[16] The budget for the Regular Army between fiscal 1932 and fiscal 1934 fell from $285.6 million to $182 million. Such reductions kept the War Department from maintaining a minimum structure for mobilization. Congress even disapproved a request for only enough tanks to equip one mechanized cavalry brigade and two infantry tank regiments. This decision came after the chief of staff, Douglas MacArthur, reported that the "trend in warfare is toward greater speed of strategic maneuver through maximum utilization of relatively fast machines for transportation; increased firepower on the battlefield . . . wider dispersion in tactical formations . . . [and] combat vehicles invulnerable to small-arms fire and capable of cross-country travel; growing dependency upon air forces for information."[17] He later said that "we are compelled to train and prepare the Army too distinctly on the 1918 pattern, whereas our effort should be to a look ahead and mold it to the requirements of future emergencies."[18] His successor, Malin Craig, remarked as late as 1938 that the Army had no effective anti-tank weapon; it needed searchlights, anti-aircraft guns, and fire control equipment. War reserves of ammunition were "far short of requirements."[19]

Well-intentioned civilians convinced that intervention in World War I had been a grave mistake became committed to the abolition of war and launched campaigns against the producers of war materiel. The Depression added to the gloom. Still, a few major publications, such as *Fortune*, warned that the armed forces were only as good as the public chose to make them. Thinking people, said the editors, understood that the military required a balance of men, materiel, and transport to carry out national strategy. But, they added, "the soldier [was] an unpleasant intrusion of fact upon [the civilian's] dogged faith in a warless world. The civilian would like to believe that if there were no soldiers, there would be no war."[20]

The officer corps retreated behind the gates of the installations and turned inward to social events like polo, receptions, and parties where alcohol flowed freely. Careers often depended upon success at coaching unit sports or upon relentless networking with senior officers to gain beneficial assignments like troop command. The seniority system led to fifty-year-old majors and a decade or more at the same rank. A future chief of staff recalled that it was a matter of some note when a unit received a recruit with a high school diploma. Junior officers had to struggle to make ends meet, and it is little wonder that the Depression went largely unnoticed among them. [21] Voluntary enlistment had resumed in 1919, after the end of the wartime draft, and enlistment incentives included retention of wartime rank and choice of unit, duty, or place of assignment. Sergeants ran the units. Junior enlisted men seldom spoke directly to officers, and they usually used the third person when they did. Civilian businessmen living near the small bases got interested in the Army only on payday. Drunkenness and fights between soldiers, or between soldiers and civilians, were common. Enlisted men received a uniform allowance, medical care, barracks housing (such as it was), and meals. It was a good deal for many who otherwise might have had not steady incomes or prospects of regular medical care. Until the pay cuts of the early 1920s, recruits received thirty dollars per month (more than in 1941), but the weekly pay of an unskilled private-sector worker at the time was about twenty-seven dollars per week.

Living conditions for most married enlisted men, and for many married junior officers, were often substandard and sometimes worse. Some families had to use community baths and toilets. Several families at Fort Benning, Georgia, lived in shacks without indoor plumbing. Some enlisted barracks were little more than huts that were freezing in the winter and blistering hot in the summer. Tight budgets and the increasing cost of food even led to cuts in mess hall fare. The desertion rate reached a staggering 7.4 percent of enlistments during one year. Continual reductions in strength led to demotion of even the best soldiers to meet the budgeted payroll. There was at least one reported murder-suicide (sergeant/wife) resulting from the stress of a pay cut. About all the War Department could do was place demoted men at the head of otherwise frozen promotion lists.[22]

Fortune magazine described the soldier as a "mixture of the clergy, the college professor and the small boy playing Indian. . . . He easily sinks to the level of the people's poor relation. . . . Yet in spite of the fact that the Army man is relieved of many of those shocks and problems that make life heroic, he strikes a note that is almost universal in human nature. The Sam Browne belts, the brief unqualified commands, the perpetual acknowledgment of salutes, the blind worship of rank, are manifestations of the primitive that lies hidden in almost every one of us." *Fortune* also noted that the Army had fewer troops in the continental United States available for combat than the British had sent against the colonies during the Revolutionary War. It pointed out that the high morale of the German army under Hitler was something "forever beyond the scope of the U.S. Army in peacetime," given its place in American society.[23]

About the only bright spot in an otherwise dismal time was the character and potential of some officers who remained in the Army. Elwood R. "Pete" Quesada, who pioneered close-air-support doctrine, was a product of the period.[24] George Patton, of course, could afford to stay in the Army. In late 1927, Lt. Col. George C. Marshall became assistant commandant of the Infantry School at Fort Benning; Gen. Henry H. Arnold, chief of the Army Air Forces in World War II, called Marshall "as strong a body of military genius as I have ever known."[25] Student officers at Benning learned the tactics and techniques of infantry operations and received an introduction to the workings of the rest of the Army. Unfortunately, the lack of modern equipment often prevented field testing of classroom theory.[26] Other service schools, such as cavalry, artillery, and engineer, produced noted World War II leaders, but many of the top generals met their future chief of staff at Fort Benning—Omar N. Bradley, J. Lawton Collins, Clarence R. Huebner, Terry de la Mesa Allen, Charles T. Lanham, and Norman D. Cota. Courtney H. Hodges, who commanded the First Army during most of the European Theater of Operations (ETO) campaign, was not one of Marshall's students, but he worked with him at Fort Benning.[27]

Marshall emphasized basics and wanted students to think on their feet. He recruited good staff and did not interfere with them. He forced the school to adopt solid and simple training philosophies, and he steered the instructors from an emphasis on formality and perfection toward improvisation based on common principles. Training standards remained high; Marshall saw to it that students gave oral defenses of their solutions.[28] Instructors and students often gathered at each other's quarters to informally discuss economics, geopolitics, or sociology in a military context.[29] Marshall left Fort Benning in June 1932 and later served with the Illinois National Guard. He did not predict the impact of the tank and the plane on future war, but he did understand the potential of such forces to disrupt enemy communications and supply.[30]

The leaders of World War II who came of age during the interwar years were generally capable men, and a few were brilliant. Those who adapted to the organizational mold were more likely to gain the career "sponsor" so necessary for the climb up the promotion ladder. The system did not always allow the best to get ahead, but it prevented the advancement of many incompetents. On the other hand, some of the future leaders "displayed serious flaws in conception and execution." They failed to grasp the compressed decision-making parameters of modern war. Maybe too many of them were more prudent than daring. But it was indeed fortunate for the nation that enough good soldiers of all ranks accepted the low pay and hardships of Depression-era service in trade for interesting assignments, travel, interpersonal exchange, and routine. The late Martin Blumenson remarked that, given the conditions of the time, "how our small interwar Army produced the leadership that got us successfully through [World War II] remains in large part a miracle, and like most miracles, a mystery."[31] Maybe this is the only explanation for future success, because there is none in funding, equipping, public acceptance, or a national tradition that respected military service outside of wartime.

CHAPTER 2

FROM FACTORY TO FOXHOLE, 1940-1942

L EADERS WATCHED EVENTS around the world, particularly what happened in Europe after Germany's invasion of the Low Countries and France in 1939–1940. Most Americans were ambivalent, hoping that the trouble overseas would not worsen the Depression. They accepted the premise that the Navy was the first line of defense, and there was little prospect anyway that war would reach the continental United States. Despite the prevailing sentiment, Gen. George C. Marshall, appointed as chief of staff of the Army on 1 September 1939, told the House Appropriations Committee in February 1940, "We must put our house in order before the sparks reach the Western Hemisphere." He wanted to focus attention on the need to expedite modernization and expansion of the Regular Army, which remained well below that authorized in the 1920 legislation.[1] The immediate source of manpower short of a draft was the National Guard. Federalization of this component, however, was a question official Washington dared not mention publicly. Yet the Organized Reserve consisted largely of "paper" units and the only solution to the manpower shortage would be a draft (Selective Service). Yet even had the manpower been instantly available, no amount of money could quickly erase two decades of neglect. As late as fiscal 1939 research and development constituted only 1.1 percent of the War Department budget. The ordnance arsenal system, responsible for manufacturing test items and limited quantities of wartime requirements, "looked like . . . a plant that had been abandoned for 20 years."[2]

Had Hitler's military been able to threaten the United States directly, there is little doubt he would found humorous the revelation that one young man from Tennessee brought his rifle when he registered for the draft. When asked if he had ever been an inmate, he responded that he had been hospitalized once for an appendectomy. Despite accusations that the nation's college students were soft and lacking the will to take on the obligation of military service, a poll found that most thought the country was worth fighting for. Selective Service registration, which began in the late summer of 1940, in the end went smoothly despite a broad-based national debate about its worth and legitimacy.[3]

Congress also intensely debated the military appropriation bills for fiscal 1941. Roosevelt had declared a national emergency after the German invasion of Poland, and this declaration was the basis for much emergency planning. However, Congress tried to save money and prepare for conflict at the same time. Members of the War Department subcommittee reminded General Marshall that the nation was still in an economic depression. To his credit, Marshall urged Congress nevertheless to fund the Army's full request for ammunition, rifles, tanks, and other equipment for a million soldiers and replacements. "They would be like gold in the vault against a financial crisis," he testified, referring to the growing lead time between design, production, and fielding of complex weapons.[4] The Army would at any rate have been hard pressed to improve quickly. Maneuvers revealed that even basic unit organizations were hopelessly obsolete.[5] *Time* magazine compared Hitler's army to its American counterpart and concluded that the latter "looked like a few nice boys with BB guns."[6]

Mobilization and Industry

RUDIMENTARY ATTEMPTS to organize industry on a national basis had first appeared during the Civil War, but until World War I the concept of reallocation of resources to support a mass army received little attention beyond talk and outline planning. The World War I effort saw competition with the Navy for resources and production capacity. Centralized army supply bureaus did little more than quarrel with each other. Washington created agencies to coordinate purchasing and allocate resources, but it never overcame shipping and material shortages.[7] When Germany invaded France in 1940, the Army did not have enough anti-aircraft guns to defend a single city. Its coast artillery guns had been idle for years. There were only fourteen modernized 105-mm howitzers and eighteen relatively modern medium tanks. Even as late as Pearl Harbor there were only 597 new-model 105-mm towed howitzers and only sixty-five of a then-required three hundred 155-mm guns. Searchlights, assault boats, trucks, and general supplies of every description were still critically short. Construction of new plants for ammunition and equipment began, and it continued around the clock.[8]

To understand further how events unfolded for the GI fighting in the ETO, it is important to review more issues related to production. While the collective memory of the World War II industrial effort enshrines icons like "Rosie the Riveter," there was in reality considerable labor unrest, along with problems in contracting, plant construction, and ordnance production. Racial strife was simmering in the industrial cities of the North and Midwest. Segments of the business community were reluctant to cooperate with the government. One historian has argued, "Public opinion was not only confused and contradictory during the war, but also manifested a callous, selfish and uncaring streak" that ultimately affected the soldier in the field.[9]

Expansion of production actually began comparatively late—there were still 8,000,000 unemployed in 1940—and total industrial output was relatively flat after 1942. Consumer spending actually rose, and while there were some sacrifices in basic goods (rationing of rubber, gasoline, and certain foods), department-store windows were often full of consumer items.[10] Entry of black workers into industries they had not previously occupied in numbers led to aggravated tensions and strikes. Though some labor leaders encouraged integration, the rank and file was often slow to accept change. Bloody riots in Detroit in 1943 left thirty-four dead and six hundred injured. An October 1943 strike at Western Electric's (a key producer of communications equipment) Baltimore plant began over integrated washrooms; the War Department took over and ran the plant for several months when it learned that production had fallen nearly 80 percent. A 1944 transit strike in Philadelphia began when competing unions disagreed on workforce integration. Commuter absenteeism at the Philadelphia Navy Yard was 72 percent on the first day after the strike vote. Roosevelt put the Army in charge of the transit system, and two regiments of infantry then training at nearby Fort Dix, New Jersey, ran it for two weeks; these soldiers lost valuable training time while doing so. GIs had also saved the New Jersey tomato crop the year before. About 5,000 men stationed in the Midwest interrupted their training in 1943 to harvest grain. Aircraft manufacturers, meat packers, tire, copper mills, forges, and foundries also turned to the Army for assistance.[11]

No single agency was responsible for national industrial mobilization planning. The services in 1922 set up a Munitions Board to coordinate planning, but it did not have its own budget until 1939. One innovation was the establishment in the early 1920s of the Army Industrial College in Washington, DC, to train officers in procurement and industrial mobilization planning.[12] Officers also "surveyed" industrial capacity, and by

1941 the War Department probably had more information than the private sector on that subject. Surveys estimated the time needed to convert civilian firms to war production, and identified capacity, floor space, requirements for essential machine tools, financial condition of firms, and the availability of skilled labor.[13]

The Army, despite the impact on the individual worker, unfortunately could not allow a corporate labor record to dictate whether a firm received a contract critical to the war effort. For example, Ford was the only producer in 1940 of an urgently needed reconnaissance vehicle. It received a contract but came under fire because of its labor record. The War Department then issued invitations for several dozen firms, including Ford, to bid on the project. Ford continued to make the best offer in terms of price and delivery date, but it would not agree to collective bargaining. Chrysler received the contract, though its bid was higher than Ford's.[14] Strikes affecting defense plants jumped from twenty to fifty-seven between late 1940 and early 1941. Man-days lost to strikes increased three times between 1940 and 1941 (up from about 7.5 million to 22 million). There were even six major strikes in the first three weeks after Pearl Harbor. Four strikes in the eastern coalfields in 1943 cost over nine million man-days of production and helped spur publication of a War Department manual on plant seizures. A Teamsters Union walkout in Chicago shut down fifty-six plants doing war work, and lost man-days hit a new high of twenty-five million not long before the Normandy invasion. Strikes also affected the production of machine tools, steel, electrical equipment, trucks, small arms, chemicals, and shipping.[15]

A 1942 survey found that 17 percent of Detroit-area workers and 4 percent of those surveyed in Pittsburgh admitted to slowing production. A worker at an aircraft engine plant in Detroit who had assisted management in developing a way to increase output of a part found his locker broken into and his clothing slashed. When union representatives at a maker of machine-gun belt links learned that one female was operating four, rather than three, production units, the union demanded the company fire worker. When the company hesitated, three hundred workers threatened to strike, and the woman lost her job. At a plant making 105-mm shell casings, workers threatened to beat two colleagues who had been turning out 592 casings per hour unless they cut their output to the contract-mandated 550. Workers at an aircraft factory in Des Moines slowed production 35 percent when they received word they would not get a pay raise. Nonunion facilities also had work slowdowns. During the height of the ETO campaign in 1944, the War Department was working on plans for the conversion of business to postwar work. Unfortunately, it also was obliged to battle a widespread belief that the war was about over. Lt. Gen. Brehon B. Somervell, commander of the Army Service Forces, and the assistant secretary of war, Robert B. Patterson, appealed for a continued sense of urgency in production.[16]

Production and the Soldier

MARSHALL'S PREDECESSOR, Malin Craig, froze development of ground weapons beginning in 1937. Budgets could not support simultaneous procurement of existing materiel for training purposes and the pursuit of developmental perfection, however desirable that was. He did not want to the Army to be caught short without a minimum of deployable inventory in the event of mobilization. Unfortunately, the rapid pace of weapons development in the late 1930s rendered designs obsolescent as soon as their design was frozen for production and there was no money for last minute changes.[17] Air leaders, meanwhile, pushed incessantly for the development of strategic bombing technology and doctrine. This led to what was probably one of the most significant events in prewar military affairs. At a November 1938 White House meeting with Craig, Marshall, Arnold, and other senior administration officials, FDR announced that the United States needed more combat aircraft to strengthen its defenses. His directive to the Army to buy 10,000 planes, however, interfered with the concept of balanced rearmament favored by ground officers. Planes meant little without supporting infrastructure like improved bases, navigation aids, and spare parts. Craig offered an alternative spending plan that included bringing five regular infantry divisions to combat strength, at a time when Germany had ninety infantry and armored divisions, Italy had forty-five, and Japan had fifty divisions in China alone. Roosevelt wanted planes and apparently was not particularly interested in balanced rearmament.[18]

The War Department staff and a few senior field officers maintained—wrongly, it turned out—that not only would big guns and heavy tanks strain limited shipping resources and raw-material supplies but that they were not appropriate to modern mobile warfare. Drawing the wrong conclusions from innovations in mobility led, for example, to a decision to limit production of heavy artillery (above 155-mm caliber). Yet when it became clear that more such artillery was useful in helping mobile forces gain maneuver space, the Army faced a year-long procurement lead time. It also found itself short of ammunition as the most intense period of fighting in the ETO began in late 1944. GIs had only a standard "frozen design" 37-mm anti-tank gun until 1943. Even its replacement was a still-inadequate 57-mm piece when the Germans had developed significantly more powerful AT weapons. About two-thirds of the medium tank inventory (which was nearing obsolescence) lacked main cannon as late as autumn 1941. Fire control and sighting instruments essential to tanks, artillery, and anti-aircraft guns were in short supply until midwar. Rifle production in August 1942 was about 68,000 against a requirement of about 200,000, and it lagged for several more months. Cargo truck delivery was also behind schedule early on—large trucks were manufactured primarily by smaller firms, not GM, Ford, or Chrysler. Heavy-duty motors were in such short supply that designers considered powering trucks with small engines mounted in tandem. This shortage of heavy trucks was one of the reasons for the failure of the logistical system in France during the summer of 1944—industry produced only 2,788 heavy (5-ton and larger) trucks through January 1944 against requirements in Europe alone of 4,100. Even the ubiquitous 2½-ton cargo truck was in short supply as late as 1943.[19]

Logistics (supply, transport, maintenance, medical, and administrative services) dictated where and when the invasion of Europe would occur; it set the pace of operations and set courses of action at all levels from Washington to the battlefield. What field commanders, or even heads of state, wanted to do was one thing; what was possible logistically was another. It did little good to produce tank turrets if factories could not turn out engines; it made no sense to tie up railroad space with completed tanks if there were no cargo ships sitting at the docks to carry them overseas. There was no reason to ship the tanks overseas if there were no ports to receive them; if there were, crewmen, fuel, ammunition, radios, and spare parts needed to be ready when they were offloaded. Soldiers in the United States had to be provided with equipment for training, then supplied with other, preferably newer, materiel for battle. Overseas, they needed not only consumables like food and ammunition but replacement end-items like tanks and trucks. Combat gear had to compete with bulldozers, cranes, asphalt, cement, and prefabricated buildings for shipping space. A single armored division, for example, required shipping space for 462 jeeps, 168 medium tanks, seventy-seven light tanks, fifty-four self-propelled howitzers, and 471 cargo trucks.[20] The Army had to train, equip, transport, and maintain around the world units of every type, from rifle companies to water purification platoons; hospitals of every description; postal and administrative units; bakery units and artillery battalions.

Moving only the soldiers who went to northwest Europe was like moving Chicago four thousand miles.

In charge of it all was the Army Service Forces (ASF), responsible for procurement, storage, and distribution of everything from bandages to bridges. The ASF procured 96,000 tanks of all types, 61,000 field guns, seven million rifles, 2.3 million trucks of all sizes, and clothing for tens of millions. ASF would have ranked among the largest industrial corporations in the world in its day. It employed hundreds of thousands of civilian and military personnel, and it included the formerly autonomous branches of the Ordnance, Quartermaster, and Medical departments, the Adjutant General Department, the Signal Corps, and the Corps of Engineers. The ASF maintained a global network of supply lines and built depots, maintained ports and railroads, issued and transported supplies, and established communications facilities to control its operations. Its lines of communication eventually stretched over 100,000 miles, from the United States to India, Australia, New Caledonia, Alaska, England, Iran, Belgium, the Soviet Union, the Philippines, and Italy. It operated on a scale that no other power or combination of powers could achieve. Yet despite this effort, as later chapters of this book will show, GIs were often under-supplied at the front.[21]

Creating an Army

Lt. Charles Cawthon was a member of the 116th Infantry Regiment, Virginia National Guard. He was not a professional soldier; he was a reporter who had received his commission at a National Guard Officer Candidate School. He wore polished russet-leather riding boots (with spurs), khaki riding breeches, and an olive-drab wool tunic—a good-looking uniform better suited to a nineteenth-century parade than a modern war. His men did not know that he had borrowed it, because the Army did not have enough uniform material for its officers. The soldiers were untrained, their doctrine was out of date, and most of their weapons were obsolete. "Never has the Republic leaned even so slightly upon a greener reed, or on one more conscious of his greenness," reflected Cawthon years later.[22]

Despite this rather miserable beginning, however, the U.S. Army completed a mobilization the scope of which dwarfed anything the nation had ever attempted. Regulations, policies, and procedures for mobilization had existed for several years, but they were hopelessly inadequate. Training, duty assignment and unit organization, camp construction, the development of doctrine and procedures, the integration of technology and industry, and the development of strategy were all facets of the creation and deployment of combat power. The troops were on the receiving end of this unprecedented effort. Yet it is hard to understate the condition of the Army at the outbreak of war in Europe in late 1939. The Regular Army (including the Air Corps) had only about 170,000 enlisted men and 13,000 officers stationed at about 130 locations in the United States and overseas. There were another 200,000 Guardsmen and several thousand individual reservists whose units existed on paper only. There were no functioning field army headquarters—the level where senior commanders implemented strategy. There were not enough ordnance, quartermaster, engineer, administrative, or medical specialists. The only modern armored units were understrength. Three of the nine Regular infantry divisions had only some 50 percent of their authorized men; the other six were worse off and all of them reflected a World War I–type organization. There were not even enough soldiers to fully man the four combat divisions earmarked for defense of the continental United States and to simultaneously train the Guard and Organized Reserve.[23]

A 1939 mobilization plan had called for a balanced force of 400,000 regulars and Guardsmen to be ready to fight within a month of call-up.[24] Such plans usually looked good on paper, but they did not anticipate such decisions as FDR's regarding aircraft production. Plans addressed continental and hemispheric defense, though the Army War College during the 1930s had developed several that addressed global operations, including war against Japan and Germany.[25] Short of a contingency the Regular Army and Guard could handle alone, the country would have to depend on Selective Service (the draft) to raise a mass army. Training this force would be a problem. The Regular Army was not large enough to absorb millions of selectees. These men would have to enter a network of reception stations, unit training centers, and enlisted replacement training centers (RTCs). Plans called for local boards to assemble and transport men to induction stations, which provided physical exams and other tests designed to weed out the unfit. They were sworn in and then transported to reception centers for "classification" according to civilian skills. They also received uniforms and final immunizations and signed up for pay allotments and life insurance. The new soldiers also took the Army General Classification Test (or AGCT—see below). Men were then available for assignment to RTCs according to requisitions from the supervising corps area (or service command), and they were also considered for officer or NCO training.[26]

One way to integrate a flood of new men was to have Guardsmen do the training. Some Guard units were already partially manned and capable of absorbing draftees. Common sense dictated that the country could not wait for war before it prepared the Guard for the task, but the only way to access the organization was to federalize it. It was also clear that the Guard needed as much lead time between training and operations as it could get. In the spring of 1940, Marshall told Congress, "Personnel happens to be our tragic shortage at the moment."[27]

Concerned civic groups and private citizens were the first to lobby Congress publicly to approve a peacetime draft and federalization of the Guard. In late June 1940, Sen. Edward R. Burke (D-Nebraska) and Rep. James W. Wadsworth (R-New York) introduced a bill for peacetime selective service.[28] The public debate was bitter, but Congress in September approved federalization of the National Guard, and it passed the Selective Training and Service Act of 1940. The term of service was one year, but the Army could take no more than 900,000 men, at a minimum age of twenty-one and a maximum of thirty-six.[29] On the night of 16 September, Marshall went on radio to address the public. He said that the next six months might be "the most critical period in the history of this nation." He added, "We expect *too much of machines* [italics in original]. We fail to recognize two things: First, that the finest plane, or tank or gun in the world is literally worthless without technicians trained as soldiers—*hardened, seasoned and highly disciplined* [italics in original] to maintain and operate it; and second, that success in combat depends primarily upon the development of the trained combat team."[30]

General Headquarters, U.S. Army (GHQ), located in Washington, D.C., was responsible for organizing ground combat units and supervising their training. Brig. Gen. (later Lt. Gen.) Lesley J. McNair was commander of GHQ. Marshall called him the "brains of the Army." As important as he was to the Army of World War II, he attained nationwide notoriety only twice. During a radio address, he told the public that the purpose of an army was to make skillful killers of men. The media had a field day. His second encounter was in 1943, after he had been wounded in North Africa. Despite shell fragments in his skull and shoulder, he walked calmly to a jeep for a three-mile ride to a field hospital. This time the media wished him a speedy recovery.[31] McNair provided decisive leadership at a time when the Army and the nation needed it, though not all of his decisions on unit organization proved sound. He supervised creation of an agile and deployable force that, for reasons as varied as logistics and production, eventually proved dangerously light for the job it had to do.

Germany invaded the Soviet Union in June 1941. Congress in July began debate on extending the Selective Service Act (regulars enlisted for three years). Guardsmen, draftees, reservists, and regulars were well integrated by that time, and failure to extend the act would destroy the integrity of units on the eve of war (for example, 75 percent of the officers in two of the regular infantry divisions were by then reservists). "The virtual disbandment or immobilization of two-thirds of our trained enlisted strength and three-fourths of our trained officer personnel at this time might well involve a national tragedy," Marshall told the Senate.[32] On the other hand, morale in the training camps was a problem—*Time* called morale "a quality that a large part of the U.S. Army conspicuously has not got." Proposals for extending draftee and Guard service drew obscenities "in thousands of tents from coast to coast." *Time's* reporter noted that the regulars, airmen, and soldiers in tank and mechanized units were thrilled to be part of something new. Blacks wanted to prove they could be good soldiers. Yet half of the four hundred troops surveyed in a Guard infantry division (the Guard/draftee mix was about sixty/forty) said they would desert at the end of their mandated year of service. Troops booed a newsreel of FDR and Marshall but cheered an isolationist senator's speech. They were bored with drill, bored with kitchen police, and bored with the routine. They resented the low pay and hated the poorly fitting uniforms.[33] The bill to extend the service of the draftees and Guardsmen passed the House by a single vote, and FDR signed it in August, just a few months before America went to war.

The War Department did not believe it would ever face a shortage of quality enlistees, given the lingering unemployment of the Depression. The Army naturally wanted only the best men, and it was quick to discharge early draftees who did not meet physical and mental standards. There was no time to teach illiterates to write, treat men suffering from mild cases of venereal disease, or find a place for those who had been in serious trouble with the law. Regulations governing physical and mental standards were high for the day, but no one could apply them to an induction center that might see several hundred, if not a few thousand men, processed in a single day (one center reportedly processed 3,000 men in nine hours). Some military jobs, such as records manager, had civilian counterparts, but few white-collar occupations matched military duties. Only late in the war did the Army develop procedures to identify and hold men with special or high-demand skills until they could be assigned to units that needed them. It was simply easier to sort people by age, physical condition, and a score on the classification test.[34] Given this turbulence, it is not surprising that too many unfit men ended up in the combat arms, particularly the infantry, early on.

The Ninety-Division Gamble

IN EARLY 1941, when the Army was still without a comprehensive plan that addressed national mobilization and arms production, Gen. Marshall directed his staff to prepare an estimate of production requirements to fight a major war. FDR, meanwhile, told both the War and Navy departments to estimate the material needed "to exceed by an appropriate amount that available to our potential enemies." The result was the Army's general blueprint for mobilization, the so-called Victory Program. Its principal author was Maj. Albert C. Wedemeyer, a War Department staff officer. He and his colleagues predicted the structure of an army that did not yet exist, outlined a strategy for a war in which the United States was not involved, and provided general production figures for an industrial base still suffering from the Depression.[35] This was not the first plan to view Germany as the primary enemy in a global war, but it recognized the requirements for a ground campaign to break German will. It was an ambitious plan for a nation that had not even properly clothed all its soldiers.

The Victory Program called for the activation of 213 combat divisions, but it was apparent soon after Pearl Harbor that the Army could not meet such ambitious goals. Limitations in shipping, equipment, competing demands from the air forces, Navy, and the needs of industry and agriculture limited the manpower available for ground units. Requirements to support operations around the world led to a very large number of logistical units. Such realities, plus the continued resistance of the Soviets, led to a decision to reduce the division ceiling to only one hundred. Activations were postponed, and Marshall made a bold decision in the spring of 1944, not long before the invasion of France, to limit the number of divisions to ninety (sixty-six infantry, sixteen armored, two cavalry, one mountain, and five airborne). Inactivation of a cavalry division in May 1944 brought the total to eighty-nine that would be completely filled and maintained at strength.[36] A smaller than planned ground combat force ended up responsible for conducting what was arguably the most significant operation of the entire war. Combat units took the fight to Germany without an advantage in manpower.

Manning and Training an Army

A WINDFALL OF DOLLARS unimaginable during the Depression could not compensate for the unforgiving rush of time, and until it could digest the lessons of combat the Army had only theory on which to base its training. This program was not perfect, and it changed continually throughout the war. It should have not been surprising that combat soldiers required a level of specialized instruction equal to that of any technician, though many believed air and ground support units should have priority for the best available men. Combat soldiers had to know how to use a dozen weapons; identify and remove mines; recognize American, Allied, and enemy planes, vehicles, and equipment on a moment's notice; use captured enemy equipment; render first aid; use a radio; read a map, and navigate cross country under extreme conditions of physical and mental stress.[37]

Policy as early as the mid-1930s recognized that the fundamental purpose of training was wartime effectiveness, thus "ensuring the domestic peace and the international security of our people." Training focused on the conduct of offensive warfare, and though the intent was to ensure cooperation between arms, the infantry was acknowledged as the "basic arm."[38] Yet the infantry, which should have had its share of the most fit and self-reliant men, received a significant proportion of lower-scoring men, because of the link between classification scoring and civilian skills—combat infantryman was most assuredly not a civilian occupation. By August 1942, for example, 89.4 percent of men in the Finance Corps had scored in the top two of five classification categories; just 27.4 percent of infantrymen were in these groups. A midwar sample of 12,000 soldiers with combat specialties revealed they were below the army average in weight, intelligence, and education and were over a half-inch shorter than the average height for all soldiers.[39] The nation had failed its potential soldiers.

The Army had two broad categories of fitness for service—limited and general. When the Army abolished the limited-service category, on the grounds that the term was a stigma, nearly all men therefore qualified for general service. As a result, many men in otherwise poor physical condition accumulated in training centers, ready for worldwide assignment. After the War Department prohibited discharge of anyone who could do useful work, a handful of men who had been diagnosed with mild cases of "psycho-neurosis" also ended up in the pool of replacements for combat units. From mid-1944, medical personnel used a more comprehensive "profile" system to evaluate the soldier's general stamina, fitness, and emotional stability.[40] The shortage of combat replacements in the ETO eventually led to the assignment of most inductees, regardless of physical condition, to ground forces units, and the reclassification of men with high AGCT scores from the air and support branches. Another drain on the pool of high-quality men potentially available to the combat arms for much of the war was the Army Specialized Training Program (ASTP). It began in 1942 to provide a flow of university-trained men by offering deferments to those who entered fields like medicine and linguistics—and in anticipation of lowering the draft age to eighteen. The Army promised successful graduates the opportunity to attend OCS, though few actually went there. The program continued through 1943, even after high casualties in Sicily caused an unexpected demand for replacements. The program finally ended in early 1944, when the Army faced disbanding ten divisions and twenty-nine separate battalions in order to supply replacements. Over thirty combat divisions received an average of 1,500 students each, and many went to the infantry regiments.[41]

Leadership in the new divisions was a mix of regulars, Guardsmen, reservists, and Officer Candidate School graduates. An infantry regiment's executive officer was probably a regular (that is, a West Point graduate); one of the three battalion commanders was probably a regular, one a reserve officer, and one a Guardsman. Up to eight of twelve line company commanders were probably OCS graduates; the remaining four were likely National Guard. One regimental commander called the OCS officers "the best that I have seen in the Army, and for the job they have to do I had just as soon have them as any graduate of the Military Academy."[42] The seventeen-week OCS program produced a steady supply of qualified junior officers (though some commanders sent their low-quality men to meet quotas for candidates). There were no formal education requirements for attendance: commanders nominated men to appear before selection boards that developed their own criteria. Instruction included lectures, case studies, and conferences. Candidates had to analyze hypothetical situations, developed in the case of Infantry OCS by a World War I Medal of Honor recipient. Returning combat veterans also spoke to candidates. Cadre evaluated candidates as they held different leadership positions during field training exercises.[43]

Perhaps the most striking aspect of the unit training program was the extent of centralized control and decentralized execution exercised by Army Ground Forces (AGF) headquarters. The concept of decentralization was discussed as early as 1935.[44] AGF controlled the subject matter and other details; field commanders were responsible for carrying out training. Staff visited units by air and used phone conferences to monitor progress. The divisions that performed best in combat, especially in their first battles, were those that had avoided the worst personnel turbulence.[45] The War Department acknowledged early on that the "book" might require changes to fit special circumstances, time, and resources available.[46] The War Department also incorporated lessons from overseas theaters. As the war went on, the program called for exposure to overhead fire and the movement of tanks over foxholes. Not only was training in squad, platoon, and company tactics outlined in detail, but there were specialized programs for staff and support elements, from cooks to anti-tank gunners. By 1944, new soldiers received four hours' training in "mental conditioning" under overhead artillery fire; sixteen hours of instruction on mines and booby traps; sixteen hours on concealment and camouflage; and instruction on hasty field fortifications, patrolling, grenades, and automatic weapons. Men received ninety-four hours of instruction in platoon and squad tactics, including a live-fire course designed to introduce them to the sights and sounds of battle.[47] Unfortunately, many improvements came after the bulk of units had gone overseas.

Events simply overcame inadequate prewar plans, and they outpaced the Army's ability to produce fully trained units in time to meet deployment requirements. Yet too many postwar historians in their quest to determine every detail of a combat action however insignificant, have neglected learning about such developments and "back end" organizational processes. These historians have incorrectly assumed that the training system was flawed in concept. In fact, the system became quite sophisticated, and had the money and national political will existed before December 1941, things would no doubt have turned out differently. It is true that too many soldiers went into combat ill trained and under-equipped, but the nation could hardly have expected otherwise, given the foundation that existed in 1940–1941. What is remarkable is that the Army managed to recognize its shortcomings and correct many of them in a relatively short time. There were significant problems and poor management, but it was impossible to expect simultaneous creation, production, and deployment of a highly proficient force where none had existed before.

Performance overseas is even more impressive when one considers such facts as the following. Seventeen of sixty-three infantry divisions examined in one study lost the equivalent of at least a year's training time as a result of losing trained men to form new units.[48] Only six divisions lost no training time, and one lost the equivalent of twenty-nine months. In April 1941, the 2d Armored Division (regular) lost 687 officers and 4,875 enlisted men as cadre for another armored division.[49] The 30th Infantry Division (National Guard) declined in strength from 12,400 men in June 1942 to only 3,000 by August; its training program stopped until it received new men. The 94th Infantry Division (draftee) lost fifty-four medical officers, sixteen chaplains, and twenty-three engineer officers shortly before it went overseas in 1944. The 106th Infantry Division, destined to suffer more than most in combat, lost 12,442 of about 14,000 men during its stateside training program.[50] One division commander remarked that fewer than half of his men were physically qualified. Some replacements received before deployment were "busted down parachutists, guard house addicts."[51]

Harvey R. Frasier, who commanded an engineer battalion, later recalled that his cadre essentially trained each other. Several Hispanic draftees from the Southwest had to learn English. Other men had to be taught to sign their names.[52] Stuart Thayer was trained as a truck driver but assigned as a loader in a tank crew when he reached the 3d Armored Division. His platoon sergeant "spent about a half hour" teaching him his job.[53] Neil Burd received no training on the weapons he would later use in combat.[54] Some of Arnold Whittaker's officers had been in an infantry division that went overseas early in the war. "They used a commonsense approach to every combat objective, and not following 'the book.' I know of many instances where following the book would result in getting our asses shot off."[55] Wallace Clement commanded a tank destroyer battalion. "Lesson plans [for training] were still being developed, in fact we usually were one day behind the instructors." He thought there should have been more training in night operations, "but we learned pretty quickly in the combat zone."[56]

The 94th Division, the subject of a later chapter, received at activation only 25 percent of its authorized rifles, and some of these had been rejected as unserviceable by another division. Almost half of the initial complement of 60-mm mortars was unserviceable. Ammunition, practice mines, and flamethrowers were scarce. A change in equipment authorization levels forced the division to return some engineer equipment. When another change reinstated the authorization, the equipment was unavailable. As late as 1943, one infantry division conducted a bayonet exercise with sticks. At Fort Hood, Texas, simulated tank destroyers maneuvered against simulated tanks.[57] Unfortunately, the AGF continued to encounter problems that affected combat performance. It had to close the big California-Arizona Maneuver Area (CAMA) in April 1944 because so many of its instructors and other personnel were transferred to new units. Only twenty of the eighty-seven combat divisions of all types activated in the States received training there.[58]

Doctrine for War

THE ARMY'S FIRST BIG TEST came during the 1941 maneuvers in the southeastern United States. These maneuvers were the largest ever conducted by the Army, and their major benefit was to give some higher-level commanders experience in maneuvering large units. Armor gained status as a branch separate from the cavalry or infantry, and horse cavalry virtually ceased to exist afterward. Problems with ground-air cooperation, however, would linger for nearly three more years. The maneuvers identified the need to organize all infantry divisions along the lines of the smaller "triangular" structure of three regiments and supporting elements.[59] The public's perception of the soldier and Army changed for the better. If Sgt. Edmond C. Wilkins's comments to his mother are any indication, the Army was on the right track. The cavalryman wrote, "I have men who if we were in actual warfare there isn't a man who I couldn't trust. . . . I know how the men feel—for I have been so tired and sleepy, weak and sick, I could lay down in a dung pile and sleep my eyes out. But I have a job to do and I must get it done. I have learned that a man must have guts, guts, and more guts. So you do not have to worry about me for when the last one goes down, I will be with them."[60]

The Army's harsh experience in World War I led officers to conclude that well-equipped soldiers imbued with an "offensive spirit" could almost single-handedly destroy an enemy in battle. Victorious generals assumed that their apparently successful methods would be adequate for the next war as well, and they also assumed there was nothing more to learn. This attitude contributed to a lack of thorough analysis of foreign developments and to the surprise of the German *blitzkreig*. Too many senior officers dismissed revolutionary ideas about restoring mobility and maneuver to the battlefield through improved communications, air power, and deep maneuver.[61] Yet one general as late as 1941 publicly advocated increasing the number of horses in cavalry units that then were mechanizing.[62]

Doctrine was a reference, a point of departure, and the expressed collective knowledge of the Army. Field manuals (FMs) contained the Army's basic doctrine. FM 100-5, *Operations*, and FM 100-10, *Administration*, were the capstone publications that addressed the conduct and support of combat operations. Whether or not they had ever heard of either manual, GIs literally lived and died by their precepts, though the Army did not intend for its leaders to adhere blindly to doctrine. The 1944 edition of FM 100-5 called for simple plans aggressively executed. The manual covering infantry battalion operations said a successful commander had "aggressiveness and the ability to take decisive action."[63] Some historians and veteran professional soldiers have rightly criticized operations for unimaginative tactics, and commanders sometimes chose shallow envelopment rather than more risky alternatives aimed at annihilating large bodies of troops. It is important to note, however, that the opportunity for maneuver of the kind practiced by the Germans in Russia and North Africa was seldom present in urbanized Western Europe. Moreover, the Germans were necessarily masters of defensive warfare, and their use of terrain often negated superior American mobility.[64]

When there was time to train and learn, there was no money. When there was money (and troops), there was no time to assimilate the lessons of modern war. Strategy should have ultimately influenced the organization of the Army, but strategy was constantly developing, and the War Department had to make training and production decisions in the absence of timely and firm strategic guidance. Training camps were not ready when the troops arrived; equipment was short; morale was low; inexperienced officers and NCOs found themselves coping with responsibilities they could not have imagined before they entered the service. Turbulence hurt unit training, and policy that attempted to match soldiers' backgrounds to military jobs led to combat units receiving more than their fair share of lower-quality recruits early on. Allocation of manpower led to the decision to limit the size of the Army to one barely large enough for the task at hand. Doctrine was not entirely adequate, but the basics were available, had leaders had time to learn and practice adequately before going overseas. But time and events caught up with the Army. Chaos often reigned, but after 7 December 1941, it was up to the GI to carry the fight to the enemy. He had no choice.

CHAPTER 3

INDOCTRINATION, 1942–1943

T UNISIA, 26 NOVEMBER 1942: Lt. Freeland Daubin Jr., had the driver of his M3 Stuart light tank move toward the German Mk IV tanks, armed with 75-mm cannon. Daubin's M3 was based on a late 1930s design, armed with a 37-mm weapon and machine guns, and intended for reconnaissance and infantry support missions. Even at only about 140 yards, the Stuart's rounds bounced off the panzer's frontal armor. "In a frenzy of desperation and fading faith in their highly-touted weapon," Daubin's crew fired over eighteen rounds at the enemy, who maneuvered effortlessly to within fifty yards of the Americans. A German AP (armor-piercing) round glanced off a wadi bank and sent dirt into the M3's open hatches. To the young American officer, it seemed as if the enemy was about to use its gun to pry him physically from the desert floor. He decided to pull back. He tried to kick the driver in the shoulder to give him the order to reverse (there was no intercom), but he could not force his foot through the expended brass shell casings that filled the fighting compartment. He hurriedly crouched down in the cramped space and yelled to the driver to back out fast and zigzag while keeping the dangerously thin frontal armor facing the enemy.

A second later, a 75-mm round "literally caved in" the Stuart's frontal armor. The driver died instantly, and the man next to him was blinded and badly injured. The loader hurriedly climbed form the turret but was killed by machine-gun fire. Daubin was wounded as he escaped. Lying in a ditch, he wondered how long it would be before he was captured or killed.[1]

America's introduction to ground combat against the Germans came at a high cost. GI performance in these first battles was the product of hurried mobilization, organization, and training. Combined U.S. and

British planning after Pearl Harbor called for early commitment of American ground forces to Europe if the Germans unexpectedly gained a strategic advantage over the Soviets or if they seemed about to collapse themselves. Underpinning this was the Germany-first strategy of the Victory Program. Planners led by Marshall rightly believed that a powerful ground invasion of the European continent aimed at the heart of Germany was the best course of action to ensure the utter defeat of the most dangerous Axis power. Neither time, resources, or American public opinion would allow a lengthy peripheral strategy, especially since the Japanese and not the Germans had attacked the United States. On the other hand, the U.S. and British Combined Chiefs of Staff deadlocked not only on the means and timing of such an operation but whether to carry it out at all. Given the state of organization and training of the U.S. Army, it did not make sense to launch a cross-Channel attack in early 1943. On the other hand, FDR agreed for political reasons, over the protests of the War Department, to send U.S. troops into action during 1942, in part to garner domestic support and to satisfy Prime Minister Winston Churchill. FDR selected then–Lt. Gen. Dwight D. Eisenhower as Commander in Chief, Allied Forces.[2] At the time, the only combat operations directed against the German homeland were bombing attacks. The United States was still a relatively junior partner in the alliance, and because it was not yet supplying the majority of resources, it did not have a good negotiating position. Whether the American military leadership was willing to admit it or not, their army was not ready to take on the Germans in northwest Europe. They had little choice but to accept Roosevelt's decision to have ground troops enter combat against Germany in 1942 in North Africa.

U.S. preparations for that invasion took place in the same "atmosphere of unrelieved improvisation and haste" that characterized mobilization. Forces due to land at Casablanca under the command of Maj. Gen. George S. Patton Jr. left the States only partially equipped. He accepted shortages in equipment in order to devote more shipping space to troops.[3] Other problems included lack of training areas in Britain for the divisions that went to the United Kingdom early in 1942, such as the 1st Armored (regular, but filled out with draftees), commanded by Maj. Gen. Orlando Ward. The division G-3, then Maj. Hamilton Howze, said that "there was really no means of training the division, or maintaining its effectiveness during [the] period of moving and relocating" from Fort Knox, to the port of New York, to Northern Ireland.[4] This division went to war equipped with a mix of obsolete M3 (Stuart) light and M3 (Grant) medium tanks. Other units also lost valuable preparation time. A ship carrying the new-model 105-mm howitzers for the 1st Infantry Division ran aground off Nova Scotia. Tools for repair of trucks and other equipment were in short supply, and logistical problems continued throughout the campaign.[5]

First Battles of a New Army

THE ARMY entered the ground war on 8 November 1942, when three task forces landed on the coast of North Africa in Operation Torch. As in any amphibious attack, troops faced the vagaries of weather, tides, beach obstacles, visibility, etc. The Western Task Force, under the command of Patton, consisted of several "sub-task forces" aiming for the Casablanca area. One sub-task force, under Maj. Gen. Lucian K. Truscott, lost the element of surprise when a French steamer flashed a warning to shore batteries. To prevent pitched battles with the French, the Allies had decided against a daylight attack and heavy naval bombardment despite the tactical risks. Rather than add to the confusion, Truscott decided to stay with the plan but to postpone the time of the attack by a half-hour. Heavy seas caused transport ships to lose formation, and there were not enough landing boats for all the troops to debark simultaneously. Navigation errors caused one unit to come ashore several thousand yards from its assigned beach. French planes bombed and strafed some landing craft and shore batteries fired at the fleet. This forced some ships farther out to sea, and the resulting thirty-mile round trip for lighters delayed the arrival of tanks and other supporting weapons ashore. Friendly naval gunfire crashed down too close to some landing sites. Late on 9 November, three rifle companies became lost while they were closing in on an airfield. When some of these men entered a building they believed to be the barracks for the security troops, they discovered that they had captured a café; over seventy customers surrendered. The airfield finally fell on 10 November.[6] Unloading operations fell behind schedule due to rough seas, accidents, and inexperienced sailors and soldiers. Patton's Center Task Force (under Maj. Gen. Lloyd W. Fredendall) endured civilian transport ships that accidentally entered the landing zone, unexpected currents, and a boat fire that ended the chance of surprise. Deep-draft lighters bottomed out on a sandbar. Some landing boats became stranded, and engineers damaged propellers and rudders using bulldozers to push them back to the water's edge. [7]

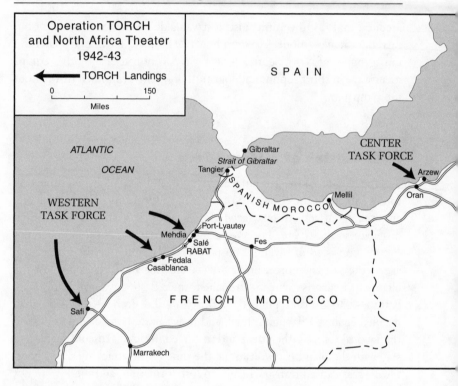

Operation TORCH
and North Africa Theater
1942-43

← TORCH Landings

0   150
Miles

SPAIN

ATLANTIC
OCEAN

Gibraltar
Strait of Gibraltar
Tangier

CENTER
TASK FORCE

Arzew

WESTERN
TASK FORCE

SPANISH MOROCCO

Mellil   Oran

Port-Lyautey
Mehdia
Salé
RABAT
Fedala
Casablanca

Fes

FRENCH   MOROCCO

Safi

Marrakech

Tunisia

AFTER THE FRENCH ACCEPTED terms of surrender for Morocco and Algeria, Eisenhower turned his attention to the Axis forces in Tunisia. Despite the impending winter rains, he chose to push east and engage the enemy. This was a risky decision, since the logistical system was unable to support large forces several hundred miles from their supply bases over a poor-to-nonexistent road and rail network. In mid-December, German forces west of Tunis stopped British columns supported by dispersed elements of the 1st Armored Division. GIs who had never been far from home now struggled for warmth and protection in central Tunisia's mountains, intermediate plateaus, and smaller hills. They were in scrub grass and cactus-covered earth that turned into a cold, brown slush during rainy weather.[8]

Renewed attacks foundered in increasingly bad weather, and in January 1943 the scene of action shifted to southern Tunisia, when Eisenhower concluded that the capture of Tunis and Bizerte was not as important as the destruction of Axis forces that might threaten Allied

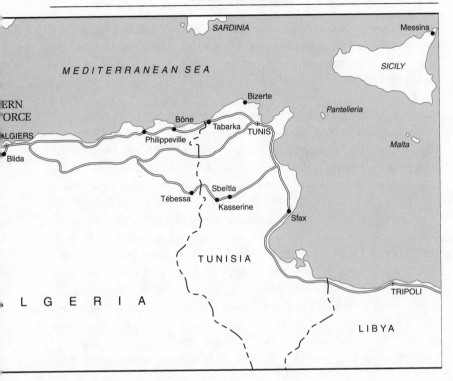

coastal positions in Morocco and Algeria. Eisenhower told Marshall that combat operations to date had violated "every accepted principle of warfare,"[9] yet he made a decision to carry the fight to the enemy. He wrote his generals about deficiencies in combat survival skills and basic leadership. Some officers failed to carry out their orders or condoned lax discipline. Soldiers did not always dig foxholes or were deficient in anti-tank marksmanship or aircraft recognition. He was not as concerned about the training methods or operational doctrine, probably because there had not yet been enough fighting to expose those weaknesses. "The only kind of discipline that is acceptable is the kind which will be carried onto the battlefield," he said.[10] General Marshall, in Casablanca for the famous Allied planning conference, told the commander of the Tank Destroyer (TD) Training Center about his having run across a poorly disciplined battalion commanded by a lieutenant colonel in his late twenties. This was the second time he had seen a badly led TD battalion, and he told the general in no uncertain terms that he was not satisfied, despite the

relative youth of commanders. For his part, Patton did not believe military bearing and discipline were up to standard.[11] The question for the
War Department was how fast it could get things right. Its observers identified problems and forwarded their reports to Washington. A report covering the period November 1942–February 1943 cited good enlisted
morale but warned that an officer's morale set the tone for the entire unit.
Small-unit commanders needed to take the initiative. Another report covering roughly the same period remarked that the 3d Infantry Division was
"determined, well-trained and well officered." Commanders knew exactly
what they wanted to do and how to do it. Soldiers needed training under
live artillery fire, and closer air-ground cooperation was imperative.[12]

There is no doubt that the U.S. Army went into combat in North
Africa unevenly trained, perhaps in some cases dangerously untrained.
Yet critics of GI performance in World War II often cite these early
reports as evidence of poor performance throughout the war. Such rea-
soning mistakenly implies at worst that the Army did little to correct the
problems or, at best, that material preponderance compensated for inept-
ness. The observer process itself indicates that the AGF was anxious to
improve battlefield performance. Bad commanders were weeded out.
Unit organizations changed. Improvements were made in doctrine.
Historians familiar with combat operations but unfamiliar with mobilization and training do not account for the dynamics of change and the cycle
of evaluation and improvement. The pace of change was so rapid that it
was hard to get all the required lessons into the chaos of the training program. Things were never perfect, but such was the complex nature of
military operations.

There were also serious problems in Allied relations. Senior British
officers, with some justification, looked down on what they perceived to
be a junior partner. British General Sir Kenneth A. N. Anderson, the
overall tactical commander in Tunisia under Eisenhower, commanded
the First British Army and had nominal control of French and
American troops. He was convinced the Americans had little promise.
General Ward, commander of the 1st Armored Division, believed
"Anderson considered the Americans privileged to serve with the
British."[13] French General Louis-Marie Koeltz commanded a corps in
central Tunisia. His superior, Alphonse Juin, commanded all French
forces in northwest Africa and, on paper at least, reported for tactical
purposes through Anderson to Eisenhower. However, Juin refused to
serve directly under the British. The U.S. II Corps was also attached to
the First British Army. The corps commander, Lloyd Fredendall, had

a white-hot temper and intensely disliked Anderson. Finally, individual battalions of the 1st Armored Division were parceled throughout the command, and General Ward found himself in charge of little. Fredendall continually bypassed Ward and dealt directly with his (Ward's) subordinates. The corps commander scathingly reproached any subordinate who asked for clarification of his habitually imprecise, confusing, often incomprehensible orders. No doubt Fredendall was in a situation that he was neither trained to handle or probably to envision. He was the product of a different army and a different time. He was not the only such example of what might be termed a generational divide in the U.S. Army officer corps.[14]

Axis units in late January 1943 hit the boundary between the British and French in Tunisia and exposed coordination problems between the Allies. Rommel, enduring significant logistical problems of his own, had about seventy operational tanks in support of about 30,000 combat troops.[15] On 30 January a panzer division slammed into French positions at Faid Pass (see map on pg. 28), opening the Kasserine battles. Fredendall managed to get a counterattack order to the commander of Ward's Combat Command A (CCA), Brig. Gen. Raymond E. McQuillin, an older officer also not up to a modern challenge. He had had about sixty tanks, 1,200 infantry, twenty-four howitzers, engineers, and a company of twelve obsolete TDs (75–mm cannon mounted on half-track chassis). He also had ineffective close air support. His counterattack, aimed at Sidi bou Zid, a village about fifteen miles west of Faid, failed, because Fredendall would not risk weakening CCA's defensive positions to assemble the amount of force needed for the attack. Enemy planes bombed and strafed the GIs, and Allied planes accidentally bombed the CCA headquarters. One tank company lost eight of its seventeen tanks during a renewed attack the next day. The Luftwaffe and artillery drove back Americans' infantry and hammered their artillery. Recriminations spread throughout the Allied command. Eisenhower wondered whether Fredendall was incompetent; Anderson and the French both questioned the competence of the U.S. Army. McQuillin blamed supporting infantry commanders, and Fredendall blamed Ward.[16]

Anderson told Fredendall and the French to block mountain passes in the area of Kasserine. Unfortunately, the U.S. 1st and 34th Infantry Divisions were separated into battalion-sized elements (about eight hundred men) that occupied positions from which they could not support each other. Tanks, infantry, and artillery from the 1st Armored Division went into positions miles from the division's other elements. Many infantry replacements had arrived with rusty skills due to considerable delays between the completion of training and their arrival in Tunisia. One regimental commander recalled that some even "lacked weapons, [others] had never fired a rifle, and none had entrenching tools or bayonets."[17]

A raging sandstorm on 14 February shielded two hundred German armored vehicles, including a handful of big Tiger tanks, supported by a few thousand infantry, all heading for forward positions east of Kasserine. These spearheads from the 10th Panzer Division surrounded and isolated parts of the 1st Armored Division. Early in the action, German fire knocked out the radio-equipped tank used to communicate with artillery. To buy time, a battalion of artillery fired from exposed positions until the Luftwaffe destroyed it as a fighting unit. Other GIs were surrounded. McQuillin's material losses were some forty-four tanks, fifty-nine half-tracks, twenty-six artillery pieces, at least a dozen TDs, and twenty-four trucks. The Germans did not exploit the initial success, since they assumed the Allies would counterattack. General Ward was, in fact, planning just this, and he radioed the stranded units to hold on. Unfortunately, his division had not yet been allowed to concentrate. Eisenhower meanwhile accepted Anderson's recommendation to retreat westward and concentrate east of Kasserine at Sbeitla. During the withdrawal, some overzealous support troops destroyed badly needed supplies, thinking they would fall into enemy hands.[18]

Ward renewed operations on 15 February. An attacking tank battalion moved out at midday but soon became enveloped by heavy dust and was hit by about twenty Luftwaffe planes. German artillery held its fire until the Americans were well within range. Air bursts forced tank commanders to "button up" and thereby lose vision. The planes kept the tankers from noticing panzers that moved on their flank, and about fifty U.S. tanks littered the desert at the end of the day. Only then did Anderson release the rest of the 1st Armored Division to Ward. The enemy hit them that night. Few GIs had been involved in night operations. Most were exhausted, nervous, confused. The destruction of an ammunition dump by U.S. engineers caused further confusion, though many troops bravely held their ground and did not withdraw until ordered to do so.[19]

American losses between 14 and 17 February were over 2,500 men, a hundred tanks, and nearly three hundred other vehicles. Two tank battalions were provisionally combined due to losses; one company each in a reconnaissance battalion and an engineer battalion had to be completely reequipped, as was an artillery battalion. Eisenhower was concerned enough at the situation that he retained under his control most of the new replacement M4 Sherman tanks still in rear-area stocks. A "horrified" Alexander told Fredendall that no one would withdraw farther west. He threw in both British and American reinforcements, and the strengthened defense impressed Rommel to the extent that he shifted his main effort to Kasserine itself. American tanks arrived in time to back up an engineer unit about to give way. Artillery from the 9th Infantry Division arrived on 21 February after completing a road march of eight hundred miles from western Algeria, in a demonstration of the inherent mobility of a U.S. division when supported by transport units. As the ground units collected themselves, the Allied command was uncertain. Fredendall did not have a clear picture of the situation. While he was at a French headquarters, his staff relocated his command post (Anderson and Koeltz also moved their headquarters). The Allied command was close to breakdown, but the Germans did not know this and called off their attack. Eisenhower relieved Fredendall and Ward. Patton temporarily became the corps commander in March, followed by Maj. Gen. Omar N. Bradley on a permanent basis in April. Significant problems in coordination between the U.S. and British forces continued to hamper operations until they ended in early May, and there was some extremely hard fighting before the Allies occupied Bizerte and Tunis.[20]

Tunisia—Conclusion

TORCH WAS THE FIRST large-scale amphibious landing after an extended ocean voyage in the U.S. Army's history. French resistance was generally inept, which was fortunate, given the chaos of the landings and the logistical buildup that followed. The initial success naturally led to predictions of quick victory, and it is therefore little wonder that the debacle in early 1943 shocked the American public. The Axis won initial success with a clear preponderance of material at critical times and places, plus the advantage of experience and skill. Yet the improvement in U.S. performance during the summer of 1943 indicates that the GI could learn quickly and that the Army as in institution could assimilate at least some of the lessons learned. What happened in Tunisia should not have surprised anyone. What is important is that the Army identified many problems and worked toward solutions.

A recent study on the 1st Armored Division notes that some officers had identified problems before the operations began but there had not been enough time to correct them.[21] On the other hand, armor commanders did not understand the capabilities and limitations of towed artillery, and they did not grasp that even self-propelled artillery had trouble keeping up with fast columns. There were shortages of artillery: the 34th Infantry Division had to use British cannon for its light batteries and World War I–vintage medium howitzers. The British guns came in handy, since one artillery battalion in the 1st Infantry Division ran out of ammunition and the 34th loaned it some pieces for which ammunition was available.[22] The trade-off of manpower for material early on led to inadequate forward logistical support of combat units, and it is no wonder that by January 1943 one of the most urgent problems facing the Americans was a shortage of cargo trucks. There were also shortages of anti-aircraft guns, carbines, howitzers, and truck parts. The condition of U.S. light tanks was described as "wretched," due to lack of maintenance, and on one occasion, when medium tanks arrived to relieve forward elements in Tunisia, light tank crews watched "as children do fire engines." Reserve stocks could not meet the demand for replacements until mid-March.[23]

Revised air doctrine emphasized the need for centralized control of aircraft under an air commander and rejected the practice of dispersed operations under ground commanders, who demanded a constant air patrol.[24] This practice wasted resources and violated the maxim that defense everywhere is defense nowhere. It was not until mid-1944, however, that air-ground operations were adequately coordinated. The War Department changed the organization of infantry and armored divisions, lengthened basic training from thirteen to seventeen weeks (which, of course, slowed the flow of replacements), and belatedly increased production of the Sherman tank and larger-caliber artillery. Tanks, not TDs, became recognized as the primary anti-tank weapon, and TDs became instead effective supporters of artillery.[25] Unfortunately, the Sherman tank was not suited for the task (see appendix B).

The manual on military courtesy and discipline noted that discipline was "the cementing force which binds the members of a unit; which endures after the leader has fallen and every substance of authority has vanished." Discipline created "a desire and determination to undertake and accomplish any mission assigned by the leader."[26] Such values take time to instill throughout the chain of command, and in 1942 time was something the Army did not have. Perhaps more could have been done in the training centers, despite rapid expansion, but too few leaders had the experience to do so early on. Rommel believed America's industrial power would be decisive, and he also admitted that the Germans "had a lot to learn from [the Americans] organizationally. One particularly striking feature was the standardization of their vehicles and spare parts." He added that the Americans adapted to modern warfare with "astonishing ... speed." He attributed this to an "extraordinary sense for the practical and by complete lack of regard for tradition and worthless theories."[27]

Husky

COMMAND DECISIONS THAT DICTATED where the GI would fight occurred not at the outset of the war but periodically throughout it. Politics and industrial production were important facets of the decision-making process, as was the ability of the U.S. Army to learn how to carry out increasingly complex operations over lengthening supply lines. The Allies at Casablanca in early 1943 decided to attack Sicily, in what was eventually called Operation Husky. This committed the United States to the Mediterranean on a larger scale than Marshall wanted. American planners had already rejected attacking Germany through Italy, because of its distance from such important military targets as the Ruhr and Saar. However, North African operations put a significant amount of resources in the Mediterranean, and using the resources already there made sense to FDR and others.

The 15th Army Group conducted the land operation, controlling the Seventh U.S. and the Eighth British Armies. Once again, Eisenhower exercised supreme command. The British had the primary task of seizing the city of Messina, located in the northeast corner of the 10,000-square-mile island. The less experienced American field army under Patton had a supporting role. Husky also saw the debut of a new family of landing craft and ships especially designed for beachhead operations, and the amphibious 2½-ton amphibious cargo truck (DUKW), nicknamed "duck."[28]

Operations began on the night of 9–10 July 1943 with a British glider assault and American airborne landing. Almost half of the gliders crashed into the sea, and the attack did little more than alert the defenders. One battalion of paratroopers from the 82d Airborne Division landed over twenty miles from its planned drop zone. Assault troops began landing well before daylight on the 10th despite a gale that delayed the landings of the new 45th Infantry Division by an hour.[29] A coordinated counterattack against the Americans was nearly impossible to put together quickly, since paratroopers had cut most of the telephone lines. Still, the commander of the Hermann Goering Panzer Division decided to attack Gela, site of the landing of the 1st Infantry Division. One German task force consisted of two battalions of truck-mounted infantry, self-propelled artillery, and seventeen Tiger tanks. Another had about ninety tanks, two dozen artillery pieces, and about a thousand combat engineers and armored reconnaissance troops.

Gela became a killing ground. Temperatures approached a hundred degrees. Flame, crashing noise, hot metal, and bullets enveloped the GIs. Panzers raked them with cannon and machine-gun fire. During the height of the counterattack a field artillery battalion loaded on DUKWs came ashore and moved directly to firing positions. A regimental cannon company (six howitzers—the product of post-Torch reorganization) and four Sherman tanks reached the riflemen in time to help stop the attack not far from the supply dumps on the beach. There had been no close air support. Naval gunfire did not join the battle until several hours after it began. While the German division was not well trained in infantry-armor cooperation, it did pose a significant threat in the critical first hours of the invasion.[30]

ALONG THE NORTH COAST

General Alexander's support of Montgomery's virtually unilateral decision to shift one of his corps to the west on 13 July, where it literally cut off the attack of the Seventh U.S. Army, is an example of continuing British doubts about the fighting ability of the GI. This decision gave the British use of a key road that had been in the U.S. zone, but it also slowed the pace of the entire operation. Patton and his subordinate corps commander, Omar Bradley, were furious. They moved the 45th Division to another part of the front, but this wasted time and resources and led Patton to focus on Palermo, located in the northwest of the island. Unlike Messina, Palermo did not block an escape route for the enemy, but it became a prestige objective. Alexander at first permitted the operation, then had second thoughts. Patton's staff claimed the message rescinding permission to move on Palermo became garbled in transmission.

At the time, most German strength was arrayed against the British in the eastern third of the island. Against the GIs, the enemy blocked mountain roads, blew bridges, and fought delaying actions. Yet between the night of 18 July and the morning of the 20th, one 3d Infantry Division rifle battalion marched fifty-four miles across rugged terrain in terrific heat, choking dust, and without extra rations or water (there were no roads for transport of extra supplies). Less than two hours after the march ended, the soldiers attacked into enemy machine-gun fire near Palermo. Engineers constructed bypasses and repaired bridges across sheer drops. Fortunately, enemy opposition fell off as the GIs neared the town, and "the Italians fell over themselves surrendering the city."[31]

A new phase in the campaign began when Mussolini's opposition deposed him on 25 July. Italy remained at war. It also became apparent that the British would be unable to take Messina without assistance, and its capture became the Seventh Army's next objective.[32] The GIs continued to fight the enemy, the elements, and the terrain. They breathed dusty air that carried the stench of open sewage and rotting animal and human remains. Disease was a problem. About 10,000 (nearly a thousand more than the number of combat wounded) GIs were incapacitated by malaria, sand-fly fever, or dysentery. Only one of two malaria-control units earmarked for the invasion arrived in time to participate in the campaign. Many troops did not think malaria could be a problem in a nontropical environment, and too many of them failed to take preventive medication, such as atabrine, until it was too late.[33]

The terrain in north-central Sicily was extremely difficult for maneuver, and a relatively few enemy soldiers could put up a stiff defense. There was no room for maneuver on a coastal plain that was a few hundred yards wide at most and had only one good, hard-surface road that passed over bridges, through tunnels, and clung to cliffsides. Lateral roads dead-ended at the mountains; all that traversed some areas were narrow footpaths gouged in the earth by the Romans. Pack mules had trouble negotiating the terrain. One of the landings intended to get behind the Germans along the road was at Brolo, about fifty miles west of Messina, on 11 August. Major General Truscott, the commander of the 3d Infantry Division, wanted to delay the landing in order for the troops attacking inland to reach supporting positions. Patton would have none of it; he had arranged for several correspondents to accompany the small convoy, and he feared they would be critical of the Army if he postponed the landing again. He stormed into Truscott's headquarters, "screamingly angry as only he could be." Truscott told Patton to find another division commander if he thought it was necessary. Patton's fury suddenly disappeared. He could not afford to lose Truscott. They had a drink.[34]

Lt. Col. Lyle A. Bernard's 2d Battalion, 30th Infantry Regiment, numbered no more than 650 of its authorized 871 soldiers. Augmenting the battalion was a naval beach-marking party, a platoon of combat

engineers, tanks, and self-propelled artillery. The GIs gained surprise
when they landed before daylight about ten miles behind German lines.
After the leaders of the engineer and tank platoons looked for a bypass
around a narrow railroad viaduct, the infantry, still with surprise in its
favor, skirmished with some defenders. GIs also identified at least four
machine-gun positions in the hills.[35] This fighting awoke every German
in the area. The local commander, who had artillery, two 20-mm anti-
aircraft guns, and parts of a panzergrenadier battalion, told his men, who
were in the hills overlooking the landing beach, to open fire. Machine-
gun bullets and 20-mm shells tore into the GIs still on the beach and in
the adjacent high ground. Bernard's headquarters radios failed. His only
link to assistance was a liaison officer's radio set. Enemy communications
were working well, however, and the commander of the 29th
Panzergrenadier Division realized that the Americans threatened to cut
off his division's withdrawal along the coast road toward Messina. He did
what German commanders always did when their units were knocked off
balance: he ordered a counterattack.[36]

Meanwhile, the five Sherman tanks and eight self-propelled guns
were having problems trying to get off the beach. While moving toward

bypasses, three tanks bellied out on the mud flats, and the other two were damaged trying to crash through a stone wall. The artillery managed to get into covered firing positions in a lemon grove before daylight brought fire from enemy guns on the high ground. The Americans managed to destroy two German reconnaissance vehicles that tried to probe the coastal flat. American fire also cut down about thirty *Landsers* who tried to separate the men on the coast from those in the high ground. About 8:00 AM, a hundred German infantry began another drive. Machine-gun fire forced them to deploy, and mortar fire trapped some on the banks of the river; many of them broke and ran. The cruiser USS *Philadelphia* provided supporting fire.[37]

Colonel Bernard's first reports were positive, but by 10:00 AM he was concerned about the strength of the enemy and was asking about the progress of the supporting ground attack. Fires had started in the dry scrub brush and burned telephone wires. Repair parties lost men to small-arms fire, and Bernard lost contact with the Navy. Because the naval commander did not know the situation ashore, and since he had received no more calls for assistance, he decided there was no need to remain at Brolo. Four Italian torpedo planes helped confirm his decision to head back to Palermo.[38] Then, about 11:00 AM, about a hundred panzergrenadiers supported by tanks reached the coast road and broke into U.S. lines. Bernard called for artillery and an air strike: "Enemy counterattack . . . request air mission . . . urgent. Also navy." Then, about 12:30 PM: "Must have everything."[39] An hour later, he reported, "Enemy counterattacking fiercely. Do Something."[40]

Truscott assumed the naval support was still at Brolo but simply out of radio contact with the infantry. He had staff officers call Seventh Army for assistance, but the only firm reply was that an air strike would come later. Relieving troops were still hours away, and Brolo was at the maximum range of the nearest artillery. Without support, the GIs could not fight off a well-executed counterattack. Fortunately, the naval commander received the urgent call and turned the cruiser and two destroyers around. They came within range at 2:00 PM. Air strikes and artillery also hit the enemy. However, just as the situation seemed in hand, radio contact between the *Philadelphia* task force and the naval shore fire-control party failed. The ships withdrew again, since the air attack seemed to be effective. American artillery was by then unable to fire safely, since the opposing sides were so close together.[41]

Without either air or naval support, the Americans on the coastal flat still drove off the enemy infantry supporting the panzers. Bernard

radioed, "Ammo very short."[42] The panzers on the beach knocked out
two of the four howitzers and the two half-tracks carrying ammunition.
A third howitzer came face to face with a German tank. The artillerymen fired first but missed, and so did the Germans. Each fired a second
round that hit the other simultaneously. Mortar ammunition was now so
short that Bernard would not allow the troops to fire any—he needed to
keep a small contingency reserve.[43] When *Philadelphia* returned late in
the day, a member of the shore fire-control party commandeered a
DUKW and headed to sea to arrange for support personally.
Misunderstanding this activity, the drivers of three other DUKWs,
loaded with ammunition for Bernard's men, turned back to sea.
Philadelphia fired on some targets but did not engage the Germans
approaching the positions on the high ground because it believed the fire
might hit friendly troops. Eight German aircraft then struck the cruiser
and supporting destroyers. They took evasive action, sustained no damage, and returned to Palermo.

Allied fighter-bombers returned, but they also put two bombs on
Bernard's CP (command post) and killed or wounded about nineteen GIs.
The planes also bombed the howitzers. Bernard ordered the men still on
the beach who could do so to move to the high ground. About 10:30 PM,
he prepared for a last-ditch stand. But there was no more German activity after the Americans regained control of the coast road and could pass
unharmed through Brolo to Messina. Relief troops reached Bernard's
men early on 12 August. The fighting cost this battalion 127 casualties,
including four officers and thirty-six enlisted men killed, it later received
the Presidential Unit Citation.[44]

ANALYSIS—SICILY

Husky cost 7,402 Seventh Army and 11,843 British casualties. Axis losses
were about 160,000 dead, wounded, and captured in thirty-eight days of
fighting. It is worth noting that with the exceptions of the 1st and 9th
Infantry Divisions, few U.S. units entered the operation with any combat
experience. This was also the first time in the war that the United States
had employed a field army in combat: Seventh Army had about 200,000
troops by the end of the campaign—it was larger than the entire pre-war
Regular Army. The operation drove the Axis from the island and opened
the Mediterranean sea lines of communication, but there was no joint
Allied plan to prevent evacuation of enemy forces. For that matter, there
was no overall operational plan. Each ally fought an independent battle to
achieve whatever goals it thought appropriate. Nevertheless, Sicily was a

proving ground that led to maturation of leaders. Bradley gained experience and professional identity; Truscott and other relatively young division
commanders proved America could produce excellent combat generals.
Junior officers and NCOs became more confident of their ability to lead
under fire, and they provided examples for the training camps. Historian
Carlo D'Este is correct in characterizing U.S. leadership as "generally
excellent." He credits Patton with presiding "over the demise of the notion
that American fighting ability was any longer suspect." Montgomery, however was one of the few senior British officers at the time who acknowledged the "rugged determination and professionalism" of the GI.[45]

On the other hand, there were logistic problems. Inventory management and accountability of supplies was often poor, and supply personnel often had to go back to beaches and waste time looking for badly
needed repair parts. Patton's logistics officer allowed an engineer special brigade, a unit dedicated to clearing and organizing beachheads,
instead of a logistics headquarters, to coordinate his supply operation.
Engineers without special training or interest in logistics, improperly
handled and sorted supplies, especially ammunition, without regard to
what the frontline troops needed. Three-quarters of U.S. ammunition
dumps had more small-arms ammunition than they needed (because it
was relatively easy for the engineers to handle) and never enough
artillery ammunition. Many 155-mm howitzers were of World War
I vintage and reached combat in an unserviceable condition. Eighteen
of the big guns were out of action within days of the invasion. Newer-
production guns performed well, but they often lacked sights and
accessories.[46]

Italy: 1943-1944

U.S. AND BRITISH CONFEREES in Washington in May 1943 confirmed
plans for continuing operations in Italy instead of mounting a cross-
Channel attack on Germany in 1943. The British Eighth Army attacked
across the straits of Messina, and the newly activated Fifth U.S. Army
conducted Operation Avalanche, a landing in the Gulf of Salerno
intended to take the Allies to Naples, a modern port that could sustain
long-term logistical requirements. A landing closer to Rome made more
sense, but it was out of the range of air cover, and aircraft carriers were
needed in the Pacific. Even Salerno was barely within range of land-based
fighters, and most of the beaches there were subject to enemy observation. Coastal defenses there varied in strength, and the Sele River split the

landing area in two. Mountains limited the depth of the beachhead and gave defenders excellent fighting positions.[47]

The operation lacked enough amphibious craft, and the Americans could not put ashore enough men at Salerno to control the large beachhead adequately in the early hours of the attack. Working against the Germans was the fact that their forces, many of whom had recently escaped from Sicily, were not fully ready for operations. GIs of the new 36th Infantry Division (National Guard) began landing at 3:30 AM on 9 September; offshore in reserve was the 45th (National Guard). Opposing the GIs or otherwise near enough to the beachhead to influence the battle were several powerful armored formations, like the 16th Panzer (with about 17,000 men, more than a hundred tanks, and thirty-six tracked assault guns), 15th Panzergrenadier, and Hermann Goering divisions. The 15th had about 12,000 soldiers, seven tanks, eighteen assault guns, and thirty-one anti-tank guns of 75-mm and 88-mm caliber. The Hermann Goering Division had an effective strength of about 15,000 and ample artillery but only thirty tanks and twenty-one assault guns.[48]

GIs went ashore carrying a canteen or two, cartridge belt, backpack filled with toilet articles and some spare clothing, mess kit, D-rations (high-calorie chocolate bars), K-rations (boxed meals), and extra ammunition. German fire pounded them: "Scared, tense, excited, some soldiers blundered across the loose sand. Others ran for cover [behind the dunes]." Some landing craft burned; others turned back to sea until control boats intercepted and returned them. Bright flares and streaks from tracer bullets colored the early morning sky. Equipment and bodies floated in the water. Staff Sgt. Quillian H. McMichen was hit in the chest and shoulder before his landing craft ground to a stop on the beach. The ramp stuck. Despite his wounds, he "kicked and pounded on the ramp till it fell." He led his men ashore until he was fatally wounded. Sgt. Manuel S. Gonzalez slipped out of a pack set afire by a tracer bullet, crawled forward, and was wounded by shell fragments but still destroyed a machine gun. A battalion commander, Lt. Col. Samuel S. Graham, gathered about seventy men and led them against mortars and machine guns. German defenders thought the GIs maneuvered skillfully.[49]

Lacking defenses in depth, the Germans at the beaches could only delay the American timetable, not throw the attack back into the water, though during one counterattack after daylight a panzer got within range of the landing craft. Lacking their own armor support in the first hours, riflemen held off such thrusts themselves. One NCO jumped on a tank and threw a grenade down an open hatch; another soldier kept some tanks at bay by removing the floor planks from a bridge across an irrigation canal. It was afternoon before most of the 36th Division artillery was ashore, and night before the supporting tank battalion had all of its Shermans on land.[50]

Progress during the next three days was satisfactory, but not all the landing forces were ashore when a big counterattack hit the U.S. sectors on 13–14 September. German artillery tore a weakened rifle battalion to pieces. One group of panzers surrounded a battalion command post. Some German commanders thought the battle was about over; indeed, the Americans were considering whether to evacuate rear command posts. Eisenhower, meanwhile, had few viable options—naval reinforcements were two or three days out, the Eighth British Army was too far away, and there was no airfield close enough for land-based aircraft to be effective. The 3d Infantry Division needed 2,000 replacements. Quick help was available only from a battalion of the 82d Airborne Division, which jumped from a height of eight hundred feet beginning about 10:30 PM on 13 September. Command decisions are detailed in the official army history, but suffice to say here that commanders like Fred L. Walker of the 36th, Truscott of the 3d, Matthew B. Ridgway of the 82d, and others, from squad leader to regimental commander, performed generally well. This was a vastly different force than that which had landed in North Africa just ten months before.[51]

Lessons streamed into the States. Walker emphasized the fundamental importance of developing good junior leaders. He said that while men were "resigned to [their] fate," they were also willing to do whatever was necessary for victory as long as they were not "sacrificed by [the] stupidity" of their leaders.[52] Maj. Gen. John Sloan, commander of the 88th Infantry Division (draftee), believed that "the training of a unit will be most strongly reflected in the results of its first campaign." He sent 108 officers and 216 enlisted men to frontline units in Italy for thirty days before his division entered combat. He said, "principles which have been developed and established in our service schools must be regarded as a broad guiding framework from which to start in the conduct of combat operations. They must not be mentally compartmented, applied rigidly, or considered as inflexible rules applicable in the same way to every situation regardless of existing peculiarities and conditions."[53] Good words from a good leader; however, the most important test was yet to begin. There was no alternative to fighting the enemy on its home ground in Germany.

CHAPTER 4

THE ENEMY

O
MAHA BEACH, DAWN, 6 JUNE 1944: Troop-carrying landing craft were traveling in line abreast, headed toward the coast of Normandy. Ahead of them were tanks fitted with flotation skirts; behind them were several larger boats with combat engineers, U.S. Navy demolition parties who would blast gaps in the beach obstacles, and bulldozers to tear through the rock shingle, dunes, and seawall. More troops and self-propelled artillery followed this wave. At 5:50 AM, the main-battery guns of the battleships *Texas* and *Arkansas* began firing on targets inland. Cruisers and destroyers joined the bombardment, which was short in duration compared with those in the Pacific. German troops at one strongpoint looked through the mist at the ragged line of boats a few thousand yards offshore. Sergeants had just told their men to stand fast when over three hundred U.S. heavy bombers dropped their loads, well inland, due to low clouds and a few seconds' delay in the release of the bombs. One sergeant thought the Americans were crazy for attacking at low tide across several hundred yards of open beach.

By 6:10 AM, the Americans were about a mile from shore. They had trouble seeing the beach through the smoke from grass fires caused by the bombardment. Their tank support was in the process of disappearing—literally. Most of the "duplex-drive" Shermans (tanks fitted with propellers and canvas flotation screens that were supposed to land a few minutes ahead of the infantry) had been swamped and were on their way to the bottom of the Channel. Supporting artillery was in about the same state. Fifteen minutes later, a shower of flaming rockets thundered toward the defenses. The first GIs came ashore about 6:30. German machine gunners squeezed the triggers of their MG-42 machine guns. Bullets flew like water from a hose.

Company A, of the 116th Infantry Regiment, a National Guard unit from Bedford, Virginia, nearly disintegrated under the fire. Ramps on some boats would not budge; other craft grounded on sandbars. Seasick

44

men scrambled over the sides. Within minutes, nineteen soldiers were dead. Bedford, population about 3,200, lost more men per capita that day than any other town in the United States. Many who reached the shore sought protection behind steel obstacles or the seawall. Sand kicked up by bullets and explosions flew into the air, along with arms and legs. Some wounded men were shot again and again as they tried to dress their own injuries. Others made repeated trips back to the water's edge to drag the wounded from the rising tide. Sometimes the wounded were shot out of their hands; sometimes the rescuers dropped dead on the wounded. The defenders continued to fire without letup. Order temporarily disappeared. The enemy defenses were unexpectedly strong.[1]

Germany's recovery from World War I and its subsequent military buildup has been the subject of thousands of books and the near-adulation of historian, buff, and professional soldier alike. Probably no army in history has been the subject of so much assumption and speculation as this one. This chapter will provide a brief overview of the subject and set the stage for the rest of this book. It will not provide the last word, but it will help give some perspective for further discussion of the abilities and performance of the U.S. Army.

Germany lacked domestic sources for many of the materials needed for modern war. Oil, for example, came from Romania, Hungary, and the USSR, and a substantial amount of industrial capacity went to the production of export goods to pay rearmament bills. New industries based on synthetics helped lower dependence on imports. Yet oil reserves were modest when the war began in 1939, and Hitler did not fully mobilize the economy until early 1944. Perhaps he reasoned that the nation's standard of living could support both war and domestic programs, particularly if he could control events. Early success probably gave him a false sense of security that he had guessed right. No doubt the staff work and professionalism of the military also bolstered his confidence. Yet the military's tradition of operational excellence could not overcome a web of government bureaucracy between Berlin and the production floor that stifled efficiency and initiative.[2]

Germany committed a larger percentage of its workforce to industrial production than the United States, and it had problems coordinating private and government efforts. Businessmen resented inefficient government approaches to management and the meddling of corrupt Nazi party hacks who wanted to control everything. Military requirements were not large enough early on to interest industry, and the military carried out much of its own development and design work.[3] One reason for the gap between what the military needed and what was actually produced was Germany's simultaneous buildup of its military infrastructure (e.g., new barracks and training areas) and of its economy. Insistence on the highest-quality craftsmanship, not fully possible if mass production was to be carried out in full, limited the quantities of arms available.[4] Germany did benefit from relatively short supply lines, but its overemphasis on state-of-the-art combat technology led to insufficient production of common articles like cargo trucks. Hitler ended up with two armies—a large, horse-drawn force and a smaller one with some of the best weapons in the world. Fortunately for the Germans, the supply lines in the west were comparatively short and they could rely on a highly developed railroad system that was often quickly repaired after air attacks.

This drive for technical perfection, coupled with a poorly run industrial base and the lack of a strong corps of management and logistics specialists, led to the eventual stagnation and collapse of the armies in the field.[5] Conversely, the U.S. Army made only minimum modifications to its weapons and combat vehicles, and the troops simply lived with what were often technologically inferior systems compared to their enemy counterparts. It was an unfortunate product of wartime decision making, and it cost many lives, but even American industry was at the mercy of unique time-and-space constraints that affected the generation and sustainment of combat power.

The army founded the modern German state, and it was a national institution in a way that the U.S. Army could never be, given American political and social tradition. The German public had historically accepted a strong military presence in its society virtually without question. Rearmament began with the creation of the Reichswehr (armed forces) in 1921. The army (Reichsheer) was limited to 100,000 men, including officers; the navy (Reichsmarine), was allowed only 15,000 officers and men. Under the restrictions of the Versailles treaty, the Reichswehr could possess no offensive weapons such as tanks, submarines, or attack aircraft. The treaty limited the production of new arms to that necessary to replace worn-out stocks. Men volunteered for twelve-year enlistments, and officers had twenty-five-year obligations. As a result of Germany's history, the military attracted quality personnel, which it recruited from specific geographic areas and assigned to units with permanent home stations. Unlike the American soldier of the time, German enlisted men received relatively high pay and on discharge had preference in civil service employment and financial support for three years while adjusting to civilian life. Those with more then ten years of service could receive training for civilian jobs while they were still on active duty. By the mid-1930s, a time when the U.S. Army had no intact combat divisions, the German Heer (army) had seven infantry divisions, authorized 12,000 men each, and three cavalry divisions of about 5,500 men.[6]

Hitler by 1936 had withdrawn Germany from the League of Nations, renounced the Versailles Treaty, become head of state, and appointed himself as supreme commander of the armed forces. He forced the military to swear an oath of personal allegiance to him, not the state; he increased the size of the army, instituted conscription, and brought the Luftwaffe (air force) into the open. A new defense law created the Wehrmacht (armed forces), consisting of the Heer, Luftwaffe, and Kriegsmarine (navy).[7] Yet even Hitler was unable or unwilling to streamline the highest levels of the armed forces staffs. Neither he nor the services would give up the power needed to create the rather autonomous theater commanders later used effectively by the United States. While American practice fostered at least some interservice unity of effort and cooperation, the German high command from the beginning lacked an effective staff doctrine for integrating land, sea, and air forces for world war. It could only coordinate the execution of operations that had often been independently planned. Hitler made the final decisions, and he apparently did not even "take notice of the army's war plans until 1937."[8] Germany, like the United States, found that rapid expansion of the armed forces diluted the impact of experienced soldiers, and the army suffered from the transfer of many good men to the Luftwaffe. Yet by 1939 the army had grown to 102 active and reserve divisions, with 730,000 active and 1.1 million reserve soldiers.[9] America's regular ground and air forces, as noted above, had fewer than 150,000 men; the Guard and Organized Reserves had about a quarter-million more.

Germany had no doctrine, per se, of *blitzkrieg*, or "lightning warfare." It was not a revolutionary doctrine, since its basic precepts of rapid and decisive maneuver went back to the nineteenth century. Even the origins of the term "blitzkrieg" are in doubt. Sources vary from *Time* magazine to Hitler. Whatever the origin, the basics of its operational concept were mechanized mobility and combined arms supported by tactical aviation. Planners envisioned a concentrated breakthrough on a narrow front to isolate enemy combat forces through neutralization of headquarters and communications facilities by air and ground attack. The focus remained operational, not necessarily strategic, in that the aim was destruction of maneuver organizations, not the destruction of rear installations for their own sake.[10]

Some observers have praised without question the penchant of German senior combat leaders to move forward and make decisions based on first hand observation. Performing this fundamental part of operational command and control was essential to success; however, one should also note that there is risk in a total focus on events at the front. Commanders must also know the limits of their logistical tether, and they must be available to their staffs in the rear. Too much forward presence can hamper the initiative of the junior commander, and such practice probably led to the relative caution with which many units fought the 1939 campaign in Poland. Coordination between the infantry and artillery was poor, and some commanders allowed even minor resistance to stop them. While the relatively small mobile forces did plow through Polish resistance, the shortage of cargo and fuel trucks tied the army to railheads and horse-drawn supply columns.[11] On the other hand, pioneers in armor and mechanization had grasped earlier than their British and American counterparts the dangers in creating tank-heavy combined arms formations. They never embraced wholesale conversion to an armor-based army. When tactical conditions allowed, German doctrine stipulated an elastic defense coupled with immediate and violent counterattack. Late in the war, however, necessity forced the Germans to adopt static, or linear, positions based on strongpoints.[12]

The 1940 campaign in the West tested an emerging capability to synchronize communications, isolate enemy troops from their support, and to find and exploit weak spots in defenses. Germany's unexpected domination of the French and British shook the world, but it also led many observers to overlook logistical weaknesses. Although successful in France, Germany lost the Battle of Britain in the summer of 1940. The Luftwaffe had sophisticated theories on strategic air doctrine, but shortsightedness led it to plan for campaigns of brief duration. For example, it did not expand pilot training after 1939, nor did it produce enough aircraft. The air arm paid the price of an arrogance that disdained its enemies and overestimated its own technology and operational expertise.[13] It is important to emphasize, however, that the Luftwaffe remained an effective tactical force until well into mid-1944, especially on the Eastern Front.

Those who criticize the United States for its "corporate management" of World War II should not praise the Germans for their almost utter neglect of the same. Optimism born of arrogance led to an attempt to manage hundreds of different and redundant types of transport vehicles, artillery, and tanks. Each of these systems required specialized maintenance expertise and repair parts (something there was never enough of).

This came to a head in the advance into the Soviet Union, when very long supply lines demanded self-contained support capability that Germany did not develop. Initial success through traditional battles of encirclement, not deep thrusts against rear areas, was costly: some 87,000 soldiers were killed in action during the first two months of the campaign. By late 1942, the Soviets had inflicted so many casualties that the German armed forces were short 800,000 men.[14]

By 1944, America caught up to its allies and opponents in terms of the ability to execute military operations of a high degree of complexity. Germany's armed forces, on the other hand, began a process of what one historian has termed "fragmentation." That is not to imply that by 1944 the Wehrmacht was unable to fight with the same degree of professionalism than it had in 1941 or 1942. On the contrary, it is an indication of its resilience and that it achieved the combat effectiveness it did despite the conditions under which it fought.[15] Early success through the effective employment of limited resources helped create the impression that the Heer had numerical and technological preponderance. This was not the case, as the qualitative preponderance was concentrated in the armored and mechanized forces of the Heer and in the Waffen SS. High morale waned over time as soldiers faced almost inhuman living conditions on all fronts. Reports as early as the winter of 1941–1942 of mental breakdowns, command failures, strained nerves, and exhaustion caused by incessant, brutal fighting filtered back to Germany.[16] This contrasts with a pervading impression among many historians that professionalism alone kept these hard-bitten soldiers solidly in control of themselves. Some recent historical research suggests that Nazi ideology played a significant role in soldier motivation. The military institution had very strong links to the Nazi movement.[17]

Regarding tactical operations in the west, there were few standard designs that determined the organization of a particular unit in a specific engagement. The basic unit of the Heer was the rifle squad, and professional development of the squad leader was one of the most important peacetime training goals. This soldier was taught to develop strict self-discipline, to set the example, to care for his men, and to be prepared to die for them. Control of fear, coolness under fire, individual initiative, and the trust and confidence of his men were essential to success. The Germans integrated the machine gun into the squad and made it the central weapon, not a supporting weapon as did the Americans. Employment of standard organizations often gave way to ad hoc infantry *kampfgruppen* (literally, battle groups) that varied in size from a reinforced rifle company to a reinforced regiment, with artillery, engineers, and possibly tanks. U.S. intelligence officers could not assume that the strength and firepower of a battle group would remain constant over a period of days just because of its formal designation. Sometimes troops from more than single divisions were banded together, and units could be transferred between the battle groups, or between divisions themselves, on short notice.[18]

Some have linked the tenacity of the German soldier to thorough training and the influence of a "primary group," or a five-to-ten-man section/squad. Cohesion in this sense refers to mutual respect, trust, sharing of a common burden or experience, and it results from living and working closely with one another. It remains an accepted belief among both soldiers and the academic community that such groups originate in bonds established either before or outside of direct combat. One study found that German soldiers accepted political symbolism only to the extent they thought it contributed to the functioning of this small group. Cohesion broke down when utter destruction threatened the small unit and all that mattered was personal survival. In this view, the culmination of years of war had finally broken these bonds by the spring of 1945. On the other hand, Allied surveys of prisoners found continued devotion to Hitler even in the latter months of the war. Sixty percent of those questioned in Western prisoner of war camps expressed confidence in him as late as the end of 1944. At a time when only one in ten prisoners believed Germany could still win the war, a third still retained confidence in Hitler and spoke of him with enthusiasm.[19]

What was the reason for such determination? Was it "grim, determined, and increasingly hopeless commitment to professional and national duty?"[20] German commanders' reports describe the poor physical and mental condition of their troops in both the East and West, and without doubt those in the East developed a greater sense of abandonment by the government and people than those in the West. Equipment breakdowns, lack of proper clothing and shelter, widespread sickness, and poor nutrition were common. Soldiers apparently concluded that they had to destroy in order to survive. Some of their tenacity in battle also seems to have stemmed from their fear of their own leaders. Germany is known to have executed about 15,000 of its soldiers during the war. As a sort of counterbalance to keep the troops under control in stressful situations, commanders sometimes allowed men to vent their anger and frustration on both enemy soldiers and civilians.[21]

Basic training was harsh and emphasized the development of character. Inductees seldom took written aptitude tests, in contrast with the GI, who might have found the enemy system unscientific in its effort to identify intangibles like willpower, mental stamina, courage, loyalty, and obedience.[22] German leaders hoped that the intentional creation of a "community" would contribute to a soldier's sense of self-worth. The emphasis on carrying out the mission, combined with coercive techniques bordering on brutality, produced a sense of "community" (Gemeinschaft) that would presumably keep this "family" together. On the other hand, American doctrine sought to inculcate individual fighting spirit. America created its army for one purpose—to fight a war, not as a vehicle for imbuing its members with a political ideology.[23]

Germany mobilized about three hundred infantry divisions and was able with some effort to rotate units (or remnants) out of the line for rest and reconstitution. On the other hand, creating so many divisions led to a significantly large amount of headquarters-level and logistical overhead. After high losses in combat, it was common for the surviving headquarters staffs and support units to be withdrawn from the line to form the basis for new units, with the addition of several thousand replacements. Sometimes staffs of units whose combat elements had been completely destroyed might be moved to assume control of other units whose headquarters had been eliminated. This sometimes happened with little or no notice—often so quickly that company commanders whose men were left in the foxholes did not know they had become part of a different division. As a result of this hurried reconstruction of units, troops simply had to rely on their own small units for survival. Such practices happened commonly in the West, and some of the most extreme examples were in the bitter Hürtgen Forest fighting in late 1944. Thousands of Luftwaffe and Kriegsmarine personnel, including hurriedly trained NCOs, filled the ranks of infantry divisions. Some of these men were still wearing their blue air force or navy uniforms when taken prisoner. GIs specifically noted this during the Battle of the Bulge.[24] The German practice of not retaining veteran units that had suffered high losses while creating entirely new units, rather than replacing casualties in the veteran units, was inefficient and ignored the strength of perpetuated organization structures. New men did not always have the benefit of learning from the veterans. It appears that a German combat replacement in the West was as likely as his American counterpart to go into battle without knowing to what organization he belonged.[25]

It is hard to generalize about intangibles such as morale in the Heer, because the service changed significantly even during the relatively short period between D-day and VE day. Morale varied between individual units and soldiers, but it is clear that intentional brutalization of soldiers, skillful manipulation by Nazi propaganda, and unique cultural factors meant that the *Landser* was a product of an experience vastly different from that of the GI. Despite these differences, there is little doubt the German soldier saw himself as a decent man. Without having anything to compare it with, the soldiers listened to the Nazi version of truth, and it gained credibility in the field. The military and the party had mutually supporting interests in giving the soldier a sense of community that made him think he was a protector of his culture and a crusader for his nation. However, this image obscured the fact that he also fought for Nazism.[26] Germany's emphasis on small-unit performance, reinforced by ideology and a sense of community, almost reached the level of strategy itself.

CHAPTER 5

NEPTUNE, JUNE–JULY 1944

ERDERET RIVER CAUSEWAY, near La Fière, Normandy, France, approx. 1045 hours (10:45 AM), 9 June 1944: Lt. Bruce H. Booker, 3d Battalion, 325th Glider Infantry Regiment, lay in a ditch, painfully wounded in both legs, unable to lead his men through the incessant machine-gun, mortar, and artillery fire. Their only route of attack was straight down a five-hundred-yard-long causeway. Booker waved at his men and called, "Get on up there, goddam it! That's where the fight is!"[1]

This was the battalion's introduction to combat. No other unit was available to make the attack. Tanks and artillery could not hold ground; it was up to the glider infantrymen to open a hole for an attack inland from Utah Beach. First one man, then another, summoned the courage to leave the relative protection of a stone wall to face the bullets. Miraculously, many survived by running as fast as they could—not low crawling—toward the enemy. Most of those who hesitated for even a second to follow their instinct to drop to the ground were killed or wounded. One man later said, "Since we had never been in combat, no one realized what hell fire we were going into."[2]

The Mission

As THE CAMPAIGN IN THE MEDITERRANEAN unfolded, a special planning staff in England worked on an outline plan for an invasion of the continent and drive into Germany. Detailed planning for the cross-Channel attack (Operation Neptune was the invasion, Overlord was the campaign to stay ashore and gain a lodgment in France) began in January 1943, long before the final decision to launch the attack. The plan eventually called for development of a large network of airfields, ports, and supply installations to sustain follow-on operations ashore. Clearance of Brittany, capture of all ports south of the Loire River, and occupation of

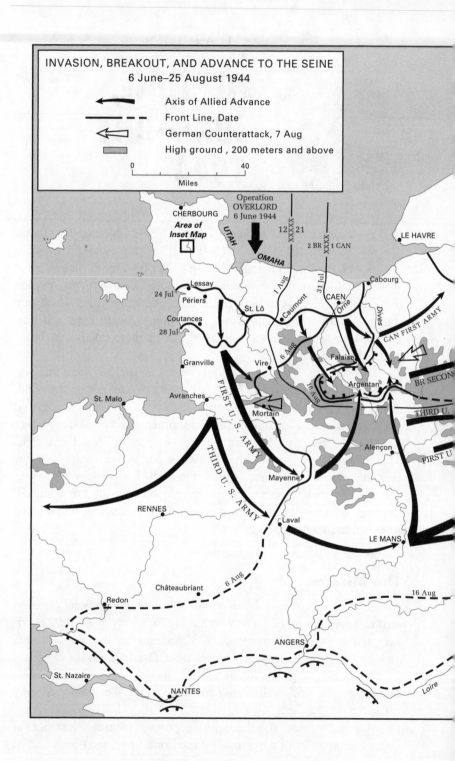

INVASION, BREAKOUT, AND ADVANCE TO THE SEINE
6 June–25 August 1944

←	Axis of Allied Advance
— —	Front Line, Date
⇐	German Counterattack, 7 Aug
▨	High ground , 200 meters and above

0   40

Miles

Operation
OVERLORD
6 June 1944

CHERBOURG

Area of
Inset Map

UTAH

12 XXXXX 21

2 BR XXX 1 CAN

LE HAVRE

OMAHA

Lessay

24 Jul

Périers

Coutances

28 Jul

St. Lô

Caumont

CAEN

Orme

Cabourg

1 Aug

31 Jul

Dives

CAN FIRST ARMY

Granville

Vire

6 Aug

Falaise

Argentan

BR SECON

St. Malo

Avranches

Mortain

FIRST U. S. ARMY

19 Aug

THIRD U.

Alençon

FIRST U

THIRD U. S. ARMY

Mayenne

RENNES

Laval

LE MANS

Châteaubriant

6 Aug

16 Aug

Redon

ANGERS

St. Nazaire

NANTES

Loire

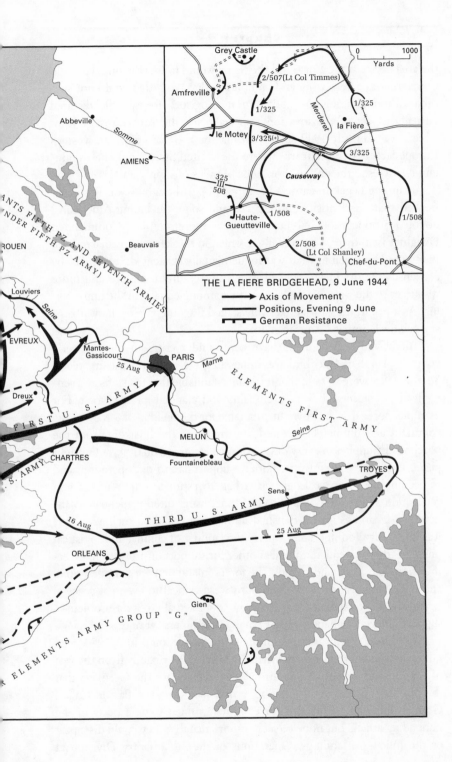

0   1000
          Yards

Grey Castle

2/507(Lt Col Timmes)

Amfreville

1/325

1/325

Merderet

le Motey   3/325(+)

la Fière

3/325

325
III
508

Causeway

1/508

1/508

Haute-
Gueutteville

2/508
(Lt Col Shanley)

Chef-du-Pont

THE LA FIERE BRIDGEHEAD, 9 June 1944
→ Axis of Movement
— Positions, Evening 9 June
┬┬┬ German Resistance

Abbeville

Somme

AMIENS

ANTS FIFTH PZ AND SEVENTH ARMIES
UNDER FIFTH PZ ARMY)

ROUEN

Louviers

Seine

EVREUX

Mantes-
Gassicourt

25 Aug

PARIS

Marne

ELEMENTS FIRST ARMY

Dreux

FIRST U. S. ARMY

Beauvais

MELUN

Seine

S. ARMY

CHARTRES

Fountainebleau

TROYES

Sens

16 Aug

THIRD U. S. ARMY

25 Aug

ORLEANS

Gien

ELEMENTS ARMY GROUP "G"
R ELEMENTS ARMY GROUP "G"

the area between the Loire and the Seine would follow the initial assault. Overlord was a very risky and complex undertaking that could not succeed without meeting several conditions. Logistics, for example, dictated virtually aspect of the invasion, especially for the Americans. A Joint Chiefs study in July 1942 supported making the main effort in western Europe largely because it was where the United States could best maintain its forces at the end of thousands of miles of supply lines.[3]

Planning began in earnest in early 1944. Although he was less experienced than his British counterparts, and some (including Americans) doubted his operational abilities, the new Supreme Allied Commander, Dwight Eisenhower, was actually a strategic thinker with a sharp mind that served him well in what was fundamentally strategy development by consensus. As the inexperienced Americans committed more and more resources to the war, they became a "first among equals" in the undertaking. As a result, the Allies effectively staked the outcome of the war on a still relatively untried American army.

Allied logistical planners have come under criticism for an overly complex plan that some think was impossible to carry out in the first place. Yet the stakes were so high that it is understandable that the staffs and senior leaders considered every eventuality and planned for the worst. For example, port capacity drove the timetable for the buildup of forces on the continent and ultimately dictated the timing of the breakout from the beachhead. Supplies of every description had to arrive on time, at the right place, and in the right quantity both to support day-to-day operations and to accumulate reserves. Logisticians had to estimate requirements and requisition supplies months ahead of time, using often inadequate planning factors and estimates that had never been tested on such a scale. It was imperative to integrate properly the landing of combat and logistical units, for they depended on one another for support or protection. Over-the-shore logistics could support the forces inland only for a limited time, and operable ports such as Cherbourg were critical to eventual success. Ironically, more combat force early on could actually pose a problem—support units could handle only so many "customers" at once.

The sheer drama and magnitude of the assault on 6 June 1944 need not be detailed here. Air forces virtually isolated Normandy from the rest of France, and deception operations helped convince the Germans that the objective of the cross-Channel attack would be the Pas de Calais. German intelligence officers correctly determined some aspects of the impending attack, but none of such importance that they could disrupt it or the follow-on landings. Operations of the 4th Infantry Division at

Utah Beach went comparatively well, because a navigation error and a strong current put the troops ashore at a lightly defended area. Ten miles away at Omaha, a regiment of the 1st Infantry Division and a regiment of the new 29th landed in the face of difficult terrain and unexpectedly strong resistance. An inexcusable intelligence oversight had failed to detect the presence of a new German infantry division. Concrete casemates, bunkers, and blockhouses were manned, and the defenders swept the beaches with fire.[4]

Strategic surprise for the overall landing was out of the question, since the Germans could easily assume that a cross-Channel attack would come in mid-1944 if at all that year. Tactical surprise was also hard to gain, though the Allies should have done better in trying to achieve it through either a night attack or with a much more powerful pre-invasion bombardment. One historian has noted that the Americans worked along "incompatible doctrines" that tried to use air attack to replace the proven effects of a naval bombardment on the order of those used with success in the Pacific.[5] However, to the extent that the cross-Channel attack was a no-fail, almost literally one-time, proposition, it was different than other assault landing operations, and some level of tactical surprise was necessary. Historians have also criticized the Americans for rejecting specially modified tanks developed by the British. These critics, however, have not explained how these tanks would have negotiated the bluffs above Omaha. The Americans did not neglect armor; however, their plan to get tanks ashore with the lead troops failed miserably.[6]

Hard fighting in France by the new army continued long after sunset on 6 June 1944, and the results indicate that the GI and his leaders were continuing to learn from past experiences. It is important to remember that only four of nineteen divisions that participated in the fighting in Normandy from 6 June to 1 August 1944 were experienced when they entered battle, and the same can be said of the myriad separate artillery, tank, TD, and supporting units. Gaining maneuver space inland required the Utah Beach assault corps, the VII, under the command of J. Lawton Collins, to clear the Cotentin Peninsula and Cherbourg. One of the divisions involved was the 82d Airborne (Maj. Gen. Matthew B. Ridgway), whose paratroopers landed astride the Merderet River behind Utah before dawn on D-day, took the village of St. Mere Eglise, and set out to block German reinforcements. The new 101st Airborne secured the VII Corps' left and maintained contact with the V Corps at Omaha. Also new to combat, the 4th Infantry Division, reinforced with a regiment from the equally inexperienced draftee 90th Infantry Division, had the critical

mission of taking Cherbourg by D+15 (see map) and opening its port.[7]
Between the invasion forces and the interior of the Cotentin were the
Douve River and its main tributary, the Merderet, which drained most of
the Cotentin Peninsula. Though the rivers had a relatively slow current
and were only fifteen to fifty yards wide under normal conditions, their
bottomlands were below sea level. The Germans held a dam that controlled the level of the rivers, and at flood stage they could restrict travel
to a handful of causeways and bridges.

Ridgway's thirty-seven-year-old assistant, Brig. Gen. James M. Gavin,
led the 82d's predawn parachute drop on D-day. Hardly any of the parachute landings went as planned. Elements of the 2d Battalion of the 507th
Parachute Infantry Regiment (PIR) were cut off west of the Merderet.
About half of the 505th PIR's 2,200 men landed in their assigned drop
zone (DZ). Elements of the 508th PIR came down throughout the area
behind the coast. Landing zones (LZs) for the 325th Glider Infantry,
under Col. Harry L. Lewis, were south of St. Mere Eglise. Plans called for
the 505th and 507th to take the Merderet bridges and causeways at La
Fière and Chef du Pont. The 508th would block enemy routes of reinforcement at the Douve crossings and extend the defensive line of the
507th. Causes of the bad drops included poor pilot training (blamed in
part on bad weather and short, late winter and spring days over England),
"green" aircraft crewmen in general, and the lack of navigators and navigation aids in some planes. Many pilots had trouble locating the DZs, and
the Germans prevented proper marking of some. Ridgway, however, had
no time to dwell on the circumstances facing him in the first hours of the
invasion. His chief of staff was injured, the division engineer was a prisoner, the ordnance officer and the G-4 (logistics officer) had been
wounded, the G-3 (division operations officer) was missing (he would
show up late on 6 June), and the G-1 (personnel officer) did not reach the
division until 7 June. Communications were so bad that Ridgway could
not be sure that the landings had occurred.[8]

Glider Infantry

JUMPING INTO BATTLE BY PARACHUTE was risky enough, but even paratroopers thought a combat landing in a glider was dangerous. The
Army's glider program, of which the 325th was a part, grew from
post–World War I civilian interest and the successful German glider
attack in May 1940 on the Belgian fort of Eben Emael. Development of

U.S. Army glider infantry began in 1941, after the initiation of its airborne program. The Army started work on troop-carrying combat gliders, but the program lacked a guiding doctrine, and the Army was unable to synchronize glider production, pilot training, and airfield development. Requirements for trained glider pilots reached 6,000. Despite the dangers of glider operations, some parachutists in the 82d "regarded Harry Lewis's gliderists with utmost scorn."[9] When twenty-year-old draftee Chester Walker arrived at Fort Bragg for training, he "did not know what a glider was; secondly, I couldn't figure out how I got in an outfit like that." To remain with his friends, Walker refused promotion or transfer during the war.[10]

The CG-4 series combat glider, called the Waco, had an 83.6-foot wingspan and was forty-eight feet long. The fuselage was a simple tubular steel frame covered with canvas; the wings were plywood covered with canvas. The cargo bay floor was of a honeycomb plywood construction that provided a load-bearing capacity greater than the empty weight of the glider. A CG-4A could carry a jeep with radio, a driver, radio operator, and one additional soldier, or even a light 75-mm howitzer and a few rounds of ammunition. The pilot and copilot sat side by side, each with his own control and basic set of instruments. Communication between the tow plane and the pilot in early models was by telephone wire loosely wrapped around the around the tow cable. If the phone cable broke, tug pilots simply lowered their landing gear to signal their intent to cut the glider free.[11]

"Gliders ready for a formation flight looked as though they meant business. . . . Covering the main runway from side to side and halfway down its length, with the noise of the C-47 engines filling the air, a glider mission in the making was one of the unforgettable sights of World War II," recalled a C-47 pilot. On takeoff, tug pilots inched their planes forward, then cut back on power when they were alongside their designated gliders. Ground crewmen secured the tow line, and a glider officer in a jeep would motion the tow pilot to ease his plane forward until there was no slack in the rope. The pilot pushed the throttles forward when he saw the green signal light indicating takeoff. The glider pilot, meanwhile, began a struggle to keep his aircraft straight—a Waco would lift off at 60 mph, but a C-47 would not take off until its speed was 85 mph. Propeller wash caused the gliders to vibrate, and canvas slapped against the metal tube frame until the release of the tow line, which brought a few minutes of silence until the landing—unless a

German bullet hit the tight canvas. That sound was a distinct drumlike pop. An inexperienced pilot might overcorrect altitude while connected to the tow plane and cause the glider pitch like a yo-yo. A loose tow line might snap back and shatter the plexiglass nose of the craft. A glider could fishtail and throw the infantry around inside. Not unheard of, especially during a strong head wind, was violent fuselage vibration that might cause a wing to snap off.[12]

"As far as we in our Squadron could see, glider troopers certainly were subjected to terrible shocks in the air, on the way down, and during the landing itself," said Martin Wolfe. Gliders did not really "land." They crashed, "more or less successfully." A glider might lose one or both wings to trees before bouncing back several feet into the air and hitting a hedgerow or wall. Some disintegrated on impact—the tail might come to rest yards from the fuselage. Dazed crew and infantry would then slowly drag themselves from the wreckage, wondering for a moment whether they were alive or dead.[13]

First Blood

IRONICALLY, SOME PARATROOPERS landed relatively close to the Merderet at Chef du Pont and at the causeway on D-day, but they did not think they were actually at their objective. They expected to hit dry ground, but, as most did not know, the enemy had inundated the bottomland. Men from each of the 82d's parachute regiments eventually converged on a railroad embankment and at La Fière itself, just a few hundred yards from the causeway, but German fire kept them down.[14] Gavin reached the area with about three hundred men (primarily from the 507th) and talked briefly with a battalion commander from 505th. He understood that the opposition was relatively light and that the paratroopers planned to have the causeway in hand soon. Things seeming under control at La Fière, he took his group to Chef du Pont, since he was unsure of the situation there. He also thought Col. Roy Lindquist, the commander of the 508th, was also heading there and the two groups should be able to take a river crossing without a lot of trouble.

However, Lindquist was actually heading to La LaFière with his own men and about forty-five more from Company G of the 507th (Capt. F. V. Schwartzwalder). He planned to seize first the house at the eastern (friendly) end of the causeway. Capt. John Dolan, whose men were already nearby and also trying to take the causeway, never got word of this activity, because of the compartmented nature of the hedgerow terrain. He had already sent out a patrol, which reached the house unobserved by the enemy. However, no officer present, including Lindquist, took charge before Ridgway arrived at midday.[15]

There were also paratroopers on the opposite (west) side of the Merderet River not far from the causeway, though no one on the eastern end with Gavin apparently knew exactly where. Lt. Louis Levy of the 507th was at the hamlet of Cauquigny (at the west end of the causeway) with another force under Lt. Joseph Kromylo. They had not crossed the causeway because they did not know which side controlled the eastern approaches. Levy did not think he had enough men to take and hold both sides of the crossing, so he secured only the west end with a machine-gun crew. He and Kromylo tried to get word to their battalion commander, whose CP was in a nearby in an apple orchard, but German fire turned them back. They could also hear the noises of combat on the east side of the Merderet, but during the early afternoon of 6 June they saw a paratrooper running toward them on the causeway.[16]

It was Captain Schwartzwalder, whose company was on the other side. After discussing the situation with the two lieutenants, he evidently thought things were under control and led his men to another objective. Levy then ran across the causeway to the house or to La Fière itself, where someone assured him reinforcements were on the way. He returned to Cauquigny to wait for the additional troops. Lindquist later went to Levy's position, where he discussed the situation before going back to La Fière and ordering a few dozen men to cross the Merderet and reinforce him.[17]

About this time, the paratroopers at Cauquigny heard tanks. Mortars or artillery suddenly burst around them. Levy, Kromylo, and a private emptied their rifles at German infantry, who quickly set up a machine gun and began to spray bullets toward the GIs. Levy then worked his way to that position, where he threw a grenade and then killed the survivors with rifle fire. One GI hit an old French-made Renault tank with a bazooka rocket. A paratroop sergeant and two privates let two more tanks pass the damaged one, then stood up and showered the vehicles with Browning Automatic Rifle (BAR) fire and grenades. One tank rolled to a halt. A German-made medium tank and more infantry came up, but the paratroopers were out of grenades and ran back to the church for cover. When other paratroopers, probably those ordered across by Lindquist, reached the church, they did not expect to have to fight tanks. Cohesion in this group broke down, and several men ran back across the causeway. The Germans had seized both Cauquigny and the western end of the causeway.[18]

Late on 6 June, enemy infantry and two tanks set out across the causeway for the east bank. In a bout of deadly close combat, a GI shot a tank commander, and other fire possibly damaged one vehicle. A second panzer passed this one, and GIs put four bazooka rockets into its turret without visible effect. The tank's main gun swung toward them, but a bazooka team fired first and hit the base of the turret. Their next round hit a track. A private ran toward the rear of the vehicle and fired another rocket without effect. It took a fourth hit to kill the panzer and its crew.[19] Gavin, meanwhile, had returned to La Fière. He radioed the commander at Chef du Pont and told him to send reinforcements. General Ridgway also reached La Fière about that time, determined to gain control of the situation.[20]

Events of 6-7 June

THE GLIDER LZs BEHIND UTAH BEACH were full of hedgerows, trees, and Germans. Gliders carrying supplies, heavy weapons, and troops came in twice on 6 June. On the 7th, follow-on glider missions code-named "Galveston" and "Hackensack" carried the 325th GIR to combat. Galveston's hundred CG-4s and Horsas (a British glider type) carrying the 1st Battalion, combat engineers, the regimental headquarters, jeeps, artillery, and ammunition, departed two airfields in England about 4:30 AM. Enemy troops opened fire as the first gliders landed about three hours later. The glider carrying the battalion headquarters practically crashed. The commander, Lt. Col. Klemm Boyd, was thrown clear and regained consciousness still partially buried in debris. For a moment he thought one of his legs had been torn off. Medics ran up and helped him find the "missing" leg, which was still attached but under the wreckage.[21] Maj. Teddy Sanford was his replacement.

One glider slammed into the treetops at seventy miles per hour. A case of mortar ammo broke loose and flew into the cockpit, crashed into the instrument panel, and hit the pilot. The craft fell to the ground, leaving its wings wrapped around the trees. Medic Chester Walker rode in a Horsa. When the pilot tried to land, the fully loaded glider would not respond to the controls, and it went down hard, leaving parts of its wings and tail in some trees. The fuselage bounced along the ground, and Walker ended up with his head between his knees. He used every bandage he had in treating men with broken limbs and lacerations.[22] Pilot Douglas Miller recalled, "In training, loaded with 2000 lbs. of sandbags, [pilots] used a minimum of 800' to land over a 20' obstacle.

In Normandy, I saw open spaces less than half that minimum." Miller put his Waco into an open space about three hundred feet in length. The left wing tore off, and the landing gear collapsed, but no one was injured.[23]

Lt. Wayne Pierce watched his pilot and copilot struggle with the controls of their overloaded glider. He ordered the men to throw out several hundred pounds of cargo, and it regained a few feet of altitude before towline cutoff. Struggling to display strength in front of his men, he hugged his pack and equipment. "I hoped the men were not watching me." Minutes later, they touched ground and rolled to a stop, undamaged and unhurt.[24] In another glider, Lt. James B. Helmer yelled at his men to brace for landing. "The wheels hit the ground and we were racing across a small field at 100 miles an hour. . . . There was a violent jolt as we hit a small ridge, then we were through the smoke and skidding on our nose toward a marsh directly ahead."[25] Lt. Richard B. Johnson's pilot pulled back hard on the controls to clear some trees at the end of a field. The impact of landing hurled the pilot and copilot through the front of the aircraft. The loading ramp broke loose, flew end over end, and tossed Johnson and his runner, who were still strapped in their seats, face down into the marshy earth.[26]

Col. Harry Lewis, the commander of the 325th, had a good landing with elements of the untried 3d Battalion. There were about 160 landing casualties, which represented some 25 percent of a full strength battalion (643 soldiers—the authorized strength of a glider infantry regiment was only some 2,300 soldiers).[27] A second after he congratulated the pilot on getting them down safely, enemy mortar and machine-gun fire came in from several directions, and everyone dashed for cover. Lewis had understood that American troops already held most of the area, and he had not received a message from Gavin instructing his regiment to "come in fighting." Though his original mission had been to get to Chef du Pont and go into division reserve, Ridgway instead ordered him to send two battalions to reinforce paratroopers at St. Mere Eglise and La Fière. Lewis also learned that the Germans were between him and the main body of the division.[28]

Gavin ordered the men at Chef du Pont to be prepared to move against either La Fière or St. Mere Eglise. Meanwhile, the enemy kept the pressure up at the causeway. About 10:00 AM on 7 June, four more old German-manned Renault tanks rumbled toward La Fière. Bazooka men met them head on, and a 57-mm anti-tank gun also got off a shot or two. One tank pushed aside bazooka teams, who fell back to reload. Either a rocket or a 57-mm AT round knocked out this tank and the *Landsers* bunched up behind it, only fifty yards from the GIs' hurriedly dug positions. When his platoon leader was "hit hard from one burst and spouted so much blood that they had to [evacuate him] in the middle of the fight," Sgt. William Owens, an inconspicuous man, older and more reserved than most of the others, rallied the survivors "just by the example of his own steadiness." Yet the Germans came on. Owens soon had only three men left. Men urged him to pull back. He refused. He sent a runner to Captain Dolan, who returned with a written message that said, "I don't know a better place than this to die."[29]

The 325th Enters the Battle

WORD OF THE INVASION'S SUCCESS finally reached Ridgway on the morning of 7 June. The bad news was that only 15 percent of the scheduled supplies were ashore and that the flow of personnel was 7,000 below plan. To speed up the drive on Cherbourg and its essential port, General Collins, the VII Corps commander, ordered the 4th Infantry Division to clear the right flank of the landing beaches instead of crossing the Merderet through an as-yet-nonexistent bridgehead. The 82d Airborne Division would continue to grapple with that task.[30]

By the morning of 8 June, the paratroopers had been worn down. Dolan's company was down to about half of its original 147 men, with sixty-six known casualties.[31] Fewer than two hundred men had been accounted for in Colonel Timmes's battalion, then under pressure in the orchard on the west bank of the Merderet. One of his officers found a route of withdrawal using a ford north of La Fière, and he eventually located Ridgway, who ordered Lewis to move a battalion (the 1st, under Major Sanford) across the Merderet, link up with Timmes, and take the causeway from the rear, through Cauquigny.[32]

Sanford's men crossed the Merderet before dawn on 9 June without incident and were nearing the orchard in the vicinity of a mansion the GIs called the "Grey Castle" when the Germans opened fire. Sanford sent one company to silence this opposition, another toward Cauquigny, and his third rifle company to block enemy reinforcements. Unfortunately, it took considerable time to silence the opposition at the "castle," and this company was unable to join the one moving toward Cauquigny. Some of these men, meanwhile, had set off trip flares, taken a wrong road, and eventually reached an open field where scouts saw an artillery position just a few yards away.

When a voice called out, "*Kamerad!*" the glider infantrymen thought the opposition was about to surrender. Men called out to hold fire, though one or two fired anyway. When some of the enemy returned the fire, the lieutenant in charge ordered an attack. It was an ambush. Bullets tore into the GIs. An enemy armored car wheeled onto the sunken road where most of the Americans were and opened fire. What started as an orderly withdrawal turned into a rout. Many of the men stopped only when they reached the orchard area. The company nearing Cauquigny was also still in trouble, and at about 5:30 AM Sanford told Lewis that the attack had failed.[33]

The 90th Infantry Division (another green unit) was meanwhile moving inland with orders to cross the Merderet and move on Cherbourg. Lewis, Ridgway, and Gavin discussed their options. Ridgway said there was no time to lose in securing the causeway at La Fière. Gavin recalled that he told Lewis "to use all the means available" to do it as soon as possible. Colonel Lewis had little choice given the terrain, enemy situation, and time available but to order a frontal attack. Gavin promised Lewis a fifteen-minute artillery preparation from the 90th Division's artillery. Lewis's only available battalion was Lt. Col. Charles Carrell's untried 3d Battalion. It was about 8:15 AM. on 9 June 1944.[34]

Lewis told 2d Lt. Vernon L. Wyant Jr., a liaison officer to division headquarters, that it was "a suicide mission."[35] In picking the commanders of his parachute regiments, Ridgway valued energy and youth, and his choice of Lewis to lead the glider regiment was "baffling and controversial." Most, however, believed Lewis was intelligent and professionally competent, and despite his age (he had entered the Army before Bradley or Eisenhower) he was physically fearless and had unlimited energy. Ridgway thought the 325th was the weakest regiment in the division and that it needed a strong-willed commander, even if he was older than his peers. Some of his officers liked him; many did not. One lieutenant thought he was a "weak man . . . short, slim, steel-rimmed glasses, sharp little face, humorless expression."[36] But others say Lewis was fair—he was hard on everyone from lieutenant to lieutenant colonel. By the end of the battle of Normandy, "there wasn't anybody in that whole outfit who wouldn't charge hell with a bucket of water" for him.[37]

Lt. Col. Frank W. Norris, commander of the supporting field artillery battalion from the 90th Infantry Division, reported that his guns could not be ready to fire before 10:30. He and his S-3 went with Gavin to a position overlooking the causeway. Norris recalled, "The Krauts were sparing nothing, so we got mortars, artillery . . . as our

Lt. Vernon Wyant, 325th Glider Infantry Regiment. [Courtesy Vernon L. Wyant]

introduction [to battle]. I waited for Gen. Gavin to get in [his foxhole]. He . . . understood how overwhelmed we were . . . and directed us, 'No, you two [Norris and the S-3] get in. I think you need it more than I do.'" Norris later remembered seeing Ridgway, Gavin, and Lewis standing at the beginning of the causeway, giving each glider infantry-man a "slap on the butt and an appropriately virile word of encourage-ment" when they began the crossing.[38]

Events climaxed to indescribable noise and chaos. Sherman tanks rumbled into position. Mortar and artillery shells crashed down. Small-arms fire picked up in intensity. Glider infantrymen waited nervously. Buckles and hooks clinked as men adjusted their web belts and shoulder straps. Radios crackled in the command post foxholes. Stomachs tight-ened. Men checked and rechecked their rifles. Gavin located Carrell, who had been injured in the glider landing, and gave him the order to attack at 10:45 AM. He apparently said something to the effect that he was ill and could not lead the attack. Gavin relieved him on the spot and replaced him with Maj. Arthur Gardner, one of the 3d Battalion's officers. Lt. Lee Travelstead later said Carrell told him he did not want to be responsible for what he honestly believed would be a futile, if not suicidal, attack, that he would do the same thing again. Travelstead also recalled thinking that Gavin and Lewis had selected the 3d Battalion to do the dirty work because it was an "orphan unit" as far as the 82d was concerned. It had not been part of the division until recently, when a third battalion was added to the glider regiments. The battalion had started the war as part of the 101st Airborne Division and had been transferred to the 82d as part of a reorganization of airborne divisions.[39] Regardless of what Carrell told Gavin or what Gavin heard, the latter was apparently con-cerned enough about the success of the attack to tell the executive officer of the 507th PIR to have its Company A (Capt. R. D. Rae) take over the attack if the glider infantry broke "in the fury of battle."[40]

Lieutenant Colonel Norris, meanwhile, ordered each of his 155-mm howitzers to fire fifteen rounds as rapidly as possible. Beginning at 10:30, dozens of high-explosive rounds slammed into the far end of the cause-way.[41] Shermans from the 746th Tank Battalion fired to supplement the artillery. Lewis recalled, "The German fire against the jump-off position held by the battalion and against the covering position held by the 507th troops was so intense, even during this artillery fire, that the men could hardly raise their heads above the ground." He wondered whether the artillery was having any effect.[42] Captain Sauls, commander of G Company, 325th, spoke briefly to some paratroop officers. They said "there were a hell of a lot of enemy on the other side of the river." Sauls saw "15 or 20" dead paratroopers. It was about 10:40 AM.[43]

German fire hit the covering stone wall and ricocheted into the buildings beyond. Sauls "winked at some of [the men], and they winked back at him." Someone made a joke about good-looking French girls who might be waiting on the other side. Sauls looked at his watch and warned the men as each minute passed. He'd been promised smoke, but there was none.[44]

10:45—Sauls led out, heading left. Lt. Donald B. Wason took charge of the group moving to the right. He was followed closely by his platoon sergeant, Staff Sgt. Wilfred L. Ericsson, and more soldiers. "They felt fire all around them and coming at them from both flanks."[45] Speed saved those who were brave enough to run fully upright without even slowing, crouching, or stopping to look for cover. Sauls was shocked to see when he looked back through the haze that only a few men were behind him. The problem was at a gap in the wall near the beginning of the causeway. The first man to run by it had taken a bullet in the head. Soldiers were bunching up behind his body. Ten minutes of indecision passed, then Lt. Frank E. Amino yelled, "Let's go on and kill the sons of bitches!" Several followed him, but others stayed behind.[46]

Wason, Ericsson, and about thirty other men survived the crossing to reach the west (Cauquigny) end of the causeway, where they fanned out into the underbrush. The firefight was intense. Sauls remained at the intersection of the causeway road and a dirt trail to direct the men as they arrived on the far side. A BAR gunner, Pfc. James D. Kittle, fired at some retreating enemy flushed from their fighting positions by Ericsson. About a dozen Germans surrendered at this point. Enemy grenades fell like rain. Fortunately, they did not cause many casualties—Sauls was nicked in the leg by a fragment. Wason was killed single-handedly attacking a machine-gun dugout. Sauls's runner, Pfc. Frank Thompson, who had been with him, spotted another position and shot the crew one at a time with his M1. "I got the bastards," he reported to Sauls.

Ericsson was hit in the back. A few minutes later, he gave his submachine gun to a friend. "Take that with you," he said. "You won't need a carbine over here." His implication was that the close in fighting required as much lead as possible.[47]

Tech. Sgt. John P. Kneale, meanwhile, was at the end of the causeway, yelling at the men as they came across. "Come on! Come on! We've got the goddam bastards on the run!" Sauls ordered him to take cover.

Within a few minutes after the attack began, wounded and dead GIs, some of whom had been hit repeatedly, blocked the uninjured men who wanted to run full out. One of the supporting tanks hit a mine (probably an American one laid earlier by a paratrooper) but did not become disabled. No one had told Sauls to delay the crossing long enough to clear the mines, and the explosion wounded seven men.[48]

From his command post, Lewis could not tell if anyone was on the other side. He ran to the bridge, stood among the dead, the wounded, and the fire, yelling, "Look, if I can stand here, then you can move, so get up and get going!" Many of them did. He followed them to make sure they went the entire way and decided it was time to call up the tanks. Running back, he went up to a Sherman and ordered the commander to get moving. The sergeant replied that he could not comply without orders from his company commander. Lewis was unable to locate the commander, but he did find an engineer officer who offered to assist. He persuaded another NCO to bring up his tank, which was also knocked out. It was still operable, however, and troops used it to pull a knocked-out panzer to the side of causeway. Lewis found Ridgway and asked him for assistance in getting the tanks across. Lewis later said "there was no time during the day when they [the tanks] did effective work in support of the battalion, and they moved reluctantly, if at all, when given specific missions."[49] The lack of tank-infantry training was apparent.

Company E, 325th

COMPANY E (CAPT. CHARLES F. MURPHY) followed Company G. Its mission was to clear the Cauquigny church vicinity and the adjacent banks of the Merderet. Murphy's 1st Platoon, under 2d Lt. Richard B. Johnson, was in two groups—under Johnson and his platoon sergeant, Tech. Sgt. Henry M. Howell. Few men heard Johnson's order to run on the relatively uncluttered right side of the causeway, and they thought he had lost his mind when he started to go across without taking cover. Howell's men, with a few G Company stragglers, became tangled in the debris and the bodies. Johnson saw a soldier whom he knew lying on his stomach. "You're going the wrong way," he said. "I can't help it, sir, I'm hit," came the plaintive reply. Johnson's men could not hear his instructions over the roar of battle. He used a .50 caliber bullet to scratch the letter E in the soot on the hull of a burned-out tank to let the men know where he was.

He later said, "I think I could feel the breeze of those bullets passing just behind me."[50]

Seconds later, a German grenade landed in a nearby manure pile, which muffled its explosion a little, but still sent a fragment slicing through Johnson's arm. He staggered, pulled the pin on his own grenade, and counted two seconds before he threw it. Probably thinking he had more time before the grenade went off, a German picked up the grenade to throw it back a moment before it exploded in his hand. Johnson then sent the crew of a German machine-gun position to the rear. A few minutes after Howell came up to discuss the situation, a machine-gun bullet passed through both of Johnson's ankles. Howell was also hit—a bullet nicked a rib and came out his back, leaving two gaping holes. Johnson crawled to Howell and tried to use the compress in his first aid packet to cover the wounds. He gave Howell a shot of morphine, but he quickly realized he had injected it below the wound— the morphine seeped out with the blood. They were both evacuated that afternoon. The NCO who took over the platoon was later killed in action.[51]

Captain Murphy was hit in the face by several small fragments. Despite losing a considerable amount of blood, he remained in command. Lt. Bruce Booker, the company executive officer, led some men across the causeway and then returned to the start point to prod stragglers. On his second trip across he was hit in both calves and sat down to await a medic. He yelled at the men to move fast across the causeway. When a group drifted back toward him, he pulled out his .45 caliber pistol, fired over their heads, and shouted at them to move out. Booker stayed in action for some time after medics treated his wounds. He crawled across the causeway, urging men on, and bandaged at least one badly injured rifleman before he was evacuated himself.[52]

Only about fifteen men of E Company's 2d Platoon (Lt. William G. Weikert) reached the church, where they took twenty-two prisoners. About eighteen men of the 3d Platoon nearly ran headlong into an enemy mortar position; the Germans had been so busy that they failed to notice the Americans, or their grenades, until it was too late.[53] Sgt. Russell Anderman "jumped in a trench where there was a wounded German. First I thought he was dead, but he was only wounded. So I kept my eyes on him and the first thing I noticed, he had grabbed his trench knife and was about to stab me. I quickly hit him with the butt of my M-1 rifle and then I let him have it with my bayonet." About thirty-five of Company E's 148 men were wounded; several more were dead.[54]

Company F

No ONE AT LA FIÈRE was sure what was happening across the causeway. Haze, dust, and smoke made it impossible to know. Few prisoners had reached American lines, because the intense fire had killed most of them. Gavin finally gave in to his uncertainty and ordered Captain Rae's paratrooper company to go across. Rae's men had apparently become so caught up in the action that they had quit giving the glider men fire support and were now simply watching the events unfold.[55] He had about eighty men with him when he reached the beginning of the causeway. German mortar and artillery fire was still heavy, and several glider infantrymen were still behind the knocked-out Sherman. His first inclination was to order these men from behind the tank. Lt. James D. Orwin, one of his officers, came up wearing a knit cap (his helmet had been blown off by the concussion of a shell) with a flower stuck under the bill. His calm manner influenced several men to move out. Orwin explained to them, "We're all going to the other side. I think you had better come along. It will be better for all of us over there."[56]

Company F, 325th (Capt. J. W. Harney), meanwhile, crossed the causeway about 11:15. Its objective was the center of the newly expanding bridgehead. German fire had finally begun to slacken. Harney's first thought after seeing the carnage in front of him was that the attack had failed.[57] Lieutenant Travelstead's men brought mortars and heavy machine guns across the causeway before noon. Sgt. Robert J. Hricik recalled seeing "the . . . artillery and mortar shells dropping on the causeway. It was very frightening, especially for a unit that was going into its first big battle." He lost no men in the crossing, and after they had stopped to catch their breath they went forward with their automatic weapons and mortars. He was talking to a lieutenant about placement of weapons when a bullet hit the officer in the head. Hricik then learned his platoon sergeant was also dead.[58]

Travelstead later believed Harney was the only officer trying to organize the shallow bridgehead. "I saw no one else even attempting any coordination of command, and, amusingly to me, even the paratroopers were calling out for any officer to lead them."[59] No one had a complete picture. Travelstead and Harney had only a very narrow view of the situation; the other company commanders and Major Gardner, Carrell's replacement, were not in contact, and each group believed it was the only one still fighting. Harney, for example, had about fifty of his own men, plus eighteen men from E Company, a dozen from G, sixteen from battalion headquarters, and about twenty of Rae's paratroopers.[60]

American artillery rained down on Cauquigny ahead of the attacking glider infantry and paratroops, but poor communications prevented the attackers from calling the artillery observer to shift the fire to a safe distance to their front. Friendly fire wounded Travelstead and killed a handful of others, including some of Harney's men.[61] Even some cooks got into the fight.[62] Captain Rae conferred with Harney, who decided there was no time for a thorough sweep of the area. His men instead seized the higher ground in the center of the penetration.[63]

There were fewer than ninety men in the expanding Merderet bridgehead. Harney had no flank protection, and he went back to the churchyard about 1:00 PM to ask Maj. Arthur Gardner to order Company E forward. For some reason, it took about two hours for the company (Captain Murphy) to move, and it kept going when it reached the forward positions. Murphy did not know that Harney had received word that Germans were heading toward their flank. Because of this, and the fact that several enemy were still fighting in the rubble of Cauquigny, Harney decided to pull his men back about two hundred yards. Murphy did not know exactly where Harney was, but he did realize that his own flank was now exposed. He shouted an order that no one heard clearly but that some interpreted as an order to pull back. An NCO from Company G saw several men approaching, and thinking they were the enemy, he decided that the bridgehead was in danger. He yelled to a paratroop officer, "For God's sake stop them if you can!"

The paratroop lieutenant stood in the middle of the road and took his pistol from its holster: "You'll keep your goddam asses right where they are. Some of my men are up there and none of you men are going to pull out." The glider infantry platoon leader regained control of his men. Enemy fire was heavy, but there had been no counterattack. The lack of good radio communication, coupled with inexperience, had led to the problems.[64]

German infantry covered by artillery and mortar fire hit the bridgehead about 6:00 PM. When his radio failed, an artillery observer sprinted two hundred yards to get a backup. Company F held its ground and beat off the attack with small-arms fire until artillery began to fall. One NCO ran out of ammunition and used his empty submachine gun as a club.[65] Colonel Lewis told Captain Rae to get all of his men into the line. Sanford's 1st Battalion, 325th, arrived later to complete the defenses.[66]

Lewis was by this time mentally and physically exhausted, and he was unaware that he suffered from terminal cancer. Late on the evening of 9 June, Lt. Vernon Wyant saw Lewis grieving at the day's events, mumbling "constantly . . . without any coherent meaning." He initially refused the suggestion of the regimental surgeon that he go to the division medical clearing station for a rest. He later took a strong sedative and was evacuated, returning a few days later in complete control of himself. This incident would have effectively ended Lewis's career regardless of the cancer.[67] A "brutal" counterattack hit the regiment after Lewis's departure. The regimental XO, Lt. Col. Herb Sitler, prepared to withdraw, though he had not issued an order to that effect, when a "livid" Gavin arrived and told him to counterattack. There was no indication that the glider infantry was about to falter, and, with other units, the 3d Battalion retook some ground.[68]

The mission of the 3d Battalion, 325th Glider Infantry, was complete. In its first day of fighting, it spearheaded a critical attack to seize a causeway that was essential to the capture of Cherbourg. The struggle for La Fière was chaotic and intense even for experienced paratroopers. The 3d Battalion did well for several reasons: it was part of an experienced glider regiment; it had undergone thorough training when it was part of the 101st Airborne; it faced an enemy whose higher headquarters were as unsure of the situation as the Americans'; and it was comparatively well supported by armor and artillery. Yet in the first hours of the fighting at La Fière itself and across the Merderet, the Germans were also well supported by armor, automatic weapons, and mortars, and it was up to the rifleman alone to seize the far end of the causeway. Gavin later recalled, "It is impossible to put into words the holocaust that took place there."[69] On a separate occasion, he agreed to Richard Johnson's invitation to speak at a postwar civic function. "Do you know why I'm doing this?" asked Gavin. Johnson replied that he did not. "You crossed that causeway, and I can't say no to any man who did."[70]

CHAPTER 6

TO THE REICH, JULY–AUGUST 1944

EAR MORTAIN, FRANCE, approximately 0400 hours (4:00 AM), 7 August 1944: Tanks of the 2d SS Panzer Division lumbered through the early morning fog toward the positions of the 1st Battalion, 120th Infantry Regiment. Lt. Murray Pulver radioed his battalion commander that he was under attack. Moments later, a mortar round knocked out the radio. Direct fire tore into a nearby building. A few yards away, a German Mark IV tank crawled relentlessly toward his CP. First Sergeant Reginald Maybee handed his commander a bazooka. Pulver crouched behind a stone wall, not ten yards from the enemy. He took aim through the primitive sight and squeezed the trigger. An electric current surged through the wire leads to the puny 2.36-inch anti-tank rocket. It hit the tank's turret, and the vehicle stopped. No one escaped, though the engine continued to run. Some distance away, a dozen SS infantrymen ran toward the GIs yelling for them to surrender. The lieutenant fired his carbine, and the others followed his lead. They dropped several of the enemy and lost none of their own. Pulver withdrew his headquarters to a safer location.[1] His 30th Infantry Division was another new organization, of National Guard heritage, that had been in combat for only a few weeks. It was the product of a system of mobilization and training that was continually undergoing changes, fits, and starts as it prepared a relatively small combat force to fight around the world.

An Overlord logistical planner is supposed to have remarked that "the number of divisions required to capture the number of ports required to maintain those divisions is always greater than the number of divisions those ports can maintain."[2] Units like the 82d Airborne and 90th Infantry Divisions described in the preceding chapter not only fought hard to gain maneuver space behind the beachheads; they also fought and bled to push the enemy out of artillery range of logistical installations and to capture Cherbourg swiftly. Plans for continued operations inland hinged on its quick capture and development as a major working port for the reception of men and supplies. Delay in its capture meant that the Americans in particular had to rely on the invasion beaches for off load of cargo. The beaches could handle the force ashore by July, but they were not capable of year-round operations, and their capacity to support a large force was limited (for example, only 71 percent of the planned tonnage had been unloaded by the end of June; the troop buildup was only 78 percent of plan [452,460 vs. 578,971]).

Critical logistical support operations got off to a slow start and did not catch up to requirements for several weeks (and for some types of supply, for months). Tactical plans assumed that Cherbourg would be operational as early as 30 June. The port was in fact not even in U.S. hands until 27 June, and it "made no contribution to the logistical support of the American forces" until well into July.[3] An engineer called the port's destruction "beyond a doubt the most complete, intensive, and best planned demolition in history." The electric generator system had been rendered unusable, and 20,000 cubic yards of masonry blocked a basin that was large enough for transatlantic liners. Cranes, quay walls, and breakwaters were heavily damaged.[4] The famous Channel storm during the third week of June was not strong by seafaring standards, but it was enough to overcome the engineering of the artificial ports devised by the British. The American port was so damaged that it would never be repaired. About a hundred landing craft and nineteen of twenty ferry barges were also destroyed. The good news was that the supply dumps inland were in good condition.[5] The question by 1 July was whether over-the-shore supply operations could fully support the two armored divisions and eleven infantry divisions, plus literally hundreds of nondivisional combat and support units, that the Americans had in France.[6]

These thirteen divisions were not a particularly large force for the task assigned to them. One way to speed the entry of combat units into France was to use shipping space otherwise allocated for supplies or transport of support units. Since the capacity of the beaches was limited and there would be no large port available until well into July, the Americans had to trade combat troops for supplies and logistical troops. Such an imbalance was acceptable only on a temporary basis, because the area of operations was still relatively small and the lines of communication were short. That situation could not remain for long, since the Allies had to gain ground to maneuver against and destroy the enemy. The ultimate success of Overlord depended on such choices made during the early weeks after the invasion. Nothing like it had ever been attempted in history, and the Allies faced a set of challenges and decisions that the Germans simply did not.[7]

Harried German generals, meanwhile, were dealing with conflicting orders from Berlin. Morale of the *Landsers* generally withstood the strain through early July. One general recalled that despite the setbacks since 6 June, soldier performance had been "surprisingly good. Their training was sufficient for defensive operations. Although the soldiers had grown tired of the war, their morale was altogether still undaunted."[8] Generalleutnant Kurt Badinski, commander of the 276th Infantry Division, recalled that the lack of major items of equipment hampered training but that morale was good and food was adequate. According to Badinski, not all of his men supported the Nazi cause, and at least 15 percent were *Volksdeutsche*, or ethnic Germans. He told interrogators after the war that the hedgerows impeded his men as much as the Americans, though since his men were on the defensive and his enemies had to expose themselves to attack, his comment appears overstated. He spoke highly of U.S. mortars, artillery, and air-ground coordination, but like many of his contemporaries, he added that the U.S. Army seemed to spare its infantrymen intentionally from close combat until artillery and air attacks had softened the objectives.[9] One must wonder why the Americans would have done otherwise.

A handful of the combat units (and support units for that matter), such as the 1st and 9th Infantry and the 2d Armored Division, had had experience in the Mediterranean or North African theaters before they fought in France. New units had to learn on the job—an opportunity for which they paid dearly. That most of these organizations ended up doing a good job and performing well is testament to the character of the soldier who endured the steep and dangerous learning curve. Given the lack of resources with which the Army entered the war, it is little wonder that the selection, mobilization, and training programs had a spotty record at first. Added to this institutional setting was the terrain inland in Normandy. Here, in the *bocage*, or hedgerow, country the bloodletting was constant and gains were measured in yards, if not feet. Operations nearly came to a stop, not only because some units had incompetent leaders executing bad plans but because the ground was so utterly conducive to the defense.[10]

A planning assumption before D-day was that the Germans would try to defeat the invasion at the beaches and then fight a delaying battle to the Seine River. That made sense; the problem was that the enemy did not follow the playbook. They held to every inch of ground.[11] All military planning involves trade-offs and allocation of risk, because resources are almost always constrained. The issue in 1944 was a matter of efficiently using the available time to ensure solid establishment of the forces ashore. It was imperative to gain and maintain superiority in ground combat power as soon as possible. With their chief advantage in mobility, not in overwhelming strength, the Americans needed to avoid long-term attrition operations. In retrospect, it is easy to criticize staffs for lack of foresight in synchronizing the flow of combat and support forces, but the logistical plans for Neptune/Overlord reflect the extent of the intellectual effort required to plan the most important military operation of the century.[12]

About eight miles inland, GIs started to encounter tens of thousands of small fields, most measuring about three hundred by two hundred yards, surrounded by centuries-old dirt embankments topped by dense hedges. They were like solid walls, up to a yard or more thick and twelve feet high. Each field had openings for wagons and livestock; none had a regular shape. Innumerable trails crossed the area, and where they passed through particularly high hedgerows they appeared to the soldiers as sunken roads covered by canopies of trees that shut out much light. There could hardly be a worse place for a new unit to receive an introduction to combat. Each hedgerow was a strongpoint. Automatic weapons, often protected by snipers, were sited for crossfire and grazing fire (where the bullets pass just inches or a few feet above the ground, intended literally to "mow down" ground troops). Trenches on the reverse sides of the hedges provided cover against all but a direct hit by mortars and artillery. Mines filled the undergrowth. Anti-tank weapons covered roads.[13] The existence of the hedges was no secret, and Allied officers who had fought there early in the war reported them to the planners, since they were convinced there would be problems getting through the area. Yet the GIs had no training to prepare for this ground, and once they were there, too many commanders failed to consider that units in hedgerow country could not practice the doctrine found in the manuals.[14]

Field Marshal Montgomery maintained that his "master plan" called for the British and Canadians to tie up the Germans at Caen so the Americans could fight through the *bocage* and gain maneuver space on the German flank.[15] Of course, the British army group did not move inland according to plan either, and some Americans, such as Omar N. Bradley, blamed the overall lack of progress in June and July on the lack of British-Canadian progress. In fact, the Americans underestimated the potential for German resistance.[16] They also suffered through the wettest summer since 1900. Bad weather prevented employment of about half of the potential air support available to First Army through July.[17] The rain-saturated ground was also a considerable problem to maneuver units in a relatively small force that depended so much on its mobility to compensate for lack of combat power. Tank-infantry coordination was poor early on, because hardly any infantry leader had worked with tanks. One reason was a shortage of tanks available for training, because the Army had wanted to stockpile them in England for the invasion. There were not enough separate tank battalions to allot one per infantry division, and there was a consequent lack of opportunity for commanders to work together.[18] Since the Americans had to keep pushing inland and there was no reserve of maneuver units to compensate for their absence in the line, there was no time to withdraw units for extended retraining.[19]

Small-unit leaders had to expose themselves to keep the men moving, and turnover due to casualties in the infantry battalions was so high that experience became a rare commodity. Units could not build up a reservoir of experience, and some wondered if the problems were due less to circumstances than to simply poor soldiers. For example, men might let a few bursts of machine-gun fire pin them down and then stay down after the fire lifted. One officer wrote in *Infantry Journal* that the enemy "worked his guns up and down and across the hedgerows, dropping his shells in the shallow ditches that ran alongside the rows, where our men insisted on taking cover at the cost of their lives again and again." Men trained in the States to fire only when they saw a target had to learn quickly that in such terrain they would seldom see a German soldier who exposed himself long enough to become a target. Not only could the GI rarely see the enemy, the terrain was such that commanders seldom knew for sure exactly where all their men were.[20] One officer noted, "No battalion commander can give you the exact location of his various units five minutes after they've jumped off."[21] On the other hand, the Germans had time to fix their positions and determine coordinates that would enable them to place artillery and mortar fire quickly.

GIs scrambled to get more automatic weapons. The German division was authorized 1,592 submachine guns and 243 light machine guns; the U.S. infantry division was authorized only 93 and 616, respectively. American tradition that the rifleman was the preeminent weapon did not work on a battlefield dominated by automatic weapons and mobile firepower. Germany developed the best individual and crew-served machine guns in the world, while too few senior leaders in the interwar U.S. Army came to grips with modern warfare.[22] Added to the problem were the interwar procurement and resource constraints. As a result, commanders redistributed the machine guns and mortars they did have from weapons platoons to rifle platoons, while supply sergeants desperately scoured rear areas for excess weapons.

Sherman tanks equipped with bulldozer blades worked reasonably well against the hedgerows, but there were just a few dozen of these tanks in France. Some units experimented with explosives, but it took at least fifty pounds of TNT to blow a hole in a hedgerow wide enough for a tank. The logistics of hauling the required explosives forced consideration of other options. Engineers estimated that a battalion of fifty-four tanks needed seventeen tons of TNT to blast through the average thirty-four separate fields to conduct an attack a mile and a half deep. Ramming the hedgerow with a tank equipped with a pipe to dig a deep hole for the explosives worked well, but an explosion would merely alert the enemy to where the tank was. By mid-July, the best-known device, first designed and assembled by soldiers in the 2d Armored Division, was in service, and ordnance units began mass production of plowlike tines to weld on the front of tanks. Tanks with these devices rammed the hedges and dug out chunks of earth.[23]

War Department observers spoke highly of German tenacity and single-mindedness. They had superb noise and light discipline; few talked or shouted unless engaged in actual combat. Tanks moved deliberately and operated relatively quietly: "They acted as if they knew exactly where they wanted to go, how, and then went there with vigor and determination." American tanks, on the other hand, made a racket. Their engines were louder and drivers had a tendency to "gun" them, making even more noise. Shouting, talking, and barking of orders characterized march columns. It was clear that leaders needed to "indoctrinate, train, and equip any group from five soldiers up so that the approach of a [German] tank is as well prepared for as the approach of an enemy plane or enemy infantrymen."[24]

A German defensive sketch reproduced in a wartime issue of the Army's journal *Military Review* shows minutely detailed defensive preparations organized up to three hedgerows deep and centered on machine guns and mortars. The Germans alternated in giving up the hedgerows a few at a time so they could place continuous fire on attackers.[25] Clammy and hot in wool uniforms impregnated against gas, weighed down with equipment, always on the move, and breathing the sickening smell of decaying human and animal flesh, men who survived became good soldiers. But that was the problem—there were not many survivors. In the first sixty days of operations, the Americans sustained 16,201 killed and 75,197 wounded in action. The 30th Infantry Division lost 968 killed, 5,097 wounded, and 297 missing by 1 August; the 90th Division lost a total of 9,639 casualties by the same date.[26]

Something had to be done. The press got wind of the problems, and Eisenhower apparently complained to Churchill about Montgomery's handling of the ground battle. Some thought that the British were "leaving all the fighting to the Americans."[27] This was not true, but the situation was serious. General Bradley's staff by mid-July had refined a plan for a breakthrough along the road between St. Lo and Periers. The basic concept was simple—air bombardment would blow a 7,000-yard-wide hole in the enemy line. Joe Collins's reinforced VII Corps would drive through it.[28] Army Air Forces leaders were not enthusiastic about the plan, since heavy and medium bombers were not suited to close support of ground troops—indeed, one postwar study determined that only 31 percent of bombs hit within five hundred feet of an aiming point. Fighter-bombers were suited for the task, but they lacked the punch of heavy bombers. Air officers warned Eisenhower of the difficulties of short-duration mass drop in a restricted area near ground troops. There was disagreement over the direction of approach of the planes—Bradley and Eisenhower received warning of the danger of flying parallel to friendly positions. Air planners wanted troops to pull back 3,000 yards, but the ground commanders unfortunately prevailed, agreeing only to a 1,500-yard withdrawal.[29]

Clouds led to postponement of the attack, named Operation Cobra, on 24 July, but not all pilots got the order. Elements of the 9th Infantry Division sustained about a hundred casualties. Planes returned the next day, and about half of the bombs hit the target area. The most famous friendly-fire casualty among over five hundred that day was Lesley McNair, who, for better or worse, had designed the units with which he died.[30] Though recriminations continued for years, air-ground relations fortunately remained solid. Generalleutnant Fritz Bayerlein, the commander of the Panzer Lehr Division, spoke of utter destruction of German command posts and of terrain that resembled the surface of the moon. The attack knocked out most of his frontline tanks. He believed the Cobra bombing was worse than anything he had seen during the war, including on the Eastern Front. There were acres upon acres of churned earth, pieces of men and animals, overturned tanks, and burned trucks.

Scattered groups of Germans fought back skillfully. Two panzer divisions moved from the British to the American sector. GIs, still

German mortar crew, 1944. [Courtesy Albert Trostorf]

shaken by the "short" bombings and delayed by the cratered ground, got off to a slow start. Yet Joe Collins was the right general to lead the break-out, and once his corps got moving the attack began to roll without letup. By the afternoon of 27 July, the 1st Infantry Division had cut a critical rail line and, with armor, was driving fast to cut off and trap an enemy corps on the west coast of the Cotentin. GIs sped through village after village, shooting up rear areas, truck convoys, and horse-drawn supply columns. German tactical communications were disrupted, and their commanders had no clear idea what was happening. A U.S. recon-naissance unit even sped through a village where General Bayerlein was holding a meeting.

An American pilot counted seventy German vehicles burning on the night of 30 July in the Avranches area. Abandoned equipment littered the roads, and there was so much dead livestock that engineers were con-cerned about the quality of water sources. Field Marshal Günther von Kluge, commander of Army Group B, called the situation a "madhouse." U.S. spearheads were about to turn into the Brittany Peninsula, and, he reported to Berlin that "the Americans will be out of the woods and they'll be able to do what they want." Hampered by damaged communi-cations, poor intelligence, and lack of equipment and supplies, as well as American speed, the Germans lost control of the situation.[31]

The Americans were learning. On 1 August, the Third U.S. Army, under George Patton, became operational. Bradley took command of the 12th Army Group and turned command of the First Army over to his deputy, Courtney H. Hodges. Like Patton, Hodges was a genuine World War I hero. At fifty-seven, he was an experienced soldier and former Chief of Infantry, but a man whom one historian characterized as lacking the "presence of Bradley or Patton." He sought no publicity and tended to play it safe. Perhaps he was also unimaginative, and it is certain that he tended to concentrate on the details to excess. Like many senior leaders, he relied on the counsel of a handful of key subordinates, Collins in particular, and some thought that his overbearing chief of staff, Bill Kean, really ran First Army. Bradley made things easier for his old friend Hodges by not taking all of the experienced staff members with him when he moved to 12th Army Group.[32] As the events of the late summer and fall went on, Hodges's troops endured the worst fighting of the European campaign, and the stress and strain wore heavily on soldiers from squad to army headquarters.

The breakout and attack deep into northern France spread the 12th Army Group thin. Third Army turned into Brittany in what some still consider a questionable effort to gain Atlantic ports that might not have been as important to the supply situation as some had thought early on.[33] The German flank east of Avranches was, meanwhile, hanging open, and Montgomery and Bradley decided it was time to destroy the enemy west of the Seine River. Bradley, however, was also concerned about the terrain corridor in the Avranches area that connected his far-flung units. Though he listened to those who thought the Germans would retreat across the Seine without a major fight, he could not ignore the possibility of a counterattack against the narrow corridor through which troops were passing. Hitler, meanwhile, had decided to counterattack the flank of 12th Army Group, cut off Third Army, and restore the shattered lines. On 2 August, he ordered an attack.[34]

General Collins issued a warning, based on air observation (and not, he later reported, specifically based on information gleaned from Ultra intelligence), about midnight of 6–7 August. He told commanders only to expect an attack within the next twelve hours, and whatever the role of Ultra in U.S. decision making, the few hours' alert gave them little time to prepare fully.[35] Had the ground troops not held during the first critical hours of the attack, advance warning would have meant little. Ultra communications intelligence was not an offset to inadequate performance. It is true that when the panzers rolled toward the GIs shortly after midnight, the 2d SS Panzer Division overran some elements of the 30th Infantry Division. However, one of the most noteworthy actions in the ETO was a stand on Hill 317, just east of Mortain. The reinforced rifle battalion there lost its commander and most of its staff. A captain took charge of the surrounded force and held stubbornly for five days a position that would have given the Germans observation of most of the VII Corps zone. Repeated attacks almost reached the crest, but on 12 August the battalion, reduced from seven hundred men to about three hundred, walked off the hill. The official history does not exaggerate in stating that this unit's stand was "one of the outstanding small unit achievements in the course of the campaign."[36]

As early as the afternoon of 7 August, Kluge was convinced the attack had failed. Tens of thousands of his men were well past the Mortain-Avranches "pocket," and the question now was how to get them out. Hodges, meanwhile, assured Bradley that he could hold at Mortain. Bradley and Montgomery then agreed to have the Third Army sweep wide around the enemy and attack them from the rear. Working with the Canadians, they would seal off the penetration. The XV Corps (Third Army) drove north from Le Mans and was on the verge of taking Argentan, several miles behind the enemy spearheads, when Bradley on 12 August ordered the corps to stop. Canadians attacking the north flank of the enemy penetration also went to ground. Bradley had become concerned that the XV Corps frontage was overextended and that the Germans might concentrate against it. He apparently was also worried that friendly-fire incidents might occur if the Americans and Canadians ran headlong into each other. After Cobra, he was probably not willing to take any such chances, and it made sense to him to let tactical air devastate the Germans.[37]

Hindsight shows that this decision was incorrect and probably allowed thousands of Germans to escape. The late Martin Blumenson was especially critical of the Allied leadership. He believed that Eisenhower, Montgomery, and Bradley focused too much on the impending future battles in Germany and did not look hard at the condition of the enemy in August. He notes that Eisenhower let Montgomery and Bradley "drift apart" and focus on personal agendas without firm guidance. Ike's "hands off" policy toward day-to-day operations was a mistake under the circumstances. Bradley thought the opportunity to destroy a large part of the Germans remaining in France was "nothing short of fantastic."[38] Supporters of Patton and Montgomery blamed him for allowing tens of thousands of enemy

troops to escape. Bradley, of course, blamed Montgomery for not pushing his own attack. Allied air power nevertheless pounded the Germans
in the meantime. One often-quoted observer said after seeing the battle
area, "It was as if an avenging angel had swept the area bent on destroying all things German." The war seemed over, and commanders were
more interested in getting to Germany than in destroying its army.
There were inviting targets to the east.[39]

It is not surprising that many saw an impending end to the war.
Enemy losses at Falaise-Argentan were staggering: 50,000 prisoners,
10,000 dead; divisions reduced to battalion strength in terms of combat
forces. The roads leading to Germany were a "choked mass of smoking
tanks, guns, trucks, field kitchens, horse-drawn wagons. Apathy, despair,
terror strained at the fabric of German discipline." Yet perhaps 35,000
men escaped, and ominously for the Allies, many of them were senior
leaders and staff officers. This was enough of a nucleus around which to
reconstitute units.[40] The Army Air Forces, in a postwar review of air
operations, reported that if a German soldier escaped the pocket and
reached the Seine River, he had a 95 percent chance of reaching relative
safety. Some 68 percent of the tanks that escaped the pocket also got
across the river, as did an estimated 89 percent of trucks.[41]

A GI said, "Over a stretch of such days, you become so dulled by
fatigue that the names of the killed and wounded they checked off each
night, the names of men who had been your best friends, might have
come out of a telephone book for all you knew. . . . [I]f there was a world
beyond this tangle of hedgerows[,] . . . you never expected to live to see
it." Combat behind the beachhead was a bloodletting. Individual soldiers
and their leaders made mistakes despite their training, which could not
have prepared them for every circumstance, and after a few days under
such conditions men simply "accepted their lot as normal."[42]

Plans for the invasion dictated where the GI would fight; prewar
decisions determined what he would fight with and how. German forces,
though mixed in their capability, conducted active defense, launched
quick counterattacks, and were often well supported by small detach-
ments of armor. They deployed and used mortars and automatic weapons
very effectively in terrain exceptionally well suited to the defense. Only
when the Americans gained room south of St. Lo did the conditions
began to change. Before that, they were unable to take full advantage of
their superior mobility. They did not do everything right, but they did
show an adeptness at improvisation and improvement. Unusually wet
weather hindered movement, and the buildup of men and materiel got off

to a slow start. The fighting in Normandy drained reserve ammunition stocks and forced GIs to curtail drastically the use of 105-mm howitzer ammunition. Tanks, rifles, mortars, and machine guns wore out and drained replacement stocks. Close combat also caused an unexpectedly high drain on infantry replacements. By mid-July, the ETO had urgently to request 25,000 replacement riflemen from the States.[43]

Meanwhile, the German commander in Paris refused to follow orders to destroy the city's infrastructure and historic fabric. Eisenhower allowed the French 2d Armored Division to enter the city first, and the U.S. 4th Infantry Division followed up. The 28th Infantry Division and other units marched triumphantly through the center of the city in a display now famous in photos, newsreels, and on a postage stamp, and then kept fighting. Yet timing was everything, and the Germans were about to get a reprieve. Summer sun, wind, and dust swirled around the GIs as they headed east. Eisenhower cabled Marshall: "The enemy forces immediately facing us are on the run. Our greatest difficulty at the moment is [logistics]. We have advanced so rapidly that further movement in large parts of the front against very weak opposition is almost impossible. . . . The closer we get to the Siegfried line the more we will be stretched . . . and eventually a period of relative inaction will be imposed upon us. The potential danger is that while we are temporarily stalled, the enemy will be able to pick up bits and pieces of forces everywhere and reorganize them swiftly for defending the Siegfried Line or the Rhine."[44] How right he was.

CHAPTER 7

AT THE WESTWALL, SEPTEMBER– OCTOBER 1944

N EAR HEMMERES, GERMANY, about 9:00 PM, 11 September 1944: A patrol from the 4th Infantry Division's 22d Infantry Regiment stood in the quiet darkness of the Our River Valley on the Belgian-German border. First Lt. Robert L. Manning, of the 3d Battalion, and 2d Lt. Clarence M. Shugart, leader of the regiment's Intelligence and Reconnaissance Platoon, flipped a coin to see who would be the first soldier of the division to enter Germany. Their orders were to assess the strength of the border defenses and bring back a jar of soil for presentation to the division commander, Maj. Gen. Raymond O. Barton. He wanted to send the package to the president.

A small nearby bridge was demolished, and no one wanted to risk sending jeeps and TDs across the shallow river at night before infantry reconnoitered the enemy side. As usual, it was up to the riflemen. Shugart won the toss, and a few minutes later, accompanied by Sgt. Wallace W. Morton, Jr., Sgt. Paul C. Karcher, and Pfc. Edward A. Reinert, he waded the Our. The men spread out and reached the hamlet of Hemmeres within a few minutes. They encountered only some very frightened civilians. This was no city—the buildings reflected the hard farm labor that sustained the residents. When they were satisfied that there were no enemy soldiers around, the men filled a cap with dirt and pocketed a few coins before they returned to Belgium. Normandy and the awful hedgerows lay hundreds of miles behind them. Resistance in Germany so far was nonexistent.[1]

Toward Germany

EVENTS IN NORTHERN FRANCE led Eisenhower and his generals to reconsider the original plans for Overlord and the follow-on operations. The campaign in France had cost the Allies nearly 40,000 killed, over 164,000 wounded, and 20,000 missing. Planners identified four routes that offered good approaches to the Ruhr industrial area, the designated key economic objective inside Germany. One route of attack was the axis Metz–Saar. What became the primary route was north of the Ardennes, where 21 Army Group (Montgomery) could use the relatively open ground. Bradley's 12th U.S. Army Group would attack through Belgium and Luxembourg. The Seventh U.S. Army, driving north from the Riviera, would support the right flank of the offensive. All armies would draw up to the Rhine before making the final attack into Germany.

Leaders originally expected that they would have to temporarily suspend operations to build up logistical bases, supply reserves, and improve the road and rail network in northern France before they turned toward Germany. These plans changed abruptly with the unexpected end to the fighting in Normandy. Eisenhower and Montgomery discussed the next moves on 23 August, as the tenuous supply distribution situation was growing apparent. Though "glittering opportunities" to destroy the enemy beckoned commanders, Eisenhower decided to pursue what some have considered "more utilitarian objectives," like the Channel ports and Antwerp, before driving headlong into Germany. There was no question that the Allies would have to capture these forward located installations at one point or another. They needed to do so before bad weather. Montgomery asked for an entire American field army to support his attacks on the ports and V-weapon launching sites. Eisenhower had already placed the airborne divisions at his disposal, and he told Bradley that First Army also would support the British. It is not extreme to consider this decision as among the most important of the war. While this reorientation of First Army's planned axis put additional Allied resources against the most important objectives inside Germany, it also split the 12th Army Group on either side of the Ardennes; original plans called for it to attack south of the Ardennes. Now, the forested mass separated the First and Third U.S. Armies, with the weight of the Allied effort on the north. This also put the American logistical effort on two major axes, but that in itself was not a risky course of action because the road network was adequate to support the traffic needed to move the supplies required at that time given the enemy situation. Eisenhower apparently understood this, and he told Montgomery to move against Antwerp "vigorously and without delay." Logistical staffs indicated First Army could receive adequate support with the resources on hand.2 The problem was that 21 Army Group did not secure Antwerp, the physical conditions began to change almost by the hour, and there were not enough transportation resources.

When Eisenhower made this decision, Cherbourg was the only large port in Allied hands (Brest would not fall until late September, and then it would be of no practical use), and it was not operating at full capacity. Most supplies for the U.S. forces still came in over the invasion beaches. The immediate problem was in distributing the supplies that reached France. Planners intended for heavy cargo trucks and railroads to carry most of the burden of moving materiel to forward dumps, but there were never enough big trucks, and the light trucks were not built to handle the workload. Railroads took time to rebuild, and frontline GIs ended up at the mercy of an argument between logistical planners and transportation officers. ETO planners reduced the estimated truck requirements from 240 companies to 160 (forty 2-ton trucks each) companies. Transportation planners had no solid operational data to back up their estimate, and the ETO G-4 staff simply disregarded it in favor of their own. Bureaucratic delays in the War Department G-4 (logistics) staff led to late approval of a transportation corps proposal to equip over one-third of the approved 160 companies with heavy trucks. Few of the vehicles arrived in France before D-day, and there were never enough of them at any rate. The ETO operations staff also rejected a transportation corps request to put two drivers in each truck to allow twenty-four-hour operations. This proposal was a way to offset partially the shortage of vehicles. Operations planners disagreed—they believed the existing organization would temporarily support continuous operations, particularly since they did not think the round-trip distances would be very long. Had operations gone according to plan, they would not have been that long, because the supporting units would have been able to set up intermediate supply dumps and facilities. Unfortunately for American planners, the Germans did not cooperate. Improvised long-haul transport operations like the "Red Ball Express" wasted manpower and resources and provided only stopgap solutions to what would become a nearly intractable problem of providing uninterrupted supply support.[3]

Montgomery advocated a heavy-fisted, forty-division attack toward the Ruhr (the so-called narrow-front attack). He maintained that a two-axis attack would disperse combat power. Eisenhower maintained that a "single thrust" would expose the Allies to a concentrated counterblow, and his decision to spread out the Allied effort remains controversial.

However, it is important to consider the logistical requirements before assuming that Eisenhower's decision was wrong. First, the British required the support of American transport units, since 1,400 British trucks were inoperable due to engine problems—and the replacement engines were also defective.[4] Some maintain that the U.S. Army's standard supply tonnage-planning factor for an infantry division was too high and that since GIs could get by with less, the concentrated attack would have been possible, because there would have been fewer supplies to haul than "official" computations might indicate. Sheer tonnage, however, was not the issue. Weight and "cube" (volume) of cargo, maintenance status of trucks, vehicle turnaround time between receiving units and dumps, synchronization of supply availability with transportation, and the impact of the weather and road conditions are a few of the factors for which people do not account. The weather and road conditions were g ood in France during the summer; unfortunately, the transportation resources were not available to exploit these temporarily satisfactory conditions.

What industry produced was unimportant if it did not reach the forward troops in time to be of use. Looking at production figures in such isolation is another error.[5] Authors also persist in citing the disparity in supply tonnage shipped to the First and Third Armies in August–September. First Army received priority of support due to its support of the British. Yet at the end of August, it received only about 2,200 tons per day, and it still had to immobilize an entire corps due to gasoline shortages. The two armies eventually received equal shares of available supplies.[6] It is also important to consider the complexities of supporting the attack across the Rhine barrier using only a handful of river crossings. Arguments oversimplify the hard grip of logistics on operations and lead people to believe that difficult decisions were in fact easy to make. The problem was that the logistical plan supporting the campaign in France simply was not flexible enough for conditions that were radically different from those envisioned by planners, who necessarily had to plan for the worst case.

Reserves of rations and medical and signal supplies were low, and while there was sufficient ammunition in France and off shore in ships, trucks had to make round trips of several hundred miles. Clothing and field equipment also needed replacement as summer drew to a close. Tanks and other vehicles operated on borrowed time because of deferral of maintenance. Third Army faced shortages of even communications wire and radio parts, for example, because fuel and ammunition received priority of transport. Despite heralded tank production statistics, First Army's forward units actually were short of replacements. Losses in July were 24 percent of its authorizations, and theater reserves ran out.[7] The summer's offensive was to come "to no dramatic end. It would sputter out."[8]

Germany's Army Group B was, meanwhile, frantically regrouping behind the concrete and steel fortifications of the Westwall, or "Siegfried Line" as the Allies called it. That complex had been neglected since 1940, and its bunkers could not mount the most modern anti-tank and machine guns. However, these defenses could put backbone even into otherwise poorly trained and equipped troops, and the Americans did not know precisely where all of the bunkers and fortifications were. Bunkers were generally twenty to thirty feet wide and up to fifty feet deep, with walls up to eight feet thick. Blocking many roads were "dragon's teeth," or pyramid-shaped reinforced concrete obstacles, set on a concrete grid about a yard thick and usually partially buried.[9] Hitler in early September reappointed the old Prussian field marshal, Gerd von Rundstedt, as OB West (Oberbefehlshaber-West, or Supreme Commander West) as a rallying symbol for the troops. Field Marshal Model reverted to the command of Army Group B. The Germans had the equivalent of twenty-seven infantry and six or seven panzer divisions against an Allied total of forty-nine divisions of all types.[10] The Allies could dictate the time and place of an attack, but the Germans had the advantage of short supply lines.

"Deeds Not Words"

THE 4TH INFANTRY DIVISION and its 22d Infantry Regiment entered the war at Utah Beach on D-day. Col. Charles T. "Buck" Lanham, who took command of the 22d in early July, put his personal mark on the regiment. He was thin, slightly built, and of average age (forty-two) for the job, but he looked older than his years. Gray hair and wire-rimmed glasses set him apart from his young subordinates. He wrote poetry, and he was known within the small officer corps of the interwar years as a thoughtful intellectual. George C. Marshall knew him, and so did Ernest Hemingway, who became a close friend. Lanham was known to have threatened immediate relief of officers who did not perform to his exacting standards. Veteran officers maintained decades later that they would have gone to almost any length to avoid him, but their respect was such that reminiscences about him could bring tears.[11]

The 22d Infantry in August lost forty officers and 828 enlisted men killed, wounded, and missing, out of an authorized strength of about 3,200. Replacements had brought it back to its authorized strength by the second week of September, when it cut through western Belgium and headed toward the increasingly compartmented ground close to Germany.[12] Despite shortages in ammunition and vehicle repair parts, the GIs remained optimistic. The regiment's daily operations report for 9 September stated, "Everyone now believes the war is practically over. The longest current estimate of the time it will take us to go through the Siegfried Line is three days after which we will do no more serious fighting. Some say we will do it in 24 hours."[13] Perhaps it was wishful thinking, but to many an acute shortage of gasoline meant only that they would have to walk, rather than ride, into Germany. At Houffalize, in the French-speaking part of Belgium, Lanham's friend Hemingway, now a correspondent, wrote of civilians "bearing gifts—cakes, baskets of eggs, and bottles of wine and brandy."[14]

First Lt. Don Warner, a Texan and then a platoon leader in Company A, later recalled, "Food and plenty of mail were flowing. In looking back, a happy carnival atmosphere prevailed; men were more than eager and no problem existed for combat patrols, duty in general, etc. In addition, most units contained French and Belgian soldiers who knew the country and were always pushing in the attack to get home . . . [A]s a platoon leader I had to read and censor outgoing mail of my platoon. All letters and V-mail contained the following: 'Go easy on my letters because this show is all but over and its possible that I'll be home for Thanksgiving or Christmas, for sure. . . .' We could see, feel and taste the end of the war."[15] The regiment's executive officer, Lt. Col. John F. Ruggles, a 1931 graduate of West Point, was not particularly elated; he thought that resistance would increase as the Germans fell back on their homeland.[16] Rank-and-file soldiers were not the only ones caught up in the euphoria of relatively easy operations after the bloodletting in Normandy. In mid-September, as he was preparing to leave for temporary duty in Washington, Maj. Gen. Leonard T. Gerow (Virginia Military Institute, 1912), the commander of V Corps, told his staff, "It is probable the war with Germany will be over before I am released to return to the V Corps."[17]

First Army commander Courtney Hodges received bad news on Sunday, 10 September. His G-4 told him there were no substantial reserves of fuel and that there was no news of additional shipments. Ammunition had not had high priority during the pursuit, but now the Americans faced the prospect of attacking the Westwall. It would take a few days to build up ammunition stocks, and Hodges decided to delay the attack until that situation improved. He did not know with certainty the condition of the defenses, but he did know that Berlin had called for tens of thousands of laborers to dig trenches and anti-tank ditches. Collins, the VII Corps commander, convinced Hodges to conduct a reconnaissance in force the next day. This was not an attack of significant size, but it would presumably be strong enough to allow First Army to get through the defenses before it halted for resupply.[18]

General Gerow of V Corps, the 4th Division's higher headquarters, also faced some significant challenges. He wanted to reinforce the left wing of his corps to maintain contact with the VII Corps, which was concentrated to support the British in the north. Yet he had a considerable amount of real estate to cover in southern Belgium and Luxembourg, since Hodges also wanted him to maintain contact with Third Army. He put the corps on line and sacrificed concentration to prevent the enemy from counterattacking against a single point. Given the supply situation and the need to keep from presenting to the enemy a gap between First and Third Armies, this line of thinking was reasonable. The 4th Infantry Division, for example, passed through south-central Belgium on a wide (for an infantry division) front of about twenty-four miles. The 28th Infantry Division, with a combat command of the 5th Armored Division, also part of V Corps, was concentrated northwest of Luxembourg City; the remainder of the armored division was spread thinly to the south and west.[19]

The Schnee Eifel

ON THE LATE AFTERNOON OF 11 SEPTEMBER, a detachment of cavalry from the 5th Armored Division made the U.S. Army's first entry into Germany, near Stoltzembourg, Luxembourg. Elements of the 28th Division crossed the Our River about two hours later, and as noted above, the patrol from the 22d Infantry Regiment also went into Germany that night. Gerow ordered his commanders to keep moving and hold whatever gains they made.[20]

German artillery had already hit the leading elements of the 22d Infantry, at midday on 11 September, and Maj. Gen. Raymond O. Barton, the commander of the 4th Division, told Colonel Lanham to consider all Germans, civilians included, to be the enemy. The shortage of gasoline kept the regiment from crossing the border in force before the afternoon of 12 September,[21] and enemy infantry engaged some of

German Westwall bunker, 1944. [Courtesy National Archives]

the dismounted patrols. There were also reports of German tanks. Only about half of the twelve TDs attached to the regiment were operable.[22]

As the regiment reached pushed into Germany, an officer hiding behind a few scrub pine trees and high weeds looked through his binoculars and saw a few enemy troops standing in the open. One of them walked into a passage that seemed to open in the side of a small hill. Lt. George D. Wilson's "stomach turned a little, and I got a slight chill." He knew this was a Westwall bunker.[23] General Barton ordered Lanham to attack the Westwall defenses at 10:00 AM on 14 September.[24] The first important objective was a ridge called Schnee Eifel (literally "snow mountain"), near the town of Prüm which was one of a handful of sizeable towns in the area with railroad sidings. The ridge was about eleven miles in length. One road ran the length of the hill mass; another paralleled about two-thirds of its length. Hill 698, the Schwarzer Mann, was the dominant point. Two creeks barred direct access from the Eifel to Prüm. The villages of Brandscheid and Sellerich lay in the shadow of the high ground.[25]

Defending the area was the I SS Panzer Corps (General der Waffen SS Georg Keppler), part of General der Panzertruppen Erich Brandenberger's 7th Army, which in turn was part of Army Group B. Keppler's troops were exhausted, and his units were so far below

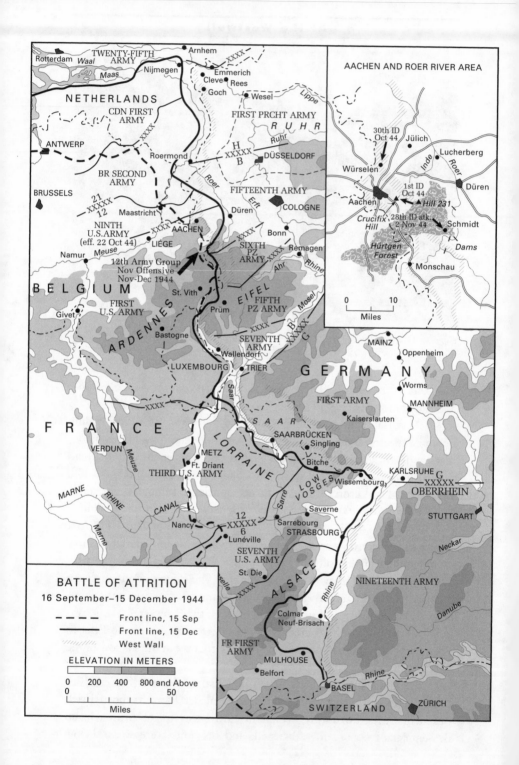

INSET: AACHEN AND ROER RIVER AREA

Jülich
30th ID
Oct 44
Würselen
Lucherberg
Inde
Roer
1st ID
Oct 44
Aachen
Hill 231
Düren
Crucifix
Hill
28th ID atk.
2 Nov 44
Schmidt
Hürtgen
Forest
Dams
Monschau

0 — 10
Miles

MAIN MAP:

Rotterdam Waal TWENTY-FIFTH ARMY Arnhem
Maas Nijmegen Emmerich
Cleve Rees
Goch Wesel
Lippe
NETHERLANDS
CDN FIRST ARMY FIRST PRCHT ARMY
R U H R
Ruhr
ANTWERP H / B
Roermond DÜSSELDORF
BR SECOND ARMY
BRUSSELS 21 / 12
Maastricht FIFTEENTH ARMY
NINTH U.S. ARMY
(eff. 22 Oct 44) AACHEN Düren COLOGNE
LIÈGE Erft
Namur Meuse Bonn
12th Army Group Remagen
Nov Offensive SIXTH PZ ARMY
Nov-Dec 1944 Rhine
B E L G I U M Ahr
FIRST U.S. ARMY EIFEL
St. Vith FIFTH PZ ARMY
Givet Prüm Mosel
A R D E N N E S B / G
Bastogne SEVENTH ARMY
Wallendorf
LUXEMBOURG TRIER
Saar
F R A N C E G E R M A N Y
MAINZ
Oppenheim
FIRST ARMY
Worms
S A A R Kaiserslautern MANNHEIM
VERDUN SAARBRÜCKEN
METZ Singling
Ft. Driant Bitche
THIRD U.S. ARMY LORRAINE KARLSRUHE G
Meuse LOW VOSGES Wissembourg OBERRHEIN
MARNE RHINE Sarre Saverne STUTTGART
CANAL Sarrebourg Neckar
Nancy 12 / 6 STRASBOURG
Lunéville SEVENTH U.S. ARMY
St. Die ALSACE NINETEENTH ARMY
Rhine Danube

BATTLE OF ATTRITION
16 September–15 December 1944

- - - - - Front line, 15 Sep
———— Front line, 15 Dec
////// West Wall

ELEVATION IN METERS
0   200   400   800 and Above
0 — 50
Miles

Colmar
Neuf-Brisach
FR FIRST ARMY
MULHOUSE
Belfort
Rhine
BASEL
ZÜRICH
SWITZERLAND

strength in early September that they hardly warranted the designation of division or regiment. The 2d SS Panzer Division, or what was left of it, was responsible for the Schnee Eifel sector. It had about a thousand high-quality panzer grenadiers and another 1,900 infantrymen who were less well trained. Heavy weapons included fourteen 75-mm anti-tank guns, about forty 105-mm and 150-mm howitzers, and a few self-propelled assault guns, but little ammunition, before 12 September. A single operable Panther tank constituted its armored force on the day the Americans entered the Reich. The division also had a weak battalion each of engineers and signal troops.[26] Yet the Americans did not quickly break through the area, because they were short on supplies, the weather was turning bad, and the Germans were reconstituting combat power literally by the minute.

Drizzle and poor visibility greeted the GIs early on 14 September. A company of supporting Sherman tanks arrived late at the link-up point where they would join the infantrymen, and this postponed the attack until noon.[27] Lt. Col. A. S. Teague's 3d Battalion (reinforced) led out, followed by the 1st (Lt. Col. John Dowdy) and 2d (Lt. Col. Glenn D. Walker) battalions of the 22d. Teague's men finally got under way about 11:30 AM. Company K, one of the three rifle companies in the 3d Battalion, with five Sherman tanks (70th Tank Battalion) and four TDs (893d TD Battalion), hit automatic-weapons and small-arms fire at the Westwall shortly after 1:00 PM. Things got worse about an hour later, when an anti-tank round slammed into a Sherman. The riflemen it was supporting were still about seventy-five yards from the edge of the woods line at the Schnee Eifel.[28] Exactly what happened next is unclear.

The other tanks and TDs stopped for a few seconds when the disabled Sherman jerked to a halt. Lanham was at his CP when the attack began. He received word that enemy fire had pinned down the infantry and that some tanks and TDs were burning. The phone line between the regimental and battalion CPs went dead. Lanham and his S-2, Capt. Howard Blazzard, accompanied by some riflemen and a French volunteer, jumped into jeeps and rushed toward the fight, where they eventually dismounted and ran toward the GIs. Lanham and Blazzard urged infantrymen by name to get up and run for the cover of the trees. Blazzard heard that some of the tanks had even reversed direction and left the riflemen unprotected. He later told Hemingway that the men got excited and came "back down across the field, dragging a few wounded and a few limping." Some of the tanks did reach the woods and continued supporting the attack. Lanham got the attention of the riflemen, fired his pistol in the direction of the enemy, and yelled for the men to move.[29]

He, Sgt. J. C. Smith, and Blazzard went farther into the woods and located a gap in the fir trees wide enough to accommodate the armor. German infantry took them under fire. They had crawled to within ten yards of a bunker and adjacent earthworks when Blazzard saw the volunteer move toward a machine-gun dugout. He yelled for him get down, but it was too late. Blazzard then hurled a grenade at the bunker, but it did no damage. Smith ran forward, grabbed the mortally wounded Frenchman by his feet, and dragged him to cover. A medic later wrote "Free French" on a casualty tag and tied it to the body; Blazzard marked out the notation and changed it to read "Company L, 22d Infantry."[30]

Lanham, meanwhile, shot a German, and Smith got two more with his carbine. Blazzard alternately crawled and ran until he got behind the bunker where he shot a German who was trying to maneuver behind his group. The wounded German fell in the middle of a dirt road and began crawling toward a ditch until one of the TDs ran over him. Blazzard and Smith got the TD to fire at the steel access door of a bunker. When the 76-mm cannon opened up, smoke, dust, and concrete fragments showered the area. But it took five more rounds to force out some of the occupants. Their faces were black from the dust raised by the concussion, and they were bleeding from the nose and mouth. Blazzard saw "legs, arms and heads scattered all over that goddam place."[31]

It took several hours for the regiment to consolidate its gains. No doubt the severity of the fighting surprised those who still held out hope for a quick end to the war. Lanham reported to Barton that the resistance was heavy and that his men had probably bypassed some of the bunkers because they could not see them all. Lanham was bitter about the tank support. He said the armor "showed timidity and almost point blank refusal to advance."[32]

The commander of Company K, Captain Whaley, recalled the battle differently. He later stated that after his men received the initial burst of fire that sent the tanks reeling, he had his lead platoons swing a few hundred yards away from the planned route of attack and then turn toward the woods. Enemy fire killed three men outright. Whaley reported that his men quickly recovered from the shock of first contact and "everyone began firing and shouting at the top of his lungs as we entered the woods and we made quite a noise."[33] Perhaps Company K did not become as disorganized as Lanham believed. No doubt the soldiers were confused when they ran up on a wide trail they assumed was the main road that ran the length of the hill mass. Whaley himself was unsure if this trail was the main road, which was the objective. Uncertainty seems to have been the issue, not a total breakdown of control of the attacking units. As far as Whaley was concerned, his company regrouped and successfully took its objective, at a cost of twenty-five casualties of what were probably not many more than a hundred men in the line.[34]

Based on the outcome of the day's fighting, Barton committed his reserve regiment (the 8th Infantry) in the relatively open ground on the northern fringe of the Schnee Eifel to try to reach the Kyll River north of Prüm. He directed Lanham to seize the village of Brandscheid, on the southern fringe of the hill. The intent was to envelop the enemy, but the 8th Infantry was unable to gain much ground. A thick mist denied the GIs effective close air support and well-defended roadblocks and blown bridges impeded ground maneuver.[35]

Not only did Brandscheid remain in enemy hands, but the riflemen noticed a steady increase in German artillery and mortar fire. A counterattack hit the 22d Infantry's 2d Battalion. Several *Landsers* infiltrated between it and the 3d Battalion, and Lanham had to send a company to clean out the penetration.[36] He had little choice but to use one of the companies then moving on Brandscheid, though this compromised the concentration there. Yet an estimated three hundred men from the 2d SS Panzer Division had "practically surrounded" elements of the 2d Battalion and had even demanded its surrender.[37] The GIs fought back and the pressure gradually eased, but the enemy had disrupted the battalion's operations for the rest of the day. Lanham ordered patrols to prevent a recurrence. Lieutenant Colonel Ruggles told one company commander to "be dam [*sic*] sure that [his patrol is] strong because it will be shot up if it isn't."[38]

The Germans could not drive the Americans from the Schnee Eifel, but their repeated counterattacks and infiltration could disrupt and delay attacks almost indefinitely. The regiment's operations journal reported, "Lots of arty. and small arms fire—can't make progress. . . . [I]t will be hell tonight."[39] Even Lanham's command post took fire.[40] Barton ordered Lanham to "take that place [Brandscheid]" on 16 September "even if [you] have to use the whole regiment."[41]

There was little progress in what had turned out to be a swirling hornet's nest of resistance. Lieutenant Colonel Dowdy's 1st Battalion faced heavy mortar fire when it moved out in a thick fog.[42] The weather also delayed the 3d Battalion at Brandscheid until after 1:00 PM. Even though the Germans shelled the battalion unmercifully, one company reached the northern fringe of the town before dark. The attack ended without further progress. The regiment's journal recorded the day's events:

10:45 AM: Crossed line of departure. There was heavy mortar fire.
10:55 AM: [Enemy] infiltration heavy from the left.
12:45 PM: Krauts moving into position . . . received pretty heavy shelling.
1:00 PM: Getting pretty heavy mortar fire.
1:45 PM: Pretty heavy fire on all 3 Bns.
3:15 PM: Catching plenty [of] hell.[43]

The regimental S-3 (operations officer), Maj. Earl "Lum" Edwards, called for two hundred rounds of 4.2-inch mortar fire on the town, but the mortars had to stop firing after sixty rounds; there was not enough ammunition to fire more and keep a reserve for contingencies. Even so, as the late summer sun dropped behind the trees, the town was "burning fiercely."[44] The 3d Battalion reported, "We are pushing out from road— taking more pill boxes—about 200 yds from Brandscheid."[45] Then, shortly before 5:00 PM, Lanham got word that Dowdy had been killed by artillery.[46] The 3d Battalion finally got into the town after dark and started clearing the buildings. However, Company C was "shot to hell . . . lost 36 men—any movement is murderous."[47]

Sellerich

OPERATIONS CONTINUED ON 17 September to comply with General Barton's orders to "seize the high ground east of Sellerich" and gain control of the approaches to Prüm.[48] The 1st Battalion, now under Maj. Robert Latimer (with attached tanks and TDs), would lead; the 2d Battalion (reinforced with a platoon each of TDs and engineers) would envelop Hill 583, north of Sellerich; the 3d Battalion, also reinforced, would finish clearing Brandscheid and secure the extreme south flank of the regiment and the 4th Infantry Division.[49] Capt. Edward Martin, the commander of Company C, thought Latimer looked "upset" on the night of 16 September as he prepared to lead the "fatal" attack on Sellerich. Martin wondered if this was due to his having assumed command just a few hours earlier. Captain Haskin, the commander of Company A, also looked "shaken up" after a close call with artillery. Latimer wanted to envelop Sellerich, but the continuing fight at Brandscheid prevented use of the best approach. The alternative route was a relatively open draw.[50]

Overcast skies and rain hampered visibility. Enemy artillery and mortar fire continued unabated—it had not let up during the preceding night—and machine-gun fire was also heavy. Men were caught in the open and cut down by fire from several directions. Latimer later said that Haskin "ran back to the Bn. CP . . . completely distraught, shaking and almost crying." Latimer ordered Lt. Peter J. Marco to take command.[51]

Company B entered the draw a few minutes later and bore the full brunt of what Martin called a "murderous band of enemy fire."[52] A TD hit a mine, and well-camouflaged anti-tank guns firing from two directions drove off the supporting tanks.[53] Riflemen instinctively threw themselves to the ground and jerked violently when bullets or shell fragments hit them. Several men from Company A nevertheless managed to reach the high ground outside Sellerich, and they had started to dig in when hellish fire hit them too. Marco radioed Latimer that his men could hold. Latimer replied that reinforcements were on the way. What he did not know was that the reinforcing unit, Company B, was itself pinned down. Company C was also under heavy fire, and moving it up would endanger the battalion's flank. Marco was wounded at some point, and Latimer eventually got Lanham's permission to get Company A out the trap. Runners went forward to deliver the message, but after some time passed and no word came from them, the battalion S-3 volunteered to go up. He was hit five times while trying to reach the remnants of the isolated company.[54] He did not know that the survivors of Company A had pulled out on their own. Casualties were apparently scattered between the Schnee Eifel woods line and Hill 520. Evacuation took several hours, and only two officers and sixty-two men reached the rear. Marco was listed as missing in action. Captain McLane, the commander of Company B, entered 1st Battalion CP about this time. Latimer "considered him a case of combat exhaustion" and sent another officer to organize the company.[55]

Lanham did not believe that the enemy resistance was as strong as Latimer reported. His view was "that Company A broke, abandoned its position without orders, and fled about two miles to the rear." He criticized Latimer "severely for failing to use all his forces to press the attack"; Lanham relieved him, his executive officer, and his S-3.[56] Maj. Clifford M. "Swede" Henley replaced Latimer on 20 September. Henley later recalled, "The surprise of my life [was] when Col. Lanham called on the phone and said, 'you are the [battalion commander], start functioning.' "[57]

Brig. Gen. C. T. Lanham (left) and Lt. Col. J. F. Ruggles in Germany, 1945. [Courtesy Donald A. Warner, Jr.]

The defeat outside Sellerich, coupled with problematic weather and persistent supply difficulties and a lack of combat power equal to the task led Barton to call off the attack on Brandscheid. Air support was also an issue. "Lum" Edwards complained, "If it isn't the weather it's something else."[58] The division was vulnerable to counterattack against its flanks because of its separation (save for a thin screen of cavalry) from the VII Corps on the north and the rest of V Corps to the south. This vulnerability was apparent on 18 and 19 September, when the Germans counterattacked the regiment.[59] By this time, the 22d could do little more than maintain patrols, which often found that the Germans had reoccupied the same defenses that combat engineers thought they had eliminated with explosives. Colonel Lanham's troops went into assembly areas in eastern Belgium during October to prepare for a major attack in November.

South of the Eifel

Two of the 28th Infantry Division's three rifle regiments entered Germany on 12 September on a fifteen-mile-wide front unprepared for an attack on fixed defenses, since they had operated for weeks in the pursuit. Troops had no flamethrowers or demolition charges at hand. Attached TD and tank units were lagging behind. Many other vehicles were in maintenance. Forward ammunition stocks could support the relatively light expenditures of a meeting engagement but not extended close combat. For example, the commander of the 28th, then-Brig. Gen. Norman D. Cota, was so concerned about the supply of artillery ammunition he placed strict controls on the firing of unobserved missions (i.e., fire adjusted by forward observers or others who could not see the target).[60]

Heavy German fire on 13 and 14 September prevented the GIs from breaking through the Westwall defenses opposite the southern portion of the V Corps zone of attack. Artillery was ineffective against the concrete bunkers. Though many of the defenders had entered the line only hours before, their positions dominated the surrounding area and it was relatively easy to slow down attackers in the open ground before them. Only when supporting armor arrived on the 15th did the enemy positions fall. Good news turned quickly to disaster, however, during an enemy counterattack supported by flamethrowers mounted on half-tracks. Already weak rifle units in the 28th sustained about 1,500 casualties in the first days at the border.[61]

The 5th Armored Division sent battalion-sized tank-infantry task forces, supported by a regiment of the 28th Division, against Wallendorf, Germany, on 14 September. Though it did not take long to drive six miles inside Germany, the "front line" was only the width of the road on which the armor traveled, and the entire column was exposed to infiltration and disruption. When visibility permitted, the Americans made good use of close air support, and they were only a few miles from Bitburg when Gerow, the corps commander, called off the operation. A strong German counterattack including tanks hit the Americans, and though fighter-bombers were effective against the panzers, they were unable for some time to locate artillery that was firing on the Wallendorf bridgehead from three directions. Air attacks damaged the Germans between 20 and 22 September, until the division and the attached infantry pulled back into Luxembourg, unable to exploit the insignificant gains.[62]

As the tactical developments described above unfolded, the Allies invaded southern France in August, and Eisenhower on 1 September assumed direct command on the continent. Two weeks later, he explained his strategy to Marshall. He called Montgomery's proposal for a so-called 'single thrust' a "scheme" and "fantastic idea" based on "wishful thinking." He rightly noted that given the overwhelming logistical support such an operation required, if it got into trouble no other units could assist, because their own logistics elements would already be tied up maintaining the "single thrust." He added that the Allies would still "have to fight one more major battle" to get through the border defenses.[63] On the Allied left, 21 Army Group was stalled at Antwerp and in eastern Holland due to the failure of the combined air-ground Market-Garden operation. Within the 12th Army Group, the First U.S. Army was halted outside of Aachen and in the Eifel. Third Army was trying to consolidate its bridgeheads across the Moselle River in France and approaching the fortified city of Metz. Behind the combat zone, support units assigned to the Communications Zone (the senior U.S. operational logistics headquarters in the ETO) were steadily moving supplies toward the front, but problems persisted with forward distribution and the inadequacies of over the shore receipt in Normandy. Cherbourg was functioning, but American planners finally had to accept the fact that Brest and the Brittany ports would serve no effective purpose. The Allies had reached what strategists call a 'culminating point'. The enemy was regrouping and refitting at a pace the Allies could not overcome. Eisenhower's forces had reached the limits of their endurance without destroying them. The Germans had time to put backbone into their defenses. In other words, the bill for carrying out the pursuit before the support infrastructure could mature had come due. There would be no Allied attack into the Reich on the heels of the summer's offensive. Eisenhower's decision to press forward was the right operational choice, but the grip of logistics upset the plans and forced the GI to fight an autumn and winter war. Germany was emerging form the summer's defeats in a position of significant strength. German troops and labor organizations were, meanwhile, increasing their fixed border defenses, reconstituting units, and increasing their inventories of materiel. They were waiting for what they knew would be an even bigger series of blows. Though the Allies still controlled the initiative (they could decide the time and place of attack), the Germans were about to take control of the outcome. As the first cool winds of autumn enveloped the battlefields, however, no one knew how bitter that struggle would become.

CHAPTER 8

BLOODY AUTUMN, OCTOBER– NOVEMBER 1944

EAR WÜRSELEN, GERMANY, 2 October 1944: Riflemen of the 1st Battalion, 117th Infantry Regiment covered engineers positioning wooden footbridges into the muddy banks of the Würm River a few miles north of Aachen. When the engineer officer in charge signaled that the flimsy bridges were ready, the infantrymen ran across them toward enemy-occupied Westwall bunkers on the far bank. Bullets and shell fragments filled the air. Black geysers of earth erupted among the men, the sounds drowning out the screams of the badly wounded. One infantry officer too impatient to wait for the bridges had already carried a twenty-foot-long board into the stream; now he threw it onto the mud of the enemy-held riverbank, turned to his men, and yelled, "There's your goddamned bridge!" Such initiative by junior leaders got Company B across in relatively good shape, but artillery nailed Company C. Seven men were dead, and another eighty were wounded inside an hour. Lt. Col. Walter Frankland, the battalion commander, committed his reserve, Company A.

Covered by BAR fire, bazooka man Gus Pantazapulos crawled to within a hundred feet of one huge concrete bunker. "Put it low, Gus," someone called as Pantazapulos took aim and fired. There was no visible damage. He fired another rocket at the same spot. When the smoke cleared, he could see that the second explosion had caused no more damage than the first. A private threw a fifty-pound charge of TNT where the rockets had hit. This also did no significant damage. A moment later, a *Landser* ran from the bunker and threw a grenade at the Americans. A GI fired back. Pvt. Marvin Sirokin dragged up a pole charge and somehow shoved it into the bunker's firing embrasure. This finally silenced the position. Sirokin was killed the same day. Someone later asked Pantazapulos what he was thinking while he crawled toward the enemy. "I wasn't thinking, I was just praying," he replied.[1]

First Army's Drive on the Rhine

VICTORY HAD SEEMED SO CLOSE just a few weeks before. Allied bombers ranged day and night over the Reich. Ground troops were approaching Germany. The Red Army's summer offensive cost the Wehrmacht 700,000 casualties in addition to the half-million lost in the West.[2] Yet despite the success of the summer battles, the failure to get the port of Antwerp working changed the face of the campaign. When Eisenhower learned that the port was unusable because the enemy still controlled its approaches and that shortages of ammunition would further delay the attack there, he warned Montgomery that operations would stop by mid-November. He reminded him that the great port had "first importance" among all other operations. Montgomery replied that there was not an ammunition shortage; rather, naval authorities, who "can know nothing [repeat] nothing" about the ground combat situation, had made an incorrect report.[3] As events unfolded, a drive to take the port itself had to wait until after capture of the Peel Marshes in Holland, and it would not receive its first cargo ship until 28 November, well after bad weather had set in.[4]

First Army commander General Hodges, meanwhile, had decided to launch a deliberate (thoroughly planned) attack to punch a hole in the German border once and for all. To assist, Bradley placed the Ninth U.S. Army with a corps headquarters, both recently arrived from the Brittany Peninsula, in the line in Luxembourg. This allowed Hodges to shorten his front and concentrate the V and VII Corps near Aachen while the XIX Corps remained on the north flank. The net gain was only one division despite the reorganization, though there was less ground to worry about.[5] Eisenhower told his subordinates that he wanted to "push hard over the Rhine. . . ."[6]

A classic military rule of thumb is that an attacker needs at least a three-to-one edge over a defender to have a chance of breaking a well-prepared defense. Operations research has in fact indicated the minimum attacker-defender ratio might realistically need to be as high as four to one or better to assure success.[7] While the Allies could dictate the time and place of an attack, commanders and staffs still had to coordinate the movement of combat units, supplies, artillery, armor, engineers, and aircraft to arrive at the critical time and place. It was not easy to synchronize these movements. Further, the Americans had to decide what to do about Aachen, a major city located on the approaches to the Cologne/Rhine plain. General Hodges preferred not to bypass it and thereby leave its garrison as a threat to his rear. There was some propaganda value for the Germans in defending the city, since it had been the seat of power of the Holy Roman Empire—the First Reich. They could not afford to waste a strong mobile force there, but the fact that the First Army could not assemble overwhelming force against it worked in their favor. Hodges decided to first envelop the city and take it only when the time was right, with the XIX Corps on the north and the VII Corps on the south. Then he could move on the expansive Cologne Plain and on to the Ruhr.[8]

The strongest band of Westwall fortifications facing the First Army was immediately north of Aachen, near the junction of the Würm and Roer rivers, where the XIX Corps would strike. Assault troops would have to cross the narrow Würm first. Its approaches were virtual marshes covered by excellent fields of fire. Many fills and cuts on a railroad running next to the enemy-held side of the river enhanced the defenses, and there were extensive minefields and anti-tank ditches. Enemy artillerymen had surveyed every crossroad and landmark as reference points for artillery. The fresh 183d Volksgrenadier Division (VGD) and the neighboring 49th Infantry Division had about 5,500 frontline troops. About forty light and medium artillery pieces, four 210-mm guns. and two large-caliber railroad guns remained from the summer's fighting.[9]

American units were learning how to fight. To prepare for the set-piece attack that would begin on 2 October, the 30th Infantry Division (Maj. Gen. Leland S. Hobbs) conducted extensive training with demolitions, flamethrowers (reports were mixed on their effectiveness), and bazookas. Engineers rehearsed bridge construction under fire, and tanks practiced cooperation with infantry. Leaders refined river-crossing procedures in a gully filled with stagnant water and banks dug to resemble those of the Würm. One battalion built a detailed sand table showing the location of concrete bunkers, anti-tank obstacles, roads, ridges, streams, draws, houses, and woods. Reconnaissance patrols helped the division accurately plot about 90 percent of the bunkers in the area. Squad leaders received aerial photos with overprinted map data showing these defenses and other landmarks. Officers of the 1st Battalion, 117th Infantry Regiment, noted that the training began from scratch, because all the experienced men had been "wiped out in previous battles and there had been a complete turnover in battalion personnel."[10]

These preparations were only possible before a deliberate attack. Despite these opportunities to practice, however, nothing would guarantee an easy victory. For example, the attack plan called for self-propelled

155-mm guns to destroy the forty-five bunkers they could take
under direct fire from friendly lines. A forward observer recalled, "[The
155-mm guns] fired direct at a range of approximately 1500 yards. In
12 rounds they fired they scored 7 hits. The only effect on the pillbox
was about 4 feet of concrete removed and some dirt off the top." Light
artillery and anti-tank guns were "almost worthless . . . even with concrete piercing fuzes." Even the largest-caliber guns took considerable
time to destroy a bunker. An eight-inch howitzer could average only one
direct hit per five rounds fired from a range of 8,000 yards.[11]

Starting at 9:00 AM on 2 October 1944, American artillery smothered
known anti-aircraft defenses. Elements of two groups of P-47 fighter-
bombers plus medium bombers hit the area with little significant effect.
The fighter-bombers missed the bunkers, and the mediums came in from
the wrong direction and could not release all their bombs without endan-
gering friendly soldiers. Some Germans did not even know an air attack
had taken place.[12] Colonel Frankland, the commander of the 1st Battalion,
117th Infantry, reported, "The net advantage of the strike was very little."
Lt. Col. Walter M. Johnson, commander of the 117th Infantry, believed
the air attack "did no good."[13]

That night, 30th Division and XIX Corps artillery disrupted the
counterattack the Germans managed to throw together. General
Corlett, the corps commander, committed the 2d Armored Division on
3 October to help expand the small bridgehead. Infantry fought house
to house in the town of Übach, located only a mile and a half east of the
Würm, but were unable to make much progress. The concentration of
armor in the bridgehead became a big target as well. Corlett's German
counterpart, General der Infanterie Friedrich Köchling, meanwhile,
pieced together a command structure for another counterattack. It was
dawn on 4 October before it got under way; it hit the 119th Infantry
and stalled. That regiment bought time for the 2d Armored Division,
which gained some ground the next day. On 6 October, however, two
battalions of *Landsers*, supported by four or five assault guns and tanks,
recaptured some bunkers and took over a hundred GI prisoners.[14]
German resistance was stubborn enough that it took the 30th Division
a week to tear a gap in the Westwall and turn southeast toward Aachen.
More than 80 percent of the division's 2,654 casualties by mid-month
were infantrymen, and more than a quarter of the infantry unit officers
were casualties. The 2d Armored Division lost fifty-two medium
tanks.[15]

Enemy artillery strength was impressive even by U.S. standards. Köchling had 239 light, medium, and heavy pieces with adequate ammunition. Four more battalions (about forty-eight pieces) arrived later.[16] For comparison, First Army's four infantry, two armored divisions and separate artillery units opposite the enemy corps had approximately 690 105-mm howitzers, 36 155-mm self-propelled guns, 216 towed 155-mm howitzers, 48 4.5-inch guns, 48 8-inch guns and howitzers, and 24 240-mm howitzers. Another 1,200 or so 75-mm tank and TD guns could supplement the other artillery. Because only about half of the First Army pieces could support the battle for Aachen without relocating, the artillery ratio was much closer than raw numbers indicate.[17] At issue was ammunition. Allocations for the week ending 5 October for the 240-mm howitzer were only 3.8 rounds per gun per day; the allocation for the 8-inch gun was 3.1 rounds without using up reserves needed for later operations or to defeat a counterattack. Inadequate unloading of ships and an attempt to build reserves at the expense of forward units were two of the main causes. By the third week of October, the restriction on the mainstay weapon of the division, the 105-mm howitzer, was thirty rounds per day, against a desired rate of sixty in First Army. Expenditures for the medium 155-mm howitzer in the same period averaged only fifteen rounds per day. The GI did not receive unlimited artillery support.[18]

The United States did have a clear superiority in tank strength. The 2d and 3d Armored Divisions averaged about 192 operable tanks each during October, and the 9 supporting separate tank battalions averaged about forty-two operable of fifty-four authorized medium tanks each.[19] The German LXXXI Corps had only forty-eight serviceable tracked assault guns, four Tiger tanks, and seven Panther tanks concentrated against the XIX Corps. Two strong reserve units, the 116th Panzer Division and the 3d Panzer Grenadier Division, had forty-one more tanks and thirty-eight more artillery pieces.[20]

German tactics during the first Westwall battles saw use of the weaker divisional units, separate *kampfgruppen* (battle groups), and separate battalions and brigades fighting to buy time for quality units. General der Panzertruppen Erich Brandenberger, commander of the 7th Army (Köchling's higher headquarters), was a capable and experienced officer and had to keep American aircraft and artillery from pinning his units down. Attrition had put inexperienced junior officers in command of battalions and NCOs in command of companies. The 246th Infantry

Division, for example, consisted of an amalgam of soldiers hurriedly drawn together into reconstituted units after the disaster in France. A U.S. intelligence report estimated that one regiment in this division was composed of new recruits and others who had been forced into service. However, the report also noted that when such units had "fixed fortifications they were capable of putting up a stubborn and occasionally fanatical resistance." On the other hand, several of the new *Volks-Grenadier* divisions had some highly competent leaders and good soldiers.[21] Field Marshall Model, commander of Army Group B, exhorted his troops to hold the Westwall: "Villages and towns to the west have become battle zones. The last battle has commenced. . . . Every village must become a strongpoint. Every block of houses a fortress. Who has a weapon and does not use it shall suffer a death of shame, for only the brave have a right to live."[22]

Crucifix Hill

CIRCUMSTANCES OF LOCATION dictated which VII Corps units would close the southern half of the ring around Aachen and link up with the northern wing (30th Infantry Division) of the attack. The 1st Infantry Division reached the outskirts of the city during the second week of September and had remained there. Maj. Gen. Clarence R. Huebner, who had enlisted in the Army in 1910 and worked his way up the ranks, was the commander. He had received a distinguished service cross in World War I as acting commander of a battalion.[23] Now his veterans were getting tired. The S-3 of the 1st Battalion, 18th Infantry, Capt. Edward W. McGregor, believed the men approached the battle with "mixed feelings. . . . [T]hey were battle veterans with a sense of destiny—a feeling that they were always selected for important tasks because they had always accomplished their mission. . . . On the other hand, there were causes for personal misgivings concerning the forthcoming operation." The euphoria of one success after another during summer "had been shattered by the abrupt increase of resistance on German soil."[24]

Col. George A. Smith Jr., the commander of the regiment, planned to attack from Eilendorf, an eastern suburb of Aachen, seize the town of Verlautenheide, and then turn west to take two important hills, designated by their elevation in meters above sea level: Hill 239 (called "Crucifix Hill" after a large religious cross at its summit) and Hill 231, called "the Ravelsberg." Taking the high ground was important because

Aachen sits in a "bowl," and the hills dominated the roads over which supplies reached the enemy garrison. The 16th Infantry Regiment would meanwhile protect the division's northeast wing and keep contact with the adjacent 3d Armored Division. The 26th Infantry would seize Aachen if the enemy refused the surrender ultimatum Huebner intended to send after the city was surrounded. The firing of four corps artillery battalions reinforced divisional artillery. The fire plan allowed only one round every two minutes—certainly not lavish support. Working in the Americans' favor, however, was the fact that the 18th Infantry was relatively rested. It had penetrated the Westwall in mid-September gone into defensive positions.[25] Lt. Col. Henry G. Learnard, the commander of the 1st Battalion, however, was not satisfied with the artillery support plan. The commander of the attached 155-mm self-propelled battery (four guns) wanted his weapons to remain in covered positions south of Eilendorf, where they would be relatively protected from enemy counter-battery fire but unable to fire directly on the defenses. Smith agreed with the battery commander. The 1st Division had none of the big guns itself; there were only thirty-six in all of First Army.[26]

From a window in a building in Eilendorf, Learnard could see Crucifix Hill. Though he could not spot them all, he knew that concrete bunkers and multiple bands of concertina wire blocked the planned route of attack. He and MacGregor could also see that many of the firing ports in the bunkers faced south, away from the direction of attack, which was east to west. There were mines too, but patrols had not been able to get close enough to plot their location. The defenders were reported to be from the 453d Replacement Battalion, with elements of the 246th Division's 352d Regiment.[27] The terrain and defenses somewhat offset the fact that these were not the highest-quality units. Learnard's plan called for Company C, reinforced with the battalion's "ranger platoon," to take the crest of Crucifix Hill and block what was one of the key roads still open to Aachen. Company A would meanwhile protect Company C's flank; Company B was in reserve. Mortars and .50 caliber machine guns would support from Eilendorf, and forward observers from the regiment's cannon company and the artillery would accompany the attackers. Attached to the battalion were two platoons of Sherman tanks and a platoon of four M-10 TDs. The weather was unfavorable—almost constant rain, low clouds, and a cold, penetrating fog.[28] Learnard, MacGregor, Capt. Bobbie E. Brown (the commander of Company C), the leaders of the attached tank and TD platoons, an observer from cannon company, and an air liaison officer reconnoitered the route of attack several times. They decided there was no alternative to a frontal attack. On the evening of 7 October, Learnard and the others learned that the attack was on for the next morning. The men climbed onto blacked-out 2½-ton cargo trucks for the trip to Brand, where they de-trucked and marched cross-country to Eilendorf, which the last elements reached by about 1:30 the next morning.[29]

Two rifle companies from the 2d Battalion headed out to clear Verlautenheide about 4:00 AM. Many of these men were new, and one platoon became disorganized as it overran one of the small villages dotting the area. This platoon recovered, and with the support of mortar fire continued toward Verlautenheide. Another platoon, however, was still in relatively open ground when the supporting artillery fire unexpectedly stopped. German machine gunners climbed from their holes and poured fire into the GIs, who dropped to the muddy earth. There were some casualties—one lieutenant was hit in both legs but kept going with one of his squads.[30]

Shortly before daylight, an estimated one hundred *Landsers* counter-attacked Verlautenheide. It was about 10:00 AM before the situation was back under control, and this was only the first of two counterattacks that day. One supporting tank platoon lost its five tanks to mines, boggy ground, artillery, and anti-tank fire. Another platoon lost two of its tanks to mines and a mechanical problem. The three remaining tanks arrived too late to be of much help to the infantry. A GI said it was "the heaviest artillery and mortar fire encountered by the men since [Normandy]." This same fire also caused about twenty casualties in Company C of the 1st Battalion.[31]

Colonel Smith ordered the 1st Battalion to get to Verlautenheide and attack Crucifix Hill, even though the 2d Battalion had not cleared the area. He refused Learnard's request to wait until the town was secure or until the artillery threat subsided. McGregor said, "utter confusion pre-vailed. . . . [S]everal houses . . . were occupied by Germans." Learnard's headquarters staff had to fight its way into the town. The field phone wire stayed in long enough for Learnard to radio for a smokescreen. Capt. Brown got his men into cellars as protection from the fire, and he had a mortar observer and a .50 caliber machine-gun crew set up on rooftops. He gave his platoon leaders the plan of attack.[32]

Brown was a former career enlisted man who had received a direct commission as a lieutenant early in the war. Had an officer senior in rank but junior in age not noticed his potential, he would never have been an officer. At age forty-one in 1944, he was much older than his peers, and about the same age as Colonel Smith. Detailed information on his early life is sketchy. He was born at Dublin, Georgia, in 1903 to Dr. Robert E. Brown Sr. and Minnie C. Brown. There was little money at home, and his father died when Bobbie was two years old. He lived for a time with an aunt and uncle, but he was a restless boy who lied about his age and tried to enlist in the Army when he was fifteen. In 1922, he finally entered the Army to stay. During a single assignment at Fort Benning, Georgia, he rose in rank from private to technical sergeant, and he served for a time as a company first sergeant. He also gained a reputation as a drinker and gambler. Brown had no formal officer's training, but his innate leadership talent got him a battlefield commission in North Africa. He led a platoon in Sicily, where he received the Silver Star. He received command of Company C over college-educated officers with combat experience who were many years younger.[33]

After checking with battalion headquarters to ensure there were no changes in the plan, at about 1:30 PM Brown led his men across the line of departure. MacGregor and the artillery liaison officer watched the progress from the upper floor of the building housing the battalion command post. Riflemen disappeared into the smoke and haze while Germans who had taken shelter in bunkers during the artillery preparation ran to their fighting positions nearby. GIs of one platoon came under fire while they were at the town cemetery. Enemy artillery began falling. When one round hit their building, MacGregor and the artillery officer "dashed madly" for the cellar, where they found Learnard talking to the Company A commander. That company had been under intense fire and had lost about twenty men wounded or killed. Learnard reminded the commander, a capable veteran who looked "extremely nervous," that he had a mission to perform. This company moved out, almost immediately came under fire again, cleared three bunkers, and took twenty-three prisoners.[34]

MacGregor, meanwhile, was unable to reach Brown by radio. What was worse, the artillery officer could not reach the forward observer who was with Brown, who, in turn, meanwhile, came under fire at the base of Crucifix Hill. With his runner and radio operator, he jumped over an embankment to get below the line of fire. He got word that the ranger platoon leader had been wounded but was still in action and that two platoons were pinned down. Taking a fifty-pound satchel charge from a platoon leader, he crawled to the bunker pinning down his 2d Platoon. A German opened the access door, saw Brown, and slammed the door shut.

Brown ran up, jerked open the door, pulled the fuze on the charge, and leaped behind the embankment. The explosion silenced the position. Now there was word that the ranger platoon leader had been wounded a second time. Mortar fire was coming in, blowing mud and debris over the GIs. Brown and his runner next took some more charges and ran toward another bunker. The runner fired a yellow smoke grenade as a signal to the 155-mm self-propelled guns back at Eilendorf to lift their fire while Brown knocked out a second bunker. This eased the burden on the 2d Platoon, but Brown was wounded in the knee.[35]

McGregor could not raise Brown by radio or relay a message to him through another unit. The wire was still out. The forward observer with Brown was also unable to get requests for fire to the rear. Radio contact between Colonel Smith and MacGregor was working all too well, however, and Smith was "constantly pressing for information concerning the progress of the attack." When the ranger platoon lieutenant received a fatal wound, an NCO took over, but the men remained under fire. "I realized now that I had been wounded again," recalled Brown, "once on the wrist and once on the chin."[36]

Only after some GIs equipped with a flamethrower cleared ground for maneuver was Company C able to get moving again. It was about 2:10 PM. Then Brown got word that his 1st Platoon leader had been wounded, though he was still with his men. More bunkers fell, and, once contact with battalion had been restored, Brown called for artillery fire. He led the company to the summit of the hill, where the wooden cross had fallen, as if in protest to the violence around it. There he placed the supporting machine guns and took stock of the situation. The battalion reserve, Company B, did not get to Verlautenheide until about 4:00 PM, but with it were five tanks and the air liaison officer who had been directing the fighter-bombers which managed to provide some support despite the weather, though not on the hill itself. MacGregor went up and told Brown that there were several enemy-occupied bunkers to his rear and recommended that he set up a perimeter defense to repel an expected counterattack.[37]

Learnard had a problem. His battalion would receive no support, because the 2d and 3d battalions were securing the area to his rear, between Verlautenheide and Eilendorf. His own Company A had not taken all of its assigned objectives; Company C had the hill, but there were an unknown number of enemy troops still around it. Company B could assist Company C, or it could plug the developing gap between A and C—but it did not have the strength to do both. Rain was now falling, the planes were gone, visibility was growing worse, and darkness was approaching. Unobserved artillery fire could be as dangerous to the GIs as to the enemy. Learnard told Brown to keep his men where they were while Company B plugged the hole between A and C.[38] About 5:30, after Brown went out to inspect a machine-gun section, the company received artillery and mortar fire, plus machine-gun fire. This time, he took a bullet through the shoulder, and the NCO with him was hit in the stomach. Brown helped him crawl to the company's medic, and then he went back to his command post, where he had a cup of coffee with his first sergeant. He still had strength to later report to Learnard at the battalion HQ, get new orders, and return to the hill.[39]

The Ravelsberg

ENEMY INDIRECT FIRE CONTINUED after dark. Brown waited for the counterattack, and the Germans did not disappoint him. MacGregor said the area "literally shook with the impact of the shells. In the inky blackness of the rain-swept night, the men of the 1st Battalion cursed and dug, prayed and waited." The fire ended sometime after 4:00 AM (9 October). Minutes later, a "wave of yelling Germans came charging up the northern and western slopes" of the hill. GI machine gunners held their fire until the enemy was nearly on them. Pvt. Ray Klawiter, of the battalion's heavy-weapons company, was at his squad sergeant's foxhole when the counterattack began. A bullet tore into his right arm, fractured a bone, and caused nerve damage. A prisoner offered to help him get to the battalion aid station, but he decided to go by himself. "You keep going with your comrades and you always keep God in your mind and prayers," he recalled.[40]

German fire also continued to fall on Verlautenheide and the other nearby towns.[41] Colonel Smith ordered Lieutenant Colonel Learnard to move against the Ravelsberg (Hill 231). Several bunkers remained in German hands, and the orders for the continued attack came only hours before the enemy counterattacked at first light on 9 October. McGregor heard that Smith had decided to use the 1st Battalion "several hours before" informing a "disgruntled" Learnard that there was no information available on the enemy defenses. Smith was also still reluctant to expose the 155-mm SPs to enemy fire, though the artillery commander eventually agreed to move them up. Until then, the 75-mm guns on the supporting tanks and 76-mm guns on the TDs had little effect on the enemy positions.[42] Companies B and I (3d Battalion) moved on Crucifix Hill after dark on 9 October. The commander of Company B inadvertently led his men to the summit of the hill rather than around it, and Company C opened fire. The commanders shouted for them to stop, but even after the companies got back on track, friendly outposts at the bottom of the hill fired on them again.[43] Company B's commander, Capt. Jesse Miller, continued on in the darkness, his column nearly running into German troops heading to Aachen. He later told McGregor that he "could have reached out and grabbed" them.[44]

Both attacking companies reached the Ravelsberg—which, unlike Crucifix Hill, was covered by underbrush and trees—undetected about midnight of 9–10 October. They captured an enemy colonel and his staff asleep in a bunker. After daylight, they captured a mess detail carrying hot food for several dozen men. Engineers cleared the road between Verlautenheide and the Ravelsberg, and Learnard moved his CP to the area.[45] At a relatively little cost (up to that time), the Americans had dominated the enemy supply route into Aachen, and the division commander, Hubner, felt confident enough to deliver the surrender ultimatum to the Aachen garrison.[46]

There was nevertheless a savage struggle over the Ravelsberg once the Germans realized that the Americans had cut their supply line into Aachen. Shortly after 6:00 PM on 11 October, infantry and tanks or assault guns hit the area. GIs fought them off, but artillery continued well after dark. Attacks resumed the next day, and men spotted enemy armor in the area. Troops continued to improve their positions and clear out bunkers as late as 19 October. During one sweep, they captured twenty-three enlisted and one officer still in one bunker. Large-caliber German artillery hammered the positions that afternoon at an estimated rate of a hundred rounds per minute.[47]

Other Struggles

Loss of the Ravelsberg led Field Marshal Model to appeal to OB West for more troops. Rundstedt gave him the 116th Panzer and the 3d Panzergrenadier Divisions (under I SS Panzer Corps) but stipulated that he should commit the units as a whole and not piecemeal as they arrived. Model nevertheless allowed such commitment of the reinforcements, because he thought there was little alternative.[48] OB West officially classified the 3d Panzergrenadier Division as "qualified for the defense." Generalmajor Walter Denkert thought morale was good, and he chose to counterattack well after daylight on 15 October in order to reduce number of hours of exposure to U.S. air attack. He had about twenty tanks available, including Tiger tanks.[49]

The attack cut communications between companies and the 2d Battalion, 16th Infantry Regiment, headquarters. The battalion reported about 12:40 PM that the enemy was infiltrating "the right flank of 'G' Company. Engaged in a small arms fight. 'I' Company is being hit from the north in considerable strength." Soldiers reported German half-tracks, then tanks, near Company I (3d Battalion, 16th). Denkert had committed the 8th and 29th Panzergrenadier Regiments. He attributed their good initial progress to effective artillery preparation.[50] The commander of the 16th Infantry, Col. F. W. Gibb, held back his tanks and TDs, probably because there was so little concrete information about the attack. He did not want to send these important assets to the wrong area; yet withholding them too long could invite disaster. He called for air support and help from the 18th Infantry. Huebner asked the VII Corps commander, Collins, for assistance, but he did not immediately commit the meager division reserve (a single battalion of infantry). Air support did not arrive until nearly 2:00 PM, and some fighter-bombers came in less than a hundred yards from the Americans. U.S. artillery was firing constantly by 1:00 PM, and about three hours later Gibb announced that the attack was over. A second drive early on 16 October, however, broke through the hard-hit Company G, 16th Infantry. The company commander requested artillery on his own position, and German infantry and tanks rumbled to within twenty yards of the American foxholes before they were stopped. GIs counted about forty enemy dead.[51]

The 30th Infantry Division was meanwhile edging toward Aachen from the north. It took the division nine days after it began its attack on 2 October to cover three miles of highly urbanized terrain between the Würm River and Aachen, along a route described by the official history as "bathed in blood and frustration." This was coal-mining country, and the Germans had turned slag piles, mines, and villages into strongpoints sown liberally with mines. Panzers unexpectedly attacked on the morning of 8 October under the cover of a thick ground fog and destroyed a rifle platoon, knocking out three of four supporting U.S. tanks. The Americans had expected to encounter only infantry elements of the Aachen garrison. The enemy also threatened both a regimental and a battalion command post. A U.S. major personally knocked out two panzers with a bazooka, and a squad leader, Staff Sgt. Jack J. Pendleton, received a posthumous Medal of Honor for deliberately drawing enemy fire from his men.[52]

General Hodges was not satisfied: "We have to close that gap," he told XIX Corps Commands Charles H. Corlett, who had no reinforcements except for a battalion of infantry. First Army's only reserve was armor located far away in V Corps. The most direct route to a link up with the 1st Infantry Division lay in the rubble-filled streets of Würselen. Against the regiment that attacked there between 13 and 15 October, the Germans concentrated up to seven battalions of light and at least two batteries of heavy artillery. One of the junior officers who participated in fighting was Capt. James M. Burt of the 2d Armored Division. He had two tanks shot out from under him, and he was wounded on 13 October. He directed artillery fire from exposed positions, reconnoitered enemy lines, rescued several wounded men, and was personally credited with holding together the infantry-tank task force of which he was part.[53] Such acts of personal gallantry could not overcome the fact that probably the entire 60th Panzergrenadier Regiment, supported by dug-in tanks and other armor, was concealed in the rubble and gardens of the town.[54]

An officer of the 116th Panzer Division recorded that his unit "held its position against all attempts to break through it, despite heavy losses and extremely unclear conditions. . . . The artillery fire roars without pause . . . with concentrated fire, the Artillery Regiment [of the 116th] succeeded in destroying an enemy unit while it was still in its assembly area." The officer asserted that the resistance had ruined the hopes of the Americans for a quick end to the war.[55] It was the afternoon of 16 October before elements of the 30th and 1st Infantry Divisions established firm contact near the Ravelsberg. The German commander at Aachen finally surrendered on 21 October.[56] Pvt. Warren Eames, a rifleman in G Company 18th Infantry, said, "Sitting out there in a foxhole at night and knowing *you* were the very front line is one of the loneliest feelings possible. You felt so exposed. It was amazing how much security you felt just being in a rear area, even thought it might be only a few hundred yards behind the main line. But there we sat, on the lookout for the enemy and surrounded by the piled up bodies of all these dead Germans."[57]

Harry Truman presented Bobbie Brown the Medal of Honor at a White House ceremony on 23 August 1945. Brown's other awards included two Silver stars, at least six Purple Hearts, a Bronze Star with combat *V* device, and the Combat Infantryman's Badge. Sgt. Max Thompson of the 18th Infantry received the Medal of Honor for single-handedly defeating elements of an 18 October attack on the Ravelsberg using a bazooka, BAR, machine gun, rifle, and hand grenades. The 1st

President Harry S. Truman presents the Medal of Honor to Capt. Bobbie Brown, 1945. [Courtesy Robert R. McCormick Research Center]

Battalion of the 18th Infantry received a Distinguished Unit Citation for its operations at Crucifix Hill.[58] Now, with the fight over for Aachen, Bradley and Hodges could go ahead with an upcoming operation that was really big—one that might finally get the Americans across the Rhine, north of the Ardennes before the end of the year.

CHAPTER 9

NO WAY OUT, NOVEMBER 1944

K OMMERSCHEIDT, GERMANY, 5 November 1944: Lt. Ray Fleig's three Sherman tanks were all that stood between a few U.S. riflemen and several panzers shooting directly at them. Enemy troops had overwhelmed nearby positions at Schmidt and now were on the edge of Kommerscheidt. Some men simply disappeared in the shell bursts; others died under grinding treads. Tracer rounds zipped toward those who tried to escape. It was sheer pandemonium.

A thick, chilling mist forced the tanks into close-range duels. At one or two hundred yards, a Sherman might kill a Panther with a couple of well-aimed rounds. Fleig's crew accounted for two German tanks, and another Sherman knocked out a third. In the relative concealment of an orchard, he saw a Panther motionless just two hundred yards away. Its long 75-mm gun barrel was pointed away from him. While the side armor plate of a Panther was relatively thin, its frontal armor was all but invulnerable to a U.S. tank or TD. Fleig nevertheless decided to risk engaging it. His crew would have only seconds to get off as many shots as it could, or without question the Panther would destroy the Sherman. "Gunner, shot [AP ammunition], tank, three hundred!" Fleig gave the fire command, calling for a solid "shot" round that used kinetic energy literally to punch a hole in the enemy armor.

Survival now depended on training. Actions were nearly simultaneous. The loader shoved a 75-mm round into the breech of the cannon. The rim of the brass casing caught two levers on the spring-loaded breechblock and tripped it closed. "Up!" called the loader as he stepped away from the gun's recoil path.

Cpl. Richard Herkowitz, an excellent gunner, announced that he had identified the tank through his telescope as he adjusted the elevation and traverse of the main gun.

Fleig commanded, "Fire."

"On the way," announced Herkowitz a moment before he pressed the foot pedal trigger. A flash erupted from the side of the Panther when the round slammed into its steel armor. The spent shell casing clanged when it hit the floor of the turret "basket" in which the Fleig, Herkowitz, and the loader rode. The loader chambered another round. "Fire." The cannon made its distinct cracklike sound. Two hits. Something was wrong. There was no distinct spark that characterized the armor-piercing round striking metal. They had fired high explosive [HE] ammunition by mistake. The frightened enemy abandoned their still-operable tank anyway. Unfortunately, the remaining armor-piercing rounds were stowed in the right hull sponson. Herkowitz frantically traversed the turret to allow the loader access to the ammunition. They had been lucky once that morning already. A near miss by an artillery shell had somehow left the turret rotating bearings undamaged. Had the bearings or turret ring been damaged, it would have taken too long for the driver to aim the gun by steering the tank even if the ammunition had easy to reach.

About this time, the Germans realized they had made a serious mistake. They climbed back on their Panther. There was a flash from their main gun. Fleig thought he could see yellow smoke corkscrew from the shell as it flew by his tank. His crew chambered and fired an AP round that somehow sliced off a couple of feet of the Panther's main gun tube. Three more rounds destroyed the German tank. Less than five minutes had passed since the Americans had first seen the Panther. This was the battalion's third day of combat.[1]

The Death Factory

HÜRTGEN FOREST. Evergreens reach to the sky and block the sun on the brightest day. Rust-colored pine needles blanket the soggy ground. Narrow valleys echo with the sounds of rushing streams. At the top of a tree-covered bluff outside the farming village of Kommerscheidt, dozens of shallow depressions mark the remains of foxholes dug in haste by GIs under tank and artillery fire. One can still find rusting ammunition clips, boot soles, grenade pins, ration cans, and shreds of rubber ponchos. Human remains are discovered occasionally. Survivors of both sides recall indescribable stress, misery, and deprivation.[2]

Both sides fought the elements and terrain, but the Germans had the advantage of the defense, and the weather conditions all but stripped the

GIs of the close air support and accurately observed artillery fire essential for maintaining an attack. Dense fields of anti-personnel mines blocked the firebreaks and trails the Americans had to use as supply routes and avenues of advance. Automatic weapons in log-reinforced dugouts surrounded by barbed wire covered these minefields. Anti-tank mines blocked every conceivable route for vehicles. German artillery and mortars were present in numbers greater than the Americans had thought possible. The GIs seldom saw their enemy, but they felt his wrath in the streams of bullets slicing through the trees.

These battles remain controversial. Some historians argue that the Americans entered the forest with no clear objective and thereby needlessly discarded what advantages they had over the enemy. On the other hand, some action was unavoidable, because the Germans would never voluntarily turn over a hundred square miles of their homeland to invaders. The problem was that the fighting was inconclusive, and it raged for months longer than it should have, contributing to the frustration and disappointment along the entire Western Front. First Army inexcusably sent all or part of ten infantry and armored divisions into the forest and immediate area to take cities, towns, hills, and road junctions, but never the really important objectives.

Recall that the First Army operated on the right (south) flank of the British army group. When the First Army reached Germany south of Aachen it ended up facing the Roer River, which stood between it and the Rhine. Yet Hodges's command was too stretched and tired to cross the Roer without pausing briefly to resupply and reorganize. Though the Roer plain north of Aachen is relatively open and flat, only two significant terrain corridors south of the city lead to the river, and the Westwall bisected both of them. The "Stolberg Corridor" was the best route, but any attack there must overcome the urban sprawl of Aachen, as the 1st Infantry Divisions and others had learned. Nearby coal mines and factories could delay armor and even swallow up entire regiments. The "Monschau Corridor" farther south had two good roads that could support operations east of the Roer. Though it was less densely built up, the ground was more difficult for vehicle traffic. Both areas lay on the fringes of the Hürtgen Forest, which shielded no targets of long-term operational importance except for a series of dams built years before the war that controlled the level of the Roer. The Germans could flood the river and cut off any units on its east bank. Though the First Army could bypass the worst of the forest by using the terrain corridors, it could not bypass the Roer except by traveling far to the south through the inhospitable Ardennes-Eifel. However, doing this would spread the available forces too thin to support the British.

The first U.S. units entered the forest in September 1944. Operations continued there for almost three months before General Hodges directed attacks aimed specifically at the dams. A few intelligence and engineer officers recognized their importance, but the evidence indicates that senior officers, who were no doubt preoccupied with crossing the Rhine, paid them little attention. General Collins, whose VII Corps entered the forest in September, even blamed the oversight on his G-2 and corps engineer. When his corps hit the Westwall south of Aachen in September, he had every reason to think the Roer River was within reach, and the first operations in the forest were justified and limited. Even after the drive to the German border ended, persistent thinking that one more attack would put the corps through the forest led to a ten-day battle in October that resulted in a thousand casualties for each mile of advance.[3] Seemingly before they knew it, the Americans enlarged the scope of the forest battle to a point from which they could not escape.

Eisenhower decided in mid-October to continue operations aimed at the Rhine despite the approach of winter, because he was convinced that lives would be saved in the long run. However, the main effort shifted from the 21 Army Group to the 12th U.S. Army Group until the British could open the port of Antwerp to shipping. The plan called for the First Army's VII Corps to make the main effort against the Roer and Rhine plain in the first week of November. Shortly thereafter, the Third U.S. Army would then attack to protect the First Army's right flank before the Americans moved on the Rhine and Ruhr.[4] Collins had two contingency plans—one for a three-division attack on 5 November and one for four divisions to attack a few days later. Each plan depended on a solid flank in the Hürtgen Forest, largely because the Americans believed that the Germans might use it to harbor a counterattack force. To secure the VII Corps flank, for the main November attack, General Hodges, the First Army commander, directed the V Corps (Gerow) to seize the town of Schmidt, located on high cleared ground above the largest Roer dam, the Schwammenauel. Remarkably, neither he nor Bradley evidently saw the need to seize the dam, even though VII Corps could not safely cross the Roer with it in German hands. Both the Schwammenauel and the second largest dam, the Urft were too important for Commanders to put it into a category of minor objectives to take during the course of more important operations. Commanders had no excuse for thinking otherwise. General Eisenhower's SHAEF staff evidently thought air attacks could eliminate the threat. The First Army engineer underestimated the potential for flooding. Supply problems, particularly with artillery ammunition, had been a distraction. Hodges in fact, told Bradley on 29 October that he did not "contemplate the immediate capture of these dams."[5] What happened next was one of the most costly divisional actions in the history of the U.S. Army. One of the units that participated was the untried 707th Tank Battalion.

Fort Knox to Scotland

Lt. Col. Richard W. Ripple's 707th Tank Battalion originated in late 1941, with the activation of the 3d Battalion, 81st Armored Regiment, 5th Armored Division. Departure of trained men as cadre for the 13th Armored Division disrupted the training program at Fort Knox. The battalion in early 1942 moved to Camp Cooke, California, for desert training, then to Tennessee in early 1943. One story had a father and son watching troops halted along a road near Knoxville. The father was urging his son to come with him to the area zoo. The boy replied, "But Dad I don't want to see the animals, I want to watch the soldiers eat."[6]

Pine Camp, New York, was the battalion's home in the second half of 1943. When the 5th Armored reorganized from the 14,000-soldier "heavy" structure to the "light," and easier to transport, size of about 10,500 troops, Ripple's battalion left the division and became the separate 707th in December. It went overseas in February 1944 on the SS *Exchange*, a former carrier of bananas. Fleig said, "The Black Hole of Calcutta could have been no worse" than *Exchange*. The ship rolled and pitched with every swell during its fourteen-day trip across the North Atlantic, highlighted by "chain reaction" episodes of seasickness. Top bunks were subject to more violent motion than those below, and the men in the top bunks became seasick before those on the lower ones. Vomit from the top bunk might cascade downward and evoke a sympathetic response from those below. When Ripple reported the situation to the ship's captain and asked the crew to clean the holds, the captain replied that he couldn't make his crew do it, because they were union members. Mercifully, *Exchange* reached Scotland in late February. After more training in England, the battalion landed in Normandy in September. Early on the afternoon of 6 October 1944, its lead elements pulled into the rest and staging area at Camp Elsenborn, Belgium, a few miles southwest of Aachen. Ripple's men threw their bedrolls to the ground without knowing what had already happened in the Hürtgen Forest.[7]

The "triangular" infantry division structure used in World War II was lighter and more mobile than its World War I and postwar counterparts. Doctrine recognized a need for close armor support of the infantry, and plans called for separate pools of tank and TD battalions to provide the support as needed. However, by the end of 1944, when leaders recognized that infantry divisions needed such augmentation nearly all the time, manpower and transportation shortfalls did not allow assignment of a tank battalion to each of the forty-two infantry divisions deployed to the ETO. Tank battalions attached to divisions seldom operated as single units. Normal practice was for one of the battalion's three medium (Sherman) tank companies to fight with an infantry regiment, though doctrine called for concentration if possible. Tanks might lead infantry attacks, probe for weak spots in defenses, or act as artillery.[8] Armor officers had to resist the temptation of infantrymen to put one or two tanks with each rifle company. Hurried attachment brought together commanders unfamiliar with the strengths and weaknesses of their respective units. Because a "buttoned-up" tank was effectively blind, an expedient externally mounted field telephone became the most important link between the foot soldier and the tanker, provided that the infantry knew it was there. Few tanks until the end of 1944 had radios that would "net" with the infantryman's. The 707th never had a chance to develop a working relationship with the unit to which it was attached at Elsenborn, the 28th Infantry Division.[9]

Attack Plans

MAJ. GEN. NORMAN D. "DUTCH" COTA, the commander of the 28th Infantry Division, learned in late October about the plan to secure a flank for VII Corps. Cota, who had distinguished himself by personal bravery on Omaha Beach, thought the plan, developed by the V Corps staff, stood little chance of success. His reinforced division would secure the road net in the Schmidt area, through which elements of an armored division would pass to seize the upper reaches of the Monschau Corridor and thereby establish the secure flank. Since only the 28th Division was available, each of its three infantry regiments had to strike a separate target: the 109th Infantry would seize the woods southwest of the village of Hürtgen; the 110th would prepare the ground for the armored division; the 112th Infantry, supported by the 707th, would move on Schmidt and the nearby villages located on ridges. The 2d Battalion, 112th, with Company C of the 707th, would hit the Vossenack ridge. The 1st Battalion would cross the Kall River and take Kommerscheidt, less than a mile west of Schmidt. The 3d Battalion would pass through the 1st to seize Schmidt. Five groups of fighter-bombers were available, depending on the weather. Their first priority was to isolate the battlefield from enemy reserves; the second was to hit the northern stretches of the Monschau Corridor; and the third priority was to drop napalm in support of the 110th Infantry.

Planners evidently thought the battle would be primarily an infantry action, because they depended so much on the ability of aircraft to isolate the battlefield and on artillery to neutralize the high ground that surrounded Vossenack on three sides (see map on pg. 125).

Hodges postponed the main VII Corps attack until after 15 November, because of the late arrival of some of the attacking formations, but he ordered the 28th Division to attack on or before 2 November, regardless of the weather or availability of air support. There were no other operations on the First Army front, and the 28th drew the attention of every German unit in the area that was not otherwise engaged.[10]

On 2 November, the division and its attachments (less the 707th) were almost at full strength—about 15,500 officers and enlisted men. The 707th had 676 enlisted men and forty-two officers against an authorized strength of 709 enlisted men and forty-one officers. It had forty-eight Sherman tanks mounting 75–mm guns and two mounting 105–mm howitzers. There were also seventeen M5 light tanks.[11] Along the final approach to the forward assembly area west of Vossenack, the tankers saw thousands of trees stripped by artillery of all vegetation. There was abandoned equipment everywhere. Some field gear even hung on the trees, blown there by exploding mines that had killed or injured hundreds of GIs. It was muddy, cold, misty, and overcast. Getting dry was nearly impossible. Darkness came in midafternoon for troops deep in the woods.

Im Hürtgenwald

U.S. ARTILLERY THUNDERED OVER the tank crews just before 9:00 AM on 2 November. The mist-filled forest erupted in smoke and debris. Explosions echoed through the canyonlike draws and on the enemy-occupied ridges opposite Vossenack. Ten Shermans from Company C supported two rifle companies of the 2d Battalion, 112th Infantry. The tank company commander, Capt. George S. West Jr. kept his other seven tanks in reserve, because there was no apparent German tank threat and consequently no need to employ all of his tanks on the open Vossenack

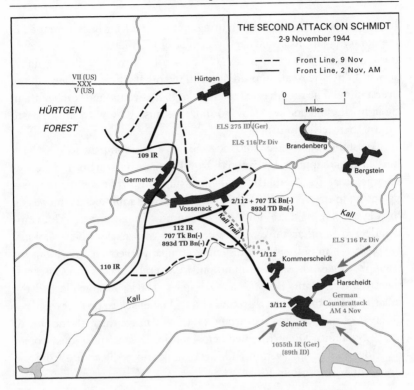

THE SECOND ATTACK ON SCHMIDT
2-9 November 1944

--- Front Line, 9 Nov
—— Front Line, 2 Nov, AM

ridge. Second Lt. William D. Quarrie's platoon fired at the steeple of the Vossenack church to eliminate the threat of snipers. One tank accidentally strayed through an American minefield, where it lost a track. Quarrie's own tank mired in the soggy earth and blocked the path engineers had already cleared through a minefield. West picked Quarrie up and moved on in his command tank toward the town, firing over the heads of the infantry. The other tanks took up positions from where they could fire on any Germans evacuating the village.[12]

Three tanks of 1st Lt. James J. Leming's platoon meanwhile lumbered toward the south side of Vossenack, exposed to enemy observation from a nearby ridge occupied by the villages of Brandenberg and Bergstein. To avoid anti-personnel mines, riflemen walked through choking engine fumes to follow the ruts made by the tank tracks. Leming's crew fired so much machine-gun ammunition that the weapons jammed from overheating, and a shell stuck in the breech of the 75-mm gun. He told his platoon sergeant, who was in his own tank, to take over and lead the infantry to the eastern end of the town. He then radioed for 2d Lt.

Joseph J. Novak (3d Platoon) to bring up more tanks, which were then in temporary positions at the nearby hamlet of Germeter. Novak evidently misunderstood the radio message, because he sent up only two tanks at first. When he finally moved out with the others, his own Sherman ran over a mine. The infantry was unaware of these events, and some of them thought the tankers were slow to move because they were unwilling to expose themselves to danger.[13]

West then received a radio message that a rifle company in Vossenack needed tank support. He wanted Novak's platoon to help, but he was unaware that the lieutenant had hit a mine and that his platoon was operating in two sections. West's tank rolled over a mine while he was on his way to investigate. With his Sherman now immobilized, West commandeered another tank and returned to Vossenack, where Colonel Ripple had him pull his back his entire company to covered positions for resupply of gasoline and ammunition.[14] Generals Gerow and Cota, and the latter's assistant, Brig. Gen. George A. Davis, meanwhile had the infantry dig in on the open ground east of Vossenack to protect the flank and rear of the battalion that would eventually move through the area to attack Schmidt. These riflemen remained in exposed positions around the clock under observation and direct tank and artillery fire from the Brandenberg-Bergstein Ridge.[15]

Fatal Victory

GENERAL COTA ORIGINALLY INTENDED for the 1st Battalion, 112th, to make the main attack on Schmidt. This battalion tried to enter the Kall River valley southeast of Vossenack and strike Schmidt from the south. Lt. Col. Carl L. Peterson, commander of the 112th, did not request tank or artillery fire, nor did he commit his reserve, even though the attack bogged down within a few yards of its start point. It is possible that instead he looked at the relatively low casualties in the battalion at Vossenack and decided the best route to Schmidt was from there west instead of the southwest.[16] Captain Hostrup (Company A, 707th) and Lt. Col. Albert Flood, commander of the 3d Battalion, 112th, met at Peterson's CP on the evening of 2 November to discuss the change in plan. Peterson told Flood to cross the Kall River gorge the next morning and take Schmidt from the west. The 1st Battalion would follow and support. Hostrup assigned his 3d Platoon (2d Lt. Richard H. Payne) to support Company K of the 112th, his 2d Platoon (2d Lt. John J. Clarke) to support Company L. The 1st Platoon, under Fleig, was the reserve. In accordance with practice, Ripple did not control the tactical operations of his companies; he acted as a staff advisor to Cota and Peterson and managed the logistical and administrative operations of his battalion. The infantry regiment and battalion commanders directed the tank companies.[17]

The temperature was almost at freezing when Company K moved out, followed by Companies I, L, and M (the heavy-weapons company). The heavily laden infantrymen found the nearly vertical walls of the Kall Gorge almost impossible to negotiate. They carried mortars, machine guns, tripods, ammunition, extra rations, water cans, and radios—there were no roads. Radio contact was intermittent, but at about 11:00 AM Hostrup saw through his binoculars that the first riflemen were in the open outside of Kommerscheidt. There was no resistance except for occasional mortar fire. He could not know that many of the infantrymen went on to take shelter in buildings, because they were too tired to dig foxholes.[18] Given the terrain, stress, and utter exhaustion that enveloped the GIs, this is not surprising. Unfortunately, these men would soon regret their choice.

Scouts from Company K edged into Schmidt about 2:00 PM; Companies L and I moved in by dusk. Flood, the 3d Battalion commander, established his CP in Kommerscheidt a few hours later. He wanted tanks, TDs, or anti-tank guns that night. However, they would have to traverse the Kall Gorge trail, which was barely passable even in good weather, to get there. Much of it was only about ten feet wide—only inches wider than a Sherman tank. A steep incline paralleled the trail on the right (from the perspective of the Americans), and there was a sheer drop on the left side. Only the beginning and end of the trail were visible on aerial photographs, and until engineers got there no one knew if it was clear. Given the importance of Schmidt and the condition of the trail, one can only conclude that the commanders and staff at V Corps and higher headquarters were dangerously overconfident in assuming this trail could support the main effort of a division attack.[19]

In the late afternoon of 3 November, officers from the 20th Engineer Combat Battalion walked the trail from Vossenack as far as the stone bridge across the Kall River. Probably because of their inexperience, they decided the trail would accommodate tanks. When Colonel Ripple received this report, he told Captain Hostrup to take his company into Schmidt. Hostrup had already reconnoitered the beginning of the trail, and he doubted his tanks could negotiate it unless engineers spent considerable time improving it. Dusk was approaching when he set out in his command tank. He felt the left side of the road crumble under the treads,

and the tank nearly slid into the gorge when the driver tried to skirt past
an outcrop of rocks. Hostrup radioed Ripple that the engineers must
widen the road and blow up the outcrop or the infantry would never see
tank support. Ripple agreed and replied that Hostrup should be prepared
to move at dawn (4 November).[20] German artillery and mortar fire hammered the Vossenack area that night and delayed the engineers' work.
One group of engineers carrying only hand tools did reach the trail after
the shelling stopped. A bulldozer that reached the site about 2:30 AM on
4 November snapped a cable shortly after it began work. Its crew drove
it to the rear.[21]

Before daylight, after the engineers reported that they had done their
best given the resources they had, Hostrup ordered Fleig's tanks to cross
the gorge. About a hundred yards from the rock outcrop, his command
tank struck a mine and blocked the trail. No one was injured. Hostrup
radioed him to get the tank out of the way. Fleig replied that if his men
had to, they would have another tank push the damaged one into the
gorge. Staff Sgt. Anthony J. Spooner, the platoon sergeant, told Fleig he
might be able to get the other tanks around the damaged one. Spooner
had his driver ease his own tank toward the left rear of the mine-damaged
one. His crew attached one end of a twenty-foot-long steel tow cable to
the shackle on the right front of the operable tank and the other end to
the left rear of the disabled tank, which now became an anchor. It helped
keep Spooner's tank on the trail long enough for him to slip by Fleig's
tank and the valley wall. The crew then switched the cable to the right
rear of the mobile tank and left front corner of the anchor tank and completed the bypass maneuver. Fleig mounted Spooner's tank after it was
clear, and he radioed Hostrup that the engineers had not widened the
trail enough for the tanks to move without risk.[22]

Hardly anything went right from that point. A hundred yards before
the one lane stone bridge over the Kall, Fleig encountered a series of
sharp turns. Despite the possibility of anti-personnel mines, he dismounted in the darkness and guided his driver in a series of backing and
turning maneuvers along a track perpendicular to the main trail.
Hostrup, meanwhile, had walked down the trail as far as the disabled
tank, where he learned that Spooner's recovery operation had been slow,
dangerous, and frustrating. Sgt. Jack L. Barton's tank had partially thrown
a track near the outcrop, and Hostrup directed another tank to pull it
straight. When the track was back in place, the driver continued while
Barton remained to assist other crews. Engineers helped Sgt. Joseph
Markey maneuver his tank by the outcropping without incident, though

it threw a track near the bottom of the gorge. The engineers also tried to use German anti-tank mines to blow off the outcrops, but they did little more than scratch the rocks.[23]

Fortunately, smaller vehicles had already found the trail passable. A supply column of tracked cargo carriers (M29 Weasels) had already passed along the trail about midnight of 3–4 November, reached Schmidt without incident, and brought out wounded soldiers. Trucks, jeeps, and M-10 TDs (893d TD Battalion) also crossed the trail, though with extreme difficulty, but the deterioration to the roadbed was evident at daylight on 4 November when Lt. John J. Clarke's four 2d Platoon tanks (the fifth tank had hit a mine in Vossenack) reached the site of Fleig's damaged one. Staff Sgt. Anthony S. Zarolinski tried to get his tank by, but because no one in this platoon knew to use tow cables as braces, the Sherman slipped off the muddy trail. Seconds after he dismounted to check on the situation, Zarolinski was killed by German artillery fire, which also wounded Lieutenant Clarke. Next was Staff Sgt. Walton R. Allen's tank, which managed to pass by using the Zarolinski's tank as a support. Unfortunately, Allen's tank, and another commanded by Sergeant Yarman, each threw a track at the outcropping. Five disabled tanks, a third of the combat power intended for infantry support at Schmidt-Kommerscheidt, now sat dead on the trail. The situation was growing desperate.[24]

When Fleig, meanwhile, pulled into Kommerscheidt, he could hear the roar of tank and artillery fire, and he saw several infantrymen running toward him. Maj. Robert T. Hazlett, the commander of the 1st Battalion, 112th, yelled that the Germans had counterattacked the 3d Battalion in Schmidt. He told Fleig to "get out there and stop those tanks." One of the infantrymen pointed in the direction of Schmidt and said there were "lots of Germans with tanks over that hill."[25]

Disaster

A MAP EXERCISE HAD SEALED the fate of the 28th Division and 707th. When the attack began, almost every German officer who could influence the battle was at a single location near Cologne. Orders went out to the 116th Panzer Division to move its reconnaissance battalion to the Kall Valley that night. The 16th Panzer Regiment (equipped with Mk IV and Panther tanks, but, contrary to American reports, no Tigers) occupied a village about a half-mile from Schmidt. The rest of the 116th followed the next night. Two battalions of the 89th Infantry Division, which was already in the area, took up blocking positions.[26]

Artillery began to pound Schmidt about 7:00 AM on 4 November. An NCO said the shelling was "so powerful, so loud, and so continuous that it seemed to form a background that you got used to. We were so tired that we didn't even hear the shells when they landed close."[27] The riflemen opened fire. The commander of Company L, 112th, called for mortar fire. At 8:30 AM, the leader of a platoon that was directly in the path of oncoming enemy tanks reported that his men could not hold. Enemy tanks were firing pointblank into the positions.[28] Fighter-bombers did not attack the Germans until after they had driven the Americans out of Schmidt. Weather had been the deciding factor; low clouds and a persistent mist "tremendously hindered" air operations throughout the battle.[29] Yet nothing could have helped the undersupported and undersupplied GIs in Schmidt. Those who could get out were gone by midmorning.

About eight Mk IV tanks and about two hundred infantry from the 16th Panzer Regiment hit Kommerscheidt, which was held by 1st Battalion, 112th Infantry, after the attack on Schmidt. The tanks stayed outside the range of bazookas and poured round after round into the village. Sergeant Spooner and two tanks had joined Fleig in Kommerscheidt earlier (the action described above). One of Fleig's crew called his attention to several American infantrymen coming from the direction of Schmidt and heading to the woods outside Kommerscheidt. He saw why these men had not joined the defenses: a Mk IV tank was nearby.[30] Brig. Gen. Davis, the assistant division commander, went to Kommerscheidt and met with Peterson, Flood, and Hazlett. Davis told Fleig to keep his tanks in place and not to withdraw them under any circumstances. He was afraid the infantry would abandon the village if they thought the tanks were leaving.[31]

The Kall Trail, 4–5 November

CAPTAIN HOSTRUP SPENT MOST of 4 November coordinating the work to clear the trail, and both he and Maj. Jack Fish, the 707th S-3, radioed Ripple to ask for more engineers. Sergeant Yarman's crew, meanwhile, had the track back on their tank, and they were ready to move at about 4:00 PM. Unfortunately, it went just a few yards before the track slid off the road wheels and damaged the left idler (rear wheel). The crew replaced the track, moved the tank, and watched in frustration as the track again slipped off. Without the proper tools to replace the idler, the crew was unable to make a permanent repair. Mechanics under Hostrup's maintenance officer, Lt. Stan Lisy later exchanged the damaged idler with one from Fleig's original tank, but it was after midnight (4–5 November) before the tank was ready to move. It traveled just a few yards before the shoulder of the trail crumbled and the track popped off the road wheels. Hostrup now had no alternative but to comply with a message from General Cota that instructing him to "roll your immobilized tanks down the slope and into the draw."[32] Payne's platoon eventually reached Kommerscheidt. Hostrup's own tank developed engine trouble, and he did not arrive until several hours later. That night (5–6 November), the German 89th Infantry Division's 1055th Regiment cut the Kall trail near the stone bridge and linked up with troops from the 116th Panzer Division. The Germans now owned the vital Kall trail.[33]

Task Force Ripple

GENERAL COTA PUT TOGETHER a tank-infantry task force under Ripple to counterattack Kommerscheidt. The fact that anyone at the division headquarters thought this plan could succeed indicates the impact of the incorrect situation reports the regiment provided the division staff. Through much of the period, the daily reports from the 112th to division inexplicably described the combat efficiency of the regiment as "excellent."[34] Ripple's "task force" consisted only of the depleted 3d Battalion, 110th Infantry (with only about two hundred riflemen, mostly

Stan Lisy, 707th Tank Battalion, 1944. [Courtesy Stan Lisy]

replacements), the handful of tanks and TDs that were already in Kommerscheidt, and his own Companies C and D.[35] How Ripple, who was not even assigned to the 28th Division, ended up in command of such a mission is simple. The commanders of the division's three rifle regiments were absorbed in the battle of their lives; General Davis was preoccupied with the fight for Vossenack and Kommerscheidt, and Cota had to manage the entire operation. The task force's infantry hit resistance in the Kall Gorge and did not reach Kommerscheidt until midday on 6 November. Yet with the Germans in control of the trail, Ripple could not call forward all the armor available to him. Later that afternoon, heavy mortar, artillery, and sniper fire pummeled the task force. The short life of Task Force Ripple ended by sundown.[36]

GIs in Kommerscheidt, meanwhile, had endured another attack in the morning. Fleig recalled, "One infantry sergeant came running towards my position. I stopped him and asked him why he was running. He mouthed the answer, 'a German tank.' I held him there talking to him to steady him, asked him if he hadn't learned in training that a tank cannot depress its guns to hit a man on the ground when it has come within 35 yards. . . . [H]e replied, 'Yessir, but I can't stand it any more.'"[37] Davis ordered Fleig and 1st Lt. Turney W. Leonard, of the 893d TD Battalion, (a handful of M-10s were present) to conduct a demonstration to draw enemy fire temporarily from the virtually unprotected infantry while other armor engaged the panzers. Fleig recalled, "I was to take my tanks up to the crest of the hill just in the rear (north) of Kommerscheidt to draw the fire of the enemy tanks. [Leonard] and his platoon were to maneuver to the right in an attempt to get behind the enemy armor" outside the town. They drew fire immediately.[38]

The End at Kommerscheidt

Artillery, mortar, and tank fire swept Kommerscheidt from end to end for half an hour on the morning of 7 November. Fires burned everywhere. Few houses stood intact. Rubble filled the streets. Lieutenant Payne's tank crew scored two hits on a Mk IV but did not put it out of action. Some infantrymen yelled to Payne that an enemy tank was on his left. His driver eased his Sherman out of a shallow draw until he could see the target. "German artillery and high velocity weapon fire was coming in damned close to me, so I pulled my tank back into the protection of the shallow draw," he said. His platoon sergeant, Andrew Lipe, and another tank commander opened fire and hit

1st Lt. Turney W. Leonard, 893rd Tank Destroyer Battalion. [Courtesy Texas A&M University]

two panzers, but Lipe's tank shuddered from a hit. He then fought from a TD until it too was hit.[39]

Someone handed Colonel Peterson a written transcription of a radio message ordering him to return to division headquarters, located a few miles away at Rott. Peterson did not question the order, and he wanted to get an accurate story of events to Cota. He turned over command of the remnants of the forces to Ripple and, with two enlisted men, set out for Rott.[40] Ripple then tried to order Company C, 112th, into action, but the company commander and "his men were in an absolute daze incapable of carrying out that order." He told them to stay put and defend the woods. Cota radioed him to hold at all costs.[41] The Germans pressed the attack relentlessly. An infantry officer said, "I saw one shell from [a] tank blow one man straight up into the air."[42]

Another indication that the division staff did not understand the situation east of the Kall was the formation on 7 November of Task Force Davis. Its mission was also to retake Schmidt. On paper, TF Davis consisted of four battalions of infantry; Companies A and C, 707th; Companies B and C, 893d TD Battalion; and some supporting units. None of these units was anywhere near full strength, and the attack never got off the ground. Generals Cota, Davis, and Gerow, meanwhile, secured General Hodges's approval to pull the men back across the Kall.[43] Col. G. M. Nelson, who had replaced Peterson, organized the remnants of the infantry battalions into a provisional company and put the other troops under Ripple. Hostrup, Fleig, and Payne were among those who led out groups of these exhausted survivors. Several wounded men had to be left behind under care of medics. Some men became lost and did not reach safety until hours or days later. Ray Fleig and six exhausted men reached Vossenack about midnight of 8–9 November. "The actual move was a nightmare," he recalled. "It was right at the freezing point and raining, darker than the inside of your hat; we were under mortar and artillery fire."[44]

Vossenack

BY 5 NOVEMBER, SEPARATE BATTLES raged at Kommerscheidt, Vossenack, and in the woods outside Germeter, where terrain prevented tanks from supporting the 109th and 110th Infantry. However, Companies B and C, 707th, played a major role at Vossenack. Enemy observers on the Brandenberg-Bergstein ridge could see almost every move an infantry-man or a tank made during daylight. Leaders had to order some of the exhausted and nervous men to eat. No one could leave his foxhole during daylight even to relieve himself. If he did, the fire would simply follow him from his hole. The rifle battalion commander (2d Battalion, 112th) was out of action with combat exhaustion. His XO, Capt. John Pruden, was in charge. Wounded men crowded the battalion's forward aid station. Misery and suffering were the *order* of the day, but the battalion had to hold the town.[45]

The tanks helped where they could, though they did not have many targets, and their short-barreled 75–mm guns were ineffective against armored vehicles on the Brandenberg-Bergstein ridge. Before daylight on 6 November, Lieutenant Lemming from C Company, 707th, told his company commander, Captain West, that Capt. George S. Granger (Company B) wanted another platoon in Vossenack. Granger told 1st Lt. Carl Anderson to "contact the G Company [112th] CO and Captain West for [information about] the situation."[46]

When Anderson's platoon reached town at daybreak, he saw incoming tracer fire from the direction of the ridge. "We started shooting," he said.[47] What he saw was the initial stage of one of the most startling events to happen during the five months of combat in the Hürtgen Forest. A large part of the 2d Battalion, 112th Infantry, was disintegrating as a fighting force. Men who had spent four days and nights under direct artillery and tank fire without the means to fight back were at the limit of their endurance. Contrary to their normal practice, the Germans did not shell Vossenack that morning. In fact, there was hardly any activity at all until an unexpected burst of small-arms fire, then a scream, broke the relative silence. It was quiet for a few seconds, then artillery shells started bursting on the open ground. Small-arms fire poured from the thickly wooded draws in front of the GIs. Without warning, one man after another climbed from his foxhole and ran as fast as his exhausted legs could move toward the center of the village. Most of the men believed they faced a rampaging attack of unknown strength.[48] Pruden wanted tank support. Captain Granger of the 707th received "an urgent radio message." The abrupt flight of the infantry, meanwhile, temporarily left Lieutenant Quarrie's tanks (Company C, 707th) and a platoon of TDs alone in the east end of town. Anderson's tanks, however, had moved to the northern edge of the village. Lieutenant Lemming said, "The whole situation was one of complete confusion. No one knew what the situation was or where the enemy or our own front lines were supposed to be." Quarrie said the Shermans fired into several houses in which GIs were taking shelter.[49]

Anderson's tanks were still firing when they reached Vossenack. Some of the Company C tankers thought the fire was "wild and at random." West, in a Company B tank since his own was damaged, drove to Anderson and shouted at him to stop. "You shot your own infantry in the back and now you're running off and leaving them!" Anderson asked West what he wanted him to do. West said to get back to the positions he had left. A concentration of enemy artillery slammed into the ground. West yelled, "Let's get the hell out of here!" Anderson saw no friendly or enemy infantry.[50]

Captain Granger radioed Anderson to go on back to Germeter, then looked around and drove to West, who was still in the Company B tank. He asked him what was happening. West replied, "Counterattack." Yet Granger saw no enemy. He then asked where the 2d Battalion headquarters was located. Yelling over the sounds of the tank engines and the fire,

West answered that he didn't know. Granger then asked him what kind of fire was coming in. West stated, "Big mortars," coming from the draw north of town. "Then I turned to look at that draw to see if I could spot the location of these enemy mortars," remarked Granger. "A heavy round came in close. I ducked. When I turned around to talk to West, the hatches on his turret were gone and so was he." A mortar shell had hit either the back deck of West's tank or just behind the vehicle. The tremendous concussion stunned Granger and tore the heavy cupola off West's tank. West died instantly. His remains dropped into the turret of his tank. Granger radioed West's driver to take the body to Germeter.[51]

Granger reached the command post of the 2d Battalion, located in the center of Vossenack. He found the commander sitting with his face buried in his hands. Looking around, Granger thought all the battalion's staff officers, except for Captain Pruden, were "dazed." Pruden had organized about sixty or seventy men into a defense near the church. Granger and Pruden talked for a few minutes, before Granger returned to his tank in time to hear a message from Lt. D. A. Sherman, a platoon leader. "Captain, it's getting too hot to handle out here. . . . We are just taking fire and doing no good." He had only two tanks still in action. Granger told him to get them under cover.[52]

Counterattack

GENERAL COTA'S ONLY REINFORCEMENT was the 146th Engineer Combat Battalion, then working on roads deep within the forest. They lost no time getting to Vossenack—some of them were still wearing their hip boots when they arrived late on the afternoon of 6 November. The commander, Lt. Col. Carl J. Isley, took over at Vossenack, and sent his troops into the line near the nearly destroyed church, which changed hands several times over the course of the battle. General Davis wanted Isley to counterattack that night, and he told Granger to keep tanks in the town. Granger remarked that as obscure as the situation was, a night attack was not feasible. Davis, who had led up some TDs, promptly told him it was none of his business. Isley finally convinced him that there would be too many problems coordinating artillery and infantry support on such short notice.[53]

American artillery began firing about 7:45 AM on 7 November. Staff Sgt. John B. Cook of the 707th saw a German infantryman run from behind a woodpile, then fall dead from by a burst from the machine guns in another tank. Cook's tank fired two rounds into a building near the church. "About 6 nuns and 30 Germans dashed out of the building," he reported. A round then jammed in the cannon. When the crew tried to pry it out, the brass casing split and powder spilled into the turret floor. Cook's driver dismounted under mortar and artillery fire to hit a ramming staff with a sledgehammer to beat the solid shot round from the breach onto tank turret floor. Soon after the driver climbed back into the tank, two artillery rounds exploded nearby. An engineer then yelled to Cook, "Watch that building to your left front. There's an enemy bazooka man in there!" An anti-tank round hit the ground behind Cook's Sherman. His gunner quickly fired two 75-mm high-explosive rounds at a building. The second round struck the corner of the building just as the enemy gunner ran into it.[54]

Granger called for air support; one P-47 dived, fired its machine guns, and dropped a bomb near Cook's tank. Another bomb hit near two tanks without doing any damage. One bomb hit a house occupied by a tank crew whose vehicle had been damaged. This crew lost one man killed and one wounded.[55] Ironically, there had been no German attack on the morning of 6 November 1944. They had intended to attack Vossenack that day, but bad weather late the night before disrupted their plans. Elements of the 116th Panzer Division entered Vossenack in force only after they realized that the U.S. infantry had left the ridge. Panzergrenadiers reached the church and set up the defenses until the tankers and engineers drove them out on 7 November.[56]

Fighting in the Vossenack-Schmidt area temporarily died out in mid-November. The 28th Infantry Division and its attachments lost over 6,100 battle and nonbattle casualties. The 707th lost thirty-one of its fifty Sherman tanks. German materiel losses are difficult to assess, but there were at least 3,000 personnel losses from all causes.[57] General Hodges ended up anchoring the south flank of the upcoming mid-November main attack on the Kall River, not the Roer. Vossenack was not completely free of Germans until early December, and Schmidt did not fall for good until February 1945. A postmortem by V Corps attributed the failure at Schmidt-Vossenack to unexpectedly stiff enemy reaction, bad weather that negated the full effect of observed artillery fire and air support, the inadequate Kall trail, and the inability to neutralize the high ground surrounding Vossenack. The division artillery headquarters had not kept close enough contact with its battalions. Commanders had failed to coordinate properly with attached units. The division had sent no patrols in the direction of Vossenack and Schmidt before the attack began and no one had known the extent of the defenses.[58]

Companies B and C of the 707th stayed at Vossenack until mid-November, then moved to Luxembourg with the 28th Division. Hostrup's decimated Company A was refitting 16 December when it was hit head on by elements of three enemy divisions in the Battle of the Bulge. The battalion's performance in early November was probably as good as or better than senior officers could have expected under the circumstances. There was no opportunity for maneuver and exploitation tactics. Given the lack of firepower and armor of the Sherman tank, the willingness of the crewmen to close with and attack superior enemy tanks is commendable. The Germans held every advantage of terrain, and they could concentrate combat power faster than the Americans, because First Army did not have enough troops simultaneously to build up for the main attack, stay in contact with Third Army, and conduct the attack on Schmidt. The losses were significant, and though eventually made up, they forced the battalion to spend a month training replacements rather than further improving its skills based on lessons learned in its first battle. The fight for Schmidt eliminated a new tank battalion from combat for several weeks and removed pressure from the Germans at a critical location just days before the beginning of the big November attack by the First Army. It was going to be a long autumn.

CHAPTER 10

HOLIDAY SEASON, NOVEMBER– DECEMBER 1944

LUCHERBERG, GERMANY, APPROXIMATELY 0600 hours (6:00 AM), 5 December 1944: German artillery fell within 150 yards in front of Company L, 415th Infantry, in this nondescript village a few miles from the rubble pile that had been the city of Düren. Five *Landsers* burrowed into a haystack ten yards from a mortar position. A GI took a submachine gun and sprayed .45 caliber bullets into the straw. One panzer lumbered toward an American 57-mm anti-tank gun. German infantrymen were on top of the position before the crewmen could fire at the tank, which lumbered farther into the town. Not far away, another AT gun crew manhandled their weapon under sniper bullets into a firing position and got off five quick shots. The enemy tank pulled to the side of the road and stopped. Sgt. George E. Burns took a bazooka and worked his way down a street to fire at another tank. He killed some enemy soldiers nearby, and the tank moved back. After getting some more rockets, he returned to the street and, in a scene that resembled a Wild West shootout, stood opposite the tank and fired from the hip. Another hit. He reloaded and fired once more, further slowing the tank. Daylight was approaching. Another cold, gray day in the Rhineland.[1]

Hard fighting after September left no doubt that the road to the Rhine would be extremely difficult. Like the autumn fog and rains that enveloped combat soldiers, frustration and strain reached high-level staffs and commanders. General Bradley designated the First Army to make the main attack in November partly because he believed Eisenhower was incapable of resisting Montgomery's unceasing calls for American support of the 21 Army Group right flank. He was afraid to lose more forces, particularly the experienced First Army, to support the British. Eisenhower could not commit the First Army to Montgomery if it were otherwise occupied in a major attack. Bradley also moved the Ninth

Army headquarters from the Ardennes to a position between the British and the First Army to separate General Hodges's command further from the British.[2] The 12th Army Group commander then directed Hodges to drive toward the Rhine at Cologne-Bonn. If the army could not get across the river, it would clear the west bank of the Rhine south to the Moselle.[3] The Ninth Army (Lt. Gen. William H. Simpson) would protect the left of the First as far as the Rhine, then swing north and link up with the Second British Army. Third Army, meanwhile, would continue its attack toward the Rhine with the intent of reaching Mainz and Worms. With three field armies, eight corps, eight armored divisions, and seventeen infantry divisions, plus separate maneuver units and supporting troops, the 12th Army Group, at over 600,000 soldiers, was four times the size of the entire Regular Army in the 1930s.[4]

Because two divisions that had been supporting the British went under First Army control later than anticipated, Bradley delayed the planned start of the First/Ninth Army attack until 10 November.[5] Third Army's attack, however, started on 8 November in a driving rainstorm, without air support but with an effective artillery barrage. The weather did not clear enough for a desired four-day window for reliable air support until 15 November.[6] General Hodges, meanwhile, wanted air power to blow a hole in the constantly improving enemy defenses in his zone of attack. Air leaders questioned whether this was possible or, given the friendly-fire losses in July, even worth attempting. Yet the ground commanders wanted the support, and the airmen developed an intricate plan for what would be the largest such attack in support of ground troops during the ETO campaign. Over 2,000 Eighth Air Force and Royal Air Force heavy and medium bombers laden with fragmentation or high-explosive bombs would pulverize towns opposite the First and Ninth Armies—such as Düren, Jülich, and Eschweiler. Fighter-bombers would blast road junctions, known enemy supply installations, and troop concentrations.[7]

A Resurgent Enemy

SENIOR GERMAN COMMANDERS in the West assumed the Allies would make a major attack in November. They realized that the activity since September was preliminary in nature. Their problem was concentrating enough reserves to keep the Allies west of the Rhine while they simultaneously built up forces for the planned counteroffensive in the Ardennes. Despite incessant Allied air and ground operations, fifty refitted or new divisions reached all fronts during the second half of 1944. Certainly the caliber of troops was sometimes questionable, there were shortages of equipment, and most logistic operations had to occur at night, but many divisions facing the Americans were quite good. These included the 11th, 21st, and 116th Panzer, Panzer Lehr, the 3d Panzergrenadier, 12th Infantry (later *Volks-Grenadier*), 17th SS Panzer, 3d Parachute, and a few of the recently formed *Volks-Grenadier* divisions. Allied bombs in fact did not prevent Germany from maintaining, and in some cases increasing, production of combat vehicles and other materiel. Westbound rail traffic through key logistics support areas near the Rhine actually increased in November. It is true that fuel and ammunition stocks declined after September, but the slowdown in Allied operations through October enabled the Germans to replace losses, even if they did not accumulate reserves. [8]

General Hodges was about ready to order the attack to begin with or without the aerial bombardment when the skies finally cleared on Thursday, 16 November. The Operation Queen air attack began at 11:30 AM. Bombing accuracy was poor, but the attack did manage virtually to wipe out some of the target cities and choke German lines of supply. Anti-aircraft fire brought down only a dozen Allied planes. Prisoner reports indicated the effectiveness of the air attack was uneven. A German NCO said, "I never saw anything like it. These kids [soldiers] didn't even dare to stick their heads out of their foxholes. . . . [T]hey were numbed 45 minutes after the bombardment. It was our luck that your ground troops did not contact us until the next day." On the other hand, some prisoners estimated their units suffered only single-digit casualty percentages.[9] Operation Queen is an example of the trade-offs of air attacks—whether it is more important to risk friendly lives in an attempt to do serious damage to the enemy than to ensure no friendly fire casualties happen at all. The Queen bomb line was so far to the rear of the enemy frontline positions that the GIs who saw the massive attack must have wondered where the bombs went.

Dr. Josef Saal, who reviewed the daily situation on German radio, announced, "There can be no doubt as to the aims of our enemies. They want to defeat the Reich before Christmas at any cost because they know that, if this is not achieved, they can expect and fear intensified and increasing German resistance. . . . For us, this greatest of all battles means that the security and right of existence of the Reich, the future of our families, and above all, of our children" was at stake.[10] Field Marshal Model had already proclaimed, "We have succeeded in a bitter struggle, in halting our withdrawal, bringing the enemy armies to a standstill. . . .

The hard-bitten defense of the Rhineland grows harder after each blow.... We win because we believe in Adolf Hitler and our Greater Germany!"[11]

The Donnerberg

COLLINS'S VII CORPS MADE THE MAIN First Army attack opposite Roer River crossing sites and the good "tank country" of the Rhine Plain. On the corps right, the 4th Infantry Division was in the middle of the miserable Hürtgen Forest. In the center, part of the 1st Division faced the same nightmare, and another part (with an attached regiment from the 9th Infantry Division) had to contend with the Stolberg Corridor. The 3d Armored Division, bridged the gap between the 1st Division and the relatively new 104th, which was on the corps left. The armor made some gains on 16 November but lost time wrestling with mud, mines, and antitank guns.

One problem was a hill called "the Donnerberg" (Hill 287), which had been in Germans hands since September. Operation Queen did not touch it. Maj. Gen. Terry de la Mesa Allen, the commander of the 104th ("Timberwolf") Infantry Division, considered the hill enough of a threat to make it his division's main objective. Though Allen was an energetic leader with considerable combat experience, he did not use all the artillery available to his division on 16 November. Perhaps he intended to achieve surprise by not signaling an attack with a bombardment, or maybe it was an oversight his staff failed to catch. Whatever the cause, from their vantage point, the defenders could not miss the Americans. The attack stalled in the mud.[12]

Facing the 104th was the 12th Infantry (renamed Volks-Grenadier) Division and the incoming 47th Infantry (also renamed Volks-Grenadier) Division.[13] Allen's 414th Infantry Regiment (Col. Anthony J. Touart) tried several times, finally with artillery support, to take the hill, but there was no progress. General Collins, always impatient, told Allen to "get moving and get moving fast."[14] Only a lack of reserves prevented an enemy counterblow, and on 17 November alone the artillery of the German LXXXI Corps fired over 13,000 rounds against the Americans.[15] The Germans could not do this without dipping into carefully husbanded ammunition reserves, but their defensive fire was deadly in scope when it had to be. Ironically, a shortage of light artillery ammunition in the 12th Army Group meant that the 104th Division and its attachments were allocated only 111,000 105-mm howitzer rounds for the entire month of

November, despite the importance of this offensive. First Army placed strict limits on what the division could fire.[16] The defenses on the Donnerberg remained unbroken until midday on 18 November, when GI persistence and six fighter-bomber sorties paid off about the same time the Germans pulled back to a second defensive line. The 104th Infantry and 3d Armored Divisions could now concentrate against the Stolberg Corridor and the city of Eschweiler.[17]

The fighting across this area was intense. One mortar crew had to fire its 81–mm rounds only fifty yards in front of friendly troops. GIs blew in doors with quarter-pound blocks of TNT.[18] Some rain-soaked elderly civilians who dodged fire from both sides to reach American lines told the S-2 of the 415th Infantry Regiment that they and 3,000 other civilians had resisted attempts by the local Nazi leaders to move them east of the Rhine. GIs searching one cellar found four *Landsers*, two women, and a seven-year-old boy. The German soldiers reported that they wanted to desert and that the civilians had offered to hide them. Another

Pvt. Duane Robey, 415th Infantry. [Courtesy Duane Robey]

young German told the GIs that he was disappointed to have been captured in his first battle. The Americans offered to send him back to own lines; he decided that he was ready to go a POW cage.[19] Thanksgiving Day was 23 November. A reporter asked some soldiers what they were thankful for. A medic said he was thankful to be alive. "I'd like a big turkey dinner, but I'm thankful for C-rations," he added. A lieutenant said that while he was thankful the fighting was finally in Germany, he would "be more thankful for clean clothes and dry shoes and for a shower."[20]

Breaking the Stalemate

STAFF OFFICERS MEASURED PROGRESS by the yard. Casualties were appalling—entire divisions became "fought out" and incapable of offensive action. The 1st and 4th Infantry Divisions grappled with some of the hardest fighting in the war inside the confines of the Hürtgen Forest. Collins originally planned for the 1st Infantry Division to widen its sector after clearing its share of the forest and gaining the Roer Plain. It was clear by the 21st that this would not happen, so he ordered the 104th Division to drive immediately on the Roer instead of waiting for the 1st to move up.[21]

Allen's "Timberwolves" operated night and day. During training in the States he had driven his men hard and set high standards that produced a draftee division capable of executing complicated tactical operations. His "Directive for Night Attacks" reflected a combination of confidence in himself as a trainer and leader, and probably more important, confidence in his soldiers. He said, "The skillful use of night attacks indicates smart aggressive leadership. . . . Attacking troops must be highly trained and imbued with a determination to close with the enemy and destroy him with the bayonet."[22] Such operations required skill in map reading, patrolling, and cross-country navigation; they demanded detailed reconnaissance, careful preparation, and clearly defined objectives. Leaders had to maintain control and secrecy, and detailed planning would account for the direction of attack, security, surprise, and secrecy of movement. Allen said, "A simple plan, flexible formations and a clear knowledge by each subordinate leader of the mission of his unit" were key.[23]

The division's night and predawn attacks ground slowly forward. Help from the 3d Armored and 1st Infantry Divisions enabled the 104th to occupy Weisweiler and gain observation of three villages located on the Inde River, a narrow barrier that emptied into the Roer. The

AACHEN AND ROER RIVER AREA

Arnhem
Rotterdam • *Waal* TWENTY-FIFTH ARMY
Maas Nijmegen
Emmerich
Cleve• Rees
Goch• • Wesel
Lippe
NETHERLANDS CDN FIRST ARMY
FIRST PRCHT ARMY
R U H R
ANTWERP
Ruhr
Roermond H XXXXX B DÜSSELDORF
BR SECOND ARMY
BRUSSELS 21 XXXXX 12
Maastricht FIFTEENTH ARMY
NINTH U.S. ARMY (eff. 22 Oct 44) XXXX AACHEN Düren *Erft* COLOGNE
Namur LIÈGE Bonn
Meuse 12th Army Group Nov Offensive Nov-Dec 1944 SIXTH PZ ARMY Remagen
Rhine
BELGIUM FIRST U.S. ARMY ST. Vith *EIFEL* FIFTH PZ ARMY *Ahr*
Givet• ARDENNES Prüm *Mosel*
Bastogne XXXX B G
Wallendorf SEVENTH ARMY
LUXEMBOURG •TRIER *Saar*
SAAR GERMANY
XXXX MAINZ Oppenheim
FRANCE FIRST ARMY Worms
VERDUN LORRAINE •Kaiserslauten MANNHEIM
METZ SAARBRÜCKEN Singling
Meuse •Ft. Driant Bitche
THIRD U.S. ARMY LOW VOSGES KARLSRUHE G XXXXX OBERRHEIN
MARNE *RHINE* CANAL *Sarre* Wissembourg
Marne Saverne STUTTGART
12 XXXXX 6 Sarrebourg *Neckar*
Nancy• STRASBOURG
Lunéville SEVENTH U.S. ARMY
St. Die *ALSACE* *Rhine* NINETEENTH ARMY
Danube

30th ID Oct 44 Jülich
Würselen Lucherberg
Inde
1st ID Oct 44 Düren *Roer*
Aachen Hill 231
Crucifix Hill 28th ID atk. 2 Nov 44 Schmidt
Hürtgen Forest *Dams*
Monschau
0 10
Miles

BATTLE OF ATTRITION
16 September–15 December 1944

– – – Front line, 15 Sep
———— Front line, 15 Dec
///// West Wall

ELEVATION IN METERS
0 200 400 800 and Above
0 50
Miles

Colmar Neuf-Brisach
FR FIRST ARMY
MULHOUSE
Belfort BASEL ZÜRICH
SWITZERLAND
Rhine

"Timberwolves" took the southernmost of these villages, Frenz, on 26 November.[24] Remnants of the 12th and 47th Volks-Grenadier Divisions, heavily armed with automatic weapons and fighting from commanding ground, prevented the GIs from clearing the west bank of the Inde River until 30 November. A counterattack by elements of the 3d Panzergrenadier Division devastated two rifle companies at the town of Inden.[25]

Reaching the Inde River cost the 104th Division forty-two officers and 496 enlisted men killed or died of wounds, and another 128 officers and 1,578 enlisted men wounded, including 139 medics (the division made an emergency request to VII Corps for replacement aid men). Mortars and artillery caused most battle casualties, and there were "a large number of traumatic amputations and shock caused by land mines."[26] The relatively high number of officer casualties indicates that leaders were up front where they usually belonged. No doubt some losses were the product of officers and NCOs exposing themselves to prod untrained replacements, but the fact remains that they were not secluded in some command post in the rear. By 2 December, only the high ground at Lucherberg stood between Allen's men and a secure Inde crossing (see map on pg. 145).

This village dominated the approaches to the Roer River in the area, and thereby had to fall in order for the Americans to gain the Rhine Plain. Given the beating the rest of the VII Corps had sustained since 16 November, it was vital for the 104th Division secure this area as soon as possible; there were no units to help if its attack slowed. The job of taking it went to the 415th Infantry.[27]

Action at Lucherberg

THERE WERE FORMIDABLE NATURAL defenses at Lucherberg: a clifflike ridge barred the southwestern approach; the Aachen-Cologne autobahn, a large lake, and spoil bank of earth were on the south; the swollen Inde and its saturated flood plain blocked the western and the northern approaches. The only practical route was through a coal-processing plant situated on an uphill slope southwest of the town. Nearly all of the town's four hundred peacetime residents had been evacuated. Most of the seventy-five buildings were of stone or masonry and provided good defensive shelters.[28] The G-2 had reported that "the cloudy, rainy weather with poor visibility and trafficability experienced during the past ten days [since 18 November] is generally an example of what can be expected in future weeks." Such weather favored the defenders by reducing American aerial observation and operations, he added.[29] Intelligence officers also identified fifteen new enemy artillery and mortar positions covering open northern approaches to the town.[30] The regiment's 3d Battalion would make the initial assault; the 2d Battalion would support with an attack across the Inde at Lamersdorf; the 1st Battalion was in reserve.[31]

Elements of the 8th and 9th Fallschirmjager Regiments had been in the area for several days.[32] There were initially about six hundred defenders, few of whom had received anything but rudimentary infantry training. Most were "reclassified" Luftwaffe air and anti-aircraft personnel.[33] Nearby were several Panther and Tiger tanks, and about 180 artillery "tubes" could fire into the town.[34] Perhaps they could not prevent the Americans from eventually crossing the Roer, but the Germans could make them pay a terrible cost and delay them until better trained reinforcements counterattacked.

Company G (1st Lt. James Millinor), 2d Battalion, attacked first to seize the brick buildings of the coal-processing plant. This would support the attack on Lucherberg itself. To preserve secrecy and surprise, when the riflemen left Lamersdorf at 11:00 PM on 2 December they carried no rounds in the chambers of their rifles. Each man also carried a half-dozen hand grenades. This would allow them to assume the first gunshot would be from a German, and they could respond with hand grenades without accidentally shooting at another soldier.[35] Whispered curses were the response when the men stepped into the ice-cold Inde and found that it was almost waist deep, not ankle deep. Troops with two .30 caliber machine guns got inside the plant without incident. The squad leader placed the guns and took five men to clear an adjacent house. Meanwhile, the remainder of G Company's 1st Platoon, with two 60-mm mortars, secured part of a building that allowed them to observe a few dozen yards in the direction of Lucherberg. They could also see the outlines of enemy fighting positions on a slag pile a few yards away. It did not take long for the Germans to realize that American soldiers were in the area, and a squad-sized counterattack came about three hours later. Two Germans got close enough to the building to toss in hand grenades, but GIs kept control of it.[36]

The 2d Platoon, meanwhile, took no casualties when it occupied four small buildings paralleling the railroad spur leading into the plant. The 3d Platoon also secured its assigned building without meeting resistance. The platoon leader, a sergeant, along with the leader of an attached mortar squad, searched the damp, pitch dark, basement of the building. They encountered a heavy steel door, placed a grenade against it, and flattened themselves against a wall before the explosion blew the door from its hinges. Inside the room, they found ten stunned Germans, who surrendered without a fight.[37]

Company E (Capt. Douglas K. Ruch) attacked with artillery support at 11:00 PM on 2 December to cut the southern approaches to Lucherberg and keep contact with the men in the processing plant. One platoon reached Haus Lützeler, a moat-ringed chateau about a half-mile southwest of the town, without trouble. A rifleman killed the lone sentry, and the platoon took nine prisoners from the basement. Another group, no doubt aware of the presence of the Americans, ambushed Ruch's rear command-post group (the executive officer, first sergeant, the company communications sergeant, wire men, and runners, plus an officer from weapons company), which had strayed into German lines. Only the first sergeant and a wire team escaped.[38]

A three-quarter moon cast a dim glow on the Inde Valley about midnight on 2–3 December as the 415th Infantry's 3d Battalion (Lt. Col. Gerald Kelleher)[39] set out for Lucherberg. Men spread mud to camouflage faded uniforms or equipment webbing as they walked silently past the outpost line. Company I's 2d Platoon went first and forded the stream by climbing on the rubble of a demolished bridge and holding onto a cable stretched above. Intermittent enemy artillery caused no casualties. First Lt. John J. Olsen, commanding the platoon, stopped a few minutes on the east bank to reorganize his men, then followed the river another five hundred yards to the south before he led them toward the east through calf-high mud toward Lucherberg. They ignored inaccurate machine-gun fire but did encounter a barbed-wire fence. More fire came in from the north, which prompted 1st Lt. David Sheridan, the leader of the 1st Platoon, and another man to go on to the town. Sheridan sent the soldier back to tell the others there were no enemy troops to their front. Olsen radioed battalion at 1:30 AM that he had two platoons ready to drive into the town. He told the men with him, "I'm making a rush to the town, come if you like, or stay and be wiped out by artillery fire in the morning."[40]

Every soldier in the 1st and 2d Platoons followed Olsen across the open ground and into wooded terrain, then pulled themselves up the clifflike slope into the town. A German tank or self-propelled gun fired almost point-blank at the lead element. The 3d Platoon got held up, lost some men, and took a while to reorganize before it reached Lucherberg. Sergeants C. F. Shotts and Francis Miller led one group to a duplex (troops called it the "double house") located next to a small orchard in the northwest part of town. Olsen took some others to the center of town as far as a house near the church. They spent about twenty minutes driving out some defenders before Olsen returned alone to the buildings near the orchard to get more men. About a dozen went back with him to the vicinity of the church, where he led them in clearing another house and taking about fifteen prisoners. Olsen started to climb through a hole into another building when a bullet hit him in the head. Lieutenants David Sheridan and Edwin Verelli came up about this time. Verelli took command as some men carried the mortally wounded Olsen inside a house. About fifty Americans in perhaps four buildings now shared Lucherberg with about five hundred Germans.[41]

Mortar observer Lt. John D. Shipley, his radioman, and a runner had become separated from the 2d Platoon. With him was Lt. Arthur A. Ulmer, an artillery forward observer. These two officers and their radiomen would play a critical role in defense against several counterattacks. A runner sent to the rear earlier by Olsen arrived minutes later and told Shipley that Olsen wanted him at the church. Shipley instead sent five men there and temporarily kept machine guns and about thirty men on the edge of town. He ran to the double house, found Sergeant Miller, and then decided to set up the machine guns there. Sergeant Shotts organized the defense.[42]

Meanwhile, Sergeant Cheatham, the platoon sergeant of Company I's 2d Platoon, was in the top floor of a house near the duplex. In the moonlight, he saw a column of men approaching from the southeast. At first he thought they might from Company I, whose exact location did he not know. A second later he realized they were enemy, and he opened up with his rifle. It was about 3:00 AM, 3 December 1944. "The situation was exceptionally confused," reported Cheatham.[43] Indeed it was.

As this firefight died down sometime before 4:00 AM, a German medical officer walked slowly toward one of the houses near the church. In the vicinity were Verelli, Sheridan, men from the 1st and 2d Platoons, and a machine-gun section, plus the mortally wounded Olsen. The German requested a truce to evacuate casualties and said his medics would see what they could do for Olsen. Verelli called for Cheatham to stop firing, and he and his men left their house. Sheridan sent for Sgt. Leon Marokus, a German speaker, to translate as he and Verelli understood little if any German, and the doctor apparently spoke little English. Cheatham's men, meanwhile, leaned their rifles on a wall by the church and started helping collect the wounded. Evidently some of the Germans did likewise. Miller could hear both German and English as he returned to organize the defenses at the double house. About forty Germans and probably fifty GIs were in the vicinity of the church.[44]

Marokus and the German doctor discussed terms and called out for everyone to stop the sporadic firing that had continued despite the truce. About this time, a German paratroop captain arrived with about thirty men, who opened fired on the Americans for a minute or two before they stopped, apparently on their own initiative. Marokus, the doctor, Shipley, and the captain started talking. The paratroop officer said he was taking them prisoner, and Marokus began arguing with him. The doctor ("a little man") backed up Marokus, reminding the paratrooper that the Americans had been helping injured Germans. Marokus defiantly stated that the captain should listen to the doctor, who was a lieutenant colonel. Naturally enough, the captain maintained that the doctor was not a combat officer and was therefore not really the senior German present. He eventually relented and gave the Americans fifteen minutes to get out of town. He kept Sheridan as a hostage, and Verelli disappeared about this time, probably taken prisoner. When the captain finally let Sheridan go, the doctor returned to German lines, and Marokus led about seventeen men to American-held buildings. Nervous soldiers on one side or the other began to fire, and when the GIs discovered that Olsen was dead, they took control of their own wounded and hustled them back to the double house. It was now about 6:00 AM.[45]

Shipley had organized a credible defense of the double house with the forty-five men at his disposal. They chopped holes through the brick and mortar for observation and fire. A command post with radios was set up in the basement. Shipley noticed several enemy soldiers moving on the house from the northwest, and he thought others were nearing the church. He grabbed a radio handset and called for mortar fire (the mortars of the 3d Battalion weapons company were still at Inden and could support) and artillery. He would eventually adjust mortar fire to hit within fifteen yards of the house. Lieutenant Ulmer adjusted at least one time-on-target (TOT) mission, but despite his best efforts German machine guns kept the house under fire all day. One of the enemy got close enough to the house to blow in a door with a bazooka, or *panzerfaust*, round. Another was able to pitch in some grenades, while one actually got inside. He claimed under interrogation that he was a "fanatical Nazi."[46] The quality of the defenders had changed.

Company L Moves Up

ONLY AFTER DAYLIGHT ON 3 December, several hours later than planned, did Company L (Capt. Francis J. Hallahan) get across the Inde and reach the coal-processing complex. Though the group with Hallahan crossed the river without a major problem, 1st Lt. Thomas Danowski, the executive officer, had more trouble with his element. Enemy fire drove it from the Inde three times, and he eventually decided to try the location used by Hallahan. By now, however, this site was under heavy fire, which had also stopped engineers from completing a temporary bridge. No good ford was available, and Danowski finally located a crossing at the village of Frenz. It was noon before the company reached the coal plant. Col. John. H. Cochran, the commander of the 415th, ordered Hallahan to take command of the men outside Lucherberg and relieve Company I. Hallahan had 102 of his own men. Company F was minutes behind. There would be no tank support, though, because the Inde was rising and the tanks could not ford it. Danowski radioed Shipley, who reported that the prisoners said a counterattack was impending early on 4 December.[47]

Hallahan got word about 4:00 AM that there was an estimated company's worth of enemy north of Lucherberg. Sporadic firing gradually picked up. Lieutenant Thompson, in charge at the church, put 60-mm mortar fire on the attackers. Riflemen on the upper floor of the double house fired downward on the enemy; Danowski thought the men did "good work with their rifles." He went to the roof, where he and Shipley observed for the 81-mm battalion mortars. One round exploded every fifteen seconds, blanketing the two-hundred-square-yard orchard. They saw that several of the enemy were armed with machine pistols and were taking cover in foxholes dug earlier by the Americans. After the fire lifted, Sergeant Cheatham led a patrol to sweep the orchard and came back with twenty prisoners. Shipley and Shotts went out and picked up machine guns and machine pistols from the dead. Many of the survivors "were too dazed and shocked to speak coherently, while others jumped out of their holes with their hands in the air."[48]

Lucherberg was a mass of smoke, noise, and confusion. Danowski said that "rifle grenades were employed by the men from the buildings, and the enemy threw grenades back." Thompson thought the 81-mm mortars were effective.[49] An NCO spotted a sniper and called for a bazooka, saying "he'd get the bastard." Before the bazooka arrived, the sniper shot him dead.[50] Lieutenant Sheridan and five men later circled around the northern edge of town and contacted Company L about

noon. Sheridan received a mortal wound, though a German medic tried
to save him. All the officers of Company I became casualties.[51]

Bridging the Inde

U.S. STRENGTH IN LUCHERBERG was about 250 by midafternoon on
4 December.[52] Tanks and towed anti-tank guns, however, were still on the
west bank of the swollen Inde. Colonel Cochrane expressed "much concern and anxiety" about the situation.[53] Soldiers from the 329th Engineer
Combat Battalion tried late on 3 December to put in a bridge at
Lamersdorf, but enemy fire led the battalion commander to move the
work to nearby Frenz. One company was already under way to that town
when the fire began to lessen at Lamersdorf and the commander reversed
his decision. Then the engineers had to wait for a bulldozer to come up
and knock down an existing stone bridge abutment to allow construction
to proceed. Enemy mortar fire picked up again about midnight, and the
engineer officer in charge of the construction site thought the shelling
might be the precursor to an attack. He ordered the men to cease work
and take up defensive positions. There was no attack, but this cost even
more time, and construction did not resume until nearly 4:00 AM. The
engineers worked hard to bolt together ten-foot sections of steel frame
and push them across the 110-foot gap—the maximum span for a Bailey
bridge without a center support.[54] It was late afternoon before the 3d
Battalion's anti-tank platoon crossed the Inde and reached Lucherberg.
More towed guns and at least five Sherman tanks reached Lucherberg.[55]

Counterattack II

GERMAN PATROLS INFILTRATED American positions on the moonlit night of
4–5 December.[56] That night also saw "the worst 15 minutes artillery barrage that the Regiment ever experienced."[57] Enemy gunners worked the
high-explosive rounds up and down the streets. A German tank broke into
town about 5:00 AM and rolled to a stop close to an AT gun position before
the GIs could man the weapon. Another gun got off five quick shots
and the tank, which was not disabled, backed away. Another panzer also
pulled back. A GI in an upper floor aimed a bazooka at a tank, but a loose
electrical wire kept it from firing. He fixed the problem and fired two
rockets at the vehicle.[58] A panzer put three rounds into a Sherman and
destroyed both a 57-mm AT gun and its prime mover.[59] Sgt. J. F. Zahora
(Company K) saw several enemy near his company CP. Infantrymen killed

four Germans and forced the others into a damaged barn, where they were trapped by mortar fire. Sharp blasts from grenades and the crack of small arms fire blended into a single roar. Machine-gun fire bullets drilled chunks of stucco and brick out of walls.[60]

Pfc. Shelby Pelfrey and Pfc. Charles Gary manned one of the 3d Battalion's organic 57-mm anti-tank guns. They had been on guard and did not have time to run to shelter when the artillery fire began. Somehow they survived, and as the fire lifted to allow the Germans to close in, Pelfrey eased himself up from the bottom of his foxhole, which was in a barn. He saw about twenty-five enemy heading toward another gun. Its crew, plus some riflemen, had taken shelter in the cellar of a house that had been hit several times by artillery. Rubble kept them from getting out. Pelfrey and Gary then saw several enemy coming their way. Gary emptied his M1, and Pelfrey, armed with only a .45 caliber pistol, did the same. This scattered the Germans for a second, but they regrouped and approached the shed from two sides, hurling grenades. The two Americans ran into a cow stall and were unhurt by the grenades. Pelfrey's pistol misfired, but Gary killed one attacker. The others ran, and the two GIs set out to free the men trapped in the building.[61]

At about 8:00 AM, Lieutenant Taylor, leader of the AT platoon, saw a German tank crew working desperately to replace a damaged track shoe. His remaining gun fired four rounds, but at least two of them ricocheted off the steel armor plate. The tank driver started his engine and got out of the line of fire. When the gun crew manhandled their 2,800-pound weapon to a better firing position near their platoon's command post, they saw a Panther only feet from the L Company headquarters. It was too dangerous to fire—it would have risked a friendly casualty. There was no shortage of targets, however, and they saw another Panther just seventy-five yards away. It took three or four rounds to stop it. The crew then took another tank under fire. It burst into flames.[62]

Meanwhile, a Panther bypassed some hastily laid anti-tank mines, and lumbered toward the Company F command post. Sergeant Swanson carried a bazooka to the upper floor of the building, but he could not get a clear shot. He ran outside but still could not fire directly at it. The tank let go a high-explosive round directly into at the headquarters, which instantly killed a forward observer, mortally wounded the company commander, and killed or wounded several others.[63]

American artillery and mortars began hitting the enemy troops still outside of Lucherberg about daylight. GIs in the town took the offensive and worked house to house looking for the enemy, and the counterattack was over by about 10:00 AM.[64] A prisoner said that the tank units had employed four "King Tiger" tanks, three Panthers, and three self-propelled assault guns. Two Tigers, one Panther, and two assault guns were either knocked out or abandoned.[65] The Germans put quite an array of firepower against the 415th Infantry and it indicated the importance they attached to Lucherberg and its key position on the approaches to the Roer and Rhine. This was an exceptionally intense and bitter close combat struggle and the performance of the 415th Infantry reflected not only the impact of Terry Allen but the state of quality of even draftee units by late 1944. Air support was not effective given the proximity of the two sides in the town, and for much of the fight they had no adequate AT and tank support. The German army had been battered but clearly had not been destroyed.

Millinor, Hallahan, Marokus, Shipley, and Miller received Silver Stars; Olsen received the Distinguished Service Cross posthumously; Danowski received a Bronze Star. Pfc. Claudie D. Soape was awarded a Silver Star for knocking out an enemy machine-gun crew single-handedly; Staff Sgt. Raymond F. Puestow received a Silver Star for talking another machine-gun crew into surrendering. Silver Stars also went to Pfc. Donald C. Fleming, who killed thirteen paratroopers, and Staff Sgt. Henry A. Ducat, who crawled across fifty yards of fire-swept ground to rescue a wounded officer. The 3d Battalion, 415th, alone killed an estimated ninety-two Germans and took 189 prisoners, at a cost of sixty-one men killed, wounded, or captured.[66] The regiment's casualties for November were forty officers and 826 enlisted men killed, wounded, or captured; for December the count was sixteen and 244, respectively. General Collins sent Allen a message congratulating the 104th Division on the capture of Lucherberg.[67] The 415th Infantry spent the days after the battle clearing the Inde-Roer Plain and, with the rest of the division, reconnoitered Roer crossings in preparation for continuing the attack.

General Allen was a superb leader who instilled into the 104th Division the lessons of his previous combat experience in North Africa and Sicily. Its performance at Lucherberg demonstrates that even relatively new draftee units could do well if they were properly trained and led. This division had the benefit of a training program based on nearly two years of lessons learned. It had entered combat only three weeks before the start of the November offensive. German opinions of the fighting capability of the U.S. Army still varied. One officer reported, "The enemy no longer considers combat a sport, but fights fanatically to hold his territorial gains. The morale of his troops is good and he attacks vigorously even in the face of losses."[68] A report from the 183d *Volks-Grenadier* Division criticized the Americans for failing to launch attacks without air or tank support (little wonder, given the weather, ammunition shortages in the forward areas and the high equipment losses), and the infantry sometimes did not properly organize defenses after taking a position. This was no doubt the result of high losses among experienced men, who would have made the newer men dig in.

Germany continued to field units with a very wide range of capability. Many were extremely good. On the other hand, there were some like Kampfgruppe Göbel, described in one U.S. report as containing of the "most bedraggled members of the Wehrmacht to show up in the [POW] cage in [some time]." Its soldiers were between seventeen and fifty years old and were from a town north of Aachen. They had been ordered to appear at their *Rathaus* (city hall) one day at noon, where they were immediately drafted into the army. They rode out the Queen bombing and entered the lines against VII Corps on 24 November.[69] Another prisoner was a young artillery lieutenant whose mother had been in the United States since 1928. He told his captors that he would rather fight for his mother's country than his father's. He cooperated willingly, reporting that while distribution of ammunition was a problem, there was plenty on hand in supply points. Another young officer prisoner appeared "soft spoken and intelligent" to his interrogators, "but digging deeper into his background, one can discover that he has been an SA [Hitler's "brownshirts"] Führer since 1930, and that he is a fanatical Nazi of the worst sort, beyond any hope—or possible reeducation." He believed his division "had to be beaten in battle; its men fought to the last and surrendered only when there was no other way out."[70]

A clerk in the headquarters of an infantry regiment said he had been told that there would "be no retreat; everyone will fight to the last—all who retreat will be shot." His regimental commander had said he would "personally shoot all cowards."[71] A prisoner taken at Lucherberg reported that his unit never had its full authorization of heavy mortars but that it was well supplied with MG 42s and that each company had six 81-mm (medium) mortars (a U.S. rifle company had only 60-mm mortars).[72] While one must acknowledge German ammunition supply issues, one cannot likewise dismiss American shortages. Looking at combat ratios makes the following statement by one German general look sensible: "With adroit, flexible combat leadership, coordinated when necessary with opportune withdrawals, even such weak forces [as the Germans] could continue fighting for several months, perhaps until the summer of 1945."[73]

Maj. Gen. Joe Collins, the commander of the VII Corps, ordered the attack to the Roer to resume on 10 December. Fourteen battalions (about 144 guns) of corps artillery participated, in addition to divisional artillery. Intelligence officers estimated German strength at twenty battalions of light guns, five battalions of medium pieces, and about two dozen tanks and self-propelled guns. Expenditures of ammunition were high in mid-December, indicating that units were dipping into their reserves, because there were still supply distribution problems.[74] German ground troop strength in the Düren vicinity included the 3d Parachute Division, with nearly 7,000 combat troops; Gruppe Engel, with the remnants of the 12th Volks-Grenadier Division; and remnants of the 246th Volks-Grenadier Division, with about a thousand men.[75] By midday on 13 December, the 104th held a four-mile front along the Roer. The 3d Armored Division and the 9th Infantry Division (the 9th had replaced the battered 1st) were in the northern fringe of the Hürtgen Forest, where the 83d Division sustained a thousand casualties in only three days.[76]

It took First Army thirty-one very long and hard-fought days (16 November–16 December) to drive only seven miles. Battle casualties in VII Corps were 15,908, including 2,448 killed. There were another 8,550 nonbattle casualties from exposure, trench foot, and combat exhaustion. The V Corps employed only part of its strength (about 25,000 men), yet it took about 3,000 casualties. Some 240 of seven hundred tanks employed in the Aachen-Hürtgen area were lost either permanently or for extended maintenance. At one point First Army had 790 artillery pieces of varying caliber, but the Germans usually stood firm until faced with annihilation. Their losses were apparently fewer than the Americans'—about 13,000. Despite the attrition, they actually increased their strength in the Inde/Roer sector over the course of the fighting, to end up with about 21,000 men there.[77] While the Americans kept the initiative, the Germans actually controlled the outcome of the battle, because they managed to limit U.S. progress to just a few miles in a period of several weeks. The deepest penetration was only twenty-two miles, and the Americans still did not get across the Roer, much less the Rhine. There is little wonder that one senior U.S. officer remarked, "The situation was that we had many times played our last card. All we could do was sit back and pray to God that nothing would happen."[78]

CHAPTER II

LORRAINE, OCTOBER– DECEMBER 1944

ORT DRIANT, METZ, France, 4 October 1944: Six officers of the 11th Infantry Regiment's 2d Battalion and an attached tank battalion assessed the plight of their units after three days of brutal fighting. Capt. Jack S. Gerrie reported that the situation was "critical." Unexpectedly heavy German counterattacks had taken a significant toll. Interlocked as the two sides were in a fight taking place both above and below ground, American air and artillery support were almost ineffective. Gerrie added,

> We have no men, our equipment is shot and we just can't go. The troops in G are done, they are just there what is left of them. . . . We may be able to hold till dark but if anything happens this afternoon I can make no predictions. The enemy arty. [artillery] is butchering these troops until we have nothing left to hold with. We cannot get out to get our wounded and there is a hell of a lot of dead and missing.

So many leaders had become casualties that any replacements who might reach the battle would have no one to learn from. Few options existed. One was to withdraw and "saturate" Fort Driant with an attack by heavy bombers. Capt. Ferris Church, the XO of the 2d Battalion, added, "All agree this cannot be held tonight by these troops."[1] A stalemate reminiscent of World War I had developed. With the apparent materiel superiority enjoyed in late 1944 by the Americans over the Germans, how had this situation occurred?

Third Army by the end of August 1944 reached the Meuse and Moselle rivers with nearly dry gas tanks. It received no fuel on the 31st, and it hardly moved at all the first week of September. It also faced the same distribution-driven shortages of other supplies as did the First Army, and as late as 10 September it was receiving only a third of its artillery ammunition requests. Winter clothing shortages were impending. Mechanics needed spare parts, tires, and antifreeze. Such problems demonstrate that the industrial power of the United States did not

157

necessarily carry forward to the foxholes with the same efficiencies that produced and transported supplies and equipment to the theaters of war. Yet even mundane items had a role to play in the generation of combat power. A half-dozen tanks or a few cargo trucks temporarily immobilized by a lack of antifreeze or tires might have tipped the tactical balance of power at a critical time and place. Ironically, when the famous summer power drive by Third Army ground to a halt in eastern France, the German defenses in Lorraine consisted of only nine infantry battalions, two batteries of artillery, and ten tanks. Few of the units were first-rate. Yet the Germans recovered quickly, and the GIs did not face a beaten enemy when they were able to renew their attack. There were other problems too. The civilian population of formerly German-controlled Lorraine was less willing to assist than citizens in Normandy. Ultra intelligence intercepts were also becoming less useful for day-to-day operations, because the Germans relied less on radio communications and more on phone lines as they fell back on their homeland.[2]

On an operational basis, the Saar industrial region, which lay inside Germany opposite Lorraine, was an important source of coal and finished products. However, it did not hold the significance of the Ruhr, and Eisenhower's emphasis on the north made sense, despite Patton's arguments to the contrary. There is also no evidence, despite what some people maintained after the war, that Third Army was a victim of "subterranean maneuvers at SHAEF." The important industrial objectives were north of the Ardennes, as was the port of Antwerp. Bradley gave First Army priority of supplies, because there was not enough distribution capacity to meet the full requirements of both field armies. Third Army also transferred the XV Corps to the neighboring Seventh Army, on its right, which was supplied through the Mediterranean ports.[3] This final turn of events left Patton and Bradley "depressed."[4]

Third Army's XII Corps, meanwhile, had been fighting German armor near Nancy and the Moselle. The fact that the army G-2 warned that the enemy was still in firm control of its retreating units indicates that the while they were in headlong retreat, the Germans had not suffered a rout; control had not broken down. However, the ever-impatient Patton apparently dismissed this assessment[5] and ordered an attack on Nancy without pausing to regroup. He did not understand that the heady days of pursuit and headlines had ended. The 3d Panzergrenadier Division, which later was so effective in the north against First Army, helped destroy the first U.S. bridgehead on the Moselle. Only when Patton and his corps commanders opted for more deliberately planned operations did they succeed in gaining river crossings. Improvisation had worked in the early summer. By September, however, time had run out for such off-the-cuff fighting. Once across the Moselle, elements of the 4th Armored Division (Regular) and the 35th Infantry Division (National Guard origins) fought off very strong counterattacks near Arracourt. Some of the fighting took place at close quarters in a forest still filled with World War I entrenchments.[6] Concurrently, the XX Corps (Maj. Gen. Walton Walker) was trying to take Metz, which barred one route of attack into Germany. This mission was beyond the capabilities of a corps with only two infantry (5th and 90th) divisions and one armored (7th), whose soldiers were still using Michelin road maps.[7]

Fort Driant

IN FRONT OF XX CORPS were several forts on dominating ground adjacent to Metz. Fort Driant was the most important position, about seven miles southwest of the city at about 370 meters in elevation. German guns there fired on the Moselle bridgehead in September, and commanders wanted it silenced before they moved east of the city. It became a matter of debate whether the Americans needed merely contain it or physically occupy it, though the decision to make a ground attack won out. Geography then forced the Americans to mount a frontal assault. The terrain at Fort Driant fell steeply into the Moselle Valley on the east, south, and north, leaving only the western approaches open for an attacker. The defenders were also superbly trained soldiers.[8] U.S. commanders certainly wanted to avoid a costly attack, but General Walker, probably did not have enough troops to envelop Metz safely and thereby neutralize the fort in a single operation. Acting in haste had already led to problems along the Moselle. For example, the 5th Infantry Division had remained so closely engaged during its bridgehead operations that it was "exceedingly difficult to absorb . . . replacements."[9] Commanders knew they could not count on consistent air support, which was limited by the "highly problematical condition of the weather in late September."[10] Sorties flown by the supporting XIX Tactical Air Command (TAC) fighter-bombers fell from 12,292 in August to 7,791 in September. Pilots also reported the "worst flak concentrations they had experienced" to date.[11] Fighter-bombers were also relatively ineffective against "hard" targets. Air photos revealed little new information, and the enemy turned back U.S. ground reconnaissance patrols. As a result, soldiers had only "meager map details" available to them when they began the operation.[12]

Such map details were important even though the Americans had access to the original plans for the imposing Driant complex. Constituting the main armament were four large guns (100-mm and 150-mm pieces) in casemates of reinforced concrete up to seven feet thick and able to retract to positions virtually flush the ground when they were not firing. Secondary positions held lighter artillery and mortars. Only the gun turrets and concrete bunkers, which could support several hundred troops, were above ground. What made this fort truly impressive was a network of underground tunnels that connected the positions. Also inside were a power plant, hospital, communications facilities, and barracks that could house up to two thousand troops. A dry moat sixty feet wide and thirty feet deep surrounded the fort, less one detached position, and barbed-wire obstacles were up to sixty feet deep. Accepted estimates put about three companies' worth of defenders from an officer candidate school.[13]

Fighter-bombers streaked in low over the riflemen on the afternoon of 27 September—some only fifty feet from the ground. Napalm canisters and 1,000 bombs tumbled from their wings and then exploded, but they did little more than shake up the defenders. Fire from 155-mm howitzers, tank destroyers, two big 240-mm guns, and four 8-inch howitzers also had little effect. When soldiers from the 11th Infantry Regiment reached the barbed wire blocking an anti-tank ditch, the Germans opened up with small arms, mortars, and machine guns. TDs moved in close and scored several hits, but they did not knock out the automatic weapons. Fire from previously undiscovered bunkers then hit the GIs. Nevertheless, Col. Charles Yuill, the regiment's commander, called off the attack, though losses were comparatively small—only eighteen men.[14] This first test was perhaps based on continuing underestimation of the enemy's resilience and overestimation of the effectiveness of close air support. After studying the results of the air effort, Brig. Gen. O. P. Weyland, the commander of the XIX TAC, remarked that such forts "were not a proper target" for aircraft.[15]

Perhaps, as one recent study suggests, Patton himself was moving against enemy strength instead of avoiding it.[16] He could have stopped operations at Metz and reinforced the bridgeheads at Nancy or consolidated the positions there and put more power at Metz. The first rebuke at Driant, however, did not lead Patton and Walker to reconsider its immediate capture despite the relatively limited forces at their disposal. On one hand, Patton often complained that the infantry he had available was neither well trained nor particularly adept at closing with the enemy.

On the other, perhaps the history of Metz and Fort Driant drew him so strongly that he was willing to risk these soldiers for a prestige objective. Much as Brest had proved a futile pursuit in August and September, Fort Driant would be an impossible target in October. It is unclear when he chose Metz over the Nancy bridgehead, but he apparently did so against the recommendations of his G-3 and chief of staff.[17]

If Patton was forgiving of Maj. Gen. S. LeRoy Irwin's failure to take the fort on the first attempt, Walker was less patient. He did not think the division's leaders were aggressive enough. Irwin maintained that his men had encountered wire, concrete bunkers, and other defenses that had not appeared on aerial photos.[18] He reminded Walker that the division had been fighting steadily for weeks, had suffered high losses already, and held a front of nearly twelve miles—very wide for a single infantry division. During September alone the division's estimated losses had been 380 killed, 569 missing, and 2,097 wounded.[19] The division had received two hundred officer and 3,773 enlisted replacements in return, and many of them saw their first combat during the October struggle for Fort Driant.[20] Integration of such a large number of men was difficult, particularly since there were few of the old men left to teach them combat skills.

Thus the 5th Division renewed its attack on 3 October. In preparation, the division had stockpiled a limited reserve of ammunition and "snakes," long pipes filled with explosive and designed to breach obstacles or minefields. Tanks dragged the snakes into position by chain and then dropped them to the ground, where other tanks could then roll up, nose them into place, and detonate them.[21] Available corps and division artillery totaled seventy-six pieces, including four each of 155-mm self-propelled guns, 8-inch howitzers, and 240-mm howitzers. Ammunition was rationed for the attack. Only three hundred rounds of 8-inch howitzer and 150 rounds of 240-mm howitzer ammunition was available at the start; the total allocation for the first five days of the battle was only 8,230 rounds of light, medium, and heavy artillery ammunition.[22] Aircraft bombs did not offset this situation, since fighter-bombers were not capable of reliably hitting pinpoint targets like the forts and were dependent on the weather. Two tanks mounting dozer blades in addition to regularly outfitted Shermans were available. Unfortunately, the crewmen assigned to these "discards of the 7th Arm'd Div." had never fired their 75-mm main guns. Eleven other tanks from the 735th Tank Battalion would also support the attack.[23] Intelligence officers reported the presence of the elite officer candidates, though inexplicably, many units received word that the fort was manned by "about 100 old men."[24]

Bad weather prevented air support at the start of the attack on 3 October. This "was a blow to the confidence of the infantry in higher headquarters' planning and a definite discouragement was evident," as the historian of Company B, 11th Infantry Regiment would report. Some men had a reasonably good idea of what lay to their front, thanks to Tech Sgt. Ernest Reeder. Early the day before, he had gone alone as far as the barbed-wire barricades at the main fort. He surveyed the company's planned route of attack and reported back to his commander, Capt. Harry Anderson. "Bullshit," said Anderson when Reeder told him he had been so far forward, but when he considered Reeder's detailed description of the terrain at the fort and the approaches to it, he changed his mind.[25]

Artillery and smoke compensated somewhat for the lack of air cover. Company B was through the wire and on the grounds of the fort within about two hours. The Germans, however, used the network of underground passages to advantage. They seemed to pop up from nowhere, fire, and then disappear. Captain Anderson's radio operator jumped into a trench he thought was empty and nearly landed on some Germans. Anderson hurled grenades at the defenders, who ran off. Under cover of some riflemen, he then ran toward a concrete structure and threw a phosphorous grenade to provide covering smoke. Unfortunately, the wind carried the thick cloud of smoke into an air duct instead of obscuring the GIs. Anderson moved closer to the structure and threw more grenades. This forced six Germans to surrender. One of them came out holding a bloody wrist with no hand.[26]

Some riflemen, meanwhile, had reached a concrete building built partially underground, with four-foot-thick walls and heavy iron gate that barred the entrance. Tank fire was ineffective. Pfc. Robert Holmlund evaded sniper bullets to climb on the roof, knock off a vent cap, and shove in explosives. He could hear the Germans "trampling over one another trying to get out." When his squad leader fell wounded, he took charge of the four men still able to fight and finally broke through the gate. The enemy had evidently fled through a tunnel. The Americans later found a stairway leading farther below ground. A burst of machine-gun fire drove them to cover.[27] Holmlund was later killed while checking the positions of his men; he received a posthumous Distinguished Service Cross.[28]

Men from Company E, 2d Battalion, had become nervous waiting for the attack to begin. "They felt if was going to be difficult, but they had no definite idea of what to expect." Five men followed each of the four tanks as they lumbered toward the wire barrier. When they were only forty yards away, the enemy opened up with machine guns and mortars.

One squad crawled through a gap in the wire and then ran about fifteen yards to a stand of trees until enemy bullets forced it to move to an even more exposed location. Covering tank fire "did not seem to reduce the [enemy resistance] much." Another squad lost one man killed and the rest wounded. Men of one platoon, meanwhile, watched helplessly as tank rounds "would only chip off a piece of concrete about the size of a K-ration box." An artillery observer called a "danger close" mission (that is, deliberately near U.S. troops). "One man killed (head taken off) when he got out of a foxhole during one of these concentrations," reported an infantryman. All but one of the unit's medics were wounded or suffered from combat exhaustion by the end of the fighting.[29]

Lt. Lee Towne's tank platoon made an abrupt change of direction during the attack when it encountered a relatively shallow ditch in front of a ten-foot-high earth berm topped by barbed wire. Machine guns in a concrete bunker covered the area. Two tanks reached the ditch, dropped their "snakes," and returned to firing positions. All of the tanks took the bunker under fire, but the high-explosive rounds from their puny 75-mm guns did no damage. Another "snake" buckled when a tank tried to push it into position. For some reason, one tank moved out alone, but in doing so it ran over the buckled "snake." Towne wanted to order this tank back but was unable to reach its commander over the radio. A moment later, a German bazooka rocket, or *panzerfaust* round, flew over his turret. Just as another tank pulled up to take the ant-tank position under fire, a TD pulled in front of it. This mistake allowed the Germans to fire another shot, which hit the tank in the turret. Towne's fellow officers had no success either. Eight rounds fired by tanks under Lt. William Bauer did not even make "a dent" in the bunkers. A *panzerfaust* round then slammed into Bauer's tank, killing him and his gunner. The crew abandoned the tank, but Towne came up and ordered them to drive it to the rear for repair.[30]

Six of eight standard Sherman tanks and the three others that mounted 105-mm howitzers stayed up front after dark. Early on 4 October, the Germans started hunting them down, and the fighting became intense. So close were the two sides that the tanks could not maneuver for fear of running over the riflemen. The commander of a tank mounting a 105-mm howitzer went to the commander of a nearby tank to ask how he could get his vehicle out of the area. A 105-mm howitzer was not suited for this kind of close combat; it was not an anti-tank weapon to begin with, and it was inaccurate against point targets beyond five hundred yards. While the tankers were discussing the situation, an infantry sergeant came up and told them to stay put, because reinforcements were on the way that might help protect the armor against the roaming enemy and their *panzerfäuste*. As the howitzer tank commander turned to walk through the mud back to his vehicle, an explosion knocked him to the ground. Another round hit his tank and killed a crewman. The four survivors, including the commander, managed to reach another tank only moments before an artillery concentration hit the area. When it was safe to leave the overcrowded tank, the crew managed to crawl to another Sherman. A crewman from this tank threw them a submachine gun and extra ammunition for the harrowing trip to their assembly area.[31] Crewmen reported, "At night the [tanks] do not have a chance of a snow ball in Hell because the Jerries can slip up on [us]." Some thought the tanks should have been pulled back at dark. Armor officers explained that the infantry did not understand that while tanks could take ground they could not hold it and that the infantry had to protect them from anti-tank fire.[32]

The 11th Infantry's reserve, Company G (Captain Gerrie), came up at dark on 3 October to attack two casemated guns. While this company was still fifty yards from the positions, the Germans counterattacked in force and killed or wounded forty men, including an officer. Gerrie reorganized the remnants and held in place. Snipers, meanwhile, opened up on Company B. "They would seemingly pop out of hidden underground holes, fire a rapid burst of burp gun fire and pop back in again." General Irwin sent in a company of the 2d Infantry Regiment, and throughout 4 October the Americans tried unsuccessfully to break into the central fort and the underground tunnel system.[33] Patton, whose men were irretrievably committed to the fort, ordered Walker to take it even "if it took every man in the XX Corps" to do so.[34]

By daylight on 5 October, the guns of enemy-occupied forts in the surrounding area opened fire on the Americans, most of whom who were still on the surface at Driant. U.S. forward observers tried to locate the positions, but a thick haze in the Moselle Valley limited the effectiveness of their counterbattery fire. The guns in Driant could not be depressed enough to hurt nearby Americans, but two howitzers in open positions fired time-fuzed rounds that detonated over the unprotected GIs. That afternoon, Companies G and B had fewer than a hundred men between them; the recently deployed Company K was also hurt. To break the deadlock, General Irwin organized a task force under his assistant commander, Brig. Gen. A. D. Warnock, to take direct control of the battle.[35] The problem was that many of the men in TF Warnock's 1st Battalion, 10th Infantry, were inadequately trained replacements.[36]

When the attack resumed at 10:00 AM on 7 October, it took four hours for Company B to gain two hundred yards and capture a complex of three concrete bunkers. It then was hit by a deadly cross fire. Mortar fire pounded the GIs in the afternoon. About 5:00 PM, the first sergeant was talking to the company commander by phone when he heard "someone yelling for grenades and then an intense burst of MG fire." There were "shots, men calling, cries of men as they were hit, and grenades exploding." A patrol dispatched later to find out what had happened failed to locate any survivors.[37]

Company C of the 10th Infantry, meanwhile, had been trying to clear a tunnel connecting two gun positions with a barracks. The passageway was only three feet wide and seven feet high. Engineers blew down an iron door, but the infantry could not continue clearing the passages until the fumes, smoke, and dust had settled. After they resumed work, they found that the enemy had returned and blocked it with piles of steel, including old weapons and a cooking stove. A heavy metal grille was on the other side of the debris, and the infantry had no alternative but to remove the metal one piece at a time, passing it up a flight of stairs because there was nowhere else to put it. Engineers used a cutting torch to remove the grille door, but they found still more debris on the other side, which they also blew down with explosives. By this time, the conditions below ground were almost unbearable. Gas masks did not filter carbon monoxide and the fumes. Power blowers made things worse. At one point the Americans heard more voices, which some interpreted as preparations to blow in the narrow tunnel. U.S. combat engineers hurriedly prepared a sixty-pound charge, which they detonated about midday on 8 October. When troops reentered the area a half-hour later, they found that the explosive had only made an eighteen-inch-deep depression in the thick wall. German troops set off a countercharge that killed three Americans and drove the rest above ground.[38]

There was confusion "beyond belief." Troops of different units were intermingled, and the space on the surface was too constricted for effective reorganization. Daylight attacks were too costly, and operations at night had become too risky and uncontrolled. Some company commanders believed their men were getting jittery with exhaustion and stress, and it was clear that the Germans controlled the tempo of the battle.[39] Warnock canceled an attack planned for the night of 8–9 October, because the fumes from the tunnels had seeped into the barracks staging area and caused some of the men to pass out.[40] Driant cost the 5th Infantry Division over five hundred casualties, a figure that represented the effective strength of about three rifle companies.[41] Meeting at Verdun on 9 October, Patton, Walker, and Bradley agreed that "the glory of taking the fort is not worth the sacrifices in men which it would demand."[42]

Patton eventually renewed the attack on Metz as part of the 12th Army Group's November offensive (discussed in chapter 10). Third Army jumped off on 8 November and achieved tactical surprise. Metz fell on the 21st to a considerably reinforced XX Corps, but Fort Driant still held out for two more weeks.[43] Poor weather prevented air activity on twelve days during November. Some fighter-bomber groups even had to change bases, when they were literally washed out by the rain.[44]

German commanders told interrogators that with so much materiel the Americans should have concluded the November attack earlier.[45] German propaganda echoed the notion that the GI depended too much on materiel and that he was a poor soldier who disliked close combat. Some German observers also believed that the Americans relied too much on doctrine and that when improvisation failed they tended to err on side of caution. On the other hand, some Germans believed that the GI was tenacious in the defense and that he quickly assimilated lessons learned on the battlefield. They praised the Americans' ability to coordinate ground, artillery, and air operations through an effective communications system. U.S. tactical leadership also received positive comment from some. A tendency quite different from operations in the summer surprised the Germans—parceling out armor to infantry units rather than concentrating it for better effectiveness.[46]

Third Army lost 298 medium and 105 light tanks and suffered 55,182 casualties (including 6,657 killed in action and 42,088 nonbattle casualties) between 1 September and 18 December, when it had to end the fall offensive and shift troops to help stem the German attack in the Ardennes. What must have been especially bothersome was a shortage of 10,184 officers and men, mostly infantry, armor, and medical specialties (there was a shortage of 8,213 infantrymen-nearly a division's worth-alone on 1 December). Trench foot was reaching epidemic proportions.[47] The Germans were outgunned in artillery, but in mid-November they still had about six hundred pieces available against Third Army's 1,000 guns including supporting TDs. Only in the first days of December did forward U.S. artillery ammunition supplies improve to the extent that they could expend ammunition at a rate of about two to one over the Germans.[48] By that time, however, the stalemate was nearly a deadlock.

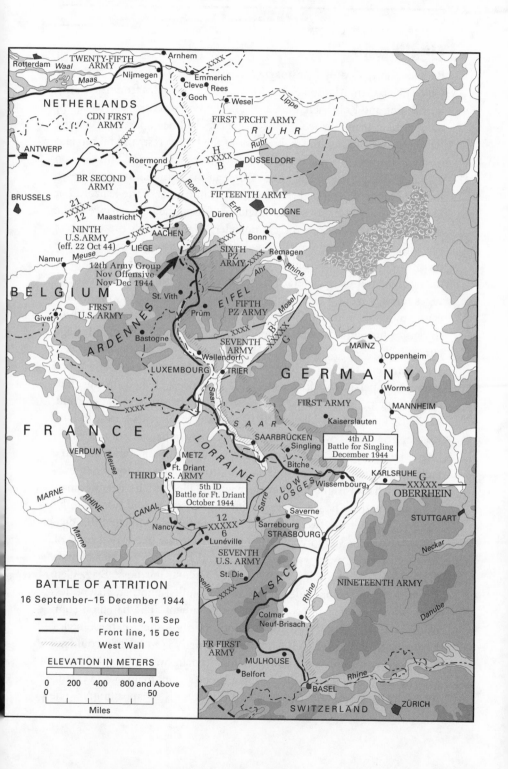

BATTLE OF ATTRITION
16 September–15 December 1944

- - - - - Front line, 15 Sep
———— Front line, 15 Dec
////////// West Wall

ELEVATION IN METERS

| 0 | 200 | 400 | 800 and Above |

0   50

Miles

Singling

By DECEMBER, THE 4th ARMORED DIVISION, part of Third Army's XII Corps (Maj. Gen. Manton S. Eddy), was just a few miles from the Reich, near Bining and Rohrbach, France.[49] The division was tired, and its equipment needed maintenance. Losses in officers had been particularly high. Patton planned to pull the division out of the line to rest, and he had also made up his mind to relieve its hard-driving commander.[50] This division was undoubtedly one of the most capable in the Army, and it would earn the admiration of General Fritz Bayerlein, commander of the Panzer Lehr Division, for its operations near Singling.[51] Given the performance of the division to date, why did the commander lose his job at the height of the autumn fighting? John S. Wood, fifty-six, was tired, having led the division throughout the campaign. Months of constant operations were taking their toll on a general who habitually led from the front, sometimes the very front. Once during the summer, while he was working forward on foot, he found a path through a minefield and sent an order back to one of his commanders, "General Dager, send the Infantry through after me."[52]

Units tend to take on the personality of their commander, and Wood stamped his personality firmly on the 4th Armored. He had already graduated from the University of Arkansas when he entered West Point, where he was commissioned in 1912. He was three years senior to both Bradley and Eisenhower, and as an artillery officer he was not part of the "Benning Group" of infantrymen. He was brilliant and outspoken to a fault, and he would let his superiors, Patton included, know unequivocally when he was right and they were wrong. He was a hard subordinate to handle, and he had no patience for superiors who did not share his vision of operations. Two types of leader eventually dominated this division. One was the stereotypical, robust combat leader like Wood and Col. Bruce C. Clarke, who was an engineer and the division chief of staff. Clarke balanced the temperament of his high-strung boss. Brig. Gen. Holmes Dager, commander of CCB, personified another, maybe less outgoing though equally competent, temperament. The battalion commanders followed suit and took on one or the other of these styles. However, Wood and the XII Corps commander, Manton Eddy, could not have been more different. Eddy, an infantryman, was a "stolid, humorless" general who never really accepted Wood's blunt manner and volatility. Historian Carlo D'Este describes their relations as "appalling."[53] The two disagreed about nearly everything, and Bruce Clarke's departure to another unit stripped Wood of a balance to his headstrong nature. There were occasional flashes in the relationship between Eddy and Wood, but nothing fatal to a career.

Then came an incident over sector boundaries. Wood virtually appropriated a sliver of Seventh Army front south of the designated 4th Armored zone of attack. This area was underutilized when Wood sought to gain more maneuver space because he did not believe the assigned route could handle the way he wanted to employ his division. This scheme worked until the Seventh Army needed the real estate and the 4th Armored ran into strong German tank units. Eddy with some justification considered this insubordination. On 1 December, when Wood's troops finally began to slow, Eddy accused him of losing his aggressiveness. A man like Wood considered this a personal insult, and their argument became loud. Wood stormed out of his headquarters after telling Eddy that he would ask no more of his men.[54] Wood had already clashed with Patton and Maj. Gen. Troy Middleton, when the 4th Armored was assigned to the VIII Corps. Wood got away with interpreting VIII Corps orders in his own way during operations in Brittany, but he could not do the same with an order from Third Army directing him farther westward into the peninsula than he thought he should go. Maybe Patton recalled in December what his headstrong subordinate had tried to do in the summer.[55] At any rate, he thought had little choice but to relieve Wood. "We are having one hell of a war, and the lack of ammunition and replacements is getting more and more serious," Patton said.[56]

Hugh Gaffey, Patton's chief of staff, took command of the 4th Armored Division at a very difficult time. On the evening of 3 December, the 25th Panzergrenadier Division and elements of the 11th Panzer Division began to withdraw toward Germany under cover of heavy artillery outside the range of U.S. guns. Early on 5 December, Gaffey ordered the 37th Tank Battalion (Lt. Col. Creighton W. Abrams), part of the 4th Armored's CCA, to move quickly on the town of Bining, which occupied ground controlling access to the communications center of Rohrbach-les-Bitche and a main route of withdrawal for the enemy. Soft ground would not allow cross-country maneuver, and the enemy artillery dominated the roads used by the 37th. Abrams, something of an emerging legend in his own right, ordered the lead tank and armored infantry elements to move quickly toward the hamlet of Singling as a springboard for outflanking Bining. The problem was that higher ground that the

French had incorporated into the old Maginot Line defenses surrounded the area. But to control Rohrbach the Americans had to have Bining; and to get Bining they had to neutralize Singling. Within minutes after starting out, Task Force Abrams lost 14 Shermans to mud and German fire. It pulled back at dusk.[57]

Gaffey intended for CCB, not CCA, to take Singling, thereby leaving Abrams free to concentrate on Rohrbach in a renewed effort. However, Abrams was in a better position to know what was going on. He could see that enemy fire from Singling would endanger any movement toward Rohrbach and that CCB was not ready to move anyway. Gaffey told him to do what he thought was best. Abrams in turn ordered Capt. James H. Leach, commander of Company B, 37th, with Company B, 51st Armored Infantry Battalion (AIB, 1st Lt. Daniel M. Belden) attached, to place suppressive fire on Singling. Supporting this were TDs and artillery, but the fire did not force the enemy out. Abrams committed "Team Leach" to direct action against Singling during mid-morning.[58]

Leach's company was short three tanks, and Belden's armored infantry company had only forty-two of its authorized 102 riflemen (the total authorization of the company was 251). Some of the companies in the 51st had had a 100 percent turn over in officers since 8 November.[59] Singling's defenses were strong: about two hundred infantry (111th Grenadier Regiment), eight to ten machine guns, three 20-mm anti-aircraft guns, a rocket launcher, five mortars, from three to five howitzers (119th Artillery Battalion), towed anti-tank guns, tracked assault guns, and at least five Panther tanks. The Germans knew the ground thoroughly, and they had had time to prepare their defenses. Singling might have been pretty in peacetime—tile-roofed houses painted in pastel colors or a drab white or gray, clustered around a brown stone church. There were about fifty houses along a main street running in a mile-long *S* pattern, with side streets branching off toward the countryside. House walls and foundations might be up to two feet thick. Garden walls were high.[60]

There was no time to make detailed plans—training took over. Leach passed the word to Belden, whose men were mounted on the tanks (it was too muddy even for half-tracks). Belden, however, was unable to get the plan to his platoon leaders, and one of them until that night thought he had been in Bining, not Singling. Some tank commanders also thought they were in Bining, and in fact the XII Corps daily operations reports for the period do not credit TF Abrams with having fought at Singling at all.[61] Leach put his tank platoons on line, and they moved fast, firing at they went. One tank developed engine trouble. Three anti-tank rounds, probably from a Panther, slammed into the 2d (tank) Platoon command tank as it swung east and entered an orchard. The platoon leader and his gunner were killed; the other three crewmen escaped as the tank started to burn. The three tanks remaining in the platoon took up firing positions.[62]

The two tank platoons carrying the infantry slowed down outside the center of the town to allow the infantry to jump off. Belden took the lead and told 2d Lt. Bill Cogwill, 3d (infantry) Platoon, to move to the left (south) of the town, and 2d Lt. Ted Price, 1st (infantry) Platoon, to secure the buildings on the right. In support was the 2d (infantry) Platoon (Lt. Norman Padgett). The three lieutenants were replacements who had been in action only since mid-November. They did not know the strength of the defenses. They thought their men would merely have to clean out some buildings. Cogwill and his radio operator reached the center of town close by a burning house. Near them was a German tracked assault gun, the commander of which was out of his hatch but evidently unaware of the Americans. Cogwill shouted for the tanks not to come up until the infantry had destroyed the enemy vehicle.[63] Captain Leach dismounted his tank and ran to Cogwill while the infantry fired at the enemy, who answered with a burst of machine-gun bullets.[64]

The four tanks of Leach's 3d Platoon were meanwhile nearing the west end of the town close to a barn that was in flames. The loader on the platoon leader's tank had seen the 2d Platoon Sherman get hit and evidently warned his platoon leader, Lt. Robert Cook, who did not absorb the fact that enemy tanks were so close by. The thick smoke obscured a retaining wall and a two-foot drop into a walled garden. Cook's tank slammed into the wall and teetered for a few seconds, threatening to turn over before it settled back down. This was certainly not a good place for a Sherman tank.

Cogwill and some of his men, meanwhile, saw two assault guns only a couple of hundred yards away from Cook's position. Cogwill warned, "There's a Kraut tank behind the third building down to the west." One of the Shermans with a 105-mm howitzer fired to knock down a section of the wall to their front so they could take the enemy under fire. The Germans replied with a round that blew a hunk of masonry from a building nearby. The tank backed off, and the two lieutenants ran to get a better look at the enemy.[65]

Second Lt. Ted Price's 1st (infantry) Platoon had only seventeen men. They had reached Singling and divided into three groups at the church, aiming to clear the north stretch of the village. Price took four men through a nearby alley, where they saw a few Germans at a small Maginot Line bunker. They tried to outflank the position but ran into a tall wire fence they could not climb without dangerously exposing themselves to fire. Unfortunately, the GI who usually carried the wire cutters had been wounded and evacuated two days before. He had taken the wire cutters with him. Tank and rifle fire forced the enemy in the bunker to give up anyway.[66]

Cogwill and a few of his men, meanwhile, were still probing the western part of the village. Through a gap in a wall, they saw two assault guns "within spitting distance," and not two hundred yards from these vehicles there were three more tanks. The Americans were finally getting a true picture of the enemy's strength. It was clear that it would be next to impossible for Team Leach to force the enemy out of the heavily defended village. All the Germans had to do was wait out the weak American force—they did not even have to risk a counterattack. Rather, they could sit tight and destroy the Sherman tanks one by one and strip the infantry of their support. Cook, Leach, Belden, and their artillery observer met at the infantry command post. The observer told them that artillery would also endanger the Americans. Leach's force had no mortars because there were not enough infantry to man them and still clear the town. Leach decided to try bazookas against the panzers.[67]

About this time, GIs saw about five more German tanks heading in their direction. Cook's Shermans were adjusting their firing positions when a white flare shot into the sky. A short but intense concentration of artillery blanketed the town; apparently the Germans were not as concerned as the Americans about friendly-fire casualties. Leach's tankers estimated a battalion's worth of fire hit them, sometimes as many as twenty shells simultaneously, for five harrowing minutes. Staff Sgt. Bernard Sowers, in charge of the 2d (tank) Platoon after the death of its lieutenant, pulled his vehicles back a few yards to the protection of one of the ubiquitous stone-wall fences. Minutes later an anti-tank round hit the crest of a low rise about a hundred yards from one of the tanks, ricocheted off the ground, and hit the turret of another tank, killing its loader. A tank commander turned his binoculars toward a bunker several hundred yards outside the village. At that instant, he saw the flash of a tank gunfire that seemed to be aimed directly at him. The round hit nearby. This Sherman tank was one of those mounting a howitzer. It did not have a power turret-traverse mechanism, and the fifteen or twenty seconds necessary to hand-crank the gun toward the enemy was too long. However, as the tank backed to cover it mired in the mud. A split second later, an anti-tank round hit the sprocket of a nearby tank. Four more rounds hit it within seconds, and it began to burn. Two crewmen were killed, and two others were wounded.[68]

The tanks of 2d and 3d Platoons were close together, idling on side streets and alleys. This was the only relatively safe place for them. Yet they were effectively immobile, because the enemy maintained the best ground and thereby the initiative. Leach went to Lieutenant Gobel's four Shermans (1st Tank Platoon), which were still in the orchard and relatively safe from long-range fire because of the ground. He warned Gobel about the approach of more enemy tanks. No sooner than Gobel began directing his tanks into better positions than a Panther pulled up only 150 yards away. The American and German tank commanders saw each other at the same time. Neither could fire immediately. The long 75-mm gun on the Panther started its slow traverse, but the American gunner, with a power-traverse 75-mm gun tank, fired first at point-blank range and set the Panther aflame with three quick rounds.[69]

Another panzer fired a smoke round and effectively disappeared behind its cover. Rockets then began to fall. Sgt. Robert Fitzgerald's 76-mm-gun Sherman set a Panther on fire with two rounds of AP. Seconds later, he saw yet another Panther about eight hundred yards away. Slow-velocity 75-mm rounds from another Sherman simply bounced off the tank's frontal armor. Fitzgerald's 76-mm high-velocity ammunition also failed to penetrate it. Two shots hit Gobel's tank, wounding him and his gunner. One of the solid-steel rounds punched a hole in the turret, ricocheted inside, and ended up beside the driver. He scrambled out of the tank. Gobel's platoon sergeant took charge of the platoon.[70]

By now it was late afternoon, and the promised reinforcements had not appeared. The fighting had been going on for about six or seven hours. Abrams now had orders to turn the town over to CCB and concentrate on Bining and Rohrbach. He was apparently unaware of the severity of the fighting at Singling; he turned to the commanders of the relieving tank battalion and the 51st AIB and proclaimed he was "ready to turn over to them their objective—and without a fight." The tank battalion commander assumed Abrams knew what he was talking about. However, when a relieving tank reached Singling, two anti-tank rounds knocked it out and killed a crewman. The other relieving tanks drove behind a ridge outside of town, but the officer in charge of the incoming armored infantry did reach Belden and Leach. They decided to use the newly arrived men to relieve Belden's soldiers in the west part of town. Abrams, who wanted more strength at Bining, radioed Leach about his status. Lieutenant Cook reported in Leach's absence that there were up to ten German tanks outside the town and several others in it. They were receiving artillery fire. Abrams told him to get the remnants of Team Leach out of Singling whether Leach made it out or not. The incoming tank company commander reported that his men would not move into the village without direct orders to do so, because of the enemy resistance and the lack of immediate tank support. Cook led out Team Leach at dark.[71] Corps artillery smothered Singling after the Americans pulled out. Elements of the new 12th Armored Division secured the town a few days later. Team Leach's fight at Singling was a success in that it enabled the capture of Bining. It was a hastily organized attack against heavy odds, with all the attendant confusion and lack of clarity about the enemy situation.[72]

As a battle, Singling was "neither a big action nor a startlingly successful one." Certainly it was made against heavy odds and its improvised nature contributed to the confusion described above. Yet it is a good example of the conditions under which the GI fought in late 1944. This includes the odds between the two sides. The XII Corps regrouped for the next phase of the attack on the Saar region, and by mid-December both it and the XX Corps were edging toward the Westwall and Germany. The fighting intensified. For example, the city of Saarlautern was itself integrated into the Westwall defenses, and the fighting there was house to house. Corps artillery observers adjusted 8-inch and 240–mm fire on individual buildings directly in front of the maneuver units.[73] Ironically, as the Americans were finally establishing a clear preponderance of fire on the enemy for the first time in weeks, attrition was taking an extremely heavy toll on the infantry. The commander of the 90th Infantry Division broke up anti-tank platoons and reduced the size of cannon companies and mortar platoons to get enough riflemen to maintain his attack. Since 1 December, this division had lost about a third of its manpower. Some rifle platoons were down to single-digit strength.[74] There were no signs of letup. As long as the Germans were on the defensive in their homeland, no amount of fire could dislodge them if they had the will to fight on. Only the continual improvement of the U.S. Army's fighting capability would enable the struggle to continue without another operational pause.

CHAPTER 12

WINTER INTERLUDE, 1944–1945

UCHHOLZ STATION, BELGIUM, 7:05 AM, 16 December 1944: First Sgt. Elmer Klug and his commander, 1st Lt. Neil Brown, Company L, 394th Infantry Regiment, 99th Infantry Division, stood in the damp cold of eastern Belgium looking at some soldiers approaching the mess line. Brown thought that a platoon was coming back too early for breakfast. They were clearly not following the schedule set up by Klug, a Regular who did not want his soldiers bunching up in line and becoming a target for artillery. Klug looked closer. "1st Platoon my ass," he remarked, "those are Germans."

Without waiting a second, Klug grabbed his carbine and squeezed off a shot that knocked down one of the oncoming soldiers, then ran to Brown and reported that there were about fifty Germans headed toward them. A few *Landsers* climbed into empty boxcars on a railroad siding by the station house that served as the company CP. At least one German got on an adjacent water tower. Klug had the platoon that was in the mess line take up defensive positions. Artillery was now falling, killing men who were carrying ammunition. One NCO fired two bazooka rockets at the boxcars but missed with both. Another sergeant also fired a bazooka, but the enemy clung to their newly won position. A bullet grazed Brown. Another man went down with a piece of metal lodged by his spine. Klug next ran to a nearby anti-tank gun crew and asked them to help. Despite the enemy artillery fire, they calmly unhitched the gun from their ¾-ton truck, set it up, and fired several rounds at the boxcars and the water tower.[1]

During a lull in the fighting, a GI searched the body of a dead German and found a copy of an order from Field Marshal von Rundstedt proclaiming that the "hour of destiny has struck! Mighty attacking armies today face the Anglo-Americans. I need say nothing else to you. Everything is at stake!"[2] Brown thought Klug was "a first-class soldier, and perfect gentleman." During the unit's withdrawal the next day, Klug broke his neck when he jumped into a foxhole to avoid artillery fire. He never regained consciousness.[3]

The Battle of the Bulge has been the best-covered ETO battle, with the possible exception of Normandy. This chapter will not revisit every important action. Rather, it will discuss aspects of that fighting that set American combat performance in context. First, the attack should have not come as a surprise. American (and Allied) intelligence officers and senior commanders simply failed to notice the full scale of the enemy buildup, which, though conducted in relative secrecy, was hard to mask completely. Without any U.S. interference, the Germans assembled over 200,000 soldiers, a thousand tanks, and two thousand artillery pieces on a sixty-mile front opposite the First Army, even as that field army pounded away at the German border. Facing this buildup was primarily the VIII Corps, which had only three infantry divisions and elements of a fourth, plus an armored division combat command and a cavalry group. One infantry division was green, and the others were exhausted and rebuilding from a mauling in the Hürtgen Forest.

Omar Bradley quite correctly called the dispersed placement of these troops a calculated risk. Whatever his reason for doing so, Bradley certainly did take a substantial risk with the disposition of First Army. General Hodges, the army commander, did not have many options given the status of the overall troop buildup. The United States did not have enough maneuver forces to substitute fresh units for the tired ones, much less enough strength to add units to the line or to place them in depth on a relatively inactive front. This thinly manned sector was the price the Americans paid for some measure of concentration during the offensive that began in November. What is more, these concentrated forces were going after objectives they could not fully exploit in the north due to the lingering question of the Roer dams.

Patton and his G-2 worried that the Germans were massing forces against the main attack near Aachen, but there was no evidence that the Germans were about to make anything other than local counterattacks there.[4] This was also the prevailing opinion of senior intelligence officers. The First Army G-2, Col. Benjamin Dickson, later claimed to have predicted the attack. Though he spent the rest of his life trying to prove that he had tried to warn others, there is no evidence in his daily reports that he was concerned about anything more than a large and uncommitted enemy reserve. He did not predict the time and place of the enemy offensive.[5] Bradley and his G-2 in late November decided there were no significant objectives in the Ardennes. They did not realize that the enemy

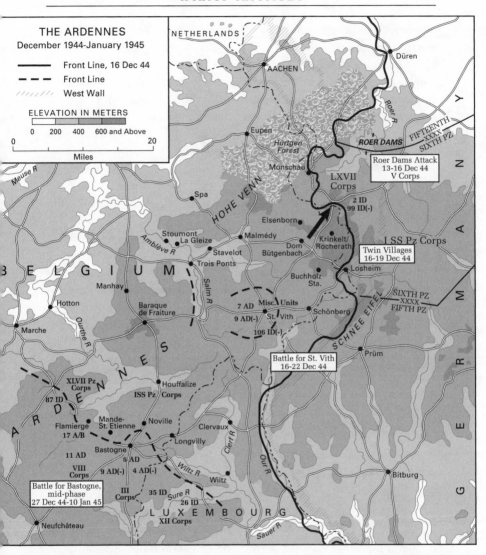

THE ARDENNES
December 1944-January 1945

——— Front Line, 16 Dec 44
- - - Front Line
/////// West Wall

ELEVATION IN METERS

| 0 | 200 | 400 | 600 and Above |

0   20

Miles

NETHERLANDS

NÉTHERLANDS

Düren

AACHEN

Eupen

Hürtgen
Forest

Monschau

Roer R

ROER DAMS

FIFTEENTH
XXXX
SIXTH PZ

Roer Dams Attack
13-16 Dec 44
V Corps

LXVII
Corps

2 ID
99 ID(-)

Spa

HOHE VENN

Elsenborn

Stoumont
La Gleize
Amblève R

Malmédy

Krinkelt/
Rocherath

I SS Pz Corps

Stavelot

Dom
Bütgenbach

Twin Villages
16-19 Dec 44

Trois Ponts

Buchholz
Sta.

Losheim

Manhay

BELGIUM

Baraque
de Fraiture

Salm R

7 AD   Miscl. Units

9 AD(-)   St. Vith

106 ID(-)

Schönberg

SCHNEE EIFEL

SIXTH PZ
XXXX
FIFTH PZ

Hotton

Ourthe R

Marche

A R D E N N E S

Battle for St. Vith
16-22 Dec 44

Prüm

XLVII Pz
Corps

Houffalize

ISS Pz Corps

87 ID

Mande-
St. Etienne

Noville

Clervaux

Clerf R

Flamierge

17 A/B

Longvilly

Bastogne

11 AD

9 AD(-)   4 AD(-)

Wiltz R

6 AD

Wiltz

Our R

Bitburg

VIII
Corps

III
Corps

35 ID

Sure R

26 ID

Battle for Bastogne,
mid-phase
27 Dec 44-10 Jan 45

Neufchâteau

L U X E M B O U R G

XII Corps

Sauer R

G E R M A N Y

Meuse R

might have a goal that was as much psychological (disrupting Allied operations) as physical (the Meuse River). Neither did Ultra signals intelligence intercepts reveal useful details. The Allies knew of Luftwaffe reconnaissance activity, but there was no additional information that linked this with the ground buildup to help form a complete picture of enemy intent. Eisenhower's G-2 even concluded that the Germans were in a new state of vulnerability.[6] Tactical intelligence officers (corps and below) did not have access to Ultra and they had no way to place events that came to their attention into a larger, operational context. Frontline units in the Ardennes were too overextended to conduct the patrols necessary to gain the firsthand enemy information that could fill in blank spots in an overall picture suggested by Ultra. Many of these units, reconstituting after losses, were too thinly manned even to prevent German infiltration. Tactical air reconnaissance did not provide enough detail and intelligence officers did not know why the enemy was concentrating command and control facilities. Air reconnaissance did report the high level of road and rail traffic in the region, but the XIX TAC, for example, had only two good days of flying weather between 1 and 16 December.[7]

In the end, the Allies knew that the enemy was gathering reserves and generally where they were assembling. Yet leaders were consumed with the events north and south of the Ardennes, and they mistakenly assumed that the enemy was thinking like they were. Commanders and their staffs did not assess enemy potential given what was known about his capabilities. Analysts simply looked at the enemy situation and effectively prescribed a course of action for German commanders. Such wishful thinking no doubt stemmed in part from the frustrations of the fall campaign. Commanders and their subordinates simply wanted that nightmare to be over. They were looking forward to gaining the Rhine. As night fell on 15 December 1944, G-2 clerks started typing daily updates that had little new information to report.[8]

At the Twin Villages

THE SURPRISE OFFENSIVE that began early on 16 December hit the VIII Corps hard. Disorganization and confusion were the natural result of the unexpectedly strong attack. Yet anxiety, distress, uncertainty, and shock do not mean that the entire VIII Corps, and by extension First Army, was nearing collapse. The initial reaction was indeed slow, largely because communications were disrupted, and it was hard to produce a coherent picture of the rapidly unfolding events. Debates between staff officers regarding the extent of the attack went on for hours during the first day. Some, for example, thought it was a limited operation intended to disrupt the ongoing drive, which had started in November. General Hodges took a long time, over twenty-four hours, to decide the situation was quite serious.[9] These were important hours, but they did not decisively affect the outcome of the battle, for at least three reasons. One was the inherent American mobility, made possible by its standardized fleet of trucks and other prime movers that could make up for some of the lost time. Another was the determination of countless small units acting effectively on their own. The third was the level of initiative of some senior commanders.

No masses of GIs ran to the rear when Army Group B slammed into them. Some inexperienced units did exhibit widespread disorganization and brief panic, due mainly to the lack of information available to them about the scope of the attack. To some of these GIs it understandably seemed like the situation was collapsing. Experienced men in almost all cases fought until they were out of ammunition, were ordered to pull back, or were cut off with no hope of escape. Retreating troops who had been hastily reformed into ad hoc units and thrown back into the fight sometimes did melt away, but most of these men hardly knew one another, and there had been no time to form even minimally capable soldier teams.

One cannot accuse an entire corps of poor performance by drawing generalized conclusions about a few units. Reports flew up the chain of command, but some of them applied to artillery and logistics organizations that had orders to move back. Their capabilities were too important to lose, and they did not need to stay up front and sacrifice themselves without a good reason. Some postwar analysts apparently picked up on such reports made immediately after the action by respected leaders from the 7th Armored Division. The well-known comments by Bruce Clarke and one of his officers not long after the war in an Armor School training text no doubt reflected the chaos in untried units outside of St. Vith in the early hours of the battle. "Great panic," "vehicles fleeing to the rear," "hopeless mass of vehicles fleeing," and "American soldiers running away" became common descriptions of the situation throughout the First Army. Yet more recent interpretations of the evidence of what happened in even recently engaged units like the 4th and 28th Divisions, provide a far more accurate and balanced picture of events and are discussed in detail in other books.[10]

GIs stood firm at places in addition to Bastogne, which was not the decisive point of action at the beginning. The enemy main effort was on the north (the German right); it was made by the 6th Panzer Army against the 2d and 99th Infantry Divisions, the 14th Cavalry Group, and other units. American resistance in the north eventually forced the Germans to focus south against Bastogne. The initial combat power ratio in the north was about six to one in favor of the Germans, whose

units included the likes of the 1st and 12th SS Panzer Divisions, supported by about eight hundred tanks and assault guns, but not by an
effective logistical structure. Here, the new U.S. 99th Infantry Division
was temporarily operating without a supporting tank battalion, and one
of its three regiments was attached to the 2d Infantry Division for an
attack on one of the Roer River dams. The north-south orientation of
this 2d Division attack was perpendicular to the east-west direction of
the enemy drive, and its axis was located just a few miles behind the line
of the 99th Division's two defending regiments. Should the enemy have
broken through this line they would have endangered the 2d Division
and the other regiment of the 99th and completely unhinged the
American defense in the north. Maj. Gen. Walter Robertson, the commander of the 2d, was concerned that the 99th would be unable to hold
long enough to allow his reinforced division to pull back from its
exposed salient. General Hodges, as noted above, was undecided at first
on the scope of the offensive, and he would not approve a withdrawal.
However, the eminently capable Robertson, on his own initiative, on the
afternoon of 16 December stopped his attack and prepared to get
his division out of danger. This was one of the critical decisions of the
battle, because of its timing and the fact that it preserved troop strength
that would prove so important in holding the north "shoulder" of the
breakthrough.[11]

Events by early 17 December proved Robertson right. Tanks and
panzergrenadiers from the 1st SS Panzer Division worked behind elements of the 99th and seized the village of Büllingen, south of the 2d
Division's attack positions. Three infantry regiments (9th and 38th from
the 2d and the 395th from the 99th) had only a single unimproved, snow-
covered road over which to pull out. A battalion from the 23d Infantry
Regiment (2d Division), meanwhile, rushed forward to backstop forward
elements of the 99th that stood between the enemy and the units that
needed to pull out. This battalion conducted a fighting withdrawal under
considerable pressure, slowing the infantry supporting the panzers and
buying enough time for the reinforced 1st Battalion, 9th Infantry, to
withdraw and dig in just outside the twin villages of Krinkelt and
Rocherath. The commander was twenty-eight-year-old Lt. Col. William
D. McKinley, a grandnephew of President William McKinley. Robertson
ordered him to hold until further notice.[12]

McKinley probably had no more than six hundred men, and when
the fight began they were reinforced by only a handful of TDs and

tanks. As the foggy darkness approached during the late afternoon of 17 December, an outpost reported the presence of tanks. The men held their fire, since they were not sure whether the vehicles were friendly or enemy. One NCO eventually left his foxhole to check and saw Germans only yards away, seemingly unaware that they were passing through a weakly held U.S. position. Some tanks moved on toward the villages; three more stayed inside the American positions and shut down their engines. GIs called for artillery and mortar fire. Tank cannon, machine guns, and rifles flashed in the darkness. U.S. artillery set one panzer on fire. Others literally tried to run over foxholes. Some soldiers took bazookas and stalked the enemy as if they were hunting animals.[13]

A larger enemy force struck from three sides about 10:30 PM. A company of tanks from the 12th SS Panzer Regiment raked the foxholes with cannon fire. A battalion of panzergrenadiers closed in from the forest early on the 18th. Pvt. William Soderman knocked out a tank with a bazooka and then engaged a platoon of enemy infantry single-handedly. He was seriously wounded later in the day after he had destroyed another tank. Someone reported seeing a man try to jam his M1 into the sprocket of a tank. McKinley himself turned around some men who had run out of ammunition and started to withdraw on their own. A rifle company commander called for artillery on his own position—there was no further word from him. Another company was almost literally overrun by the enemy armor. Colonel McKinley and his S-3 were the last out after Robertson ordered a withdrawal that afternoon. The youthful battalion commander reportedly stayed long enough to shake the hand of every survivor as he escaped. Only 217 of about six hundred who started the battle got out.[14]

The desperate close combat outside the twin villages forced the 12th SS Panzer Division to divert its effort to a road to the south that led from Büllingen to Bütgenbach. It would not cut off the elements of the 2d and 99th Divisions that had been in the forest on 16 December. Instead, they set up part of what became a solid northern defensive shoulder Meanwhile, elements of the 1st Infantry Division, barely two weeks out of the Hürtgen Forest, began to arrive outside Bütgenbach early on 17 December. The significantly understrength 2d Battalion, 26th Infantry, dug in near the road used by the SS division. The commander, Lt. Col. Derrell M. Daniel, was a reserve officer who held a PhD in entomology from Cornell University. He declared, "We fight and die here." They too held.[15]

Roadblock

SOUTH OF THE EVENTS DESCRIBED above, the 5th Panzer Army aimed for the vital road network around St. Vith, Belgium. While this was not the initial German main effort, it became so because of the defense discussed above. Manteuffel's army quickly cut off and destroyed the two green regiments of the 106th Infantry Division in the Schnee Eifel (see chapter 7) before they moved on St. Vith, the site of the division headquarters. In line for only a few days, the regiments of the "Golden Lion" Division were simply overmatched. As the magnitude of the attack became clear, SHAEF alerted units to reinforce the northern and southern shoulders of what was becoming a sixty-mile-wide penetration. One of these units diverted to St. Vith to stem the tide at the center long enough for the defense to become set was the 7th Armored Division, which had been in Holland. Brig. Gen. Bruce C. Clarke, formerly of the 4th Armored Division (see chapter 11) commanded its CCB. He reached St. Vith on 17 December, a few hours ahead of the main march columns of the combat command. The exhausted commander of the 106th, Maj. Gen. Alan W. Jones, deferred to Clarke, who took immediate steps to stabilize the situation and lend moral support to the inexperienced infantry division commander.[16]

Probing attacks hit on 18 December, and the main attacks began a day or so later. Clarke and his boss, Brig. Gen. Robert W. Hasbrouck, realized that the St. Vith defense was creating a reverse salient into the enemy penetration. Their men would buy some time for other units to improve defenses to the west, but each hour they remained in place brought closer the likelihood that they would fight surrounded. To conserve supplies, Clarke ordered artillery to fire only when the situation was critical. Convoys ran gauntlets of German ambushes when they went to the rear for supplies.[17]

Eisenhower, meanwhile, placed the American forces on the southern flank of the penetration under Bradley and those on the north under Field Marshal Montgomery, because the expanding enemy salient had all but cut reliable communications between Bradley (whose HQ was in Luxembourg) and his subordinates to the north, including Hodges. Montgomery advocated building the defense as far to the west as the Meuse River. Hodges, on the other hand, wanted to hold St. Vith, and so did the others.[18]

Fighting at St. Vith grew in intensity through 22 December. The Shermans ran low on high-explosive ammunition, the type effective against ground troops. After the enemy overran an armored infantry company, Clarke decided that he had no choice but to pull the defense back a thousand yards to the west.[19] Maj. Gen. Matthew B. Ridgway, commander of the XVIII Airborne Corps, which took charge of the St. Vith sector on 22 December, was extremely upset by the withdrawal. To their credit, Hasbrouck and Clarke stood up to Ridgway's scathing criticism. A paratrooper might be accustomed to fighting cut off from support, but it made no sense to waste armor in the same manner. Nothing Hasbrouck said satisfied Ridgway, however, and Ridgway went forward to see Clarke and the commander of the surviving regiment from the 106th Division. Clarke said the units were about 50 percent effective. This was not good enough either, and only when an old friend, Brig. Gen. William M. Hoge of the 9th Armored Division, told him the situation was as bad as reported, did Ridgway order a phased withdrawal across the Salm River, west of the St. Vith positions. Here, the 82d Airborne Division and other units were building up a new line. The problem was that about 20,000 Americans would have only two or three poor roads available to them, and the 2d SS Panzer Division was already probing the 82d.[20]

Evacuation of the salient required units spread over many square miles to reach feeder trails and roads that led to the three crossings over the Salm. Such a march was difficult to synchronize even under good weather conditions. Cross-country movement might have been impossible had it not been for a bitterly cold weather front that made the ground just hard enough to give the vehicles some traction. Tanks and TDs often had to stop and engage closely following German armor that threatened to kill vulnerable support vehicles. Though the 7th Armored Division had lost a third of its tanks and about 5,000 GIs from all units around St. Vith were casualties, the Germans lost a week they could not make up. Even Field Marshal Montgomery acknowledged that the Americans conducted a brilliant defense.[21]

Flamierge

ONLY FORTY-FOUR OF THE SIXTY-ONE combat divisions that would eventually fight in the ETO were even on the continent on 16 December 1944, and of these only thirty-six had at least a month's experience.[22] The shift in command that split U.S. and British responsibilities put Patton in charge of retaking the southern half of the battlefield. Perhaps Third Army should have counterattacked closer to the base of the penetration and thereby cut off more of the enemy than would be endangered by an attack farther to the west, but it is important to note that the Allies at that

time did not need to take unnecessary risks with the units they would need
for the final attack into Germany. America's supply of trained combat
manpower was getting low. Senior leaders erred on the side of caution.
Eisenhower had to think about the continuation of the campaign, and the
Allies could not sustain losses that would delay the drive to the Rhine and
give the Germans yet another break to refit.[23] Third Army opened a corridor to Bastogne on 26 December, but as late as January 1945 Patton
remarked that replacements and ammunition supply were "the two things
which bother us."[24] Despite the U.S. counterattack, the Germans continued to build strength at Bastogne. Between Christmas and New Year's
Day 1945, the number of their divisions, weak as they might have been,
in the area grew from three to nine.[25]

Elements of the new 17th Airborne Division (Maj. Gen. William
"Bud" Miley) occupied Meuse River blocking positions beginning
Christmas night under VIII Corps control. Miley then received a series
of orders beginning on 2 January that took the division to the Bastogne
area, where it relieved an armored division and attacked at daylight on
4 January despite a shortage of trucks delayed arrival of part of the division. Miley said the corps directive was, "a large order for a new division.
However, the high command was insistent at this time that there was
nothing in front of us. By high command, I mean Third Army was presenting this view to VIII Corps. The latter didn't figure it would be that
easy, they said in passing the estimate on to us, but even their calculations
were an underestimation of the enemy situation."[26]

It was indeed. Many of the GIs had been airborne-school troops and
were thus highly trained, but there was no substitute for combat experience. Still, the men showed exceptional courage and endurance over
unfamiliar terrain and in hip-deep snowdrifts. The 2d Battalion (Lt. Col.
A. C. Miller) of the 513th Parachute Infantry (Col. James W. Coutts)
used grenades and bayonets to gain the starting point for an attack to
clear a zone west of Bastogne. One officer recalled that most casualties
were from small-arms fire but that one lieutenant "was hit directly by an
88 [mm gun] shell."[27]

Fog prevented effective artillery and air support. Samuel Calhoun, a
platoon leader in Miller's battalion later recalled, "The Germans let me
and my left and right scouts get to the field and then cut loose on us,
killing about eight of the men and badly wounding another five to eight.
Both scouts ... were dead, my runner was killed right beside me."
Ammunition was short, but Calhoun had to disregard an order to conserve smoke shells so that medics could get some protection when they

attended to the wounded.[28] Patton's staff apparently had not realized that the Germans intended to continue determined attacks on Bastogne, and the VIII Corps almost literally ran into an enemy attack aimed at pushing in the north and northeastern sections of the Bastogne line. The Germans had only about fifty-five tanks in the area, but it did not take many to wreak havoc on an airborne unit.[29] Miley summed up the situation: "[Third] Army was still insisting there was nothing in front of us. Our patrols indicated that they were still out there. We couldn't tell how many. But Army said they were all pulling away from our front. And so we pushed."[30]

The 513th moved out on 7 January against the village of Flamierge, located about four miles northwest of Bastogne. Fog and snow continued to blanket the battlefield. Five Sherman tanks were present, but so were a half-dozen panzers. The battalion commander, Maj. Morris Anderson, loaded men from two parachute infantry companies onto the Shermans, but three of them hit mines. Enemy fire knocked out another, and the fifth simply stopped. They all remained in place to cover the infantry, who had to continue the attack on foot. Due to radio problems, Anderson had to shout orders, wave his arms, or rely on runners to communicate with his companies. Their only support was from their organic mortars and limited artillery. The GIs fired from the hip and threw grenades to clear the buildings. Supplies reached Flamierge that night.[31]

Early the next morning, some fifteen or twenty German armored vehicles and several hundred infantry hit the village and surrounding area. Supporting TDs had pulled out the night before. The paratroopers stayed put, but they were soon intermingled with the enemy. Some of the Germans evidently had flamethrowers, and a few of the panzers lined up and poured fire into the Americans. Miller pulled his survivors out only after they ran low on ammunition.[32] Miley moved another regiment behind the 513th and ordered Anderson to withdraw from Flamierge on the night of 8–9 January. Poor communications forced messengers to bring the new order to Anderson personally, who by this time was wounded but still in the village. He would recall, "This was the most uncomfortable night of my life. I was lying on a snow covered straw pile and was terribly cold. The messages took an hour to come through, and then I realized that our town would have to be given up." Yet he was confident that his men could have held out if they had more ammunition.[33]

On 2 January Coutts's regiment had 144 officers and 2,290 enlisted men; two weeks later, after counting replacements, it had eighty-one officers and 1,036 men.[34] Patton, of course, had a different perspective. He

believed the division overstated its casualties and considered relieving
Miley, who "did not impress me when I met him at Bastogne. . . . He told
me he did not know where his right regiment was, yet he was not out
looking for it. . . . We can still lose this war. . . . I can never get over the
stupidity of our green troops."[35] Losses were indeed high, but Patton's
own staff contributed to the problems with its inaccurate assessments of
the enemy situation. Frustrated as Patton might have been, what happened with the 17th Airborne and other units in their first battles was to
have been expected.

Retrospect

THE BATTLE OF THE BULGE was the largest single battle in the history of
the U.S. Army in terms of men involved and geographical scope. The
average daily American battle strength was about 610,000, and casualties
hit 82,000, with about 17,000 killed by late January 1945. This high ratio
indicates the severity of the fighting. The British sustained about 1,500
casualties. German losses are nearly impossible to assess, but historians
place their losses between 81,000 and 103,000. Concurrent fighting in
Alsace, not discussed in this book, cost the Americans another 11,000
men and about 23,000 German casualties.[36] The Germans spent
resources they could not replace; if they had remained behind their border defenses, they would have added weeks, if not months, to the war.

It is important to place into perspective the importance of U.S. air
power, artillery, and materiel in the battle. Determining the impact of
air power is hard. A sample count on the ground of German armored
vehicles destroyed in battle could verify only about 10 percent of pilot
claims. The Germans were also able to repair damaged rail lines as fast or
faster than the Allies could bomb them, and the Allies never completely
isolated the battlefield by air.[37] Close air support was very effective when
the conditions were right, but spot shortages of aircraft, particularly night
fighters, and allocations of planes to interdiction instead of ground support forced the ground troops to fight a harder battle.[38]

The impact of artillery is also hard to assess with accuracy. German
guns could not keep up with the maneuver forces, whereas because of
superior mobility the Americans could ensure their own troops were
almost always within range of friendly weapons. Consumption drew
American reserve stocks to new lows, and the Germans faced both limitations in supply and in trained observers. They never accumulated enough
reserve ammunition, but allocations for the Americans were no more than

about half of what tactical commanders wanted. This battle also saw the introduction of the proximity fuze (POZIT), which used radio signals to explode an artillery round reliably over the heads of troops, thereby materially increasing fragmentation effect. If not decisive, its morale impact was important, for very different reasons, for both sides.[39] The U.S. defense suffered early on because so many guns were on the road—heavy pieces (8 inch and 240-mm) might take a full day or even two to set up after a normal tactical move. These weapons had the longest reach and the most hitting power, but they were few in number. For example, First and Third Armies combined had at the end of the battle only thirty-six 8-inch howitzers.[40] Determining the impact of materiel is more complicated than simply counting numbers of systems. For example, the defense of St. Vith owes as much to leadership as it does to numbers of tanks.

Other Hazards

GIs ALSO FACED NONCOMBAT hazards that drained the pool of available combat forces. "Trench foot," for example, was a diagnostic term that described cold-weather injuries caused by prolonged exposure to moisture at just above freezing. Soldiers could prevent trench foot by removing footgear, massaging their feet, and changing into dry socks. Treatment of mild cases was relatively easy; advanced cases could require amputation. It reached epidemic levels in the ETO during the winter of 1944–1945, stripping the equivalent of more than three infantry divisions (about 46,000 soldiers) from the front. Over 9 percent of all casualties hospitalized during the campaign were due to trench foot, and nearly every trench-foot casualty was a frontline soldier.[41] One regiment lost five hundred of its 3,200 men to trench foot and exposure during the first days of the Bulge. Cold-weather injuries rendered an entire regiment in the 90th Division combat ineffective. Medical officers in the ETO knew about the experiences in Italy of the winter of 1943–1944, but that theater's full report somehow reached the ETO only in early 1945. Lower-level units instituted measures to reduce the impact, but they could not always cope, and leaders sometimes failed to enforce them. However, small unit officers and NCOs were not responsible for poorly designed or ill-fitting footwear, a lack of overshoes, and circumstances wherein soldiers had no opportunity to care properly for their feet. Overshoes, for example, had no arch support, rubber soles that were too thin, and leaky canvas uppers. Eisenhower's chief surgeon remarked, "The footwear furnished U.S. troops is, in general, lousy."[42]

Not only was footwear "lousy"; so was the winter combat uniform. War Department planning and coordination with the ETO regarding clothing was abysmal. The ETO placed orders too late to ensure receipt from the States and distribution in time for bad weather, even though operations in Italy had identified problems with existing clothing. The Quartermaster Department had designed a good replacement combat uniform that used the layering principle for warmth and met with success in Italy. This outfit would have replaced, among other items, a light field jacket that dated from the late 1930s and an older heavy wool overcoat. The War Department was unable to convince ETO quartermasters that the new uniforms would be available in quantity by late 1944, and the quartermaster chose not to requisition it, instead choosing the all-wool British-design (the so-called "Eisenhower jacket") instead. Unfortunately, it was in short supply too, and the ETO's rejection of the new combat uniform condemned the troops to living and fighting without a proper winter uniform for wet cold climates.[43]

As late as July 1944, the ETO quartermaster accepted the old design field jacket as a substitute pending delivery of the wool jacket, even though the War Department warned that it would not be available in quantity for another six months. He cited as one reason the complexity of stocking and handling multiple items of clothing. The events of the summer appeared to bear this out; it had briefly looked as if the war might be over before the end of the year and there was no need to burden an already tenuous transportation situation with unnecessary cargo. Consumption figures for the summer, however, indicated the very high level of wear and tear on clothing. This prompted the ETO to increase belatedly its requisition for winter uniforms. The War Department could not meet the requirement, and many frontline troops were forced to use the old jacket or the heavy overcoat, which, when soaked with mud and rain, could literally become too heavy for an exhausted soldier to wear.[44] Too many rear-echelon troops also took for their own use winter clothing intended for frontline men. It was late winter before the uniform used in Italy, a design already two years old, reached ETO troops in quantity. Poor coordination between U.S. Army agencies led to casualties on the order of those that a German attack might bring about.

Mental exhaustion was an equally grave problem. Infantry private Lester Atwell later recalled, "In the end you crack up or you get killed; another guy comes up and takes your place and it starts all over again. The only thing I have to hope for . . . is to pick up a wound that's not too serious. I know that's the only was I'll ever get out of this alive."[45]

Combat exhaustion (CE) caused unexpectedly high nonbattle losses. Medical personnel used this term to describe conditions occurring mainly among frontline troops during combat and, to a lesser extent, immediately before. It had been coined for psychological reasons to fix in the soldier's mind the idea that rest could cure his problem—"exhaustion" carried less stigma than "breakdown." CE was not a "reportable" condition in the ETO, but it certainly caused most of the theater's nearly 102,000 neuropsychiatric casualties, which over the years have led some to question the adequacy of the GI. One type of CE was temporary and occurred just before entry into battle or during the first days of combat. It was common among infantry replacements who had not received proper indoctrination into their unit. Symptoms included vomiting, violent pounding of the heart, a sinking feeling in the stomach, shaking, trembling, cold sweat, a feeling of weakness, and loss of bowel or bladder control. The second form affected experienced men; symptoms included irritability, loss of interest, decreased efficiency, and carelessness.[46]

Treatment began, and with luck ended, as close to the front as a battalion aid station, a few hundred yards behind the forward foxholes. A GI might get a day or two of rest, a hot meal, and a shot of whiskey or a sedative before he returned to the line. Disagreements sometimes arose between unit commanders and military psychologists, with each side accusing the other of not seeing the situation his way. Medical personnel in some units recognized that the replacement system itself caused many problems.[47]

One method of preventing such casualties might have been relief and rotation of entire divisions, but the army was too small to allow it to do so routinely, even had more use been made of rear-echelon soldiers. Improvements in training were intended to reduce the effects of fear reactions that led to disabling strain. Leaders eventually understood that exhaustion was to some extent preventable in an organization with a strong chain of command and a well-developed sense of esprit and belonging.[48] This was hard to develop given the Stateside process of "stripping" divisions well along in their training of men to serve as cadre for new organizations. There was a noticeable drop in the incidence of CE during the pursuit to Germany, which some believed was a result of higher expectations for personal survival. The savage battles of autumn, on the other hand, forced men to stay in the line for extended periods. Many of the "older" men believed they had already done their part, but as with all GIs, the only ways out of combat they had were wounds, victory, or death. No wonder news circulated that troops could get a short break in a rear area if they exhibited the symptoms of "exhaustion." To the credit of the GI, however, there was no appreciable increase in admissions to hospitals or aid stations for combat exhaustion during the Battle of the Bulge.[49]

GIs believed with good reason that they were little more than expendable parts of an enormous, impersonal machine in total control of their fates. Periods of monotony and boredom gave reflective young men time to wonder if they really were indestructible. "They thought the Army intended to keep them in action until everybody was killed. . . . All the men have hope of getting back, but most of the hope is that you'll get hit some place that won't kill you. That's all they think about," said one man.[50] Combat soldiers had to accept killing as part of routine business. "I'll tell you," said one veteran rifleman, "a man sure feels funny inside the first time he squeezes down on a kraut."[51]

Yet stress seemingly pervaded their lives and never let up. One man confided, "I myself don't believe I could stand [anymore] the shelling. . . . If one shell dropped near me [again], I believe I'd blow my top."[52] GI Frank Stephens said, "The longer we survived, the more nervous about our own future we became. By the time I was wounded on 8 January 1945, I was ready for a shoulder wound and an escape from the weather and combat."[53]

Battle had many variables: terrain, weather, adequacy of supply, competence of leadership, intensity of combat, morale, casualties, enemy resistance, and fatigue. Men had to adjust quickly to sudden and violent death, confusion, discomfort, deprivation from sexual and social stimuli, to the sight and sound of wounded or dead men, and heightened instincts for personal safety. Rarely did a soldier face any of these singly. GIs listed prayer, unwillingness to let someone down, the need to finish the job, hatred of the enemy, and what they were fighting for, in that order, as reasons they stayed with it.[54] One can only guess whether any ETO GIs knew that, based on experience in Italy, rifle companies would have a nearly complete turnover of both officers and enlisted men every two or three months. Infantrymen (all specialties) would account for casualties far in excess of their percentage of divisional manpower (riflemen were only 11 percent of total infantry division strength, yet they suffered the majority of casualties). Life at the front was so difficult that even combat veterans were more likely than a new replacement to say that a dishonorable discharge was not one of the worst things that could happen to them.[55]

Officers, especially at the company level, had to fit in the group structure. They had a certain amount of coercive power at their disposal, but they also had to gain the trust and confidence of their men—it was obvious when an officer did not know his job. Unfortunately, high officer losses in combat often forced unprepared lieutenants into company command. Some did superbly; others held on long enough to get men killed through ill-advised tactics. It was also common for nineteen- or twenty-year-olds to begin a battle as a private and find themselves leading squads if not platoons within a few days' time. Yet many officers and NCOs became casualties because they were up front leading their units; men did not necessarily want their officers very far out front—units did not need their experienced leaders performing unnecessary heroics. Force of personality counted, and wartime interviews indicate that there were times, particularly in the hardest-fought actions, when platoon leaders and NCOs had to prod new men from their holes with their rifles. Sometimes the enlisted men were more experienced than their officers, and it was hard for new officers to command immediately the respect of hard-bitten veterans.[56] Leaders, like junior-ranking men, had to learn by doing in action.

CHAPTER I3

THE ROER DAMS, JANUARY– FEBRUARY 1945

NEAR KESTERNICH, GERMANY, 30 January 1945: John B. Babcock, a twenty-two-year-old NCO in the 310th Infantry Regiment, 78th ("Lightning") Infantry Division, saw a fellow sergeant leaning over a fence, apparently cutting some wire from the path of the attack. It was biting cold, the kind of penetrating wet cold found in that part of Europe. Babcock's platoon was on the attack, and he waded through the snow to assist the man. Unfortunately, he was not cutting wire. He was "as stone-dead as the lambs I had helped butcher back on the farm. . . . If unfamiliarity with violent human death required dramatic confirmation, the pinkish-white crater above his left eye convinced and sickened me. A chunk of his forehead had been shot away. . . . He'd simply been snuffed out by a burst of machine gun bullets he never saw coming from a kraut soldier who probably didn't know his bullets were striking a human target."[1]

General Hodges and his First Army staff were both tired. Their tendency toward micromanagement had paid dividends in the complex planning for Overlord. Now, however, was no time for unimaginative thinking or for what turned into a near obsession with obtaining information from the forward units. As the historian of that headquarters noted, staff operations were "often characterized by uninspired planning, questionable boundary placement, inadequate concentration of forces . . . and a tendency to press attacks past the point of a reasonable goal."[2] Boundaries within the 1st Division and between that division and the 104th in the November attack were too complex and required alteration from almost the beginning; Hodges and his staff let V Corps push the attack of the 28th Division at Schmidt far too long without paying proper attention to the Roer dams and their importance to gaining the Rhine plain.

Only in late November did the army staff and its commander awaken to the fact that the dams silently controlled their operations. Air attacks failed to compensate for the lack of foresight and planning, and only then did army headquarters implement a plan for a ground attack specifically aimed at the dams. This was a two-wing operation that began on 13 December. The southernmost attack was that mentioned in the previous chapter—by the 2d Infantry Division and the attached regiment from the 99th, on the Urft Dam. A new infantry division led the drive on the north. This was the draftee 78th, assigned to V Corps and commanded by Maj. Gen. Edwin P. Parker Jr. Its mission was to seize the Schwammenauel Dam rapidly while protecting the south flank of the VII Corps' drive toward the Roer and Rhine. Only two of the 78th Division's three regiments were available—the 309th and the 310th. The 311th Infantry was covering part of the Hürtgen Forest, because a regiment from another division (the 8th) had fought itself out there. General Parker's new division had a standard "package" of attachments, but the reserve was only two rifle companies.[3]

Kesternich

TANKS ACCOMPANIED 78TH DIVISION riflemen moving through a freezing mist across the pastureland west of the Schwammenauel Dam on 13 December 1944. An important intermediate objective was the village of Kesternich, which occupied a key ridge. Troops from a company of the 309th reported late in the day that the town was "filled" with Germans, and the company commander did not press the attack. He later said that the tank crewmen "were afraid" of roadblocks, mines, and anti-tank guns. The tankers told him they had lost many of their vehicles before in combat and thought they had good reason to be cautious. Such problems continued the next day. After a preparatory artillery bombardment, the infantry climbed from their foxholes and remounted the tanks before they learned the armor would not move unless a bulldozer came up to clear a path ahead of them. Capt. Richey V. Graham was arguing with the tank battalion commander and one of his platoon leaders when an exploding mortar shell wounded the lieutenant, Graham, and three others. The tank battalion commander, standing five feet away, was not touched. A rifle platoon leader who volunteered to lead the attack anyway was killed, and Graham was evacuated with his wounds.[4]

General der Infanterie Otto Hitzfeld's LXVII Corps held the area. His goal was to buy time and to help ensure the Americans did not interrupt preparations for the upcoming Ardennes attack. He later acknowledged that the defenders, particularly the 272d Volks Grenadier Division, successfully halted the U.S. drive. "We still had confidence in our military command—albeit more and more doubts were arising. The German soldier had been trained in such a way, as to carry through even against all odds."[5]

The commander of the 2d Battalion, 309th, spent the night of 13–14 December in a foxhole outside Kesternich. He and his executive officer could not find their artillery observer, and the battalion's 81-mm mortars were all that was available to support the renewed attack. Everyone was exhausted, and sleep had been almost impossible the preceding night because of intermittent artillery and mortar fire. Parker ordered the 2d Battalion of the 310th to support. However, this battalion's staff had made no plans for such a mission, though it was the kind of task the commander should have anticipated. They had little detailed knowledge of enemy dispositions and strength. Part of one company tried to bypass a concrete bunker and ended up in a minefield. When the riflemen began setting off the mines, machine-gun and mortar fire erupted around them. Artillery then thundered into the earth, and anti-tank guns poured fire at the supporting tanks. Casualties approached 25 percent before the Americans finally reached Kesternich, having braved several hundred rounds of enemy artillery on their way.

Problems with control arose immediately. Men seemed to disappear into the houses. The two rifle companies in the village before noon did not have enough men both to thoroughly clear the town of the enemy and simultaneously set up defenses against the habitual German counterattack. Leadership casualties had been heavy as well. The radios were not working, and so the battalion commander went in person to report to the commander of the 309th. The commander of the 272d Volks-Grenadier Division knew that the loss of Kesternich would split his force in two and give the Americans excellent observation of a large stretch of the Roer Valley. They might even drive the Germans from these positions that were to important to the north flank of the upcoming attack. Though he had no reserve, he would still have to counterattack.

German artillery started to fall sometime later, covering the approach of armor that quickly tore into the ineffective U.S. defense and caught many GIs outside their partially completed positions. Isolated groups of men held out in the buildings, while others tried to reach the road leading out of town to the west. Leaders had trouble even accounting for all their soldiers as the Germans pushed the remnants of the defending units from building to building. No one knows exactly what else happened that night. Some patrols managed to reenter Kesternich but had to withdraw, since they could not reinforce their positions. Only fifty-three enlisted men and three officers from Companies F and G of the 310th Infantry Regiment are known to have escaped from Kesternich after the counterattack. A few more men trickled out a handful at a time for several more days. As an example of the high price of learning, casualties in the 2d Battalion, 310th Infantry, were over five hundred of 871 men authorized.[6]

The Roer Valley

STRATEGIC CONSIDERATIONS LED TO the next phase in operations, which got underway after the "Bulge." Eisenhower still wanted to build a firm defensive line along the Rhine and use the bulk of the Allied armies against the Ruhr industrial area. There would be a secondary thrust against Frankfurt, through a terrain corridor between the southern Ardennes and the city of Kassel, though the British preferred to weight the attack in the north, where the ground was more suitable for mobile operations. The Combined Chiefs of Staff did not accept Eisenhower's plan until 2 February. They instructed him to cross the Rhine as soon as possible and not to wait until the armies cleared all enemy formations from the west bank of the river. General Bradley, meanwhile, secured the Supreme Commander's approval to continue operations temporarily in the Ardennes-Eifel with an attack that started on 27 January in hip-deep snow. Thick ground fog gave little assurance of air cover or observed artillery fire. Only on one day in a two week period through mid-January did the weather permit all-day air support. On only two other days could the fighter-bombers fly at all. Trucks hauling ammunition and supplies could hardly negotiate the ice-covered roads. Once again, success depended on the will of the individual soldier, but by 1 February, some units were again facing the Westwall on the general line reached in late September 1944. Also on 1 February, Eisenhower ordered Bradley to end the attack of those divisions that would transfer to the Ninth U.S. Army for the upcoming attack to close to the Rhine in conjunction with the 21 Army Group. The British army group would attack not later than 8 February, and the Ninth U.S. Army would move not later than the 10th.[7] There was one issue, however, that the Ninth Army would have to resolve—the Germans still controlled the level of the Roer River and thereby access to the Rhine Plain.

The materiel situation was improved in early 1945 over that in late 1944. The Allies could reconstitute losses faster and more completely than their enemy. Superiority in artillery by February was 2.5 to one, roughly ten to one in tanks, over three to one in aircraft, and 2.5 to one in all troops. On the other hand, there were lingering problems with ammunition distribution, and with supply of rounds of certain calibers. The German situation was not altogether desperate: tank and assault-gun production was steady at 1,600 per month between November 1944 and February 1945, and there were still reserves of manpower. Germany raised eight new divisions, composed mainly of seventeen-to-twenty-year-olds, as late as February,[8] though it might have done better to reconstitute existing units. Additionally, the Germans still grappled with unending logistical complexities in the distribution of their remaining fuel and ammunition.

There were no large-scale operations in the Roer Valley during the Battle of the Bulge, from mid-December through January. The Ninth Army took over some of the First Army's front and with it responsibility for the 78th Division. To help train the inexperienced men and gauge the status of the defenses in the area of the big Schwammenauel Dam, the division staff, with the assistance of Ninth Army engineers, prepared detailed terrain studies, and the infantry regiments conducted patrols to take prisoners who might have information. Westwall bunkers studded the division's area of operations. There were anti-tank obstacles, extensive minefields, and trench systems. The venerable 272d Volks-Grenadier Division still had about 6,000 men available for action, enough to make attackers pay a high cost for every foot of advance. There were also elements of the 62d Volks-Grenadier Division, with about 4,000 soldiers. Lt. Gen. William H. Simpson, commander of the Ninth Army, allocated the 78th Division artillery 30,000 rounds for preparatory fire. Its commander, General Parker, wanted 60,000 for his renewed attack starting on 30 January. Simpson's staff, facing supply distribution problems decided to base ammunition allocations on the division's limited expenditures during its period of recent inactivity. This disagreement in the end did not cause significant problems; in fact, prisoners stated that the U.S. attack caught them by surprise, since so little artillery had been fired.[9]

Infantry and armor, supported by British "flail" tanks, set out early on 30 January 1945 for the first steps of the attack on the Schwammenauel Dam. Kesternich, still in German hands, was a main goal. The division's plan of attack reflected significant maturing of its commanders and staff. For example, the 2d Battalion of the 311th used detailed street maps of the town that assigned a number to each building. Lt. Col. Richard W. Keyes, the battalion commander, would control the battle by tracking these numbers. This attack got off to a difficult beginning. Armored infantrymen from the supporting 5th Armored Division found it hard to see through the windblown snow, and their half-tracks became stuck in the drifts. They had to dismount some distance from their objective and then stop in the open under fire just to catch their breath. Those who could walked in the ruts made in the snow by tanks, to avoid anti-personnel mines. When a wire obstacle threatened to slow their momentum, an infantry platoon leader mounted a tank, told the commander what direction to go, and yelled at his men to follow. A few minutes later, the tank hit a mine, and the concussion threw the lieutenant to the ground, stunned but otherwise unhurt. A soldier helped him locate a bangalore torpedo, which he used to blow a gap in the wire. The detonation also set off several mines, which actually helped make a path for the GIs. The lieutenant then directed a tank through this passage, reorganized his platoon, and participated in the battle until he was wounded. Staff Sgt. Jonah Edward Kelley led his squad's attack until he was mortally wounded. He received the Medal of Honor. Actions such as this helped get the Americans back into the western part of Kesternich.[10]

Fighter-bomber support at tree-top level despite the doubtful weather improved soldier morale regardless of its direct impact at the front.[11] Colonel Keyes learned that the assault squads were having trouble identifying the buildings because most of them were badly damaged or nothing but piles of debris. Capt. John Rowan, the commander of Company E, radioed Keyes that he had committed his three platoons but could not make any progress. He recommended that the battalion dig in and prepare to defend. Keyes told him the battalion was not going to rest; it was going to take the town. He said later, "The tank-infantry coordination was not favorable. The tanks seemed to expect the infantry to lead them, and the infantry was prone to wait for the tanks." Kesternich at that point was nearly leveled and it was exceedingly difficult for the Sherman tanks to maneuver through. Darkness came on 30 January with the GIs in control of about half of the town.[12]

Close-in fighting continued the next day. A short artillery preparation opened the final push through the town, but heavy small-arms fire continued to pour from the remains of many buildings. German artillery fire remained intense. U.S. artillery fired smoke on the high ground outside the town to block enemy observation. Keyes thought the attack was about to stall. He vowed to "get the town" anyway.[13] The soldiers did—

the town, with its commanding view of the Schwammenauel Reservoir, was in their hands by dark. Time was of the essence. There was a lot riding on the performance of a single infantry division.

Schwammenauel Dam

BRADLEY REASSIGNED the 78th Infantry Division to the First Army's V Corps on 2 February. His plan called for the army group to "go over to the defensive, except that the First Army, using the 78th and the 8th and possibly one or two more divisions will clear up the dam situation as soon as possible." Hodges's order called for capture of the dams "at the earliest possible moment," since the planned start of the Ninth Army (and 21 Army Group) attack toward the Rhine was 8 February.[14] In the end, the mission fell to the 9th and 78th Divisions. During the next three days, the latter division conducted a series of attacks to extend its gains toward the Schwammenauel Dam.

The seizure of Kesternich allowed U.S. artillery to interdict enemy supply and communications routes and also to fire on most of the positions that blocked entry into Schmidt, which was still in enemy hands after the abortive November 1944 attack by the 28th Division. The artillery, though, could not hit every piece of important ground, and three hamlets along the Roer south of the dam had to be neutralized before the main attack. Keyes's battalion received replacements after Kesternich, but few of these men had been around long enough to even know the names of their platoon leaders before they jumped off. One company had only one officer and had received about forty replacements just two hours before the attack. Squad leaders and platoon sergeants had to talk to each man individually and tell him what to do. Men got lost in the early morning darkness of the canyonlike draws. German defenses included log-covered earth bunkers connected by several deep trenches.[15]

Pressure on Parker to take the dam as swiftly as possible became unrelenting. It started at SHAEF, rolled down to the regiments, and led to last-minute changes in the attack plans that only confused those responsible for carrying them out. The division staff had trouble understanding the intent of the corps commander, now Maj. Gen. C. Ralph Huebner, former commander of the 1st Infantry Division.[16] Also, this was not a lightly defended area. Two combat historians surveying it in late February noted that anti-tank obstacles were near "every highway" and they "abounded in mine fields, [bunkers], and troop shelters. On commanding slopes, facing southwest, all along the road, there could be seen an almost continuous line of concrete positions which defended almost all avenues of approach against attack." Supplementing these defenses were anti-tank ditches, concertina wire, trenches, and dug-in mortar and machine-gun positions.[17]

The final attack on the dam began on 5 February. It was a three-pronged operation that sent the 309th Infantry against Kommerscheidt, the 311th toward Schmidt from the southwest, and a battalion of the 310th, plus elements of an armored division, toward the town from the south. As usual, the armor was available for a limited time only. Parker intended for the 310th to support the 309th, which he designated as making the division's main effort, in the initial stages of the attack. The 310th would then pass through the lines of the 309th to seize Schmidt.[18] This plan had the benefit of maintaining unrelenting pressure on the enemy and the division was executing it when Huebner told Parker to have the 309th Infantry continue its attack on Schmidt rather than holding it up for the 310th to pass through. The new scheme of maneuver added

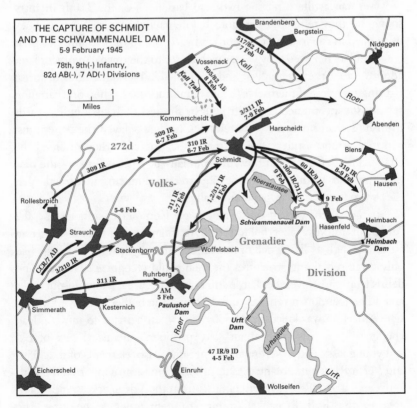

THE CAPTURE OF SCHMIDT
AND THE SCHWAMMENAUEL DAM
5-9 February 1945

78th, 9th(-) Infantry,
82d AB(-), 7 AD(-) Divisions

0   1
Miles

nothing to the offense. Huebner's interference only caused confusion, because both regiments were on the move and it was extremely difficult to stop an attack in that terrain after it had begun. Troops of the 310th ended up standing in the rain all day without permission to take shelter because they had to be ready to follow the 309th on little if any notice. Lt. Col. Charles A. McKinney, the division G-3, called the V Corps G-3 on the afternoon of 5 February to ask whether the corps commander intended for the division to continue operations that night; McKinney said the division was not ready, because it had not made plans to operate after dark in such compartmented ground. He learned in no uncertain terms that the division would keep moving until dark and that only then could it halt and untangle the regiments. "Remember," said Col. John G. Hill, the corps G-3, "the main objective is the dam. [Don't] waste too much time clearing up [your rear area.]" Huebner was "very anxious" for the division to capture the dam as soon as possible.[19] Perhaps he was too eager since his instructions had led to the confusion to begin with.

German artillery hit the two lead battalions of the 310th Infantry soon after they renewed operations before daylight on 6 February. They were deep in the forest a few thousand yards south of Schmidt, but their commanders believed they were much closer to the town. An officer later admitted that they were "lost and befuddled." The difficulties of forest fighting manifested themselves again at midmorning, when one battalion reported it was pinned to the ground by fire less than six hundred yards from its starting point. A counterattack further delayed the Americans, and mortar and artillery fire hit them not long after they resumed the attack. The defenders cut one rifle company to pieces. Some of the new men ran back to the battalion headquarters announcing incorrectly that they were the sole survivors of an ambush.[20]

Parker then worked out a new plan. Kommerscheidt, lost by the Americans in November, fell to the 309th Infantry on 7 February after an attack through a "living hell of mortar and artillery fire." The village had only three remaining structures the men could recognize as houses, and debris from the November battle still littered the area. Knocked-out tanks and TDs, abandoned vehicles, and decomposing bodies were everywhere. One American was killed by a booby trap when he tried to move a dead enemy soldier. GIs took about sixty prisoners, the usual mix of old and young, assigned to several different units. Also, elements of the 505th and 517th Parachute Infantry (82d Airborne Division) supported the 78th between 4 and 7 February with attacks from the Vossenack–Brandenberg area to the Kall River.[21] Contrary to contemporary boasting, the ultimate success of the Schmidt operation rested with the 78th, not the paratroopers.

Lt. Col. Andy Lipscomb, commander of the 3d Battalion, 311th, was on the southwest approach to Schmidt with the supporting Company A, 774th Tank Battalion. Their attack began at noon on 7 February, but nothing went even remotely according to plan. Intense artillery fire pummeled the tanks and infantrymen not long after they left their assembly area. They lost more time clearing anti-tank and anti-personnel mines from the road between the assembly area and the attack position. It was "practically impossible to move at any speed," Lipscomb would recall. Men were wounded in the assembly area, on their way to the attack position, and waiting for the order to attack. Minutes after the attack finally began, about 2:30 PM, anti-tank fire slammed into the lead Sherman. It started to burn, and the others pulled behind cover. Some tanks with the infantry still riding on them went back to the line of departure. One of Lipscomb's company commanders ordered his men off the tanks and reorganized them for an attack on foot. Lipscomb ran up and ordered the tanks to get back under way, but the tank commanders found reasons not to continue. Lt. Col. Harry Lutz, commander of a battalion in the 310th, was also present, and he reportedly "begged" the tankers to support the riflemen. Infantry officers also offered to lead the tanks personally, but in the end no one attacked but the riflemen. Artillery fire killed three officers and wounded eight enlisted men. The commander of the 311th, Col. Chester Willingham, said he would not have planned the attack in the same way had he known that tanks would not participate.[22]

Schmidt was no more recognizable as a town than Kommerscheidt. Buildings had been destroyed. A wet slime coupled with a stench seemed to cover everything.[23] That night (7–8 February) the 311th established an all-around defense, and tanks and TDs reached the town.[24] A false report that all of Schmidt was in American hands led Parker to order a battalion of the 310th to pass with the armor [25] through the lines of the 311th on the morning of 8 February so the division could maintain pressure against the dam. Officers from the 311th warned the commander of the leading company of the 310th that there had been several firefights the night before. They could not guarantee the security of the area once the attacking battalion passed through it. When the operation got underway about noon, this battalion had no artillery support, because no one was sure exactly where all the American units at Schmidt were and the gunners did not want to risk friendly-fire casualties.[26] Worse yet, an estimated ten to fifteen enemy tanks were in the area. GIs patrolling east of the town had one bazooka launcher and two rockets, and they were unable to score a hit on the armor they encountered, but the Germans ended up staying put. Later analysis in fact indicated that elements of up to ten companies, including men from the 3d Panzer Division, were in the immediate area. They were supported by two 120-mm and fifteen 80-mm mortars.[27]

By 8 February reports had come in to Parker that the men were "getting groggy" as a result of the unrelenting pace of the attack.[28] He relieved the commander of the 310th because of a mix-up in the delivery of an order to set up a roadblock outside of Schmidt.[29] Still, Hodges let Parker know he was not satisfied with the progress. The Ninth Army was scheduled to attack in two days, and the Schwammenauel Dam was still in German hands. Hodges could not see "why the artillery available to the 78th could not "blast a road . . . straight to the dam," but he did not visit the area and so did not understand the nature of the terrain in the Roer Valley. Hodges also phoned Huebner to express his impatience. Not long afterward, however, Maj. Gen. Louis A. Craig, the veteran commander of the 9th Infantry Division, arrived at V Corps headquarters on a routine visit after his division had secured the nearby Urft Dam. The corps commander told Craig to use one of his own more experienced rifle regiments to take the Schwammenauel Dam and for his headquarters to take overall control of the attack.[30] Parker was effectively out of a direct role in the final stages of the fight, controlling only the 310th Infantry.

Soldiers from that regiment moved out toward the high ground above the dam on the morning of 9 February, despite having had "no rest, no blankets and no chow." Tanks did not arrive until after the infantry had seized their initial objectives.[31] The 311th Infantry Regiment, meanwhile, was sealing off the dam from the possibility of reinforcement from the north and northwest. Craig's own men were also skirting the high ground between Schmidt and the dam to help secure an attack position for the 309th Regiment (78th Division). That regiment's 1st Battalion (Lt. Col. Robert Schellman) spent the evening of 9 February in an assembly area digging holes for protection against German artillery. Schellman, a young graduate of West Point who would eventually become a major general and command the 3d Infantry Division, expected to make that attack early the next morning. He and his company commanders were surprised to receive Col. "Duke" Ondrick's order to begin the attack immediately. No doubt Ondrick thought a daytime attack would be costly, and there is little doubt that he too was feeling the pressure. Schellman and his S-3 gathered the company commanders to explain the situation and issue a hasty attack order. So loud were the sounds of the artillery preparation that he had to shout the orders into each officer's ear in turn.[32]

Underbrush and darkness forced the two leading companies to move single file across the densely forested steep hills above the reservoir (the slope was one yard vertically for every seven horizontal). Debris from artillery-shredded trees added to the difficulty of the footing. One officer remembered that the only redeeming feature of the night was that the noise from the artillery and the water rushing through the spillway drowned out the noise the men were making as they contended with the terrain. Schellman set up his forward CP in a small dugout previously used by the Germans. He was in intermittent radio contact with his company commanders. Scouts and platoon leaders stopped periodically to check directions with their company commanders. To maintain security, they covered themselves with ponchos and read their aerial photographs by flashlight. Negotiating the broken ground was so difficult that the commander of Company B, Capt. Donald Cotherd, was "amazed" to learn that his men had reached their initial objective at the base of the dam without detection. He deployed his platoons on line for the final attack. Not long afterward, 2d Lt. John Bigart (2d Platoon, Company B) stumbled into a German foxhole.[33]

"The next few minutes were truly a nightmare," Bigart recalled after the war. "Apparently this was the first inkling the Germans had that an attack was under way. Their reaction was immediate and violent. Flares burst directly above . . . and machine gun and small arms fire [from the powerhouse] swept the position. . . . The flares also disclosed to B Company that they were right in the middle of a line of German foxholes." Riflemen eliminated these defenders and poured small-arms and bazooka fire into the powerhouse. Bazookas were hard to carry cross country, but the men were glad they had brought them. While they were not particularly effective against tanks, they could easily put a hole in nonreinforced masonry. It was hard under the dim light of flares and fires to tell friend from enemy, and several surrendering Germans were killed before the firing stopped. This fighting lasted about fifteen minutes.[34]

Company A also literally fell over the enemy defenses. One platoon took advantage of the confusion to continue its attack toward the building housing the dam's intake gates, which was the company's objective. Soldiers used grenades and point-blank small-arms fire to silence the position. Another platoon reached a knob overlooking the dam. GIs covered each other with rifle fire as they moved in short rushes to silence the resistance. About this time, they heard the unmistakable sound of explosions coming from the powerhouse and the control valves. Those who had a good view of the dam itself reported that it looked intact, though water was pouring from the reservoir in a deafening torrent. Capt. John Miller, the commander of Company A, called for the supporting combat engineers to come up. Riflemen led them along the road that ran the length of the structure toward an entrance leading to a tunnel that ran through its concrete core. "Everyone in the battalion was thinking of this tunnel now," said Bigart, "seeing it packed with demolitions, with the Germans waiting for the opportune moment to press a button and send it sky high" and the Americans with it.[35]

About 11:00 PM, flares unexpectedly shot into the sky. Machine-gun bullets drove the GIs back to cover. Schellman called for artillery. About thirty battalions of division and corps guns opened up, and the men could literally feel the ground shake when the rounds hit. The defenders' fire slackened finally, as the GIs reached the far side of the dam. There they saw that the Germans had destroyed the spillway bridge, which they had intended to use to access the tunnel. Using ropes was out of the question, because the spillway was forty feet deep and fifty feet wide. There was one other way to reach the tunnel, however. There was an access door built into the face of the dam. Schellman ordered Bigart's platoon across a bridge over the lower spillway to protect the engineers who had no choice but to slide two hundred feet down the face of the dam and try to stop before they hit the water.[36]

It was about 1:00 AM, 10 February 1945. Commanders wanted reports from the attacking troops. The 309th S-3 told the 9th Division that there was no information. Inside the tunnel, meanwhile, the engineers had begun work in knee-deep water, high air pressure, and stifling humidity. They had to complete one of the most important missions of the European campaign, ensuring there were no demolition charges that could breach the dam. Colonel Ondrick contacted Schellman's XO and urged him to "throw the chips in the middle of the table—[if the Germans do not] blow the dam, we'll take it away from them."[37] Only a minute later he radioed again, "Got to have [the engineer's] report on [their] investigation down there. Don't care how you get it [a report] but it is necessary."[38] He also instructed Schellman to hold. "Dig in nicely and hold. Don't want too much [*sic*] people around there—Disperse, Dig in, and protect.... I want [the engineer report] on amount of water flowing and in what places. What is the amt [*sic*] of demolitions in the dam, and how far have our people got in the dam?" The report so many were waiting for came soon afterward. The dam was not wired for a catastrophic explosion.[39]

Daylight on 10 February brought significantly less enemy infantry resistance, though it did lead to unexpectedly heavy artillery and mortar fire. U.S. counterbattery-fire missions against the suspected location of the enemy artillery and mortars achieved only moderate success. One such mission brought friendly artillery down on Schellman's men. Engineers estimated that about 500,000 pounds of TNT would have been needed to destroy the dam beyond repair. That did not happen, but the damaged control valves released enough water to cause a slow flood of the Roer and delay the Ninth Army's attack from 10 until 23 February. German General Hasso von Manteuffel refused to comply with Hitler's order to destroy the dam.[40]

Fighting the weather, terrain, higher headquarters, and the enemy, the inexperienced 78th Infantry Division learned and adapted. Some men failed, and others performed unexpectedly well. Operations between 1 and 10 February 1945 cost the division about ninety-seven men killed, 887 wounded, 296 nonbattle casualties, and eighty-one missing in action. After receiving 559 replacements, the division was still short thirty-nine officers and over four hundred enlisted men. The 311th Infantry, for example, on 30 January had 149 officers and 2,966 enlisted men. On 2 February, the regiment had sixty-one officers and 1,645 enlisted men.[41] General Parker's men executed an extremely important mission using a rather complex, but sensible plan under the circumstances. Given his resources and what he no doubt understood about the importance of the attack, Parker's plan was designed to maintain constant pressure on the defenders. While V Corps and First Army were justified in maintaining a close watch on the attack, Huebner and Hodges became too involved in its execution. Perhaps as a result of the tremendous pressure to seize the dams as soon as possible, Huebner caused the very disruptions he sought to overcome.

General der Infanterie Karl Püchler, commander of the LXXIV Corps, later said that countering the effects of U.S. artillery was a priority. Measures included building infantry defenses in depth, using concentrated counterbattery fire when possible, integrating anti-tank defenses (also in depth), emphasizing camouflage, and ensuring that resupply and troop movements took place at night. He added that the terrain and weather also played an important role in mitigating the effects of American air and artillery firepower. He was impressed by the degree of planning that was evident in U.S. operations, and, of course, he remarked about the effectives of mortar and artillery support. Püchler was also impressed by the Americans' ability to coordinate the infantry, armor, and artillery arms. He thought their outposts were generally alert and effective and that reconnaissance patrols displayed "excellent teamwork." He was critical of what appeared to be a failure to exploit local successes, and he noted that despite the effectiveness of American fire, German casualties in these last weeks were "really quite moderate in number and the same can be said of the loss of materiel on our [artillery] positions."[42] Püchler's comment about moderate casualties reflects the importance of the infantryman and the limitations of indirect firepower.

Bradley's G-4 reported that artillery and mortar ammunition supplies in forward dumps were inadequate to meet operational needs and allow them to establish a small reserve for contingencies without strict rationing. Deficiencies in eight-inch howitzer ammunition were 22 percent; 39 percent in 240-mm howitzer ammunition. Production shortfalls in the States during December for these two calibers and for 155-mm gun ammunition were part of the reason. SHAEF logisticians even withheld some shipments to the army groups so that they could establish reserve stocks at their [theater] level. Expenditures by both the 6th and 12th Army Groups in December fighting off the German offensives in the Colmar Pocket and Ardennes significantly lowered inventories and affected the supply at the artillery units themselves as late as February. Conflicts also arose between logisticians in the army groups, the ETO, and the War Department. Washington maintained that the theater consistently overestimated its requirements, thereby unnecessarily taking up shipping space. The ETO countered that the War Department's lower estimates of requirements were based on usage reports that did not reflect how the theater purposely restricted allocations to combat units so that it could build up reserves. Without knowing how difficult the Rhine crossing would be, the army groups were reluctant to reduce their estimated requirements. It was mid-March 1945 before the dumps at all echelons had adequate stocks and the theater and War Department had resolved their differences on supply policy. Yet the ETO never solved its distribution problems. The challenges of cross-leveling inventories as artillery units transferred between corps and armies, for example, was a problem to the end, and it was one reason that forward units endured restrictions on and rationing of ammunition.[43] The situation with fuel, particularly gasoline, improved with lower demand and as engineers pushed pipelines as far east as Paris, Maastricht, and Saarbourg by February. Stocks by March were at their highest levels, but the fighting by then was entering its final phases. Railcars carried fuel from the pipeline heads to army rail-heads, where cars were decanted directly into five-gallon cans or tanker trucks for delivery to the division service areas or for division pickup.[44]

After nine months of very hard fighting, the Rhine was finally a realistic goal. Ninth Army was concentrated north of Aachen. First Army was preparing to clear the Eifel. The Third Army, meanwhile had completed operations in an area south of the ancient city of Trier. These battles were limited in scope, as far as the higher echelons were concerned. To the fighting soldier, however, they were as desperate as any to date.

CHAPTER 14

ACROSS THE SAAR RIVER, JANUARY– FEBRUARY 1945

N EAR THIONVILLE, FRANCE, 8 January 1945: Slowly moving troop trains carrying the 376th Infantry Regiment (94th Infantry Division) rattled across Lorraine. Each unheated boxcar carried about thirty men. There were no lights. The only approximation of comfort was a few inches of yellow straw on the plank floor. Occasional rest stops offered some relief, but unannounced departures forced many to cut their latrine trips short and run back to the train holding up their field trousers. Many men thought French railroad workers took all night to move the trains just a few miles—it did take three days for the train to get from Brittany to sidings near Thionville. Upon arrival, train crewmen unlatched the sliding doors while the men gathered their equipment and jumped out to form up in their squads and platoons. Cargo trucks idled nearby, and not all of them had canvas tops. Frostbite and frozen skin began to appear before the trucks rolled into a XX Corps staging area.[1]

George Patton had been concerned for over two months about "that triangle between the Moselle and Saar Rivers," nestled in the southwest corner of the Rhineland with its apex near the ancient city of Trier, Germany.[2] It stretches about seventeen miles from north to south and is about thirteen miles across at its widest point. It had no substantive for-tifications until 1939, when construction began on a belt of obstacles up to two miles thick at the base of the triangle. German soldiers called these defenses the "Orscholz Switch." They helped block the approaches to Trier, which was the southern anchor of the Westwall defenses in the Eifel. Sharply compartmented countryside with patches of densely wooded ground reinforced the man-made defenses, which Third Army had tested without success in the last weeks of 1944. Losses had been comparatively high, and the attack was called off at the start of the Battle of the Bulge. When the Third Army renewed operations there

208

in January 1945, the relatively untried 94th Infantry Division (Maj. Gen. Harry J. Maloney) made the main effort. It operated for days without significant tank and air support against one of the best German divisions of the war.[3]

Tettingen and Butzdorf

MALONEY'S DIVISION ENTERED THE LINE in Brittany in the late summer of 1944. This assignment gave the men some experience in patrolling, building fighting positions, and adjusting artillery fire, but there was no opportunity to conduct battalion or regimental-sized maneuver operations.[4] Such relatively limited activity made life easier in the near term on the combat soldier, but in the long run harsher initial experience would have led to lower casualties. The plan was for the division's 301st and 376th Infantry Regiments to move against the Orscholz Switch; its 302d Infantry was in reserve. Major General Walker, commander of the XX Corps, told Maloney to probe the Switch line with attacks not to exceed a reinforced battalion in size. This would give the men experience in high-intensity combat and draw the enemy into the open for concerted artillery and air attack when possible.[5]

Sunday, 14 January 1945, dawned with a fourteen-degree temperature and good visibility. Soldiers of the 1st Battalion, 376th slung bandoleers of ammunition across their chests and stuffed a box or two of K-rations into their pockets while artillery sailed overhead to the villages of Tettingen and Butzdorf. These nondescript farming towns lay in the southwestern part of the triangle. A company each of TDs (607th TD Battalion), engineers (Company C, 319th Engineer Combat Battalion), and 4.2-inch mortars (Company C, 81st Chemical Battalion) were in support.[6] Two understrength regiments from the 416th Infantry Division (Generalleutnant Kurt Pflieger) manned the defenses. Pflieger recalled after the war that his men were relatively well trained but tired and needed an extended rest and refit with new equipment. His only reserve was an untrained replacement battalion. He had an adequate supply of mortars and artillery, but shortages of ammunition restricted engagements to the most important targets.[7] The relatively good condition of the Germans, coupled with the logistic and operational restrictions on the Americans, meant that the odds would be generally even.

Companies A and C of the 376th followed about two hundred yards behind the artillery preparation, crossing open ground. They were in Tettingen, the southern hamlet of the pair, by about 8:15 AM. Brig.

Gen. Henry B. Cheadle, the assistant division commander, was in the headquarters of the 376th, and about 8:20 AM he told Col. Harold H. McClune, a former enlisted soldier in command of the regiment, to push the attack into Butzdorf. Lt. Col. Russell M. Miner, the commander of the 1st Battalion, ordered Capt. Carl J. Shetler's Company A to lead. Miner did not permit even a few minutes' delay to reorganize.[8]

If the initial progress had surprised the Germans, they were ready to react at Butzdorf. Fire increased in intensity as soon as the GIs moved out into choking gray smoke of burning buildings. Troops heard hear the distinct, hollow, "popping" sound from the nearby high ground—mortars. One man recalled, "It was like standing at the bottom of a well and helplessly being stoned by a group of small boys at the top."[9] When the Americans started clearing Butzdorf, many of the enemy pulled back to the northern fringe of the village, where they continued to return fire. Shell fragments mortally wounded Shetler. GIs drove off an ineffectual counterattack of about forty Germans before noon.[10]

The narrow-tracked TDs had a hard time in the snow, and there was no tank support for the men now occupying a pencil-like penetration about four hundred yards wide and 2,000 yards long into the Orscholz Switch. Decreasing visibility formed a backdrop for vastly increased enemy shelling. Fire slammed into the Butzdorf, blowing walls, chimneys, and roofs to pieces. About two hundred *Landsers* from the 416th Division's replacement battalion counterattacked the village and recaptured some buildings. Some enemy reached Tettingen, where fighting was close and brutal. It took three hours to clear up the situation, but the Americans held on to the two villages as 15 January ended.[11]

Maloney's men had succeeded too well in drawing out the enemy from his defenses. More action was on the way, too, in the form of the 11th Panzer Division (Generalleutnant Wend von Wietersheim). This highly experienced and competent division had not fought in the Ardennes. Now it had orders to conduct a strong raid out of the Switch toward east bank of the Moselle overlooking the Luxembourg frontier to relieve pressure on the remnants of the units pulling back from the Ardennes salient. Fuel, road, and bridge conditions forced Wietersheim to leave his Panther tanks on the east bank of the Saar River, but he did have thirty Mk IVs armed with powerful 75-mm main guns, about thirty assault guns, and two relatively full-strength panzergrenadier regiments totaling about 4,000 men. It was a powerful force that overmatched that of the 94th. The axis of the attack, coincidentally, was planned for the Tettingen-Butzdorf area. U.S. reconnaissance flights on 16 January reported German armor entering the triangle, and the GIs went on alert that night. A handful of Sherman tanks finally arrived.[12]

Maj. Walther Schaefer-Kehnert commanded the 3d Battalion, 119th Panzerartillerie Regiment. The twenty-six-year-old officer had fought in France, the Balkans, Russia, and in the West. His battalion had several Soviet-made heavy mortars, a battery of four 105-mm howitzers, and two batteries of 150-mm howitzers. Ammunition supplies were often low, but the division always got by, because American air attacks never completely stopped resupply. Fighting spirit was strong until the end of the war, and there is no indication that the division was anything other than a highly professional and resolute organization. Kehnert later recalled that his fellow officers enjoyed only one privilege that the enlisted men did not—to always be in the place of danger. He remembered the bonds that grew from fighting and living closely together, though the officers demanded the respect due their rank. Morale was "professional to the very end," with "no breakdown of discipline."[13] Oberstleutnant Karl Thieme, thirty-one, commanded the 110th Panzergrenadier Regiment.

Oberstleutnant Karl Thieme, commander of the 110th Panzergrenadier Regiment. [Courtesy Karl Thieme]

He had seen combat in Poland, Russia, and Yugoslavia, had been wounded six times, had received a Knight's Cross for heroism at Kursk, and would receive the swords to his Knight's Cross before the end of the war. He recalled, "In the 11th Panzer Division, the feeling was: 'We are better than the enemy.'" Toward the end of the war, however, "a kind of fatalism developed. For me and my friends this started when the battle at Kursk in 1943 was lost. . . . We felt caught in the inescapable fate of our nation, but this hardly affected the professionalism of the [soldiers]."[14]

German artillery fire began to hammer Tettingen and Butzdorf early on 18 January and lasted for twenty-five minutes. From a nearby town came panzergrenadiers, infantry, combat engineers, and tanks from the 15th Panzer Regiment. Some of the enemy infantry got into a house in Butzdorf. U.S. mines or fire trapped others while they were still outside the towns. One American private scored a bazooka hit on a tank's tracks. Several bazooka rounds fired at half-tacks carrying panzergrenadiers failed to explode, but two privates took .30 caliber machine guns from their tripod mounts and fired from the hip at the enemy who tried to dismount. Supporting the defenders were division artillery, the regiment's own cannon company, and battalion and company mortars. The crew of a 57-mm anti-tank gun got off a shot at a panzer but was soon hit by a mortar round that damaged the gun and wounded most of the men.[15]

Pfc. Virgil E. Hamilton sped across the open area between the two villages in a jeep loaded with a bazooka and rockets to deliver to some riflemen. With him were Corporals Bernie H. Heck and Earl N. Vulgamore. They soon found themselves staring at four panzers. Hamilton whipped the steering wheel hard and got behind a farmhouse. The others quickly assembled the bazooka for Hamilton, who scored a hit on a tank just forty yards away. His second round hit near a German crewman who had just opened his hatch. Another tank could not find a good target and sat long enough for the GIs to fire at it. A fourth backed away. Hamilton and the others later apologized to the riflemen for giving them a "somewhat used bazooka without ammunition."[16]

The first wave of the attack was over by about 9:00 AM. Artillery disrupted another attack a few hours later, but some tanks took up positions and pounded the Americans for several minutes. About 2:30 PM, the 110th Panzergrenadier Regiment struck Butzdorf. GIs in Tettingen were powerless to help, since German fire controlled the ground between the villages. Colonel Miner did not have enough men to reinforce the position in the towns. The Americans had resorted to blowing holes in walls to move between buildings without exposing themselves to the fire now sweeping up and down the streets. Maloney authorized the 376th to give up Butzdorf. That night artillery fired covering barrages while the riflemen carried out the badly wounded on doors.[17] The German raid was over, though the Germans did succeed in gaining another village, Nenning, a few days later.

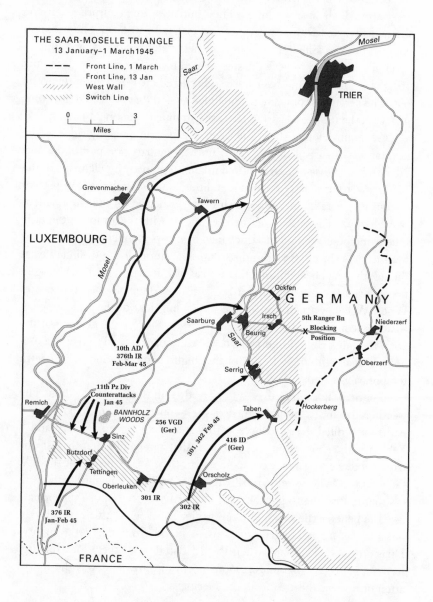

THE SAAR-MOSELLE TRIANGLE
13 January–1 March 1945

- - - Front Line, 1 March
——— Front Line, 13 Jan
////// West Wall
\\\\\\ Switch Line

0   3
| | |
Miles

Orscholz and Bannholz Woods

A LIMITED-SCALE ATTACK at Orscholz, the eastern anchor of the Switch, on 20 January was a disaster. Combined with a successful penetration at Tettingen, a breakthrough at Orscholz might have led to a wide rupture of the enemy line. Unfortunately, a combination of terrible weather and inexperience led to failure. Soldiers of the 301st Infantry attacked in a snowstorm with little visibility. They initially gained surprise, but the Germans reacted with a vengeance and isolated 250 men. The battalion commander was killed, TDs could not negotiate the terrain, and follow-up attacks could not relieve the surrounded men. The commander of the 301st chose not to reinforce failure and ordered the GIs to fight their way out. The surviving company commander replied that he "could not comply" with the order and surrendered the stranded men on 22 January.[18]

General Maloney chose the town of Sinz and a nearby ridge as the next targets. Also available, but only until 27 January, was part of the new 8th Armored Division. An armored infantry company hit elements of the 11th Panzer Division at Nenning, and this, coupled with the slow pace of operations overall, led Walker to lift the restriction on the employment of Maloney's division. He put two regiments with the armor to the task. One battalion encountered a thick field of anti-personnel mines. Two platoon leaders stayed in action directing evacuation of the wounded even though they had been injured themselves by mines. Intense machine-gun fire delayed the infantry, and a big anti-tank ditch stopped the armor. When Walker warned him of the impending loss of the tank support, Maloney committed his reserve. GIs were in Sinz by the evening of the 26th, though it cost six Shermans to kill eight panzers and gain only a toe-hold. Walker withdrew the armor that night, and operations by the 94th temporarily ceased.[19]

February brought a thaw and a steady rain that lasted for days. The weather grounded aircraft, turned the supply routes into bottomless paths, and filled every foxhole with water. Between 30 January and 8 February, the supporting XIX Tactical Air Command could fly just one day, and those missions were in support of the VIII Corps, not the XX. General von Wietersheim, meanwhile, was trying to convince his superiors that it was time to put the 11th Panzer Division to more appropriate use. Elements of the 256th Volksgrenadier Division eventually relieved it, but not before it exacted some more blood from the 94th Infantry Division on 10 February, when the 2d Battalion of the 376th Infantry moved against the Bannholz woods north of Sinz. This was the fourth attempt to seize the area from the Germans.[20]

Capt. G. Philip Whitman, the thirty-one-year-old commander of F Company, had worked as an investment banker in Boston and New York before the war. He had received an ROTC commission in 1935 upon his graduation from Boston University. Today, everyone had a bad feeling about this attack; Whitman was sure he would be wounded or killed.[21] Problems began in the assembly area—the bazooka teams did not arrive on time—and Whitman decided to wait for them before starting the attack. The supporting company, G, jumped off on time, but it headed too far to the left to support Company F. Whitman called in the clear on his radio for the other unit to move to its right. His 2d Platoon (1st Lt. Gordon Weston), meanwhile, was under orders to stay in contact with the other company. Weston did so all too well, veering off the planned route with a third of Whitman's combat power. Fortunately, most of the errant men reached their assigned sector without attracting much German attention.[22]

Fire caught the 1st Platoon (1st Lt. Wilford Wilson), attached machine guns, Whitman's command group, and his mortars in an open field outside the woods. Two German armored vehicles then started firing at individuals who managed to reach the tree line. Some of them bravely returned fire and tried to keep the crewmen buttoned up long enough for some of the bazooka men (they had finally arrived) to get in close. However, they ran out of ammunition, and the armor continued to roam the firebreaks and trails with impunity. Whitman's radio was out. He and the mortar platoon leader ran toward the section of woods that was the company objective, and on their way met Tech. Sgt. Mario Scapoli, who was with two squads of Mason's platoon. Mason was severely wounded and had been taken to the battalion aid station. Whitman ordered these men to secure the objective, but they dug in several yards from the right location. He got them moving and went to look for more men. Minutes later Scapoli's group ran headlong into a line of entrenched German infantry.[23]

Pvt. Anthony J. Kapela was the only medic left, and he had both to treat the wounded and help them get to the edge of the woods. Kapela had already been recommended for a Silver Star for actions a few days before.[24] Whitman, meanwhile, having unloaded a full magazine from his carbine at three Germans, ran back to Scapoli and told him there were enemy instead of the 2d Platoon on his left. He then alternately ran and crawled toward Company G's location until a shell exploded overhead in the trees, showering him and others with hot metal and wood splinters. Whitman was down for a time, and then he recovered and located his 2d Platoon and Company G. He told Weston to get his men to Scapoli's last

Combat medic Anthony Kapela, 376th Infantry Regiment. [Courtesy Anthony Kapela]

known location, where they found thirteen survivors who had been driven back by a counterattack.[25]

Whitman and the commander of Company G reviewed the situation in the early afternoon. They believed there was no hope of taking the woods, that all they could do was try to get as many out as possible. Supporting artillery kept more enemy tanks from getting into the woods, but it was impossible for the depleted rifle companies to take the area.[26] About 3:30 PM, a battalion staff officer told them to "hang on" and wait for Company E. A half-hour later, Whitman, barely able to walk with a leg wound, decided that he had had enough. Scapoli helped him to the edge of the trees, where they found two wiremen with a field telephone. For the first time since the attack began, he could speak directly to the battalion commander, Lt. Col. O. C. Martin, who told him that he was bringing up the relieving company. "Sorry, Colonel," replied Whitman, "it's too late. We are coming out. We are being murdered."[27] Fewer than thirty Company F soldiers of 124 who began the attack came out of the Bannholz Woods. Whitman and Mason were wounded; Wilson was dead.[28] Colonel Martin recalled that morale in the company was low at the end of the fighting that day.[29] "It was a morning of terror and confusion, where the enemy was just as apt to appear behind you as in front of you."[30]

Clearing the Triangle

LIMITED ATTACKS ENDED ON 15 February 1945. Corps and division staffs developed a plan to clear the Triangle, cross the Saar River, and prepare to support an attack on Trier. Patton had doubts about the leadership of the 94th Infantry Division. He had recently told Maloney "somewhat angrily" that his division's rate of nonbattle casualties was the highest within Third Army. He added that if the division did not improve, "Maloney himself would become a nonbattle casualty." Patton also talked to representatives from each rifle company in the division and praised them for their successes. He was not completely satisfied, though, telling them "very frankly that the 94th had lost more men as prisoners of war than all the other troops I had commanded during my entire military service. . . . I then patted General Maloney on the back." He left believing that the 94th Infantry Division would improve.[31]

The departure of the 11th Panzer Division removed a major threat, but Eisenhower was determined to retain a strong reserve, in the form of the experienced 10th Armored Division. He would allow Patton to have it only if the renewed attacks by the 94th Division broke cleanly through the Switch line. Plans called for Maloney's 301st and 302d Regiments to turn the German flank west of Orscholz and take Saar crossings at Serrig, Rodt, and Taben. The armor, with the 376th Infantry attached, would push north and east to take crossings opposite Ockfen and Ayl.[32] A hard rain was falling early on 19 February when the attack began. Resistance was stiff in some places and weak in others, reflecting the eroding capabilities of the units that stayed behind after the departure of the 11th Panzer. The Americans had made their breakthrough by dark and moved quickly to sweep the interior of the triangle. Eisenhower's operations officer had approved use of the armored division only within the confines of the triangle. This did not include committing it across the Saar River, but that restriction had little effect on Patton and Walker, who saw the chance to finally clear the area as far as Trier.[33]

It did not take long to exploit the penetrations that developed after the GIs broke through the hard shell of resistance. Prisoners indicated that even the Trier area was lightly defended. Contrary to the intent of SHAEF, the 10th Armored Division (Maj. Gen. William H. H. Morris Jr.) was ready on 21 February to stay in the fight and cross the Saar.[34] There was one problem, though: no one had ordered forward any assault boats. The XX Corps G-3 later recalled that the Third Army had not prepared for a river crossing or engineering operations to begin so early in the exploitation of the triangle.[35] The attack was moving so fast that there was also no time for thorough reconnaissance, and delay in crossing gave the Germans time to strengthen defenses.[36] It is unclear exactly why the corps and army staffs neglected to anticipate an early requirement for bridging equipment, but it certainly was a possibility they and their commanders should have anticipated.

Colonel McClune's 376th Regiment, attached to the 10th Armored, reached Ayl shortly after the defenders left, but the hour for the river crossing came and went without the arrival of either engineers or assault boats. An officer from the armored division's engineer battalion finally arrived on the afternoon of 21 February with handful of men to announce only that the rest of his unit's trucks were lost. It was late afternoon when the equipment finally arrived, and Morris and McClune directed that crossings go at two sites. Enemy machine gunners on the east bank of the Saar River poured so much fire across the narrow river valley that soldiers from a chemical battalion manning smoke generators dared not expose themselves to refuel the engines. Riflemen had to haul the heavy canvas and wood assault boats across the flood plain in full view of the enemy. Fire killed or wounded two of the three rifle battalion commanders, and McClune took personal charge of the crossing until he was wounded by shell fragments and evacuated to an aid station. There was little he could do, though, and the attack lost momentum. Additional boats did not reach Ayl until about 10:00 PM, and the 376th tried another crossing an hour later. The infantry eventually reached the east bank and attacked the enemy entrenched in the bluffs. Stiff resistance and the inability of U.S. tanks to get across the Saar until a bridge was built made expansion of the bridgehead nearly impossible.[37]

Walker had intended for Ockfen to be the main crossing site, but the relatively unopposed emplacement of tank-capable Class 40 bridges at Taben and Serrig changed the plan. Walker and Morris decided to redirect the half-tracks and tanks of the 10th Armored to the less risky and more suitable bridge crossing at Taben, which the 302d Infantry had already seized. The dismounted armored infantry would meanwhile cross at Ockfen through a 376th bridgehead and join the vehicles at the high ground at Irsch, a town on the river's east bank. From there, the armor would head east on the highway toward the town of Zerf and then turn north on Trier.[38] The armored infantrymen completed their crossing at Ockfen by midday on 24 February.[39] One officer later said the fight in the hills above the Saar was "worse than Bastogne. We lost more vehicles and men. The enemy was sitting on the hills where we couldn't find them to get at them with artillery. . . . There was not enough infantry left at the end to flush out the hills and clear out the gun positions."[40]

"We Have Something Urgent Coming Up"

To SECURE THE CRITICAL ZERF AREA, Walker turned to the 5th Ranger Battalion.[41] For the past several days, these men, under Lt. Col. Richard P. Sullivan, had maintained an outpost line in the Saar valley. They now had a "true Ranger job. . . . [L]ead the way through virgin enemy territory until you find yourselves all alone, surrounded by the enemy . . . and hold no matter what the enemy throws at you—at any cost!" remarked one man.[42] The battalion was the product of Army interest early in the war in the highly trained commando units created by the British. Volunteers had to be experienced officers and NCOs in excellent health and superb physical condition. They had to pass a mental aptitude test and undergo extremely intensive physical conditioning. Prospective rangers qualified with several weapons, and while they did not undergo airborne training, they had to be prepared to use a parachute.[43] William Boyd said that the training "really helped us; we got to know our weapons and we were geared up in our type of work. Also, we got to know each other and respected each other, which helps when you are in [situations] of confusion and death. Our relationship with our officers was the best right from the . . . platoon leader to the Bn. commander. . . . I was lucky to have had two platoon leaders that were the best as a person and leader. Both were KIA."[44] The battalion was activated at Camp Forrest, Tennessee, in September 1943. Including its medical detachment, it had an authorized strength of twenty-seven officers and 489 enlisted men.[45] Walter N. McIlwain, wartime first sergeant of Company

B who was to retire from the Army as a lieutenant colonel, would recall, "I don't believe there could have been any better trained, better motivated, or better led unit."[46]

Sullivan, the battalion commander, a twenty-seven-year-old native of Massachusetts,[47] arrived at General Maloney's headquarters at about 11:00 AM on 23 February, where the corps and division G-3s briefed him on the mission. His battalion would pass that night through the bridgehead at Taben, move seven thousand yards undetected over difficult and unfamiliar ground behind enemy lines, cut the Irsch-Zerf road, and wait for relief by the 10th Armored Division. Sullivan and his S-3 then went to the 302d Infantry headquarters, while the battalion XO directed assembly of the widely dispersed companies.[48] Raymond M. Herlihy, a Company D platoon leader who had been a first sergeant before he received a battlefield commission, would remember, "Now we were together and would fight, not piecemeal or disjointed, but as a unit. . . . [I]t meant a great deal to your pride and integrity and every Ranger would do his utmost to succeed."[49] Tom Sloboda, the first sergeant of Company C, however, "had a funny feeling that we were going to have a rough time."[50]

Chilling darkness shrouded the Saar Valley by the time the last of the ranger companies reached Taben, where intermittent German artillery fire had been little more than a nuisance until two rounds nailed a platoon from Company A (Capt. Charles H. "Ace" Parker) and caused twenty-four casualties. "Most of 1st platoon is gone," reported the S-3.[51]

At 8:00 PM, as Company B led the battalion, minus its rear command post and administrative and supply elements, to the two-foot-wide footbridges across the Saar, more artillery hit the area.[52] Sullivan and Capt. Edward Luther, the S-3, with the 2d Platoon of Company B, under 1st Lt. Lou Gombosi, reached the headquarters of the 302d Infantry, where that regiment's XO said that his unit had been unable to expand its bridgehead. This news was "considerably different" from what he had been told earlier in the day, and Sullivan knew it meant that his men would have to negotiate more enemy-held territory than expected. He sent Gombosi's platoon back to intercept the main body of the battalion and guide it to them, and he went with Luther to reconnoiter the ground ahead. They returned to the 302d headquarters area, where they joined the rest of the battalion, which Gombosi had led up. About 11:00 PM, Sullivan briefed the company commanders, set his compass for an azimuth of ten degrees and led the battalion toward the enemy.[53]

From the river valley, the Irsch-Zerf road ran east about a mile and a half across fairly flat ground, then uphill toward the southeast before it intersected a line of Westwall bunkers south of Trier. The final objective was about another mile to the east.[54] Only one east-west logging trail ran through the forest in a direction favorable to the route of attack. Companies C (Capt. Jack A. Snyder), D (Capt. George R. Miller), and F (1st Lt. John J. Reville) marched in column on the battalion's left; Companies A (Captain Parker), E (1st Lt. James F. Greene Jr.) and B (Capt. Bernard M. Pepper) were on the right.[55] Pressed by time and hampered by the difficult ground, bad weather, and pitch-black darkness, they moved at arm's length but still lost contact with one another. Artillery caused several more casualties and "obliterated" a forward observer team. Enemy patrols operated throughout the area. There were several skirmishes and casualties. "We were making too much noise passing through the brush," Sullivan later recalled. With the extra gear they carried, the men could hardly avoid making a racket. Handles on the mines rattled, tired men dropped ammunition boxes or bumped into each other. They came under more artillery fire sometime later.[56] Under the circumstances it is not hard to understand that Company A veered off course and cut through the Company B column. Unfortunately, this separated Gombosi's men and the weapons platoon from the rest of his company (B).[57]

Sullivan halted the battalion at a checkpoint before daybreak on 24 February, hoping the separated platoons would catch up. He did not know that they would be gone for most of the action. An enemy patrol hit Company D. One of its platoons swung wide to engage the enemy flank while another "fixed" them, prevented them from maneuvering. The rangers took about fifty prisoners and lost two men killed.[58] Sullivan sent out patrols, which located an alternate way from the area by 8:30 AM. He told his artillery observer to ensure that friendly batteries knew the new route.[59]

After another brief halt about 9:30 AM, enemy troops hit Company D again. Captain Miller sent Herlihy's platoon to outflank them. Grenade explosions flashed in the shadows. Bullets ripped through the trees, snapping limbs and plowing into soldiers with sickening thuds. "There was no artillery nor mortars—only rifles and machine guns. The fight was intense—very intense," recalled Herlihy.[60]

As the rangers pushed ahead through the forest, they captured both individual Germans and a group of about thirty at a complex of earth-covered bunkers. Another prisoner was a German army doctor, taken when his vehicle strayed too close to the rangers as they neared the objective. He was stunned to find Americans so far behind the lines.[61] Nearing the objective, Sullivan took a chance and selected a relatively exposed route that would keep the battalion on schedule. They had had little success in bypassing defenders in the forest, and time was important. Intermittent enemy artillery was still hitting the area. The 10th Armored Division was fighting at Irsch and would soon be on the main road leading toward the rangers' objective. After a patrol found that a settlement called Kalfertshaus, located just south of the objective, was occupied only by a few terrified civilians, the men ran across the open area in groups after dark at fifteen-minute intervals. When most of the rangers settled down for some sleep, Sullivan sent a patrol to reconnoiter two nearby buildings. The men took more prisoners and lost one man killed.[62]

Early on 25 February, the rangers finished clearing the Kalfertshaus area and an enemy armored vehicle fired a few rounds before it withdrew.[63] Company E cut the Irsch-Zerf road and occupied the objective ahead of the rest of the battalion. It was a poor defensive position, only about eight hundred by eight hundred yards in size, and the enemy could use the surrounding woods as covered avenues of approach. It was hard to see farther than a man could throw a hand grenade, and since nearly everyone had to occupy a place on the perimeter, the Kalfertshaus area was reopened to enemy occupation.

"From that point," Sullivan would recall, "we had trouble."[64] Company A, which had left a few men near the Kalfertshaus, was hit first by artillery about 3:45 PM, then by about two hundred enemy "heavily armed with automatic weapons and *panzerfaust*."[65] Sullivan noted, "We did everything we could for [Company A] with supporting fire and told them to withdraw to the southernmost part of the battalion defense position."[66] Company D also reported trouble. First, armored vehicles halted outside the perimeter and were firing directly at the foxholes. However, the two sides were too close for the safe adjustment of artillery. Someone then told Captain Miller that German trucks were slowing down to drop off infantrymen.[67] These were about four hundred soldiers from Gebirgsregiment 136 of the 2d Gebirgsdivision (mountain division). Their division commander had ordered them to kill the Americans "to the last man."[68] Ray Herlihy's platoon, however, "piled them up. It became obvious we would experience ammo problems. Finally, I called Bn. Hqts. and explained our status. I radioed for artillery fire directly on our position. The men were advised to get down and the artillery opened up loud and long . . . the effect was devastating."[69]

The attack was over by dark. Yet the Germans were still able to prevent an artillery liaison plane from accurately dropping extra ammunition to the rangers, who spent the night improving their positions. It was a good thing they did, because the next major counterattack hit about 3:00 AM on the 26th.[70] Stellungskampfgruppe XII, under the command of Maj. Otto Kuppitsch, had about three hundred men. It had been raised in Heidelberg and comprised soldiers of widely varying capability. Its armament consisted mainly of small arms and machine guns, but it was well supported by mortars and artillery. Kuppitsch's mission was to support the mountain division and move "without delay to the west and link up with those units . . . near Irsch."[71]

Captain Miller (Company D) shifted BAR fire from one threatened spot to another. Captain Parker (Company A) took a dozen men to reinforce E, which had lost some ground and a few men. Company C (Capt. Jack A. Snyder) pulled back to form its own defense and held in place. Men recalled that the Germans charged headlong toward them, often shouting for them to surrender. Sullivan radioed for more artillery.[72] Snyder reported that after one barrage enemy dead lay every ten yards throughout the area.[73] Parker recalled, "It was impossible to identify between friendly and enemy troops. Artillery fire was heavy and close in and the only way to identify small-arms fire was to recognize the sound of friendly or enemy weapons."[74]

German rockets ("screaming meemies," as the GIs called them) remained a threat after the defeat of the ground attack. Tom Sloboda recalled, "One of the line Sgts. came to check on something (I don't remember what it was). We sat there for a while chewing the fat when he said he was going back to his position and left. He was not more than 15 or 20 feet from the C.P. when we heard one of those screaming meemies coming in. Everybody hit the floor. After about 2 or 3 minutes we went out to see the damage and there was the Sgt. lying on the ground. We had to roll him onto a raincoat to take him to the Bn. C.P. I think every bone in his body was broken [by the concussion]."[75]

Relief of the Rangers

TANKS AND HALF-TRACKS, meanwhile, did not reach Irsch until the afternoon of 24 February, and even then they were several miles from the rangers' blocking position. Gombosi's Company B platoon, which was separated from the rest of its battalion, eventually reached Serrig, one of the Saar crossing sites. Gombosi and his men could have remained there, for they knew that trying to link up with their battalion would be difficult in the extreme. About this time, Lt. Col. Jack Riley of the 10th Armored Division's 21st Tank Battalion was in Serrig with his own men and elements of an armored infantry battalion. He was under orders to link up with the rangers as soon as possible. Gombosi asked if his men could go with them. They moved out over nearly impassable back roads trying to reach the balance of the armored infantry, who were still on foot and fighting with the 94th Division opposite Ockfen.[76]

At the edge of Irsch, the lieutenant in charge of a tank platoon reported to Riley that no friendly troops were in sight. The tanks edged into the town as far as a roadblock. After firing on it to drive out any defenders, they decided it was unmanned and drove on as a third tank slowly rolled up. Just then, the sharp crack of an anti-tank gun echoed between the buildings, and the newly arrived tank jerked to a halt. Flames sprouted from it an instant later. A *panzerfaust* round then slammed into the thin armor of the platoon's fourth tank. Landsers put an *ofenrohr* (German equivalent of a bazooka, literally "stovepipe") rocket into another tank. Two M-5 light tanks came under fire from a panzer. The only one that did not catch fire had been hit in an empty fuel tank. It was almost dark on 24 February.[77]

Riley's S-3 ran to Gombosi and his platoon sergeant, Tech. Sgt. McIlwain, and told them to help.[78] Gombosi's background as a farmer, woodsman, hunter, and agriculture teacher had served him well so far. *Battle Experiences*, a report by Headquarters, ETO, described his methods. GIs could often locate German crew-served weapons positions by listening for conversations and other noises. The lieutenant reported that enemy soldiers often walked and talked quite openly unless they knew Americans were nearby. He often crawled to within fifteen or twenty feet of their positions without detection. He tried to take experienced men on patrols, and before the mission he explained the details of the operation so that each man knew what to do.[79]

Bill Boyd, of Company E, was with Gombosi's platoon. At the start of the operation, Boyd was at a field hospital in France recovering from a wound. "One day our battalion ambulance came to the hospital and I spotted it and told the driver I was going to go back with him [Boyd had not been discharged from the hospital]. The next day we left, I didn't tell anybody because I thought they would [otherwise] not let me go. I joined up with a platoon of Rangers from B Co. and we joined up with the 10th Arm'd. Div., which, by the way, was my old Div. when I volunteered for the Rangers."[80]

Burning tanks and exploding ammunition illuminated Irsch, and the rangers clearly saw about two dozen wounded enemy sitting propped up against a damaged building. One group of GIs burst into a tavern and found several elderly civilians drinking beer. The rangers took over sixty prisoners and set up roadblocks.[81] About 9:00 PM, the first of the armored infantry arrived on foot and began to clear the town, taking over two hundred prisoners. Riley later received orders to move east, link up with the rangers, and take Zerf. During that phase, German tank fire knocked out the two lead Shermans and hit the half-tracks carrying Gombosi's men just seconds after they dismounted.[82]

Intense artillery fire hit the column after daylight on 26 February. The infantry riding in the half-tracks could do little more than hunker down and wish they could crawl into their helmets. It took several hours to reach the rangers' blocking position.[83] Staff Sgt. Boyd found Sullivan and eagerly reported how he had "escaped" from the hospital to return to his unit. Sullivan replied that he had known he would do so to be with his buddies.[84]

Harassing artillery and rocket fire hit the rangers late that afternoon and continued into the night. Maj. Hugo Hefflefinger, the XO, and the S-4 brought up supplies and took back prisoners. A status report to 94th Division headquarters noted, "Ammo was almost expended. Estimated 200 enemy killed. Fighting strength [of the battalion], 250 EM and 16 officers. . . . Getting artillery in there."[85]

Dense fog blanketed the area early on 27 February, when an estimated two hundred enemy infantry blundered into the perimeter. The growling of Company A's St. Bernard mascot alerted the men, who set up a hasty ambush. Machine-gun bullets from three sides ripped into the intruders, and about 145 of them surrendered. An unknown number were killed or wounded. Prisoners reported two conflicting reasons for their apparent error: some said their unit stumbled by accident onto the Americans; others said they had had orders to attack.[86]

The same day, Walker ordered Maloney to expand the Saar River bridgeheads and support the 10th Armored Division's attack on Trier. Maloney's staff developed a plan that called for the capture of several key hills east of the river, and it would require a very high degree of control to coordinate the attacks of six rifle battalions on the objectives. Maloney also attached the 5th Ranger Battalion to the 301st Infantry Regiment.[87] Col. Roy Haggerty, the commander of the regiment, ordered the rangers to stay in place pending receipt of further orders. He gave Sullivan four TDs, four tanks, and two half-tracks with .50 caliber machine guns. The exhausted Sullivan had no choice but to continue an operation that had

*Lt. Col. R. P. Sullivan, commander of the 5th Ranger
Battalion in 1944–1945.* [Courtesy R. P. Sullivan]

expanded far beyond anything for which he had planned. In turn, he warned Haggerty not to let the infantry "come to our position at night without letting us know. Otherwise, we will shoot the hell out of you."

Haggerty replied he would notify the rangers when his troops were present. Nonetheless, a rifle company accidentally entered an area in which the rangers had previously heard small-arms fire. Possibly the company commander assumed that no one would shoot at them, because they were in friendly territory. It is unclear whether he tried to contact the rangers, but it is clear that some riflemen headed directly toward their foxholes. Rangers ordered them to stop and identify themselves. It is unknown whether or not they did, but the rangers later maintained that they gave a challenge and waited for the countersign. When no response came, the rangers opened fire. A moment later, they learned they were firing at Americans. Three infantrymen were killed and seven were wounded. Sullivan "was very sorry but as far as we were concerned I had notified everyone where we were. Where they had given the password they had gotten through all right. Where they didn't they were shot at. I don't know where the 302d Regt was at that time. The passage of information should have gotten through to the 302d Inf from the 301st Inf. I felt I had done everything in my power to divert such a situation."[88]

Not only was the ranger battalion not relieved, it received orders to attack to the south. There was continual enemy fire, and disruptive, though not overwhelming counterattacks. A prisoner said the 2d Gebirgs division had a "personal grudge and were simply out to destroy" the ranger battalion.[89]

Attack and counterattack followed, then stalemate after 28 February. U.S. artillery, which had had little impact in this heavily forested area until this point, finally began concerted counterbattery fire, which lasted for hours. This effort shifted to direct support of the rangers in a renewal on 2 March of the push to the south. Captain Parker decided on a desperate measure to gain control over the situation. To the shock of his ranking prisoner, he ordered several Germans to get into the open. Using a working telephone located in a bunker, he told the officer to contact his headquarters and tell his commander to stop the artillery before it killed some of his own men. The plan worked for a while, but German armor still managed to stay in action.[90]

Enemy artillery eventually returned and lasted for hours without letup, saturating the hill where the rangers were operating. Gombosi later said, "As soon as the SP [self-propelled artillery] fire lifted the Germans infiltrated through the pine trees, and occupied foxholes within our lines, at times right next to our men. Due to the heavy underbrush we had practically no field of fire. The Germans set up a machine-gun position about 30 yards from my CP foxhole. We were trying to hold an area of about 200 square yards with less than 20 men. We were so close to the Germans that when one of them made a lot of noise, I thought it was one of my men and called to him to be quiet." By 4 March, only Gombosi, McIlwain, and two other men were left in the platoon.[91] Once, when he was digging a foxhole, Gombosi decided to stop work and move to a spot where he had better observation; several hours later, rocket fire slammed into the place where he had been. When he had time to check on the position, he saw a fifteen-foot-diameter crater.[92]

Fewer than two hundred utterly exhausted men staggered from a bloody, crater-filled hill nine days after the start of what was supposed to have been a forty-eight-hour mission. Sullivan had taken 378 men and twenty officers into battle on 23 February. By 4 March, casualties were two officers and forty-five enlisted men killed; nine officers and 206 men wounded, many of who fell at the final objective after the original mission.[93] Enemy casualties through the period at the roadblock were about three hundred killed and 328 prisoners. After a rest and refit, the 5th Ranger Battalion saw additional combat, supervised military government operations, and guarded prisoners. It was in Austria at the end of the war.[94]

Elements of the 10th Armored Division had meanwhile headed north to Trier, and on 1 March were fighting roadblocks outside the ancient town. The approaches were such that the armor had no way to bypass the hastily prepared obstacles. Under a full moon that night, GIs overran the last defenses and reached the Moselle River at the Römerbrücke, where there are pilings dating to the Romans. Troops prevented the Germans from connecting a blasting machine detonator to explosives, and the remaining residents awoke the next morning to the sound of American tanks and half-tracks rumbling along the cobblestone streets. Besides a drunken officer who had failed to see to the destruction of the bridge, GIs captured another seventeen officers having a late-night party not far away.[95]

Fighting in the Saar-Moselle triangle began in January and climaxed with the assault on Trier in early March 1945. The relatively new 94th Infantry Division began the fight with limited combat experience; it had not yet conducted offensive operations at a regimental or division scale. It fought evenly matched early on, and while the 11th Panzer Division was present, it was also outgunned. Support from the 8th Armored Division was tentative and only after the entry of the 10th Armored Division into the battle did the XX Corps finally exploit the early gains of the 94th. At the Saar crossings, the Germans made excellent use of the high ground, and the weather and terrain forced commanders to separate the armored infantry from their half-tracks and tanks. These conditions helped offset the armored division's mobility. Even an elite unit like the 5th Ranger Battalion faced significant challenges. Attacks against it were persistent and often well supported by artillery and other indirect fire. Such units were neither manned nor equipped for sustained, high-intensity combat, though they habitually fought that way. Another indication that the Americans did not always have overwhelming combat power is the fact that the ranger battalion had to continue operations for several more days than planned, at an extremely high cost in specially trained men.

By the first days of March, Bradley's north flank was alongside the Ninth Army's burgeoning offensive toward the Rhine. First and Third Armies were closing in on the great river too, in operation Lumberbjack. Patton had two options after clearing the Saar-Moselle triangle and taking Trier. Third Army could turn to the south and secure the Saar industrial area, or it could continue through the contested Eifel Highlands and the Moselle Valley to Koblenz. A complementary 6th Army Group attack, Undertone, was also under way. Bradley had misgivings about the 6th Army Group's attack, and he secured Eisenhower's approval for Third Army to expand its part of Lumberbjack by making a major attack south across the Moselle to link up with the 6th. Enemy units were in growing confusion, ordered to hold at all costs east of the Rhine despite the pull of common sense to escape an impending trap. The intransigence of Hitler and his senior commanders contributed to the ultimate destruction of what was left of his armies.

Though the wet weather made cross-country travel very difficult for maneuver units in the 12th Army Group, those that could remain on the roads gained speed as they headed east. All was going well until the evening of 7 March, when SHAEF began a "raiding mission" on Bradley's forces to use as reinforcements for the 6th Army Group. Bradley was "furious" and in danger of losing the argument to keep his army group intact—that is, until he got a call about a bridge across the Rhine.[96]

CHAPTER 15

"LIKE A BOLT FROM THE BLUE," MARCH– APRIL 1945

AMUR, BELGIUM, EVENING, 7 March 1945: Maj. Gen. Harold R. Bull, Eisenhower's G-3, was in an after-dinner conference with Omar Bradley, lobbying for the transfer of combat divisions from the First Army to the 6th Army Group, when Courtney Hodges called with some electrifying news. A corps had seized a Rhine River bridge at Remagen and was pushing forces across the river. Bradley knew this would upset the plan for the British (with the Ninth U.S. Army) to cross the Rhine first later in the month. He turned to Bull and declared with a grin, "There goes your ballgame. . . . Courtney's gotten across the Rhine on a bridge."[1]

However, Remagen was not on the list of potential crossing sites. In other words, the planner's war had "gone to pieces." The two generals argued about the situation for hours. Staff officers hovered around Bradley, who sat opposite Bull in a leather chair next to a planning map. Bull did not believe that any crossing between Koblenz and Mainz offered the potential that a crossing north of the Ardennes did. There was something to be said for this position, since Remagen was so far from the important Ruhr industrial area. Bradley phoned Eisenhower, who told him to hold the bridgehead and get as much combat power across the river as he could.[2]

Roer to the Rhine

HOW COULD AN UNEXPECTED CROSSING of the Rhine cause a problem at this time in the war? Plans had envisioned a Rhine crossing as soon as practicable during the campaign. Staffs at all levels of command had spent many hours exploring supply and engineer bridging requirements, line haul transport capacity, artillery support, deception plans, wire and radio communications requirements, and camouflage. Engineers also studied every aspect of the Rhine's flood history and the topography of the entire river valley. It was a planning effort second only to Overlord. Eisenhower correctly believed that any crossing operation would be "a tactical and engineering operation of the greatest magnitude," and he vowed to "spare no efforts in allotting such operations the maximum support possible."[3] For example, staffs from 21 Army Group began their work in October 1944, at a time when the Allies' logistical situation was doubtful and German resurgence had all but guaranteed the war would continue through winter. General Simpson's Ninth U.S. Army staff planned on using naval landing craft and tracked amphibious landing vehicles. Officers estimated a requirement for 138,000 tons of supplies, largely road and bridge construction material and ammunition, to be on hand before the attack. Like Overlord, the assault across the Rhine had to be a no-fail undertaking.[4]

Eisenhower as late as mid-January 1945 reiterated that the Allies should not batter needlessly against defenses everywhere on the front, and he agreed with Montgomery's call for a concentrated blow weighted in the north. On the other hand, the Allies could not afford to commit a large force to engage German positions that would be left west of the Rhine if the final attack was limited to a narrow front. Letting the Air Forces perform such a task against a relatively unopposed Third Army flank in France in August 1944 was one thing. It was a different matter with consistently undependable flying weather and enemy forces fighting at home with short supply lines.

Bradley's G-3 Plans chief had stated in late 1944 that there were no suitable crossing sites between Koblenz and Mainz, an area that included Remagen.[5] In other words, he too recommended the northern approaches to the river and thereby the Ruhr. By February 1945, after months of discussion, a compromise plan called for the Allies to clear the enemy from the west bank of the Rhine, reach the river on a broad front, and make the main effort in the north. There was something for everybody in that decision. Yet early 1945 was not a time to take unnecessary risks. In addition to the operational concerns about by-passed enemy units noted above, there was a logistical basis for decisions that led to crossings on a broad front. Even the Ruhr's modern road system had limited capacity, especially under wear and tear from heavy military vehicles. A flood of such traffic might cause gridlock; the flow of men and materiel across the Rhine could stop unless there were several bridgeheads with defensible approaches and the assurance that engineers could construct and maintain high-capacity tactical bridging. Events at Remagen eventually demonstrated that concern about traffic congestion was well founded.

Another reason for conducting a large-scale supplementary attack south of the British zone was that the Americans wanted, and deserved, to be in on the kill. The first step in this direction was the Ninth Army's crossing of the Roer west of Cologne, beginning on 23 February, as the floodwaters from the Roer dams started to recede. By the first week of March, objectives of the 12th Army Group were those prescribed under Operation Lumberjack. The army group would clear the enemy from the area west of the Rhine north of the Moselle and capture Cologne.[6] Deeper targets included the Frankfurt-Kassel area, where the army group would probably draw enemy reserves into battle.[7] Lumberjack began on schedule against less than 100,000 frontline enemy troops of Army Group B. Resistance was light in most places,[8] and one wonders to what extent the average German soldier thought this was the beginning of the end. Third Army's attack slowed due to paved roads severely damaged by military traffic and secondary roads turned to slush by a late winter thaw. Divisions' frontages were reduced to the width of the roads on which they operated. Dense ground fog and steady rain often eliminated air support, and there were still some resolute Germans in well-organized positions.[9] First Army, however, broke out of the confines of the Eifel and reached the sprawling Cologne Plain. Gone at last was the rugged ground that had slowed operations since October.

Senior American commanders could now realistically discuss the possibility of capturing a Rhine bridge intact, though few believed the Germans would let one fall into their hands. In fact, as early as February they had authorized air attacks against bridges, since, they assumed, the Germans would destroy them anyway. Destruction of the spans at Neuss and Oberkassel in the Ninth Army zone seemed to validate this line of thinking.[10] GIs actually crossed the bridge at Ürdingen, but they could not exploit the coup before the enemy brought it down too.[11]

One of the participants in Lumberjack was First Army's III Corps. When the operation began, the corps front line was about thirty-five air miles from the Rhine. It had to first cross the Roer south of Düren, then the Erft River about fifteen miles west of the Rhine. It would then link up with Third Army's northern wing along the Ahr River, which emptied into the Rhine near the town of Remagen. To get his units (1st Infantry, 9th Infantry, 78th Infantry, and the 9th Armored Division) across the Roer as fast as possible at the lowest human cost, the corps commander, Maj. Gen. John Millikin, sent them singly through existing Roer bridgeheads rather than trying to capture new ones that might allow a faster crossing. This marked the beginning of an exploitation that reminded some of the previous summer's pursuit across France. Within a few days, elements of the corps were less than seven miles from the Rhine. Unfortunately, the exhausting pace of operations had taken a toll on the infantry. "The mud and daytime attacks alone would have been enough to produce fatigue, but hardly was there a commander who did not continue to push his men . . . to overcome the advantage that flat, open fields afforded the enemy in observation."[12] Maj. Gen. John W. Leonard, commander of the 9th Armored Division, said that even jeeps had trouble in the muddy Rhine Plain.[13]

Command Views

JOHN MILLIKIN, FIFTY-SIX, had commanded the III Corps since October 1943. The corps had deployed to Europe in August 1944 and was eventually assigned to the Third Army. It performed well during the latter stages of the Ardennes campaign, but Millikin and Patton never got along. Patton thought Millikin was "very amateurish compared to the other corps commanders. I don't like him and never have."[14] These misgivings might have stemmed in part from the fact that Millikin had not led a division in combat before he took command of a corps. Another reason may have been that Millikin's father-in-law was former chief of staff Peyton C. March, who had been John J. Pershing's World War I rival for power in the army. Patton had been Pershing's protégé.[15] It is unknown whether Courtney Hodges had reservations about the III Corps' transfer to First Army. Perhaps the cavalryman-led III Corps did not fit well into the infantry-led First Army. It was hard to "work directly under the eye of Courtney Hodges, particularly in any operation that was critical enough to strain Hodges's nerves and to focus on the First Army attention that might become embarrassing to Hodges himself."[16]

Yet by the end of February Hodges was telling an aide that "III Corps . . . now seems to have struck its stride." Hodges and Millikin on 28 February met for two hours to discuss upcoming operations.[17] One must presume that Hodges reviewed the corps' performance to date and that he might have mentioned the capture of a Rhine bridge,[18] but no specific directives on the matter resulted from the session. Millikin and his division commanders had no doubt considered the possibility of taking a bridge, though Hodges's stated priority in Lumberjack was to reach the Ahr River and contact Third Army. The first known date that

Millikin and Hodges specifically discussed the possibility of taking the Remagen Bridge was 4 March, but it was hard to devise a scenario in which the Germans would not destroy the span to keep it from falling into American hands. Hodges's chief of staff on 7 March told Millikin that the corps should take a bridge if it had the opportunity to do so; however, the First Army was not the main effort, and it could not spend its resources to conduct an attack aimed specifically at crossing the Rhine at the expense of linking up with the Third Army.[19]

Millikin's orders to his division commanders through 4 March reflected compliance with stated plans. To reinforce the importance of reaching the Ahr, Hodges on the night of 5 March increased the width of the III Corps front opposite that river, thereby forcing the corps to devote more troops to the Ahr instead of the Rhine and Remagen. Despite this, Millikin told General Leonard of the 9th Armored Division to "attack aggressively in an effort to seize the Ahr River bridges and possibly the Rhine River bridge [at Remagen] intact."[20] He pointed at a map and told Leonard to look at the "little black strip of bridge at Remagen. . . . If you happen to get that, your name will go down in glory."[21]

The chief of staff of Army Group B, Generalmajor Carl Wagener, believed that the Ardennes attack had upset American plans and cost them freedom of action. Berlin rejected the sensible alternative of fighting delaying actions west of the Rhine and they ultimately shortened the war themselves. The Germans expected the main Allied attack to take place north of the Ardennes after the Americans had neutralized the Schwammenauel Dam. All reserves were committed by 1 March.[22] By then, a single word characterized the German situation in the Rhineland—confusion. Until March, *Wehrkreise*, or military districts, were responsible for securing the river line behind the withdrawing units that manned defenses. *Wehrkreis* commanders, who reported directly to the Waffen SS, jealously controlled their prerogatives and engaged in turf battles with field units. Anti-aircraft troops were vital to the defense of Rhine crossing sites, but they were part of the Luftwaffe, not the army, and they answered to neither the army nor the Nazi Party. At Remagen, an army officer was "combat commander" of the immediate bridge area, but he had only limited authority over other nearby troops. An engineer officer was responsible for the bridge itself, an anti-aircraft officer exercised independent control of his units, and the Nazi Party controlled the local "people's army," or Volksstrum.[23]

Generalmajor Walther Botsch was probably the only person who fully understood the situation in the Remagen area. Unfortunately for his

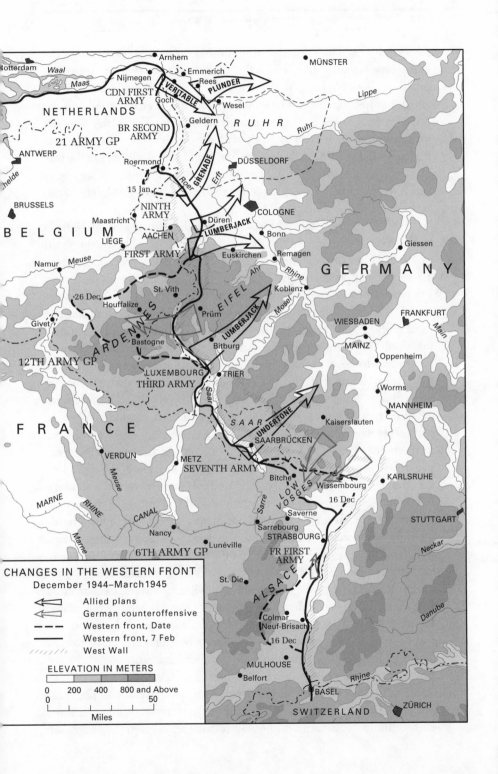

MÜNSTER

Arnhem
Emmerich
Rees
Nijmegen
PLUNDER
Waal
Maas
otterdam
CDN FIRST
ARMY
VERITABLE
Goch
Wesel
Lippe
NETHERLANDS
Geldern
R U H R
Ruhr
BR SECOND
ARMY
21 ARMY GP
DÜSSELDORF
ANTWERP
Roermond
GRENADE
Roer
Erft
helde
15 Jan
BRUSSELS
NINTH
ARMY
COLOGNE
Maastricht
Düren
LUMBERJACK
B E L G I U M
AACHEN
Bonn
LIÈGE
Giessen
Namur
Meuse
FIRST ARMY
Euskirchen
Remagen
G E R M A N Y
26 Dec
St. Vith
A R D E N N E S
E I F E L
Koblenz
Ahr
Rhine
Houffalize
Prüm
FRANKFURT
Givet
LUMBERJACK
WIESBADEN
Bastogne
Bitburg
Mosel
MAINZ
12TH ARMY GP
Oppenheim
LUXEMBOURG
TRIER
THIRD ARMY
Saar
Worms
MANNHEIM
S A A R
Kaiserslauten
F R A N C E
UNDERTONE
VERDUN
METZ
SAARBRÜCKEN
KARLSRUHE
SEVENTH ARMY
Bitche
Meuse
Wissembourg
LOW
VOSGES
16 Dec
MARNE
RHINE
Sarre
Saverne
STUTTGART
CANAL
Nancy
Sarrebourg
Lunéville
STRASBOURG
Neckar
6TH ARMY GP
FR FIRST
ARMY
CHANGES IN THE WESTERN FRONT
December 1944–March 1945
St. Die
A L S A C E
Danube

⟸ Allied plans
⟸ German counteroffensive
– – – Western front, Date
—— Western front, 7 Feb
/////// West Wall
Colmar
Neuf-Brisach
16 Dec

ELEVATION IN METERS

0	200	400	800 and Above

MULHOUSE
Belfort
Rhine
0   50
BASEL
ZÜRICH
Miles
SWITZERLAND

successor, Botsch was ordered late on 6 March to take command of the LIII Corps, on such short notice that he did not have time to explain the situation. Botsch's boss, the commander of the 15th Army, ordered another corps commander to send someone to check personally on the situation at Remagen. This general sent his aide, Maj. Hans Scheller, with a few men, in two vehicles with instructions to take charge at Remagen and ensure the bridge was prepared for demolition. On the way to the town, the aide's vehicle became separated from the other one—which carried the radio. It was nearly midnight (6–7 March) when Scheller arrived at Remagen.[24]

Big stone towers stained black with decades of soot and grime from trains stood at each end of the Rhine bridge, which had been completed in 1916. Horse-drawn wagons, some pulling artillery pieces, lumbered across wooden planks laid over the rails and disappeared into the Erpler Ley tunnel entrance in the bluff on the east bank of the river. Hauptmann Karl Friesenhahn, the engineer officer who was immediately responsible for the bridge, had orders on the morning of 7 March to put in demolitions only when the Americans were within eight kilometers. But such orders had to be in written form from the commander responsible for the tactical defenses (troops at Cologne had recently destroyed a bridge prematurely), Hauptmann Willi Bratge, and even then the final order could be given only when destruction seemed "unavoidable." When he had earlier phoned Army Group B (Model's command) directly to ask for instructions, Bratge had been told by a duty officer that no one was particularly worried about Remagen. Bonn, it appeared, was in the most danger. Bratge had fewer than forty men under his direct control, and many of the anti-aircraft troops that morning joined troops fleeing to the east. At about 11:15 AM on 7 March, Major Scheller arrived at Bratge's headquarters to announce that he was now in command. Reports then arrived indicating that the Americans were on the high ground west of Remagen, but Scheller thought that it was still too early to destroy the bridge.[25]

As the III Corps swept toward the Ahr River, General Leonard told Brig. Gen. William M. Hoge, commander of the 9th Armored's Combat Command B (CCB), to take bridge if he could, though he knew that success might upset strategic plans.[26] Hoge sent one task force toward Ahr crossings west of Remagen and another under Lt. Col. Leonard Engeman (built around his own 14th Tank Battalion) toward the confluence of the Ahr and Rhine at Remagen. This was a liberal interpretation of the III Corps mission to give priority to Ahr crossings, and CCB had no specific orders to take a bridge, but it made sense given the geography of the area. Remagen sits in the Rhine Valley, with high ground on both east and west. The commander of Company A, 27th Armored Infantry Battalion, part of the task force, was 1st Lt. Karl Timmermann, son of an American father and a German mother. Timmermann's men moved out at 7:00 AM. A reconnaissance platoon and a platoon of new M-26 Pershing tanks accompanied the column, but there was no air support.[27]

About three hours later, 1st Lt. Harold E. Larsen, a liaison pilot from the 16th Armored Field Artillery Battalion, flew his unarmed single-engine plane toward the Remagen area. Bad weather had prevented flights on the preceding days, but as Larsen and his observer approached the Rhine Valley the clouds thinned out, and he began seeing enemy ground troops "fleeing eastward in an attempt to escape across the river." Then, at about 10:30, when he was still about two miles from the Rhine, he saw that the Ludendorff Bridge was intact. It was impossible for him to determine if it was capable of carrying heavy traffic. He radioed the news to his battalion commander, who in turn relayed the message to Hoge's headquarters.[28]

Just before noon, Timmermann's lead platoon entered the wooded high ground northwest of the town. GIs in the lead half-track dismounted and found an abandoned anti-tank gun pointed in their direction. Then they saw an opening in the trees. Timmermann rushed to find platoon leader 2d Lt. Emmett J. Burrows (the only officer besides Timmermann in the depleted company) standing at the edge of the tree line high above the Rhine. "Hey, Tim, take a look at that!" The railroad bridge was still intact.[29]

"Dammit, that's the Rhine; I didn't think it was that close," replied Timmermann. He radioed Colonel Engeman, the task force commander, who arrived within minutes. Not far behind was Timmermann's own battalion commander, Maj. Murray Deevers, and the commander of Company C, 27th, 1st Lt. William E. McMaster. They requested artillery fire using time-delayed fuses. These fuses would explode the rounds above the bridge and shower fragments on the enemy without causing great physical damage to the structure. The supporting artillery battalion refused to fire the mission because there were reports that friendly troops were in the area. No one could make the artillery fire-direction-center staff understand that these "friendlies" were the men who were asking for the fire in the first place. On the other hand, the reply might have been taken as tacit permission to take the bridge despite the orders to push to the Ahr. Deevers ordered Timmermann's and McMaster's companies into Remagen.

Maj. Ben Cothran, Hoge's S-3, came up about that time. The general had sent him to tell Engeman to go on and take the bridge if it was intact. Cothran radioed Hoge with the news. Engeman in turn ordered Timmermann to get his infantry moving immediately down the bluff and into the town. The force went in dismounted, however, and lost time. Engeman also told the lieutenant in charge of some of the big, new Pershing tanks to "barrel down the hill and go through the town and cover the bridge with tank fire, and if anybody attempted to demolish the bridge to liquidate them."[30]

Hoge arrived about 2:30 PM and kicked the attack into overdrive. He was not satisfied with what he thought was its slow pace. Engeman replied that he was "doing every damn thing possible." Though Company A was on foot, he had sent Company C into town by half-track.[31] Hoge weighed the odds of losing a battalion if the Germans blew the bridge while troops were on it. "I knew it was right," he later said. "I felt inside me that I could never live with the knowledge that I had given up that opportunity without making a try for it. . . . [H]ere was the opportunity of a lifetime."[32]

In town, meanwhile, Company A met little resistance, though Lieutenant Burrow's platoon apparently took some fire from a machine gun near the city hall. Two of the Pershings silenced the weapon and accompanied the riflemen toward the bridge. The men were hugging buildings to avoid snipers.[33] Most residents had put out white flags. Lieutenant McMaster (Company C) later said that if they had resisted, "we would have cut the town to ribbons."[34]

It was shortly after 3:00 PM. Prisoner reports reached Hoge that the bridge would be blown in forty-five minutes. He immediately informed Engeman.[35] Meanwhile, at the bridge, Major Deevers approached Timmermann and asked him if he could get his company across the bridge. "Well, we can try, sir," replied Timmermann. "Go ahead," directed Deevers. "What if it blows up in my face?" asked the lieutenant. Deevers did not say a word.[36]

A few riflemen and one or two of the Pershings were approaching the bridge when the road in front of them erupted in noise, smoke, and a shower of rocks and dirt. Engineer Friesenhahn had set off the cratering charge designed to keep tanks off the bridge. Scheller and Bratge were in the tunnel under the Erpler Ley Bluff. Friesenhahn was running across the span to see if Scheller would allow him to destroy the bridge itself when the concussion from an exploding tank round knocked him down. He lay dazed and barely conscious, hardly noticing the bullets zinging overhead.

Chaos reigned in the tunnel under the bluff. Terrified adults and children cowered in the shadows. Reluctant soldiers waited for a chance to surrender. Blinding, thick, white smoke from white-phosphorous shells drifted inside.

Friesenhahn was out for nearly fifteen minutes, and his men did not set off any more explosives during that time. Bratge, meanwhile, ran outside the tunnel, where he saw the American tanks firing round after round toward the tunnel. He found the stunned Friesenhahn and yelled at him to locate Scheller, who alone could give the order to bring down the bridge. Scheller gave the order, and Bratge watched as a lieutenant carefully wrote the exact wording and time. It was 3:20 PM when the major told Friesenhahn to set off the main charge. Friesenhahn then said he must also have a written copy of the order but quickly decided that there was no time for someone to write it. He took the firing device and gave the winding key a twist. Nothing. He turned the key again and again. Still nothing. There was not enough time to assemble a team to find the break in the wiring, but he found a sergeant willing to go out and ignite the charge by hand. The sergeant completed the mission and ran back toward the tunnel through the American fire.[37]

Engeman, meanwhile, had ordered the supporting engineer platoon leader, Lt. Hugh Mott, to check the bridge for explosives. He added that riflemen were at the bridge and would cover him.[38] Moments later, a thundering explosion erupted on the bridge. Thousands of tons of steel actually lifted up and seemed to hang for a second in the air. The GIs threw themselves to the ground. Those who dreaded crossing against what still could have been significant resistance on a bridge that might collapse under them breathed a sigh of relief for a second or two. But as the dust cleared, it was obvious they would have to go—the bridge was still intact. Sgt. Anthony Samele told platoon leader, Sgt. Mike Chinchar, "C'mon, Mike, we'll just walk it over."[39]

"Move on!" yelled Deevers.

Chinchar was the first to go. Timmermann was the first officer across. Chinchar told Pfc. Art Massie to "leapfrog me up as far as that blown hole [caused by the explosion]." Massie replied, "I don't want to go, but I will." With them was Sgt. Alex Drabik, who was the first American to reach the east bank. What concerned the men most, aside from the possibility of incineration by another explosion, was the possibility that enemy guns were in the Erpler Ley tunnel. Lieutenant Mott and his engineers were with them all the way. One of them reported, "We were cutting all the wires in sight and I suppose we cut a lot of communication wires, but we were playing it safe." Riflemen quickly shot out the electrical connection boxes. The engineers found that the blasting caps on some of the dud charges had themselves functioned properly. Four charges on the decking, however, were intact. One unexploded charge weighed an estimated five hundred pounds. After his men disarmed all the explosives they could find, Mott made a quick inspection of the bridge and declared it safe for infantry. He told Engeman that he could have it ready for tanks in two hours if he could get replacement planks.[40]

During the engineer inspection, the riflemen continued to work their way toward the east. One of the tanks still on the west side fired on snipers in a barge on the river. Platoon leader Staff Sgt. Joe DiLisio single-handedly cleared one of the bridge towers, while Chinchar and two men cleared the other located on the east bank. Drabik and some others reached the east bank and set up defensive positions in some bomb craters.[41]

When General Hoge told General Leonard about the capture of the bridge, Leonard remarked, "That's a hell of a note. Now we've got a bull by the tail, and caused a lot of trouble. But let's push it and put it up to corps." Leonard was aware of the overall plan but would not stifle the initiative of his leaders. He added, "We did some scratching of our heads at first, but General Hoge and I agreed that we couldn't even think of coming back once we had pushed across. The only thing to do was exploit the bridgehead."[42]

Millikin was away from his headquarters visiting the command post of the 78th Infantry Division. The III Corps chief of staff received word of the crossing about 4:30 PM, and it took several minutes for him to reach the corps commander and get his personal approval to shift the main effort from the Ahr crossings to Remagen. He also wanted the 9th Armored Division to exploit the bridgehead.[43]

Courtney Hodges received the news about 6:00 PM. He was determined to take "full advantage . . . of this great opportunity," and he told Millikin to go ahead and reinforce the new bridgehead.[44] Millikin's staff got things moving relatively quickly, considering that the entire operation had been unplanned. Before midnight, three battalions of artillery were in position to support the dozen tanks and about two hundred infantry across the river. That was the good news. The bad news was that the limited road net in the area would soon be hopelessly clogged with traffic.

Exploitation of the Bridgehead

PLATOON-SIZED GERMAN counterattacks hit Engeman's task force throughout the night of 7–8 March. His primary concerns were how to get the bridge ready for heavy equipment and how to keep the road clear for traffic that must cross the Rhine as soon as possible to secure the area and exploit the crossing. He and Major Deevers agreed that in light of the limited manpower available, they would have the infantry set up road-blocks on the high ground on the far side of the river. It was 10:00 PM, before Lieutenant Mott reported that the bridge was ready for traffic. Before many vehicles could cross, however, a TD got stuck in a gap in the planking and shut down the bridge until early the next morning.[45]

Neither side was ready to do battle on the east bank of the Rhine. In a deliberate attack, III Corps would have moved its units across the river in the order they would be used, and divisional units would have kept their integrity. But to take advantage of this unexpected opportunity, units had to move across the river as they became available. It was a very complex task to shift thousands of vehicles of every description from one direction of attack to another and to reorient communications circuits and even supply routes. Order could quickly disappear under such circumstances and turn an unprecedented opportunity into an

The collapsed Ludendorff Railroad Bridge at Remagen, Germany, March 1945. [Courtesy National Archives]

unsupportable disaster. Traffic control, not planning for anti-aircraft defense or construction of additional tactical bridges, became the most important task under such a river-crossing scenario. It was also important to build tactical bridges to supplement the Ludendorff Bridge, since it would have to be shut down at some point for repair. To gain control of, and establish unity of command over, the attacking units in the bridgehead, Millikin attached them to CCB, 9th Armored. Two of the first reinforcing units to come up were the 311th Regiment (78th Infantry Division) and 47th Regiment (9th Infantry Division). General Millikin ordered "maximum effort to exploit [the] bridgehead."[46]

Millikin soon replaced Hoge as site commander with Maj. Gen. General Louis A. Craig, commander of the 9th Infantry Division. This was not a slight to the very capable Hoge; rather, the corps commander believed the nature of the operation warranted an infantryman's experience. Craig began to set priorities for unit movement across the Rhine, while the 9th Armored controlled movement of units through Remagen and across the bridge. This helped simplify command lines, but Craig still had to deal with nine different headquarters in command of the soldiers across the river.[47]

Engeman's men were understandably jittery during the first hours after the crossing. Support was slow in coming, and there was a lingering chance that the Germans might still demolish the bridge behind them. A rumor of an impending withdrawal swept through the ranks not long after dark. Several men drifted back toward Remagen in a pattern of disorganization that lasted no more than an hour until Engeman's staff discovered what was happening and got the men back across.[48] Soldiers who crossed the Ludendorff Bridge after daylight on 8 March noticed a large wooden sign, blue with white letters, hanging from one of the bridge towers: "Cross the Rhine with Dry Feet, Courtesy 9th Arm'd. Div." An infantrymen told one of the tankers where he could put his courtesy. Elmer R. Wagner, a rifle squad leader in the 3d Battalion, 47th Infantry, later said, "The weather was miserably wet and the ground was sloppy. We couldn't lay down when we did stop. Men fell asleep when standing or walking." Platoon leader Roy Gordon saw "the body of a German soldier lying partially in the road, his lower body squashed flat by passing trucks."[49]

German Reactions

MILLIKIN AND HIS G-3 STRUCTURED the expansion of the bridgehead by three "phase lines" that would control the attack eastward. The first phase line marked the range of enemy small-arms fire. Reaching the second would push the Germans back far enough to eliminate observed artillery fire. The third extended beyond the range of most known enemy artillery.[50] For the first few days, however, the infantrymen could be little more than firemen, rushing from one threatened sector to another, because the expansion was going slowly. As a result, the Germans managed to keep the Americans from concentrating their force at a single location. Yet they were as unready for a battle as the GIs. Neither side had reserves. Many German combat units were still on the west bank, trying as hard as their enemy to cross the Rhine. Most senior officers were on the road working to organize the crumbling resistance when the Americans reached the river, and they were not in a position be of much influence on events. There was no chance that they could organize a defense strong enough to stop the Americans at water's edge. It was the morning of 8 March before the stalwart 11th Panzer Division, with about 4,000 men, twenty-five tanks, and eighteen artillery pieces, was ready to move to Remagen.[51] That division's assistant G-3 would recall that the move to the bridgehead was "ghastly . . . full of reminders of how desperate was our situation." When the lead elements of the division finally reached the area on 10 March, officers found it very hard to get a good picture of the situation. Model visited the division and gave the usual orders to hold at all costs, but he offered nothing in the way of practical support. The 11th Panzer G-3 thought that it "would be a fight to the death. Most believed they had nothing left to lose."[52]

Model designated an old warhorse, Generalleutnant Fritz Bayerlein, as the single commander at Remagen. Besides the 11th Panzer, he had the shell of the Panzer Lehr Division, with about three hundred men and fifteen tanks; another fifteen tanks and six hundred men that constituted the combat remnants of the 9th Panzer Division; plus five more tanks and some infantry from the 106th Panzer Brigade. Had the Germans been able to make even a moderately strong counterattack during the first forty-eight hours or so, they likely would have eliminated the bridgehead. As it was, they still hit the Americans very hard as they struggled against the commanding ground occupied by the *Landsers*. More German artillery and infantry reached the area on 13 March, but again, the defenders did not immediately counterattack. Model wanted the newly arriving units to reconstitute others and build up a cordon. Nevertheless, local resistance forced the Americans to fight hard for every foot of ground.[53]

As the struggle in the hills dragged out, the Germans also launched air and artillery attacks against the bridge, floated mines down the river, and even fired V-2 rockets at it. They employed swimmers with explosives on the night of 17–18 March. Against such threats the Americans deployed substantial anti-aircraft defenses, searchlights to detect water-borne threats, and aircraft cover when the weather permitted. The so-called *kampfschwimmer* were young, well-trained soldiers, all of them probably under thirty years of age. They arrived at Remagen after a flight from Vienna to Frankfurt, followed by a truck trip to the battle area. But once on the river, American small-arms fire and explosives placed in the water drove them to shore, where they were captured.[54]

Crossing on the bridge was dangerous with or without the enemy fire. Shell fragments and spent anti-aircraft rounds were about as dangerous to the engineers, MPs, and combat troops as bombs and bullets from the Luftwaffe were.[55] Carlos Esteva, a private in the 9th Infantry Division, later said that Remagen "was littered with tracks and half-tracks with dead GIs." An officer recalled that crossing the [Ludendorff] bridge was hairy. While the shelling was sporadic, the speed allowed was only five miles per hour and the whine of that shrapnel ricocheting off the girders was unnerving." Staff Sgt. Al DiRisio saw "a captain and his driver in a jeep burning like an inferno, a direct hit. Death was instant for them." One GI saw a jeep and driver literally disappear when artillery hit them.[56] The commander of the 9th Armored Division's Combat Command R, Col. Walter Burnside, would remember, "The first time I crossed the bridge, when the shells started whistling and chugging over, every infantry man hit the flooring and hugged it, and I did likewise. Then I discovered how much this held them up and held up the troops behind them."[57] Burnside's comment about the shelling holding up infantry on the railroad bridge (and on the tactical bridges that were also going in) is important. The bottleneck of a weakened permanent bridge and the time needed to build tactical bridging contributed to the piecemeal reinforcement and slow expansion of the bridgehead—a delay that eventually drew Hodges's ire.

Bridging the Rhine

ENGINEER SURVEY TEAMS ARRIVED in Remagen during the morning of 8 March to begin planning for construction of alternate bridges. U.S. Naval Unit 1, attached to First Army and equipped with twenty-four landing craft (LCVPs), began operating on 9 March. It eventually transported 13,800 troops and 406 vehicles across the Rhine, marked water obstacles, and assisted in the construction of the bridges.[58] A treadway (tactical bridge built from a metal roadway laid on pontoon rafts) built by the 291st Engineer Combat Battalion opened on the afternoon of 11 March. During its construction, enemy fire had knocked out four cranes, three dump trucks, two air compressors, and thirty-two floats (with 312 feet of completed bridge). Several men had been wounded or killed. The battalion commander, Lt. Col. David E. Pergrin, would say, "It was an open question whether we would get the whole bridge in before German fire expended our resources and manpower."[59] Six other engineer battalions and two bridge companies were employed at Remagen in addition to the 291st and Naval Unit 1. These units operated ferries, installed protective booms, and built six bridges.[60]

It is remarkable that the bridge withstood the strain of traffic, artillery concussions, and effects of the demolitions as long as it did. It had closed and reopened for traffic more than once as temporary repairs failed and permanent rehabilitation began. The upstream truss was "virtually useless"; the downstream truss was taking the load. About 2:00 PM on 17 March, Lt. Colonel Clayton A. Rust, commander of the 276th Engineer Combat Battalion, responsible for maintaining the span, was inspecting the repair work. He heard a sharp crack and turned around to see a vertical hangar breaking loose from its turnbuckles. Sounds like gunshots came sporadically and increased in frequency as rivet heads sheared and tore loose. The old bridge deck began to tremble and vibrate. Dust rose from the temporary wooden floor. Colonel Rust and the other engineers ran for their lives. "I found myself running, in effect, on a side hill. The next instance instant I was engulfed in water. I had no sensation of falling at all," he reported soon afterward. A girder pinned him underwater for a few seconds—long enough for him to believe his lungs would burst. Suddenly, he floated to the surface, another girder probably having dislodged the one pinning him. The current carried him to the treadway bridge, where engineers pulled him from the river. Twenty-eight men died and nearly a hundred were injured when the bridge fell into the Rhine.[61]

Millikin's Relief

COURTNEY HODGES was "not . . . very satisfied with the situation. Apparently there has not been sufficient control applied by the Corps over the troops on the other side; there is a lack of accurate information; and the transfer across the other side of the 9th Div. as has been desired has not been sufficiently expedited."[62]

His aide, Maj. William C. Sylvan, also recorded that the bridgehead "does not look too promising. Today [9 March], as before, the greatest difficulty the [First Army] headquarters had was in obtaining correct and speedy information on the disposition of troops, what had crossed and what had not crossed. . . . There still does not seem to be a sufficient control by [III] Corps of the whole situation. . . . There is no attempt made to hide the fact that everybody here wishes the bridgehead command had fallen to General Collins."[63] Hodges thought that the progress of the 9th and 78th Infantry Divisions was "not anywhere as much as [he] had hoped for."[64]

Hodges knew from Ultra that the Germans were trying to amass enough combat power to destroy the bridgehead.[65] Until 11 March, when he first visited the east bank of the Rhine, Millikin had oriented the direction of the bridgehead expansion toward the east and southeast, no doubt thinking this would enable his corps to support SHAEF plans for the bridgehead to divert German attention from 21 Army Group. Because of concerns about traffic congestion, he did not move the corps forward headquarters across the river during the first days of the operation.[66]

Troops from the 78th Division finally cut the Ruhr-Frankfurt autobahn on 16 March, but it had been very hard to push the Germans back far enough to get the bridge out of the range of artillery.[67] Hodges wanted III Corps to attack toward the north, where it would ease pressure against the VII Corps. Yet he did not give Millikin specific orders regarding the direction of attack until 15 March, though he had an apparently "strenuous discussion" with him on the issue overall. Millikin's G-3 staff thought the reason for giving priority to a northern route was to assist the favored VII Corps. Millikin nevertheless complied in part by shifting the weight of the 9th Division's attack to the northeast.[68] Yet this did nothing to push enemy guns out of range. Adding to the impression that General Millikin was perhaps not in complete control of events was message traffic from III Corps to First Army. For example, the 9 March III Corps situation report states that a regiment of the 78th Infantry Division was across the Rhine and "progressing slowly *north*" [emphasis added], when the regiment in fact was headed east from the northern part of the bridgehead.[69] Given the inherent confusion in the situation, it is not surprising that the corps staff did not know with certainty at any given hour which units were in the bridgehead and which had been designated to move across but had remained on the west bank waiting for a place in the congestion. Collins remarked to Hodges that it was a shame "that VII Corps had not been the people to establish the bridgehead. . . . [A]t the end of the first day, he would have been out at the Autobahn."[70] The auto-bahn is less than ten miles east of the Remagen crossing site. The roads, however, wind across steep and compartmented countryside.

Millikin later told an interviewer, "I suppose I should have done some things differently." Reflecting on the operation, he acknowledged that he might have "gotten the divisions across faster than I actually did." Lt. Col. Norman B. Edwards, the assistant corps G-3, acknowledged only a few days after the capture of the bridgehead that the corps should have attacked "toward the autobahn much more boldly and in widely sep-arated spearheads" rather than in a measured advance. He thought that the commanders were "a little cautious in pushing forward" and that they gave the Germans time to shift reserves into the bridgehead.[71]

Hodges and Bradley on 15 March discussed Millikin's relief. "Mind you," Hodges told Bradley, "I have only the greatest admiration and respect for the GIs doing the fighting out there, but I think they have had bad leadership in this bridgehead battle."[72] Hodges had managed to find fault with every step Millikin took. The III Corps staff, in fact, believed the First Army commander had even compiled a "dossier" of issues with the corps commander's performance and that he had sent it to Bradley, who did not believe "that they constituted very serious charges."[73] It did not matter. Bradley replaced Millikin with Maj. Gen. James A. Van Fleet. Hodges broke the news. "I have some bad news for you," he began. He told the corps commander that he had lost his job but that he could come by First Army headquarters the next day if he wished to discuss the relief in person with Hodges. When the army commander was finished, Millikin replied, "Sir, I have some bad news for you too. The railroad bridge has just collapsed."[74]

Colonel Edwards said, "When I saw Gen. Millikin he had tears in his eyes and he said he told General Hodges that he had done his best or words to that effect."[75] Millikin later said, "Somebody along the line did not like the way I did the thing, so that's why I'm no longer a member of III Corps."[76] Remagen was a poor location for a river crossing, and because there were no key objectives in the immediate area, no one had planned for taking or exploiting the Ludendorff Bridge. Units that had conducted a road march were not physically organized for such a hasty attack. German resistance was never decisive at a single point, but it was strong enough under the circumstances to balance the limited number of men Eisenhower allotted to the bridgehead. Officers from the III Corps headquarters believed that Hodges and his staff took undue credit for capture of the Ludendorff Bridge. Then, when it became evident that some were not happy that this coup upset SHAEF plans, the First Army staff blamed the corps for having done so.[77] What could have been the culminating moment of John Millikin's career ended in reassignment to command an armored division in the last weeks of the war, and the end of his career.

On the night of 23–24 March, the 21 Army Group's Rhine crossing in the north began in earnest. That army group and the Ninth U.S. Army had amassed enough ammunition to blow a hole, almost literally, in the enemy defenses. Third Army, meanwhile, had gained crossings near Oppenheim. Remagen remained important to First Army and the 12th Army Group, but events and headlines moved to other places. Perhaps the most interesting epitaph to the whole story is a poem written by "Sagitarrius," an unnamed observer of events in the late winter of 1945. Its first stanza is:

> You know Remagen Bridge was seized
> A week or two ago
> The High Command was hardly pleased,
> It almost wrecked the show.
> The bridge they thought as good as blown
> When Ike's assault began;
> Allied Headquarters had their own
> Supreme strategic plan.[78]

CHAPTER 16

GENESIS TO GREATNESS, SPRING 1945

W HEN THE REMAGEN BRIDGE collapsed, there were less than sixty
days left in the ETO campaign. The Allies were at the Rhine
along most of the 450-mile front. General Eisenhower's armies
consisted of some ninety combat divisions, plus hundreds of
thousands of logistical and other nondivisional combat and support personnel, and an equal number of airmen in support. There had never been
anything like this potent force in the history of the West, and there never
would be again, in terms of soldiers reporting to a single theater commander—three army groups (6th, 12th, and 21). As spring approached,
Eisenhower rethought his original strategy of having the armies first clear
the entire west bank of the Rhine before crossing the river. He had
planned, and indeed still would, direct the 21 Army Group to make the
main attack against the Ruhr from the north, with part of the 12th Army
Group driving against it on the south. However, when Eisenhower
learned that the Soviets were less than fifty miles from Berlin while the
Allies were still more than three hundred miles from the city, with little
prospect of reaching it ahead of Soviets, other objectives appeared to be
in order.

One option was an attack east to link up with the Red Army and
thereby cut Germany in two. Other considerations included an attack
on the "National Redoubt," the alleged enclave deep in Bavaria from
where the Nazi die-hards would set up their last defenses. Though the
Ruhr never left the top tier of Allied ground objectives, some thought
that it had been made less important by the shifting of factories to locations deeper in Germany. Events were moving fast, and decisions had to
be made. Both Montgomery's and Bradley's army groups made significant
progress within their zones of attack once they were across the Rhine.
First Army's breakout from the Remagen bridgehead took it as far east as
Marburg and Giessen by 28 March. Third Army was nearing Mainz, after

249

driving through the Saar-Palatinate and capturing 68,000 POWs. The 6th Army Group, meanwhile, was across the Rhine near Worms.[1]

Despite the progress in the late winter and early spring, leaders were still concerned about replacing casualties. U.S. battle and nonbattle losses were over 134,000 in December 1944, 136,000 in January 1945, 91,000 in February, and 101,000 in March.[2] The replacement situation, exacerbated by the fighting in the Ardennes, became so critical that the War Department accelerated the shipment of one airborne, two armored, and three infantry divisions overseas. Three other infantry divisions that had not completed their training programs lost their infantry regiments to early shipment to the Seventh U.S. Army in the Vosges. Another newly arrived infantry division also lost about 25 percent of its enlisted strength as replacements for Ardennes casualties. Belatedly, the Army also permitted formation of black rifle platoons and assignment of black soldiers to several divisions. By all accounts, these men performed admirably.[3]

Historians have criticized the U.S. replacement system for years, and many have argued that the German system for maintaining combat power made more sense, because it processed men in groups. There were two basic choices available to the U.S. Army. One could keep existing units in the line and replace individuals/small units or let attrition reduce these units to ineffectiveness and raise entirely new ones. The United States took the latter path in the Civil War and the former in World War II. Without having raised a large number of units from which to draw individual replacements or to use as a rotational pool, the Army in World War II forced troops to remain in the line for extended periods. This degraded or eliminated entirely the chance to rest or conduct refresher training. Infantry rifle units suffered most, because they sustained some 94.25 percent of all infantry division casualties, even though they did not constitute an overwhelming amount of divisional strength. Infantry divisions themselves sustained 67.8 percent of all casualties.[4]

According to ETO figures, four infantry divisions lost over 200 percent of their strength between D-day and VE day. Thirteen more lost over 120 percent casualties.[5] No wonder some observers thought infantry units were poor performers who needed help blasting their way across Europe. Though the U.S. Army's system of individual replacement received much well-justified criticism, however, the fact remains that it was the only army that maintained its ground combat forces at nearly full strength throughout the war (even in World War I, the Army had to break up infantry divisions to form replacement pools). This feat impressed even the Germans.[6]

Units received replacements according to projected requirements that drove training allocations in the States. As a result, the pipeline for replacements was a long one, much like that for materiel. Replacements ideally should have reached their new units able to integrate quickly into existing roles and missions. Unfortunately, the Army Ground Forces failed to expand its training capacity after it assumed the training mission from the Army Service Forces early in 1942. Recruits usually underwent basic training in units, and installations took on the mission of training loss replacements who would be assigned to overseas organizations. There was inadequate coordination between those projecting losses and those operating the training centers. Planners knew that men had to be able to fight when they joined units in the field, but the strains of time and the inefficiencies of a hastily organized system took their toll on individual effectiveness.[7] Such administrative failures included long delays between completion of training and entry into units, cursory medical examinations, and equipment shortages. Many replacements endured conditions en route that destroyed "their morale and [eliminated] the effects of their training." Soldiers might spend months in the pipeline without the support of their own leaders and friends. They became physically soft, lost discipline, and saw their combat skills degenerate.[8] Units in battle received men ill prepared for what they were about to face. It was a matter of a good plan very poorly executed.

Trouble developed in Italy in the winter of 1943–1944, as the replacement system broke down in the United States due to its inability to meet unforeseen demand, especially for infantrymen. There were enough divisions then in the United States to have allowed temporary replacement and rotation of those in combat, but shipping was inadequate to get them overseas before they were needed elsewhere for actual operations. Commanders in the Pacific reported the same situation. Alternatives included the drafting and overseas assignment of eighteen-year-olds, which the public at first opposed and the Army promised not to do. However, losses in France after D-day were so great that, to maintain this policy, the War Department had to send virtually every draftee over eighteen, regardless of ability or physical condition, to combat units. Ironically, "youth, vigor and alertness were concentrated in the artillery. . . . Infantry and armor, which needed the men with the highest endurance, had to fill out their ranks with physically least qualified . . . men." Too many infantry replacements who arrived overseas until late 1944 fit this category.[9] No doubt most of them tried to do the right thing, but the odds were squarely against them. In short, the grinding attrition of war in Europe surprised War Department planners. It was not a war of slashing mobile operations. Rather, it was a war of movement interspersed by unexpectedly brutal close combat actions fought by units supplied and staffed by an extremely long supply chain. Air power did not win the war, nor did intense armored operations. The interwar technocrats were wrong.

The ETO, meanwhile, continued its all-or-nothing fight against the Germans, and demand for replacements quickly outpaced the forecast supply. Replacement depot capacity in the theater was over 65,000, but by mid-July 1944 imbalances according to specialty were growing to an unmanageable extent. Average daily losses in July were 1,529, mostly in the infantry. Officials established a retraining program for non-infantry troops, but it was not fully effective until late in the year. Senior line officers did not understand the intricacies of the personnel classification and assignment system, and they did not grasp the fact that men needed refresher and specialized instruction on local conditions after they reached their ultimate units of assignment. Untrained personnel operated many specialized replacement units. They were also understaffed and lacked basic supplies such as tents, cots, heaters, and laundry facilities. There were interruptions in mail service. Poor requirements estimation led to a lack of winter clothing. Even rifles and other small arms were in short supply. Refresher training was poor, and morale among the replacements was abysmal. Returning veterans, who also passed through depots, often treated the new men badly, passing "malicious misinformation" to them, and causing "the gravest morale problem."[10]

Eisenhower sent a commission to Washington in late 1944 to hammer out the problems with the War Department, and Marshall offered him Lt. Gen. Ben Lear, who had succeeded McNair at Army Ground Forces, to help. The ETO combed rear areas for able-bodied infantry, armor, mechanized cavalry, and artillery replacements and considered breaking up the last two armored divisions shipped to Europe. Lear established an officer training school and persuaded Eisenhower to support a plan to declare all able-bodied white soldiers less than thirty-one years of age then assigned to support organizations as fit for combat duty. Not only was there disagreement between the War Department and the ETO on the operation of the system but the two American army groups did not agree on the details of allocation of replacements. Theater policy was to allocate men based on relative divisional strengths and operational missions. During the Bulge, for example, the theater allocated Bradley's army group infantrymen on an eight-to-one proportion over Devers's army group. Replacement armor-crewmen allocation was on a ten-to-one basis. The theater and the 6th Army Group (Devers) did not reconcile their conflict until late January 1945, despite the fact that the army group was also fighting hard in the Vosges.[11] A War Department program to group individual replacements into ad hoc squads and platoons before shipment overseas began a few months before the end of the war. The intent was to allow men who had shared common Army backgrounds to remain together as long as possible. This program had merit, but the war ended before it could be properly evaluated.[12]

The logistic situation also did not materially improve until well into 1945. As late as February, the 12th Army Group reported that ammunition reserves for 4.5-inch guns were only 16 percent of requirements, 240-mm howitzer ammunition was 61 percent, and 8-inch howitzer ammunition supply 78 percent. This was despite the fact that units had husbanded supplies in February and early March to amass reserves to support operations across the Rhine.[13] It is true that by the time the 12th Army Group crossed the river the situation had markedly improved; however, it came about only through hand-to-mouth supply practices and plaintive calls for artillery fire that went partially or totally unanswered during the preceding months of heavy combat.

It was still taking a long time to clear supplies from the ports, because the Communications Zone had not been able to establish an adequate chain of intermediate depots. Emergency transportation operations such as the "Red Ball," "Red Lion," and "XYZ" routes were stopgaps at best, pending adequate rail service. Rail was the most efficient method of transporting supplies long distances, but it took months after D-day to repair and organize the French rail system. Only after October 1944 did railroad movements account for a majority of supply shipments to the field armies. The reasons for the slow deliveries were varied. Supply officers tended to use rolling stock as portable warehouses, and they did not promptly return empty cars to the transportation corps. This created an artificial, but nonetheless "critical," shortage of cars by November. Then, when the weather turned bad, evidence of poor track maintenance appeared, in the form of derailments.[14]

Most problems endured by the frontline units can be attributed to hasty organization, training of logistic personnel, breakdown of administrative control processes, unanticipated progress in 1944, and a transportation and distribution system unable to cope with the strain placed on it. At the end of April 1945, there were over 159,000 soldiers operating the transportation system for the U.S. forces alone in the ETO. They handled over 30 million tons of cargo, handled over 9,500 ship arrivals, and moved nearly 4.2 million soldiers and 806,000 vehicles.[15] No other Allied or enemy army faced a comparable task. It is all but impossible to determine the full extent of rear-echelon misappropriation and graft, and therefore the impact of such factors on the frontline soldier, though some students of the campaign have tried to make a cottage industry of alleging that logistical troops were one step removed from the Germans in the damage they caused. In such cases, overstatement is as dangerous as understatement.

To the Elbe River

MONTGOMERY'S RHINE CROSSING was comparable to Overlord in numbers of soldiers involved and supply support—he had over 1,280,000 men.[16] One aspect of the assault was Operation Varsity, an airborne drop of two divisions across the Rhine ahead of the ground attack but within range of supporting artillery. The spectacular crossing itself began on the night of 23–24 March, and by the end of the month 21 Army Group had troops thirty miles east of the river. On 29 March First Army turned toward Paderborn, where it would link up with the Ninth Army and form the "Ruhr Pocket." The 3d Armored Division, reinforced, encountered stiff resistance from students in an SS replacement training center. About sixty panzers stalled the Americans on the night of 30–31 March, and the division lost its able commander, Maj. Gen. Maurice Rose, to enemy fire. The Ninth U.S. Army sent a combat command from the 2d Armored Division to assist, and on 1 April the two armies closed the ring around much of Army Group B. The final prisoner count was about 320,000, including pre-Nazi German chancellor Franz von Papen. Model committed suicide, and the list of his generals taken prisoner was impressive: Bayerlein (LIII Corps), Lüttwitz (XLVII Corps), Waldenburg (116th Panzer Division), and Denkert (3d Panzergrenadier Division).[17] Other prisoners included old men, boys, female technicians, Hitler Youth, and "monocled Prussians, enough to gladden the heart of a Hollywood casting director."[18]

By late April 1945, the 12th Army Group was the largest field command in the history of the United States. Totaling 1.2 million soldiers, it was nine times the size of the entire Army just six years before. Across the ETO in all units, there were about 786,000 infantrymen, 323,000 engineers, 313,000 artillerymen, and 628,000 service troops.[19]

The Allies were ready for the final stab into Germany. Third Army on 4 April discovered a trove of precious jewels and other loot, including an estimated $250 million worth of gold bullion and coins, deep in a salt mine. GIs the same day captured the first concentration camp taken by the western Allies. By the evening of 11 April, elements of the Ninth Army's 2d Armored Division were on the Elbe near Magdeburg.[20] Other great cities fell: Erfurt, Jena, Bayreuth, and Nürnberg. German troops defended some places to the death but hardly appeared in others. At Heilbronn, elements of the 17th SS Panzergrenadier Division nearly drove an infantry battalion back into the Neckar River and delayed construction of a bridge. Resistance at Crailsheim brought another attack to a halt and threatened to cut off spearheads. Cargo planes used a captured airfield to bring in supplies and evacuate the wounded.[21]

Hitler committed suicide on 30 April. Adm. Karl Dönitz was now leader of the disintegrating Reich. German units began to surrender as fast as they could find a single GI or small unit. Generaloberst Alfred Jodl, chief of the Wehrmacht operations staff, signed the surrender document at 2:41 AM on 7 May, to become effective the next night at 11:01 PM. Frontline GIs accepted the news with relief, seldom with wild jubilation—they were just glad to be alive.[22] Charles Cawthon, who had had to borrow a uniform when his National Guard unit was mobilized in 1941, was a major in 1945. He later recalled that the reaction of the average soldier to the news of German surrender was "in keeping with the mood in which he had fought the war: conviction, determination, unstinted effort, no little courage and sacrifice—and little exultation."[23] Eisenhower's 7 May 1945 message to the Combined Chiefs of Staff was likewise understated: "The mission of this Allied force was fulfilled at 0241 local time, May 7th, 1945."[24]

The greatest campaign in the history of the U.S. Army was over. In eleven months of combat, ground and air casualties were over 586,000, with 135,576 dead.[25] A relatively small army that had not always been well supported or supplied up front had completed its mission. But it did not go home. Over sixty years later, many thousands of soldiers remained on duty in Germany and elsewhere in Central Europe.

Summing Up

ANALYSIS OF THE PERFORMANCE of the U.S. Army in the ETO has been clouded with the postwar statements of captured German officers explaining their defeat, historians superficially aware of the difficulties of projecting and supporting combat power, otherwise authoritative persons who oversimplify warfighting in their effort to make a point, and journalists who do not fully consider the context of their observations. Discussion is usually limited to combat operations, anyway. Though combat does not occur in isolation, it is still hard to find works that even address, much less give a professional discussion of, mobilization, organization, training, or logistics. Such discussion is usually limited to national-level issues of production, with the assumption that everything produced that did not go down with a torpedoed ship probably ended up in the hands of a frontline soldier. In fact, second-guessing regarding the conduct of the campaign began before the war was over. People were right to critique the U.S. Army, but too many observers attributed German defeat only to a flood of materiel.

Yet supplies and technology did not substitute for soldier and leader skills, will and character. Production made victory possible but not automatic. Sheer weakness of the enemy was not, and could not have been, the only reason the GI prevailed. As one of the more balanced works has noted, statistics need interpreters. They do not address skill, quality (or lack thereof) of weapons, or intangibles.[26] As this book has shown, units seldom had a significant materiel advantage where and when it counted. The ETO campaign was the first and only one for the vast majority of units. Yet too few widely read authors have provided balanced and thorough explanations of why the American army, and ground combat forces in particular, succeeded despite significant odds against them.

Historian T. N. Dupuy tried in the 1970s to quantify the results of engagements and prove that overwhelmed Germans outfought the Allies on a man-for-man basis. A set of mathematical models he designed attempted to predict combat effectiveness. This was a noble goal, originally funded by the Department of Defense. Unfortunately, it also provided a considerable amount of ammunition for those who wanted to believe the German army was somehow "better" than the U.S. Army. No model can duplicate or account for the intangibles of human behavior. Armies do not fight "at a measurable percentage of a notional capacity for battle"—they just fight better, about the same, or worse, than their opponent. Dupuy even calculated a "score effectiveness" indicating that one German *Landser* equaled 1.55 GIs.

A major problem with the model was a set of poorly chosen data points, and even Dupuy cautioned readers that his figures were contradictory and confusing. (How else can one account for the fact that tactical or operational victory often causes as much confusion to the victor as to the loser?) The model had more than seventy variables, which included weapons effects, terrain factors, weather effects, air superiority, and mobility. Yet there could be no variables for such vital aspects of fighting as morale or experience, and he developed no basis for measuring logistical effectiveness. His analysis of thirty-nine 1943 and 1944 U.S. and German division-level engagements (he added ten more shortly before his death in the early 1990s) had the United States attacking in all but three. While its individual comparisons, like performance of one model of tank over another, are solid, the model unfortunately mixed U.S. armored and infantry divisions with German panzer divisions, parachute divisions, corps, and field armies. In nine other cases, the U.S. units were involved in their first days or weeks of combat. As historian John S. Brown noted, "It seems no accident that [Colonel Dupuy's book] labels one of its subchapters, *Fudge Factors*." One example will suffice. Dupuy gave a "score effectiveness" of 1.13 to a German division attacking the 4th U.S. infantry Division in the early days of the Bulge. The 4th got a rating of 0.87, but Dupuy does not mention that the U.S. division had only days before left the death trap of the Hürtgen Forest, where it had sustained 6,000 casualties in three weeks of fighting.[27]

Appropriate issues for comparison do not lend themselves to quantification, but they might be: How far off their "prime" were the German divisions of 1943–1944? How much of an advantage did American equipment standardization offer? To what extent did better logistical support result in increased combat efficiency in a relatively small and inexperienced U.S. Army? Was there a balance between the complex German replacement system, which favored the soldier but broke down completely, and the U.S. system, which was unfair to the individual but enabled units to stay in the fight?[28] These and many other basic questions of organization and administration are not glamorous objects of study, but they deserve evaluation because such issues represent the basic components of warfighting.

Historian Martin Van Creveld clearly holds the organization, training, and warrior ethos of the German army in high esteem, and he has tried to show as well that Montgomery's concept of a "single front" approach was logistically supportable. His comparison of U.S. and German armies covers many topics, some more effectively than others. He acknowledges the ultimate success of the GI and also the dangers of producing a military that unquestioningly obeys even criminal orders. He identifies many of the problems the U.S. Army encountered, but it is more difficult for a reader to isolate German army shortcomings, other than generalities of instances of its brutality. With regard to the Americans, many of his conclusions are questionable or lack historical context. For example, after assessing U.S. officer casualties, he reports that not enough men in the service forces became casualties and that most wounded officers were pampered after they entered medical channels. It is hard to understand how rear-echelon officers were supposed to have done their job supporting combat forces if they were themselves in the frontline foxholes. A look at detailed records indicates that officers in combat units generally paid at least a "fair share" in blood in terms of their numbers and the case studies above demonstrate this. Further, leaders did their men no good if they were dead. Leaders had to be where they could best influence the battle, whether it was with the lead squads or where they were within reach of subordinate commanders needing guidance. Many new officers on both sides were thrust into situations for which they were unprepared. There was simply not always time to give newly commissioned lieutenants a few months' experience in a tactical unit in the States before assignment overseas.[29]

Max Hastings concludes that as the products of a democracy the GI was somehow unable to fight as determinedly as, say, a panzergrenadier. Arms presumably compensated for the shortcoming of democratic soldiers.[30] Likewise, John Ellis wonders why GIs were "prone to rely simply on material superiority to blast a way through German positions." He incorrectly asserts that Eisenhower had no significant supply constraints except for August and September 1944.[31] And so it has gone for decades.

One flawed thesis accepted for years was that few GIs ever fired their weapons in battle. This originated with one of America's most renowned military observers, Samuel Lyman Atwood Marshall. "SLAM" was a reporter-turned-historian who fabricated World War I service (he was commissioned after the armistice and never served in combat). Shortly after the end of World War II, he published a study claiming that only a small percentage of riflemen had ever fired their weapons. He based his conclusions on postcombat interviews reportedly made with thousands of GIs, beginning in the Pacific in 1943. He concluded that at most a only a quarter of combat soldiers ever fired their weapons in combat and that therefore the outcome of a battle often rested in the hands of a relatively few men who worked together in small groups, depending on each other for moral support. Marshall claimed to have interviewed soldiers who were assigned to about four hundred infantry rifle companies. This number later climbed to 603. His standard of using up to four days to debrief a company would have meant he was still interviewing soldiers at the end of 1946—which he was not. One researcher could find no supporting documentation of so many interviews in his surviving notebooks.

Though Marshall was an astute commentator, who rightly wanted to keep his postwar readers from assuming that technology could compensate for human factors in battle, too many people found it convenient and tempting to accept without question everything he reported. Many veteran leaders recalled things differently during and just after the war, while memories were still fresh. Even interviews conducted by historical teams under Marshall's supervision indicated that the percentage of firers was much greater. One of the war's most distinguished combat leaders, Harry Kinnard of the 101st Airborne, never heard that failure to fire was a problem. Gen. Bruce Clarke, a hero of the Bulge fighting, thought Marshall made "ridiculous and dangerous assertions." Gen. James Gavin, commander of the 82d Airborne Division, said, "All of our infantry fired their weapons. I know because I was there and took part." One combat veteran wondered, "Did the SOB [Marshall] think we clubbed the Germans to death?"[32]

Expansion in only five years of a hollow, ineffective army of fewer than 150,000 to one of about eight million soldiers, deployed on nearly every continent, was an impressive achievement, though it was not done without significant problems. With the possible exception of the British army, no other ground force had to organize and train soldiers and units capable of operating around the world—and not even the British deployed and sustained a comparable amount of combat power to climates ranging from Morocco to Alaska. Frenetic mobilization shortchanged the GI, in that leaders and staffs probably had at least as much to learn as the field soldier. Unit and individual training, the quality of armament and other equipment, logistical infrastructure, and, above all, leadership, are the foundation of an effective military organization. These factors built the force that air and sea services transported to the theaters of operation. These organizations had to arrive at distant air and sea ports at the right time with the right mix of combat and support units to influence events and exercise the nation's will. Once it entered combat, the force had to receive supplies and equipment of the right types and quantities at the right place and time to maintain its operational momentum. These were extremely complex processes.

Manpower and materiel attrition still grew to an alarming level. The War Department's efforts to economize on manpower by creating rather small divisions backed up with pools of separate (nondivisional) combat and support units ended up forcing leaders to improvise continually their responses to tactical challenges. These improvisations often hurt the combat soldier. Losses, particularly within the infantry regiments, were extreme, and relatively few of these men survived without serious injury. One need only compare the size of the combat force with its accomplishments to grasp exactly what a few hundred thousand young Americans did.

The Army that lost at Kasserine was not the same one that so brilliantly reacted to the opportunity at Remagen. The changes between early 1943 and early 1945 were significant, and they reinforce why analysts cannot use snapshots of performance. For example, America produced some exceptionally capable small-unit and operational-level leaders by 1944–1945. While generalship and planning at the corps and field-army level were not always up to par, one must remember that few of these officers (nor even division commanders, for that matter) had had any more combat experience than their subordinates before their units entered battle. Fewer still had anywhere near the experience of their enemies. However, by early 1945 many senior U.S. leaders were beginning to show that they too had learned their trade. Lack of resources as much as lack of imagination (the Hürtgen and a few other places excluded) led to the bitter battles of tactical attrition that occurred through February 1945.

Given the circumstances under which it fought, the German army was surprisingly resilient and capable. It was a relatively strong force until the last weeks of the war. The U.S. Strategic Bombing Survey's study of German logistics reached several conclusions. Germany should have distributed material according to a policy that ensured new divisions did not receive priority over experienced and battle-hardened ones and thus allowed veteran units to be always less effective than they could have been. Materiel shortages caused by Allied attacks on railroads was as much a manpower issue as one of equipment denial. Railroads were often repaired and returned to use in within hours after an attack, but such response came at a cost in manpower that would have been better used at the front. Reconstruction operations in Bavaria, for example, occupied up to 80,000 people.[33]

On hand in France on D-day was enough small-arms and machine-gun ammunition for twenty days of normal fighting, and enough artillery ammunition for thirty days' defensive fighting or a week's worth of heavy offensive combat. There are no definite figures on the amount of equipment left behind or destroyed in France after Mortain, though it was no doubt very significant. Yet at the start of the American offensive in November 1944, the German armor situation had improved considerably, and units had an average of 80 percent of their authorized artillery pieces. As telling, enough ammunition was in the forward positions for six days of normal fighting at the start of the U.S. attack. Critical German shortages were cargo trucks, signal equipment, and mines. As the report noted, "On the whole divisions were fairly well supplied and equipped. Allied air attacks had decreased in density over the previous campaigns in Normandy and eastern France." German logisticians had no need to disperse supply dumps further, and losses were "negligible" between the end of the fighting in France and the beginning of operations in November. Even when Allied air attacks hit supply installations, operations were usually disrupted for "only short periods. Losses were negligible and could be replaced quickly." The army that launched the Battle of the Bulge was relatively well equipped with weapons but suffered form a lack of fuel and trucks to push forward supplies in quantity.[34] Still, the Germans benefited from supply lines considerably shorter than those of their enemies. The balance of materiel was closer than many assume. The Americans maintained an advantage, but as this book has noted, it was not overwhelming everywhere and everytime.

Germany had some superb leaders of all ranks at all levels of command. Having lost the World War I, their best thinkers were not prisoners of institutional memory. While their bureaucracy had its flaws, it seems to have been more willing than that in Washington to tolerate independent thinking. Yet while Germany had some of the most advanced weapons of the time, it remained a continental power in both thought and action, unable to sustain its forces over the long term. The same military bureaucracy that accepted the finest in engineering also allowed dozens of designs of single items of equipment rather than a handful they could mass-produce and get into the fight.[35] Despite centuries of military tradition, superb soldiers, and great leaders, the *Heer* ultimately failed because of arrogance and the inability or unwillingness of its leadership (and the national leadership as well) to value support functions.[36] Some believe the United States erred in overemphasizing what they derisively term "industrial management" of warfare,[37] as if trading ammunition for lives was somehow less than honorable or gave the United States a somehow unfair competitive advantage. The Germans failed in large part to acknowledge that manpower alone could not compensate for developments in modern warfare.

Generalmajor Carl Wagener, the chief of staff of Army Group B at the end of the war, attributed bitter German resistance to soldier loyalty and duty. "Even if the [German] Supreme Command's continuation of the war were a criminal offense, a soldier would have made a terrible decision if he had broken his oath, disobeyed orders, or capitulated. It is a contradiction of common law and moral law to answer one crime with another." The *Landser*, he added, "did not believe in the possibility of a negotiated peace," especially under the circumstances of unconditional surrender.[38] General der Infanterie Otto Hitzfeld, commander of LXVII Corps, said that the Germans relied on "tenacious delaying actions" if units were not strong enough to attack: "Every foot of terrain had to be defended up to the last man." [39]

The U.S. Army had to maintain its mobility to survive against such staunch resistance, but the weather, terrain, enemy resistance, and tactical mistakes often narrowed the odds. Most U.S. generals understood emerging doctrine, but physical circumstances and logistical support often prevented even the best of them from fully practicing it. The global nature of the war also inhibited the Americans' ability to generate combat power in Europe. The United States faced unique global requirements that contributed to the inefficient allocation of manpower and materiel, as noted above. Hundreds of thousands of troops were needed to man port-reconstitution units, to maintain tens of thousands of miles lines of communication to the USSR, to operate a worldwide communications network, and to rehabilitate roads and railroads in remote parts of the world. The ETO had to compete with the Pacific for resources, and extremely long lines of communication tied up a considerable amount of manpower and equipment in transit. One figure cited for support manpower in the ETO alone is over 979,000 by 1 May 1945, out of a U.S. total strength of about 2.8 million.[40] Some arguments then and now regarding 'tooth to tail' are justified, and it is true that support units often spend lot of time taking care of themselves. The fact remains, however, that the right level of support to combat soldiers is that needed to get soldiers on the objective to stay. The Army had trouble balancing what was needed with inexcusable inefficiencies in allocation of quality manpower and supplies between the support and the combat arms.

Mobilization began late, effectively only after the fall of France, when it was hard to foresee the eventual scope of the war. America was in many ways intellectually ready to prosecute a global war in that its higher-level staffs had experience in developing such plans. [41] On the operational and tactical levels, however, it was quite unready in 1942, when it began offensive combat operations. Staffs had given plenty of thought to industrial mobilization, but there had been no money to buy equipment. Some young officers were mentally prepared to execute operations at a modern pace, but they had had no practical experience in leading units, nor had the structure of their units fully adapted to the latest doctrine and lessons from battle. It was mid-1943 before the Army could initiate a wide-ranging reorganization of its combat forces based on lessons learned to date.[42]

Development of combat power required access to fit manpower, a base of technology, raw materials, shipping, training sites, logistical infrastructure, and ability to develop and assimilate new doctrine and procedures. That there were significant problems should not be a surprise, though it seemingly has been exactly that to some. The early campaigns in North Africa, Sicily, and Italy exposed many shortfalls that often bordered on the disastrous. Readiness was "uneven." There were equipment and training shortfalls. Many support units in North Africa were still equipped with the World War I–vintage Springfield rifle. Stripping trained units to provide cadres for new ones and slowness of production ensured that some units were destined to fail. Ironically, the best-trained units were not the ones to meet the enemy first, in Tunisia.[43]

Sicily and Italy were proving grounds that gave leaders experience and allowed the Army to continue its transformation before it landed in northwest Europe. The Overlord plan was "fraught with difficulty," and there was no guarantee that it would succeed.[44] Not only was the invasion itself risky, but the Army continued operations even as it incorporated inexperienced units into its inventory. It did not even reach its peak ETO strength until early 1945. The critical and generally most intense fighting actually took place before the Army was fully deployed overseas.[45] Physical constraints and logistical realities forced a relatively slow troop buildup on the Continent and led to chronic shortages of ammunition, fuel, and replacement troops—often, but not always, driven by the lack of transportation and other problems related to distribution. The sheer magnitude and importance of the cross-Channel invasion put a heavy weight on the shoulders of inexperienced planning staffs. Observers have criticized the logistical plan for its emphasis on getting ashore at the expense of thorough planning for follow-on operations. Yet getting ashore and staying there were the chief problems. They were not easy tasks, and the ramifications of a logistical failure offshore would have likely outweighed any that occurred inland. Hindsight indicates that the Overlord plan went too far in trying to anticipate every contingency; one wonders whether the critics have actually read the plan and its annexes. Regardless, the United States risked the outcome of the war in a one-round confrontation with the enemy in his home territory. It was a weighty responsibility for a new army.

Well-executed logistics cannot win a war, but poorly executed logistics operations can lose one. American success was not the inevitable consequence of materiel advantage. Logistics did not determine all tactical courses of action, but logistical constraints usually determined where and when the armies would strike. They affected where U.S. forces were located after their arrival in the United Kingdom and accordingly where they landed in France. Such constraints tied the combat forces to the iron grip of supply, from the beaches to the Elbe. Seldom did the American soldier fight with an overwhelming preponderance of materiel. What abundance there was came for the most part after the beginning of 1945. There was a long chain of events between the factory and the fox-hole. There were not enough heavy trucks, due both to production constraints and infighting between staffs in Washington and overseas. U.S. tanks were obsolescent and automatic weapons had a slow rate of fire. Faulty loss estimates and inattention to organization and administration of the replacement depots contributed to a crisis in availability of combat replacements. Other supplies, such as spare parts and smaller-caliber artillery and mortar ammunition, were short at one time or another. Reducing production of heavy artillery ammunition was ill advised, given the relatively limited numbers of heavy-caliber guns in the inventory to begin with. All of these often ignored factors led to relatively even odds at the front for much of the campaign.[46] It is remarkable that the average GI and his leaders did so well under these conditions.

The supply system broke down in France, and it was unable to recover quickly enough to prevent a stalemate by September 1944. The Germans received the gift of time in which to execute a masterful example of regeneration of combat power on ever-shortening lines of communication. The War Department was also part of the problem. Its computations for production and replacement of equipment were based on World War I experience and data from other theaters during World War II; figures did not always match ETO requirements and experience. Yet worldwide supply required a considerable amount of equipment in the pipeline, and the average lag time between requisitions and delivery from the U.S. industrial base was 120 days. It was 135 days for tanks. With an estimated 11 percent replacement rate and a total allowance of 4,000 medium tanks in the ETO, about 2,000 Sherman tanks were needed in the pipeline. The same factors applied to other materiel.[47] It remains a challenge to anticipate future combat needs, and the logistician cannot really begin work until the operational concept is finished, provided that it ever is.

Once the forces were established ashore, they found that there was little room for operational maneuver on an urbanized continent. There was certainly far less maneuver space there than in the Soviet Union. On a tactical level, the terrain itself forced maneuver units into narrow avenues of approach. Troops often had literally to punch through the enemy defenses on narrow frontages. Such hindrances have confronted armies for centuries, and no technology can overcome them.[48] Hedgerow fighting was brutal. Some believe that the lack of fast progress behind the beaches was an indicator of what poor soldiers the GI and his leaders were. Yet the Germans had the advantages in such terrain. The Allies in Normandy never had more than thirty-four divisions on a front of about a hundred miles. Writers have taken Montgomery's arguments, sensible as they may have been with respect to ending the war as soon as possible, at face value, without understanding the requirements for supporting such operations as he proposed. The question was not whether the Allies could have shifted and concentrated the weight of their attacks but rather whether could they have sustained the offensive after it began. The answer is probably no.[49] Germany's swift recovery, the delay in taking Antwerp, and Allied logistical problems no doubt encouraged the Germans just as they forced the Allies to reconsider their plans. The Allies finally hit a wall in November 1944—a wall built of German resurgence and an unexpectedly hard fight everywhere from Lorraine to Holland. On one hand, some senior staff officers and leaders failed to identify the meaning of the German buildup that led to the December counteroffensive. On the other, the performances by officers like Hasbrouck and Clarke equaled any other in the war.

British Brigadier Hubert Essame, a World War II combat veteran, has remarked, "It is an oversimplification to say that the Germans were defeated by superior materiel might. The country favored the defense and the British and American armies had to develop the necessary techniques in the heat of battle itself."[50] The Army activated 3,830 units of all types; trained 122,000 men through the Officer Candidate School; developed, modified, accepted, or rejected 10,450 items of equipment; and expanded 800 percent in size within five years. Ground troops represented 37 percent of all soldiers deployed overseas but sustained about 80 percent of the casualties. Infantrymen represented only 14 percent of overseas strength in June 1945.[51] Certainly the Army could have done better in organizing and equipping its units. There was a considerable amount of overhead in the Army Service Forces and Army Air Forces. Army Ground Forces policies themselves led to stripping of units in training and projecting and sustaining combat power on a scale never seen before required a considerable amount of overhead. The problem was balance, and that was one issue the Army never really overcame.

What is remarkable is that so many observers since the war have believed that since things did not go perfectly the Army somehow failed in its biggest test. They see a model in the German army, without understanding the full set of organizational, logistical, and structural requirements that go into generating combat power on a global basis. The German army had some absolutely superb and innovative soldiers, and it remained a very potent force until very late in the struggle. On the other hand, while the ETO was the U.S. Army's main effort, it was not the only effort. America had a significantly different set of requirements than did Germany. It had clear advantages over its enemies, but its enemies also had advantages.

The United States chose a head-on approach to defeating Germany, but its army was not large enough large for the task. The Army spent most of its time on the offense, and thereby in a more exposed operational position than the defenders. GIs could not always blast their way through the enemy positions. Some units performed well; others failed, and there were changes of leadership in all levels of unit from corps to platoon. Units could not always practice doctrine. Some devised tactics suited to their particular needs, after a painful learning curve. These lessons were necessary though brutal and they do not change.

Production created possibilities and conditions for success, but only operations on the ground ensured success. America could not somehow purchase victory with its industry. The only answer was in developing and using its combat forces in a more effective manner than its enemies. Richard Overy makes this point clearly, by stating that the only way the Allies could defeat the Axis was by defeating them in battle.[52] Given the strategic, organizational, logistical, and tactical factors, the accomplishments of the American combat soldier in the ETO deserve a second look. Some U.S. units had serious problems of organization and ability to execute their missions. Some were as good as any that fought in the war on either side. Such units bore the brunt of the fighting and proved that the citizen soldier, if properly trained and led, was up to great challenges. The U.S. Army outfought its enemy by skillful handling of organizations that were better suited for a war of mobility and maneuver that the enemy actually did not allow them to fight. Often literally stuck in the mud on the wrong side of the terrain, these organizations did not always have a technological advantage. Frontline soldiers were frightened to death, and often cold, tired, and hungry. They knew a level of mental and physical exhaustion incomprehensible to civilians. Some of them saw their best friends suddenly injured or dismembered. There were three ways out—the end of the war, death, or a wound. Yet they persevered. They secured the victory with sheer guts as well as steel and explosives. Could the generals have done better? Certainly some of them should have done a better job and others who should have been relieved were not. Yet even with the hindsight of six decades, when one considers the totality of the mission and what it took to organize and deploy the Army, the outcome is impressive. Were the best people always in the right roles? Certainly not—no one turned in a flawless performance, but given the state of the U.S. Army in 1940, that should not be a surprise. Enough good leaders like Collins, Simpson, and Allen were at the right place and time to ensure success.

If there is a real "lesson" of the campaign in Europe, it is the importance of perseverance of both organizations and individuals. A constabulary became a global military force while fighting a multifront war. A War Department with a bureaucracy epitomized by insular culture ended up managing its resources with early computers and global telecommunications. Units changed in organization; indeed, at war's end there were organizations that had not existed when mobilization began. An army with horse cavalry units in 1941 had portable surgical hospitals and petroleum-products laboratories deployed overseas in 1943.

Germany was battered in 1944–early 1945 but was not defeated until the end, and not until combat soldiers stood in its greatest cities and occupied its industrial heartland. The Army and GI of 1940–1942 would not have accomplished this task. Gen. William E. DePuy, who was a battalion commander and division G-3 in the ETO before he was thirty years of age, remarked, "It is hard to overstate how ineffective [we were] in the beginning and how very effective [we were] at the end."[53]

Winston Churchill called the Army a "prodigy of organization, of improvisation." The pace of its transformation from constabulary to global power was, he said, a "wonder of military history." He added, "it remains to me a mystery as yet unexplained" how the prewar U.S. Army was able quickly both to raise a mass force and find enough leaders to move it "faster and farther than masses have ever been moved in war before."[54] This is the real story of a campaign carried on to the bitter end.

APPENDIX A

TABLE OF COMPARATIVE OFFICER RANKS

U.S. ARMY	GERMAN ARMY
General of the Army	Generalfeldmarschall
General	Generaloberst
Lieutenant General	General der:
	Infanterie
	Artillerie
	Panzertruppen
Major General	Generalleutnant
Brigadier General	Generalmajor
Colonel	Oberst
Lieutenant Colonel	Oberstleutnant
Major	Major
Captain	Hauptmann
1st Lieutenant	Oberleutnant
2d Lieutenant	Leutnant

APPENDIX B

THE U.S. ARMOR PROBLEM

O NE OF THE SIGNIFICANT IRONIES of the Army's rebuilding going into World War II was that the "most mechanized nation on earth" failed to develop adequate tanks and anti-armor doctrine. There were several causes, but the end result was that tank crewmen battled superior German armor with under-armed and under-armored vehicles. Army doctrine as developed on the eve of its entry into the war called for tank destroyers (TD) to be the tank killer, while tanks were to support the ground soldier and exploit breakthroughs. In the end, both vehicles were inadequate, and the underlying doctrine had fundamental flaws.[1] The TD concept was based largely on the assumption that the Germans conducted "all-tank" operations, when actually only about 10 percent of that Army was ever mechanized.[2] Leaders saw what were shocking developments in Europe and found a threat they believed they should address with massed anti-tank weapons assigned to specially trained and organized battalion-sized units. To counter the assumed moral and psychological superiority of armor, TD soldiers would be indoctrinated with an aggressive, elite spirit complete with a motto ("seek, strike, destroy") to indicate TDs would take the initiative, and a shoulder patch depicting a black panther crushing a tank in its jaws.[3]

Lack of appropriations was only part of the problems of armor and counter-armor technology in the U.S. What money there was ended up devoted to two paths of development. Entrenched infantry interests gained control of the remnants of the World War I Tank Corps and steered tank development toward lightly armed and armored tanks that

270

would operate in direct support of the infantry. Institutional bureaucrats in the cavalry branch, meanwhile, would not accept the demise of the horse. Several chiefs of that branch forced development of its mechanized doctrine toward supplement of the horse. No amount of money flowing from Congress could force such thinking to change. Only the creation of the separate armored force in mid-1940 allowed progressive officers latitude to expand the role of the tank in line with that being developed overseas. Yet even this positive development failed to overcome all internal cavalry and infantry biases. Armor organization reflected continuing emphasis on traditional cavalry missions of reconnaissance, security, and limited exploitation of breakthroughs coupled with infantry support as required. Tanks themselves, like horse-mounted units, could seize ground but could not hold it without infantry support. Tanks were also vulnerable to isolation and defeat in detail. As the Army learned the hard way, it needed a force that fully integrated mobility, firepower, and air support.[4]

Interwar experiments solidified the place of the tank in the conduct of combat operations by the Army. Senior leaders long before had concluded from the experience of World War I that the rifleman was the preeminent weapon and that technology like the tank was nothing more than a supporting weapon, though some acknowledged that it was an offensive weapon. Infantrymen won the first internal fight for control of the new weapon, when legislation in 1920 put tanks under their control. Exercises by temporary experimental units did lead to discussion about using tanks in roles other than infantry support. Yet public discussion was limited and there was little productive development as the infantry and cavalry bureaucrats hunkered down to keep the resources they still had in a Depression-era military. For example, the chief of infantry in 1932 told Congress that tanks were "merely parts of the Infantry's armament." This line of thinking persisted in official doctrine and policy through the 1930s, and armament remained machine guns and a light (37-mm) cannon at best.[5]

The Ordnance Department, the bureaucracy responsible for weapons development, received no firm guidance from the War Department staff other than the policy statement that the tank was to support the "uninterrupted advance of the rifleman in the attack." Weight limits became tied to the capacity of engineer tactical bridging rather than technical specifications or doctrine based on combat concepts. Ordnance officers understandably did not believe they had a coherent development policy with which to work. While senior leader vision remained trapped in the past, there was little reason for the Army to throw good money after old thinking. The tank development budget between 1925 and 1930 was only about $60,000 per year, though large automobile manufacturers were spending up to $20 million per year. As late as 1939 the chief of ordnance "begged for $10,000 solely for development of diesel engines for tanks."[6]

Ordnance officers, at the urging of some cavalrymen, had already mounted a 75-mm howitzer in an experimental tank, and ironically, a few years later, some German observers remarked that the United States led the world in development of armor organization and design. As the official history noted, if that was sincere opinion and not flattery, the Army had certainly lost its edge by 1938 as nothing seems to have moved the pace of thinking. Even after he heard about a German tank experimentally mounting an 88-mm gun, the chief of infantry declared that even a 75-mm design proposal was not necessary given the infantry support role of the tank.[7] Reports about the effectiveness of new anti-tank weapons during the Spanish Civil War finally led to some reassessment of the need for heavier tanks. Unfortunately, even as the war began in Europe, the Ordnance Department began development of a medium tank armed with a 75-mm howitzer suited to the infantry support role but incapable of killing comparable armor.

Developments after the beginning of the war also failed to spur reconsideration of the role of the tank. Officers still did not see the issue as anything more than developing a vehicle that was survivable against anti-tank weapons and fixed defenses only. It was mid-1940 before the chief of infantry asked the Ordnance Department to investigate increasing armor protection and firepower of a then-experimental medium design. This timing coincided with the creation of the Armored Force.[8]

The M3 medium (Grant) carried a 75-mm short-barrel gun in a sponson, because no foundry in 1941 could cast a turret large enough for the weapon. It was an interim design at best, though not interim enough to keep it from going into combat with the 1st Armored Division. Production of the ubiquitous medium M4-series (Sherman) began in 1942. Despite Ordnance Department suggestions that the using arms adopt a heavier tank, the decision was made to standardize the M4 series, largely for logistical (shipping and maintenance standardization) reasons. A sixty-ton heavy tank had been designed, but the Army Ground Forces saw no use for it. Though more heavily armed and armored German tanks, including the Tiger, entered combat by early 1943, this was well after initial production decisions had been made in the United States and there was no way to quickly change them.[9]

Maneuvers in 1940 and 1941 led to the revision of Armored Force organization and doctrine, though the armored division remained "tank-heavy" and light on infantry. Officers believed the maneuvers also validated the theory that the anti-tank gun should be the primary anti-tank weapon. Lesley J. McNair, the powerful General Headquarters chief of staff and later commander of Army Ground Forces, ignored the concerns of infantrymen who believed the French in 1940 had placed too much reliance on the anti-tank gun. McNair, an artilleryman, lacked the vision to understand that tanks were the best anti-tank weapon. He maintained that the inherent stability of a stationary gun made it superior to any gun on a mobile platform, and he directed establishment of what became the tank destroyer arm.[10]

By mid-1942, stopgap self-propelled TDs mounted 37-mm and 75-mm guns on truck and half-track chassis. These hastily modified vehicles were unsuited to the close combat forced upon them by their inadequate short-range guns. Success in Tunisia was due in large part to overconfident German commanders who disregarded local security, or to Americans who operated in dispersed, not concentrated, formations—they soon learned that massed TDs made good targets. At El Guettar, for example, full-tracked M-10 TDs, armed with a 76-mm gun that was more powerful than that mounted on M4 tanks, helped devastate a panzer battalion. But the cost was seven of the twelve M-10s engaged. Commanders usually broke up TD battalions and attached their companies directly to divisions. Their typical use in the ETO was as additional artillery or close-support weapons for the infantry. In the TD, the Army had a solution to a problem that did not exist except in the minds of the media and military observers who were enthralled with technology and overlooked the importance of air and infantry support to tanks. The Army had invented a solution for a defensive problem but was itself primarily engaged in offensive operations.[11]

With the exception of the self-propelled TDs and a few models of light and medium tanks that were diesel-powered, another problem with U.S. tanks was their gasoline engines. There were some questions regarding reliability of diesel engines, though the Armored Force favored them at first. Yet by early 1942, the ASF already had growing concerns about the availability of diesel fuel in remote theaters and the logistical problems inherent in adoption of several types of engines. Domestic refining capacity was limited and gasoline was needed for aircraft and in the production of some explosives and synthetic rubber. Facing unique logistical challenges that its enemies did not, the U.S. Army in mid-1942 had to decide what type of power plant to standardize in order for production decisions to be made. It opted for gasoline engines.[12]

As the campaign in Europe approached, all the GI had on which to rely was the reliability and slightly greater operational range of the Sherman. Combined with TD doctrine that suggested the tank was not the best anti-tank weapon, the Sherman not only was too light but undergunned. TDs carried the higher-velocity 76-mm gun and later the hard-hitting 90-mm cannon. Few Shermans ever carried an equivalent main weapon. If the panzers were mechanically unreliable, too complex, and "over-engineered," they were at least much more survivable than their U.S. counterparts. Germany also recognized much earlier that the tank had to be able to overcome all types of weapons. Tragically, the Army Ground Forces, for all its ability to organize and train soldiers, simply would not consider heaver tanks, because its leadership somehow could not conceive that tank-against-tank combat could become the norm.[13]

The Ordnance Department could design stopgaps in the form of up-armoring and up-gunning Shermans, and the field could report its experiences in the hope that someone would put good ideas to production, but nothing seemed to move the bureaucracy. The Ground Forces, confronted with the facts of armored warfare by late 1944, criticized the Ordnance Department for not having designed a better tank.[14] GIs lost confidence in the M4. Design work on heavier tanks, had, meanwhile, continued, and the War Department, finally listening to field reports, forced McNair's Army Ground Forces to accept a new design called the T 26. This vehicle, with a 90-mm gun and a low silhouette, weighed over forty tons and could take on Panthers and Tigers. Unfortunately, it was already 1944, and production was very slow until early 1945, when a handful reached Germany in time to fight at Cologne and Remagen. Only about two hundred were in the hands of soldiers by VE Day. The Army Ground Forces blamed Ordnance for striving for perfection at the expense of production, and the Ordnance Department blamed the Ground Forces for impeding its work.[15]

APPENDIX C

BATTLE AND NON-BATTLE CASUALTIES, JUNE 1944–MAY 1945

1944

Year and Month	Total	Battle	Non-battle
June	n/a	39,367	n/a
July	63,424	51,424	12,000
August	59,503	42,535	16,968
September	63,179	42,183	20,996
October	59,981	31,617	28,364
November	118,698	62,437	56,261
December	134,421	77,726	56,695

1945

Year and Month	Total	Battle	Non-battle
January	136,747	69,119	67,628
February	91,545	39,414	52,131
March	101,156	53,209	47,947
April	87,209	41,058	46,151
May (1–8)	14,178	2,028	12,150

Source: Ruppenthal, *Logistical Support of the Armies*, Vol. II, 317.

NOTES

Abbreviations in the notes are:

AAR After Action Report

CI Combat Interview

LOI Letter of Instructions

PR Periodic Report

RG National Archives Record Group

RO Report of Operations

USFET GB US Forces European Theater General Board

INTRODUCTION

1. Leo A. Hoegh and Howard J. Doyle, *Timberwolf Tracks: The History of the 104th Infantry Division, 1942-1945* (Washington, D.C.: Infantry Journal Press, 1946), 214. Duane A. Robey, *The Memories of an Infantryman in the I&R Platoon*, n.d., provided by D.A. Roby to the author, 127–34. This action was also reported by *The Stars and Stripes* on 5 January 1945. The enlisted men received the Silver Star; Pruitt was awarded the Distinguished Service Cross. A former regimental staff officer, Gen. John R. Dean Jr. (Ret.), corroborated the above accounts in an interview at Ft. Myer, VA, on February 10, 1996.

CHAPTER 1

1. Timothy K. Nenninger, *The Leavenworth Schools and the Old Army* (Westport, Conn. Greenwood Press, 1978), 83–84.
2. The best study of the pre-1900 army is Edward M. Coffman, *The Old Army, A Portrait of the American Army in Peacetime 1784-1898* (New York: Oxford University Press, 1986), see especially Chapter 8. Also see Coffman, *The Regulars, The American Army 1898-1941* (Cambridge: Harvard University Press, 2004), particularly Chapter 5, hereafter cited as Coffman, *The Regulars*.
3. Public Law 35, 64th Cong., 1st Sess. (3 June 1916): 197–211.
4. Edward M. Coffman, *The War to End All Wars: The American Military Experience in World War I* (Lexington: University Press of Kentucky, 1998), 11.
5. Russell F. Weigley, *The History of the United States Army* (Bloomington: Indiana University Press, 1984), 351.
6. Paul F. Braim, *The Test of Battle: The American Expeditionary Force in the Meuse-Argonne Campaign* (Newark: University of Delaware Press, 1987), 146, hereafter cited as Braim, *Test of Battle*. Marvin A. Kriedberg and Merton G. Henry, *History of Military Mobilization in the United States Army 1775-1946* (Washington, D.C.: GPO 1955), gives

the strength of the army as 133,111 on 1 April 1917, and 3,884,417, on 11 November 1918, see pages 221, 247. Hereafter cited as Kriedberg, *Mobilization*. The Pentagon Library holds several dozen examples of the reprinted foreign publications.

7. Braim, *Test of Battle*, 149–51.
8. James W. Rainey, "The Questionable Training of the AEF in World War I," *Parameters* 22, No. 4 (Winter 1992-1993): 100.
9. Edward M. Coffman, "Conflicts in American Planning, an Aspect of World War I Strategy," *Military Review* 43 (1963): 78–90.
10. Public Law 242, 66th Cong., 2d Sess. (4 June 1920): 759, 69, 84, hereafter cited as PL 242.
11. Mark S. Watson, *Chief of Staff: Prewar Plans and Preparations*, The U.S. Army in World War II (Washington, D.C.: GPO, 1950), Chapter 1, especially 33–35. Hereafter cited as Watson, *Chief of Staff*.
12. Coffman, *The Regulars*, 234.
13. Watson, *Chief of Staff*, 16; Kriedberg, *Mobilization*, 379.
14. David E. Johnson, *Fast Tanks and Heavy Bombers: Innovation in the U.S. Army 1917-1945* (Ithaca, N.Y.: Cornell University Press, 1998), 90. Hereafter cited as Johnson, *Fast Tanks*.
15. Watson, *Chief of Staff*, 21–22; Thomas W. Collier, "The Army and the Great Depression," *Parameters* 18, No. 3 (1988): 103.
16. War Department, *Annual Report of the Chief of Staff* (Washington, D.C.: GPO, 1933), 3–8.
17. *Ibid.*, 13–19; 31.
18. War Department, *Annual Report of the Chief of Staff* (Washington, D.C.: GPO, 1934), 12.
19. War Department, *Annual Report of the Secretary of War* (Washington, D.C.: GPO, 1938), 33–35.
20. "The People's Army," *Fortune* 24, (August 1941): 97.
21. Gene Smith, "The Seventeenth Largest Army," *American Heritage* 43, No. 8 (1992): 101.
22. Robert K. Griffith, Jr., *Men Wanted for the U.S. Army: America's Experience With the All-Volunteer Army Between the World Wars* (Westport, Conn. Greenwood Press, 1982), 1–36; 85–110.
23. "Who's in the Army Now?" and "Why an Army," *Fortune* 12 (September 1935), 39–40; 132–136.
24. Coffman, *The Regulars*, 282.
25. Quoted in Jeffery S. Underwood, *The Wings of Democracy: The Influence of Air Power on the Roosevelt Administration, 1933-1941* (College Station: Texas A&M University Press, 1991), 120. Hereafter cited as Underwood, *Wings of Democracy*.
26. William O. Odom, *After the Trenches: The Transformation of U.S. Army Doctrine 1918-1939* (College Station: Texas A&M University Press, 1999), 213. Hereafter cited as Odom, *After the Trenches*.
27. Forrest C. Pogue, *George C. Marshall: Education of a General, 1880-1939* (New York: The Viking Press, 1963), 248–49. Hereafter cited as Pogue, *Education of a General*.
28. George C. Marshall, *The Papers of George Catlett Marshall*, Vol. I, "The Soldierly Spirit: December 1880-July 1939," ed. Larry I. Bland and Sharon Ritenour (Baltimore: The Johns Hopkins University Press, 1981), 321, hereafter cited as Marshall, *Papers*, Vol. I; Pogue, *Education of a General*, 254–56.
29. J. Lawton Collins, *Lightnin' Joe: An Autobiography* (Novato, CA: Presidio Press, 1994), 51–52.
30. Pogue, *Education of a General*, 291–292.
31. Martin Blumenson, "America's World War II Leaders in Europe: Some Thoughts," *Parameters* 19, No. 4 (1989): 13.

CHAPTER 2

1. George C. Marshall, *Testimony on Military Establishment Appropriation Bill for 1941* (Washington, D.C.: GPO, 1940), 3; Watson, *Chief of Staff*, 16; PL 242, 759.

2. Watson, *Chief of Staff*, 31; Harry C. Thomson and Lida Mayo, *The Ordnance Department: Procurement and Supply*, The United States Army in World War II (Washington, D.C.: GPO, 1960), 5. Hereafter cited as Thomson, *Procurement*.

3. Lee Kennet, *GI* (New York: Schribner's, 1987), 5–7.

4. George C. Marshall, *The Papers of George Catlett Marshall*, Vol. II, "'We Cannot Delay,' July 1, 1939–December 6, 1941,'" ed. Larry I. Bland, Sharon R. Ritenour and Clarence E. Wunderkind, Jr., (Baltimore: The Johns Hopkins University Press, 1986), 163. Hereafter cited as Marshall, *Papers*, Vol. II.

5. John B. Wilson, *Maneuver and Firepower: The Evolution of Divisions and Separate Brigades* (Washington, D.C.: GPO, 1998), see Chapter 6.

6. "National Affairs," *Time* 35, No. 22 (27 May 1940): 19.

7. Kriedberg, *Mobilization*, 123–28; 318–328.

8. Thomson, *Procurement*, Table 1, p.25; Table 8, p.70; 83; Table 9, p.84.

9. Alan L. Gropman, *Mobilizing U.S. Industry in World War II* (Washington, D.C.: National Defense University Press, 1996), 6n. Hereafter cited as Gorman, *Mobilizing Industry*.

10. *Ibid.*, 2; 6n, 135.

11. Byron Fairchild and Johnathan Grossman, *The Army and Industrial Manpower*, The United States Army in World War II (Washington, D.C.: GPO, 1959), 157; 160–67; 181, hereafter cited as Fairchild, *Industrial Manpower*. The specific impact on future combat performance has to the author's knowledge not been a subject of scholarly research, but there can be little doubt that it was negative.

12. Gropman, *Mobilizing Industry*, 11; Fairchild, *Industrial Manpower*, 4.

13. R. Elburton Smith, *The Army and Economic Mobilization*, The United States Army and World War II (Washington, D.C.: GPO, 1985), 62–5. So-called 'educational orders' for production of small quantities specialized goods were of considerable value in determining production capacity.

14. Fairchild, *Industrial Manpower*, 38–9.

15. *Ibid.*, 57–75; 80–81

16. *Ibid.*

17. Constance M. Green, Harry C. Thomson and Peter C. Roots, *The Ordnance Department: Planning Munitions for War*, The United States Army in World War II (Washington, D.C.: GPO, 1955), 177, hereafter cited as Green, *Planning Munitions*; Johnson, *Fast Tanks*, 114–15.

18. Underwood, *Wings of Democracy*, 132–39.

19. Thomson, *Procurement*, 81–89; 100–03; 144–50; 173–74; 272–92.

20. War Department, Field Manual 101–10, *Staff Officers' Field Manual, Organization, Technical and Logistical Data* (Washington, D.C.: GPO, 10 October 1943), 120; 149.

21. War Department, *Logistics in World War II, Final Report of the Army Service Forces* (Washington, D.C.: GPO, reprint 1993), Chart 5, pp. 25–31; "US Army Supply Lines," chart between pp. 54–55.

22. Charles W. Cawthon, *Other Clay* (Niwot, CO: University Press of Colorado, 1990), xii–xiii, 1–2.

23. Steson Conn, *Highlights of Mobilization, World War II, 1938-1942*, U.S. Army Center of Military History file 2–3.7AF.B1; War Department, *Biennial Reports of the Chief of Staff of the United States Army to the Secretary of War 1 July 1939–30 June 1945* (Washington, D.C.: GPO, reprint 1996), 3–4; 27.

24. War Department, Mobilization Regulation 1, *General Mobilization*, 1 April 1940.

25. Henry G. Gole, *The Road to Rainbow: Army Planning for Global War, 1934-1940* (Annapolis: U.S. Naval Institute Press, 2003), hereafter cited as Gole, *Road to Rainbow*.

26. War Department, Mobilization Regulation 1-7, *Reception of Selected Service Men*, 1 October 1940; War Department Pamphlet 12-8, *The Evaluation, Classification and Assignment of Military Personnel of the United States Army*, 28 July 1944. The AGCT did not measure IQ; it was an attempt to determine the ability to learn. The total score on a multiple choice test of simple arithmetic, block counting, and matching synonyms put men into one of five categories. Officer candidates, for example, generally came from the Category I pool. Deferring to the pressures of time, the army gave more credence to science over subjective analysis. There was a tendency to assign high-scoring men in good physical condition to specialties that were comparable to their civilian trade. Higher scoring men were more likely to have had an established trade in civilian life, and they often got the assignment of their choice, which was usually not a combat branch.

27. Watson, *Chief of Staff*, 193–94; Marshall, *Papers*, Vol. I., 231.

28. Kennett, *GI*, 3–6.

29. Public Law 783, 76th Cong., 3d Sess.: 865. The first Guard divisions mobilized (30th, 41st, 44th, 45th) were from states whose comparatively small industrial base would be least disturbed by the loss of manpower—including New York, North Carolina, Tennessee, Oklahoma, New Mexico, Idaho, and Washington). After mobilization, the divisions averaged only 40 percent of their authorized wartime strength. See Chief National Guard Bureau, *Annual Report for Fiscal Year 1941* (Washington, D.C.: GPO, 1941), 19; 83–89.

30. Marshall, *Papers*, Vol. II, 309.

31. E. J. Kahn Jr., *McNair-Educator of an Army* (Washington, D.C.: Infantry Journal Press, 1946), 6–8; 50.

32. Statement of General George C. Marshall in Connection with Retention of Selectees and Reserve Components in the Military Service Beyond One Year, Before the Committee on Military Affairs of the United States Senate, 9 July 1941 (Washington, D.C.: GPO 1941), 2–4.

33. "National Defense," *Time* 37, No. 7 (18 August 1941), 35–36.

34. Kennett, *GI*, Chapter 2; War Department Mobilization Regulation 1–915, *Standards of Physical Examination During Mobilization*, October 1943.

35. Charles E. Kirkpatrick, *An Unknown Future and a Doubtful Present–Writing the Victory Plan of 1941* (Washington, D.C.: GPO, 1990), 1.

36. Maurice Matloff, "The 90-Division Gamble," in *Command Decisions*, ed. Kent Roberts Greenfield (Washington, D.C.: GPO: 1960), 366; 370; 374.

37. Robert R. Palmer et. al., *The Procurement and Training of Ground Combat Troops*, The United States Army in World War II (Washington, D.C.: GPO, 1948), 2. Hereafter cited as Palmer, *Procurement and Training*.

38. War Department, Training Regulation 10–5, 10 August 1935, 1–4.

39. Palmer, *Procurement and Training*, 6–10; 14–17.

40. *Ibid.*, 48–50; Supplement to Mobilization Regulation 1–9, *Physical Profile Serial*, 30 June 1945.

41. Palmer, *Procurement and Training*, 24–39.

42. *Ibid.*, 96.

43. *Ibid.*, 334–40.

44. War Department, Training Regulation 10–5, 6.

45. John S. Brown, "Winning Teams: Mobilization-Related Correlates of Success in American World War II Infantry Divisions" (master's thesis, U.S. Army Command and General Staff College, 1985), 10; 14–17; 170–71.

46. War Department, Mobilization Training Plan 17–1, 31 January 1942, 1.

47. War Department, Mobilization Training Plan 7–1, 12 September 1943, 1–2.

48. John S. Brown, *Draftee Division* (Lexington: University Press of Kentucky, 1986), 164–67.

49. Donald E. Houston, *Hell on Wheels* (San Rafael, Calif. Presidio Press, 1977), 52.

50. Palmer, *Procurement and Training*, 457; 472–73.

51. *Ibid.*, 476–77.

52. Harvey R. Frasier, *The 51st Again* (Shippensburg, PA: White Mane, 1992), 10.

53. Stuart Thayer, letter to author, 2 September 1997.

54. Neil Burd, letter to author, n.d.

55. Arnold Whittaker, letter to author, 29 November 1997.

56. Wallace Clement, letter to author, 15 July 1997.

57. Palmer, *Procurement and Training*, 464–65.

58. HQ, Army Ground Forces, Army Ground Forces Study No. 15, *The Desert Training Center and CAMA* (Washington, D.C.: GPO, 1946), 9–14; 30, 60, 88.

59. Christopher R. Gabel, *The U.S. Army GHQ Maneuvers of 1941* (Washington, D.C.: GPO, 1991), 185–193.

60. Edmond C. Wilkins, letter to Mary E. Wilkins, 20 November 1941, author's files. Wilkins was killed in action in Italy in May 1944.

61. Odom, *After the Trenches*, Chapter 3 reviews the early post-WWI years.

62. Timothy K. Nenninger, "A Revised Mechanization Policy," *Armor* 78 No. 5 (September-October 1969): 45–49.

63. War Department, Field Manual 100-5, *Operations*, 15 June 1944, 32; Field Manual 7–20 *Rifle Battalion*, 1 October 1944, 5.

64. Christopher Gabel, e-mail to author, 6 January 2000.

CHAPTER 3

1. Freeland Daubin, Jr., "The Battle of Happy Valley," (Ft. Knox: U.S. Army Armor School Advanced Officer's Class #1, 24 April 1948), 1–4.

2. Martin Blumenson, "Kasserine Pass," ed. Charles E. Heller and William A. Stofft, *America's First Battles 1776-1965* (Lawrence: University Press of Kansas, 1986), 240–42. Hereafter cited as Blumenson, "Kasserine Pass." Department of the Army, *Algeria-French Morocco 8 November 1942-11 November 1942* (Washington, D.C.: GPO, n.d.), 4–5. Hereafter cited as Department of the Army, *Algeria*. War came to North Africa in 1940 when the Italians attacked British forces. Hitler in 1941 sent in troops under the command of Erwin Rommel, but an Italian theater commander directed operations. A powerful Axis drive in mid-1942 through Libya captured the British defenses at Tobruk. Retreating British forces halted Rommel in July at El Alamein. In October, a British counterattack drove them into southern Tunisia.

3. George F. Howe, *Northwest Africa: Seizing the Initiative in the West*, The United States Army in World War II (Washington, D.C.: GPO, 1957), 61–66, hereafter cited as Howe, *Seizing the Initiative*.

4. Information provided by Mark A. Reardon from Orlando Ward Papers, Box 1, U.S. Army Military History Institute, Carlisle Barracks, PA. Ward was an artilleryman who had been the War Department Secretary of the General Staff before the war. Marshall offered him a chance to go to the new Armored Force in mid-1941.

5. Lida Mayo, *The Ordnance Department: On Beachhead and Battlefront*, The United States Army in World War II (Washington, D.C.: GPO, 1968), 104, hereafter cited as Mayo, *Beachhead and Battlefront*.

6. Howe, *Seizing the Initiative*, 153–158; Department of the Army, *Algeria*, 13.

7. Department of the Army, *Algeria*, 22. The attack included an ill-fated, British-planned operation to seize the Oran harbor. About four hundred U.S. troops participated, but only 47 GIs reached the docks. Bad weather and poor communications also broke up an attempted airborne landing. Some French units strongly resisted the 1st Infantry Division, though Oran surrendered on 10 November.

8. Department of the Army, *Tunisia* (Washington, D.C.: GPO, n.d.), 7–10.
9. *Ibid.*, 11–15.
10. Dwight D. Eisenhower, *The Papers of Dwight David Eisenhower, The War Years*, Vol. II, ed. Alfred D. Chandler, Jr. (Baltimore: The Johns Hopkins University Press, 1971), 904–05, hereafter cited as Eisenhower *Papers*, Vol. II.
11. Marshall, *Marshall Papers*, Vol. 3 (Baltimore: The Johns Hopkins University Press, 1991), 520–521.
12. Lt. Col. J. R. Dryden, Jr., memorandum to HQ, Army Ground Forces, 17 March 1943; Col. Harry Mc K. Roper, memorandum to HQ, Army Ground Forces, 22 March 1943; Lt. Col. W. H. Schaefer and Maj. Franklin T. Gardner, memorandum to HQ, Army Ground Forces, 10 February 1943.
13. Orlando Ward Papers, Box 1, contains an unpublished biographical mss by Russell Gugler.
14. Howe, *Northwest Africa*, 378, 399–400; analysis provided by Mark Reardon to author 16 July 2001. The 59-year-old corps commander had trained troops in France during WWI, attended Command and General Staff College and the Army War College, and was promoted to brigadier general in 1939. He took command of II Corps in 1941, but turned it over to another officer before TORCH. Eisenhower accepted Marshall's suggestion that Fredendall resume command of the corps for TORCH since he knew the staff and had a reputation as a forceful leader.
15. Howe, *Northwest Africa*, 370–371.
16. Blumenson, "Kasserine Pass," 245–46.
17. *Ibid.*, 246–47.
18. *Ibid.*, 248; 250–51.
19. *Ibid.*, 25–54; Howe, *Seizing the Initiative*, 430–32; Historian Mark Reardon, who has read unit journals and records in detail, maintains that the actual level of confusion and disorganization was likely not as bad as that described by Blumenson and some others (email to author, 16 July, 2001).
20. Department of the Army, *Tunisia*, 17, 24–25; Howe, *Seizing the Initiative*, 466, 478; Blumenson, "Kasserine Pass," 255, 257–60.
21. Mark. T. Calhoun, "Defeat at Kasserine: American Armor Doctrine, Training, and Battle Command in Northwest Africa, World War II" (master's thesis, U.S. Army Command and General Staff College, Ft. Leavenworth, KS, 2003), 74–75.
22. David W. Hazen, "The Role of Field Artillery in the Battle of Kasserine Pass" (master's thesis, U.S. Army Command and General Staff College, Ft. Leavenworth, KS, 1963), 145–48; 159–66, 171; Mark Reardon, email to author, July 4, 2001.
23. Mayo, *Beachhead and Battlefront*, 132–41.
24. Daniel R. Mortensen, *A Pattern for Joint Operations: World War II Close Air Support in North Africa* (Washington, D.C.: Office of Air Force History and U.S. Army Center of Military History, 1987), 78.
25. Blumenson, "Kasserine Pass," 262–63.
26. War Department, Field Manual 21–50, *Military Courtesy and Discipline* (Washington, D.C.: GPO, June 15, 1942), 1.
27. Erwin Rommel, *The Rommel Papers*, ed. B. H. Lidell Hart (New York: DaCapo, n.d.), 404, 521.
28. Department of the Army, *Sicily* (Washington, D.C.: GPO, n.d.), 4–6; 10. A disturbing incident was the friendly fire disaster on the night of 11-12 July when anti-aircraft gunners offshore and on land shot down 23 American transport planes carrying troops of the 82d Airborne Division. Not everyone had been informed of the impending operation and the Luftwaffe had been active during the day.
29. Albert N. Garland, *Sicily and the Surrender of Italy*, The United States Army in World War II (Washington, D.C.: GPO, 1965), Chapter VI, especially 115–146, hereafter

cited as Garland, *Sicily*. While the other assault divisions had been preparing for the invasion by training in North Africa, the 45th Infantry Division had been at sea. It had limited preparation time, but it took every assigned objective.

30. *Ibid.*, 163–174.

31. Department of the Army, *Sicily*, 14–16; Rupert Prohme, *History of the 30th Infantry Regiment in World War II* (Washington, D.C.: Infantry Journal Press, 1947), 52–56. Hereafter cited as Prohme, *30th Infantry*; Charles B. MacDonald, *The Mighty Endeavor* (New York: Oxford University Press, 1969), 154.

32. Department of the Army, *Sicily*, 16–17; Garland, *Sicily*, 389.

33. Charles M. White, *The Medical Department: Medical Service in the Mediterranean and Minor Theaters*, The United States Army in World War II (Washington, D.C.: GPO, 1965), 173.

34. Lucian K. Truscott, *Command Missions*, (Novato, CA: Presidio Press, reprint, 1990), 234–35, hereafter cited as Truscott, *Command Missions*.

35. The story of Brolo is from Truscott, *Command Missions*, 236–41; Prohme, *30th Infantry*, 65–68; and Garland, *Sicily*, 388–405.

36. Garland, *Sicily*, 396–97.

37. *Ibid.*, 398.

38. *Ibid.*, 399.

39. Truscott, *Command Missions*, 237–38.

40. *Ibid.*, 238.

41. Garland, *Sicily*, 401; Prohme, *30th Infantry*, 67.

42. Truscott, *Command Missions*, 239.

43. Garland, *Sicily*, 402; Prohme, *30th Infantry*, 68.

44. Garland, *Sicily*, 403; Prohme, *30th Infantry*, 69.

45. Carlo D'Este, *Bitter Victory, The Battle for Sicily–1943* (Glasgow: William Collins Sons, 1988), 559–60.

46. Mayo, *Beachhead and Battlefront*, 166–69.

47. Department of the Army, *Naples-Foggia* (Washington, D.C.: GPO, n.d.), 3–5.

48. Martin Blumenson, *Salerno to Cassino*, The United States Army in World War II (Washington, D.C.: GPO, 1969), 74-78; 96–98.

49. *Ibid.*, 77–79.

50. *Ibid.*, 79–81.

51. *Ibid.*, 119–130. The Germans could neither push the Americans into the sea nor firmly cordon the beachhead. They conducted a skillful withdrawal north of Naples. By the time of the disastrous December 1943–January 1944 attacks along the Rapido River, it was clear that the Allies had run out of steam. Large numbers of reinforcements were out of the question if the Allies were to build up the forces needed for an invasion of France in 1944. Churchill became sponsor of an attack at Anzio, behind the "Gustav" defense line in an operation that had promise but utterly poor execution at high levels. By mid-February, the Germans outnumbered the Allies there, and they began a series of counterattacks that lasted for weeks. The U.S. VI Corps was out of the beachhead in late May and at the outskirts of Rome by early June.

52. Walker, *From Texas to Rome*, 437.

53. Fred L. Walker, "Experiences with the 36th Division in Italy," *Military Review* 24, No. 10, (1945): 19.

CHAPTER 4

1. The author is indebted to Col. D. E. Nash, U.S. Army (Ret.), an expert on the German military, for his review of this chapter in draft. Of course any inaccuracies are my responsibility. Sources on the first minutes on OMAHA Beach include Edward Ellsberg,

The Far Shore (New York: Popular Library, 1960), 172–82; Department of the Army, *OMAHA Beach* (Washington, D.C.: GPO, 1945), 38–48. Paul Carrell, *Invasion: They're Coming!* (New York: Bantam, 1973), Chapter 2, discusses the German perspective.

2. Richard Overy, *War and Economy in the Third Reich*, (Oxford: Clarendon Press, 1995), especially Chapter III. Hereafter cited as Overy, *War and Economy*. He also argues (235–36) that Hitler planned for a long war and large-scale mobilization.

3. Army Industrial College, "The German War Economy," (Washington, D.C., 29 October 1945), 2.

4. Overy, *War and Economy*, 250.

5. D. E. Nash, interview with author, 5 May 2005.

6. Robert M. Kennedy, *The German Campaign in Poland 1939* (Washington, D.C.: GPO, 1956), 8–14. Hereafter cited as Kennedy, *Campaign in Poland*.

7. *Ibid.*, 20.

8. Manfred Messerschmidt, "German Military Effectiveness Between 1919 and 1939," ed. Allan R. Millett and Williamson Murray, *Military Effectiveness: The Interwar Period*, (Boston: Allen & Unwin, 1988), 225.

9. Kennedy, *Campaign in Poland*, 24–25.

10. Samuel J. Newland, "Blitzkrieg in Retrospect," *Military Review* 84, No. 5 (2004): 86–89.

11. *Ibid*, 86; Kennedy, *Campaign in Poland*, 130–35, provides an overview of the campaign's outcome and lessons for the Germans. A German infantry division at the time used about 5,000 horses.

12. D. E. Nash, email to author, 28 April 1997.

13. Williamson Murray, *Strategy for Defeat, The Luftwaffe 1939-1945* (Maxwell, Ala: Air University Press, 1983), 302.

14. Department of the Army, *The German Campaign in Russia–Planning and Operations (1940-1942)* (Washington, D.C.: GPO, 1955), 71, 88, 169.

15. D. E. Nash, comments on the draft chapter, April 2005.

16. Omer Bartov, *Hitler's Army* (New York: Oxford University Press, 1992), 21. Hereafter cited as Bartov, *Hitler's Army*. Bartov focuses on the Eastern Front, but comparable conditions existed elsewhere.

17. There was considerable Nazi influence in the regular military. See Roger Beaumont, "Wehrmacht Mystique Revisited," *Military Review* 70, No. 2 (1990): 64–75; Stephen G. Fritz, *Frontsoldaten*, (Lexington: University Press of Kentucky, 1995), Chapter 8.

18. Nash comment on the draft chapter. See also War Department, Military Intelligence Division, *The German Squad in Combat*, (Washington, D.C., January 1943). One cannot rely on standard tables of organization to determine the composition of a battle group at a particular time. American intelligence officers could not assume the strength and firepower of a battle group would stay constant over time and they had to assume the worst.

19. Determining why the German army endured as long as it did has been a cottage industry. Edward A. Shills and Morris Janowitz, "Cohesion and Disintegration in the Wehrmacht in World War II," *Public Opinion Quarterly*, 12, No. 2 (1948), 280–315, was probably the first widely distributed report on German cohesion. Other scholars such as Bartov and Fritz have expanded on and balanced early findings.

20. Omer Bartov, "The Conduct of War: Soldiers and the Barbarization of Warfare," *The Journal of Military History* 62 (December 1992 Supplement), S-45.

21. Bartov, *Hitler's Army*, Chapter 2, 29–58.

22. Fritz, *Frontsoldaten*, 12.

23. *Ibid.*, 159.

24. D. E. Nash. email to author, 28 April 1997.

25. Robert S. Rush, "Germans Facing the Twenty Second in Hürtgen," unpublished mss, 1997, copy in author's possession, 16–18.

26. Fritz, *Frontsoldaten*, 241–43.

CHAPTER 5

1. War Department Special Staff, Regimental Unit Study #4, *Forcing of the Merderet Causeway at LaFière, France,* August 1944, 20. Hereafter cited as RUS #4.
2. Chester W. Walker, letter to author, 19 May 1992.
3. Memorandum, Operations in Western Europe, 14 July 1942, *Records of the Joint Chiefs of Staff, European Theater of Operations, 1942-1945,* microfilm, Reel 1, Frame 88, The Pentagon Library.
4. Department of the Army, *Normandy* (Washington, D.C.: GPO, n.d.), 7-20.
5. Adrian R. Lewis, *Omaha Beach: A Flawed Victory* (Chapel Hill, N.C.: The University of North Carolina Press, 2001), 292-93.
6. The author is indebted to Dr. Christopher Gabel of the U.S. Army Combat Studies Institute, Ft. Leavenworth, KS, for his thoughts on the imponderables of OMAHA and other aspects of the campaign.
7. 4th Infantry Division, FO #1, 12 May 1944; First U.S. Army memo to VII Corps, subject, Modification to VII Corps Plan, 30 May 1944; 82d Airborne Division Plan, 26 May 1944.
8. Clay Blair, *Ridgway's Paratroopers: The American Airborne in World War II* (New York: Dial Press, 1985), 278-79.
9. *Ibid.,* 63.
10. Chester W. Walker, letter to author, 30 March 1992.
11. Gerard M. Devlin, *Silent Wings* (New York: St. Martin's Press, 1985), 64-67. Hereafter cited as Devlin, *Silent Wings.*
12. Martin Wolfe, *Green Light! A Troop Carrier Squadron's War From Normandy to the Rhine* (Washington, D.C.: Office of Air Force History, 1993), 319-21.
13. *Ibid.,* 147, 329.
14. War Department Special Staff, Regimental Unit Study #5, Preliminary Operations Around the Leafier Bridgehead, Merderet River, Normandy, n.d., 19-20, copy in author's files. Hereafter cited as RUS #5.
15. *Ibid.,* 21-26.
16. *Ibid.,* 33-36.
17. *Ibid.,* 38-41.
18. *Ibid.,* 41-49.
19. *Ibid.,* 57-61.
20. *Ibid.,* 61-63.
21. Devlin, *Ridgway's Paratroopers,* 198.
22. Chester Walker letter to author, not dated, received April 1993.
23. Douglas Miller, letter to author, 3 April 1993.
24. Wayne Pierce, "Normandy! Let's Go!, My First 60 Hrs!" Unpublished recollections dated 1989, copy in author's files provided by Wayne Pierce.
25. James B. Helmer in *The Glider Tow Line,* publication of the 325th Glider Infantry Association, Winter 1993-1994, n.p.
26. Richard B. Johnson, reminiscences completed in December 1976. Copy in author's files provided by Lee Travelstead. Johnson was a pre-war graduate of Harvard Law School who enlisted as a private.
27. War Department, Table of Organization (T/O) 7-51, 5 September 1942, with changes, through 24 May 1944 (the organization of the regiment changed before Normandy from a two battalion to a three battalion structure); Report, "Initial Operations of 325th Glider Infantry," typescript in 82d Airborne CI #170, prepared about September 1944, 3, hereafter cited as "Initial Operations." Air movements are in Annex No. 3 to 82 Airborne Division report, Action in Normandy, France, June-July 1944, RG 407, NARA.
28. "Initial Operations," 3-6.

29. RUS #5, 69–72.
30. Department of the Army, *Utah Beach to Cherbourg* (Washington, D.C.: GPO, 1947), 75.
31. RUS #5, 75.
32. *Ibid.*, 77–78; Initial Operations, 6.
33. RUS #5, 79–85.
34. Statement of Brig. Gen. James M. Gavin, typescript in 82d Airborne Division CI #170, 11–12, hereafter cited as Gavin Statement.
35. Vernon Wyant, letter to author, 26 October 1993.
36. Blair, *Ridgway's Paratroopers*, 50–51; 95–96.
37. U.S. Army War College interview with Maj. Gen. Teddy Sanford, 103–04.
38. Quoted in John Colby, *War From the Ground Up: the 90th Division in World War II* (Austin, TX: Nortex, 1991), 21, 23.
39. Lee Travelstead letter to author, 17 April 1992. Max Hastings in *Overlord* (New York: Simon & Schuster, 1984), 154, says that Carrell did not "feel well." Blair, *Ridgway's Paratroopers*, 322, reports that Carrell told Gavin that he was "sick." Gavin does not specifically mention this incident in his statement included in the CI files; neither does Lewis.
40. Gavin Statement, 12–13.
41. Colby, *War From the Ground Up*, 22.
42. "Initial Operations," 8–10.
43. *Crossing of Merderet by 325–3*, 1–2. Combined combat interview transcript, 82d Airborne Division CI #170.
44. *Ibid.*, 3. This transcript, operational records and the RUS track well, though the direct quotes appear only in the RUS.
45. *Ibid.*, 3–4.
46. *Ibid.*, 6.
47. *Ibid.*; the Ericsson quote is from RUS #4, 16.
48. *Ibid.*
49. "Initial Observations," 9–10.
50. Richard B. Johnson reminiscences provide by Lee Travelstead to author, n.d.
51. *Ibid.*; Crossing of Merderet by 325–3, 8.
52. RUS #4, 18–20.
53. Crossing of Merderet by 325–3, 9.
54. Russell Anderman letter to author, n.d., received in early 1993. The strength figure is from RUS #4, 22. Crossing of Merderet by 325–3, p. 10, notes that 30 men were lost in the crossing.
55. Gavin described the chaos at the crossing site and the "uncertainty" pervading the situation (p. 14). RUS #4, 26–27, provides the situation with Rae's men. When the author was actively corresponding with glider veterans in the early 1990's, one consistent theme was that Gavin too quickly assumed the inexperienced battalion was having trouble and that he did not need to send in the paratroopers. "Initial Operations," 14, indicates that Lieutenant Colonel Sitler requested the paratrooper support. The differences of opinion were even apparent to the contemporary interviewers (see RUS #4, 31).
56. RUS #4, 33–34.
57. *Ibid.*, 27.
58. Robert Hricik, letter to author, 29 January 1993.
59. Lee Travelstead, typescript provided to the author in 1993.
60. Strength figures are from RUS #4 and CI files. Low relative strengths are quite believable and discrepancies in such reporting are common.
61. Information provided by Lee Travelstead in the author's files; RUS #4, 39–40.
62. *Ibid.*, 44, mentions the cooks.
63. Crossing of Merderet by 325–3, 11.

64. This account is from RUS #4, 54–61; Continuation of Merderet Crossing, narrative typescript in the 82d Airborne Division CI Files, 7–11.
65. RUS #4, 63–65.
66. *Ibid.*, 66–67.
67. Vernon L. Wyant, Jr., untitled report in *The Glider Tow Line* (Winter 1991-92), 4–5.
68. Blair, *Ridgway's Paratroopers*, 325–26.
69. Wyant in *The Glider Tow Line* (Winter 1991-92), 4.
70. Johnson reminiscences provided to author, 11. Lewis died in 1945; Johnson passed away about 1977. Sanford reached the rank of major general and died in 1992 at age 84. Ridgway would not approve a Distinguished Service Cross for Lewis, but he did recommend him for promotion to brigadier general (see Blair, 325).

CHAPTER 6

1. Mark J. Reardon, *Victory at Mortain-Stopping Hitler's Panzer Counteroffensive* (Lawrence: University Press of Kansas, 2002), 99–101.
2. Quoted in U.S. Army War College, *Case Study: Operation Overlord*, Vol. V, *Sustainment* (Carlisle Barracks, PA: 1990), v.
3. Roland G. Ruppenthal, *Logistical Support of the Armies*, Volume I, The United States Army in World War II (Washington, D.C.: GPO, 1953), 415–16; 421. Hereafter cited as Ruppenthal. *Logistical Support, Vol. I.*
4. Gordon A. Harrison, *Cross Channel Attack*, The United States Army in World War II (Washington, D.C.: GPO, 1951), 441.
5. Ruppenthal, *Logistical Support*, Volume I, 406–07; 10–11; 13.
6. _____ *Logistical Support of the Armies*, Volume II, The United States Army in World War II (Washington, D.C.: GPO, 1959), 282. Hereafter cited as Ruppenthal, *Logistical Support, Vol. II.* The divisions were: 1st, 2d, 4th, 9th, 29th, 30th, 79th, 83d, 90th, 82d and 101st Airborne and 2d and 3d Armored.
7. Historical Section, G-4, Communications Zone, European Theater of Operations, Outline of Operation Overlord, (Center of Military History file number 8–3.4 AA v.7), n.d., 1.
8. Henirich Eberbach, *Report on the Fighting of Panzergruppe West (Fifth Pz. Army) from July 3-9 August 1944*, MS B-840, 1 June 1948, 8.
9. Kurt Badinski, *Report on Combat Commitment of 276 ID in Normandy*, MS B-526, 14 April 1947, 3–5; 56.
10. One need spend only a few hours in this area to gain an appreciation of the terrain conditions that must have faced the Americans.
11. U.S. Forces European Theater (USFET), General Board, Study 1, *Strategy of the Campaign in Western Europe*, n.p. (1946), 6–9.
12. Copies of the VII Corps plan and extracts of the First Army plan are from RG 407, NARA.
13. Harrison, *Cross Channel Attack*, 284.
14. James Jay Carafano, *After D-Day: Operation Cobra and the Normandy Breakout* (Boulder: Lynne Rienner, 2000), 26–28. Hereafter cited as Carafano, *After D-Day*.
15. Bernard L. Montgomery, *The Memoirs of Field-Marshal Montgomery* (New York: Signet, 1959), 230. Hereafter cited as Montgomery, *Memoirs.*
16. Carafano, *After D-Day*, 29.
17. Martin Blumenson, *Breakout and Pursuit*, The United States Army in World War II (Washington, D.C.: GPO, 1961), 178.
18. John Ellis, *Brute Force* (New York: Viking, 1990), 356–57.
19. Richard S. Faulkner, "Learning the Hard Way, The Coordination Between Infantry Divisions and Separate Tank Battalions During the Breakout from Normandy," *Armor* 99 (July-August 1990): 24–29.

20. Henry G. Spencer, "Baptism in the Hedgerows," *Infantry Journal* 55, No. 4 (1944): 10; "The Hedgerow Country's Tricky and Mean," *Infantry Journal* 55, No. 4 (1944): 15.

21. European Theater of Operations, Notes from Normandy, No. 27, 5 July 1944.

22. Joseph Balkoski, *Beyond the Beachhead*, (Harrisburg, Pa.: Stackpole, 1989), 280–81; Odom, *After the Trenches*, Chapter 11, 199–212.

23. Michael D. Doubler, *Busting the Bocage: American Combined Arms Operations in France, 6 June–31 July 1944* (Ft. Leavenworth: Combat Studies Institute, 1988), 30–34.

24. "German Tank Tactics in France," *Military Review* 24, No. 10 (1945): 3–5.

25. "Employment of Tanks and Infantry in Normandy," *Military Review* 24, No. 9 (1944): 13–17. The defensive sketch is reproduced on page 14.

26. HQ 12th Army Group, G-1 Daily Summary, 7 August 1944, reproduced in Appendix 13, USFET General Board Study #8, *G-1 Reports and Reporting Procedures in European Theater of Operations*, n.d.; *First US Army Report of Operations 20 October 1943–1 August 1944*; Annex #4, G-1 Section, 83.

27. Montgomery, *Memoirs*, 236.

28. Blumenson, *Breakout and Pursuit*, 230–37.

29. U.S. Army Air Forces Evaluation Board, ETO, *The Effectiveness of Third Phase Tactical Air Operations in the European Theater, 5 May 1944–8 May 1945*, reproduced in U.S. Army War College Case Study, *Operation Overlord, Volume III, Air Operations* (Carlisle Barracks, Pa., 1992), 140–41. Hereafter cited as *Third Phase*. Ian Gooderson, "Heavy and Medium Bombers: How Successful Were They in the Tactical Close Air Support Role During World War II?" *Journal of Strategic Studies* 15, No. 3 (1992): 367–399, notes that 600 bombs were needed to guarantee a 95 percent chance of one hit on a bridge. A USAAF ETO study determined that 18 medium bombers were needed to guarantee a reasonable chance of a hit on a small (point) target, and even then, the enemy infantry might well survive if their heavy equipment did not.

30. Blumenson, *Breakout and Pursuit*, 234–37.

31. *Ibid.*, 273; 322–23.

32. David W. Hogan, Jr., *A Command Post at War, First Army Headquarters in Europe 1943-1945* (Washington, D.C.: GPO, 2000), 121–22. Hereafter cited as Hogan, *Command Post at War*.

33. There has been some scholarly research on this issue, but clearly the last word has not been written. Studies have not integrated tactical supply requirements with actual consumption, supply offload and transit inland (throughput) from the beaches and Cherbourg after its repair, maintenance availability records for the logistic units themselves and the effects of weather and terrain on supply routes (to name a few issues). The plan to take the ports was sensible when originally devised, but the persistent emphasis on the Brittany ports bears further study to assess the real impact of diverting resources to their capture.

34. Department of the Army, *Northern France* (Washington, D.C.: GPO, n.d.), 14–15.

35. Collins, *Lightnin' Joe*, 250–51, notes that corps commanders did not get ULTRA intelligence.

36. Department of the Army, *Northern France*, 15; Blumenson, *Breakout and Pursuit*, 488; War Department General Order #3, 8 January 1945.

37. Department of the Army, *Normandy*, 17. The role, if any, of ULTRA in Bradley's decision is unclear in secondary sources, even those published after public release of the ULTRA operation.

38. Martin Blumenson, *The War Between the Generals* (New York: Morrow, 1993), 262–63; Omar N. Bradley, *A General's Life* (New York: Simon and Schuster, 1983), 296.

39. Department of the Army, *Northern France*, 19–20.

40. Charles B. MacDonald, *The Mighty Endeavor* (New York: Oxford University Press, 1969), 317–18.

41. U.S. Army Air Forces, *Third Phase*, 131.
42. Blumenson, *Breakout and Pursuit*, 176–77.
43. *Ibid.*, 178–79.
44. Chandler, *Eisenhower Papers*, 2118–19.

CHAPTER 7

1. 22d Infantry Regiment S-3 Journal entries 11 September 1944 (2240; 2242 hrs.); 12 September 1944 (0532 hrs.); HQ, 22d Infantry Regiment report, subject: Patrol Entry into Germany, 21 September 1944.
2. Charles B. MacDonald, *The Siegfried Line Campaign*, The United States Army in World War II (Washington, D.C.: GPO, 1963), 6–9; Eisenhower, *Papers*, 2091.
3. Joseph Bykofsky and Harold Larson, *The Transportation Corps: Operations Overseas*, The United States Army in World War II (Washington, D.C.: GPO, 1957), 239–41; Ruppenthal, *Logistical Support I*, 571.
4. *The Administrative History of the Operations of 21 Army Group on the Continent of Europe 6 June 1944–8 May 1945*, November 1945, n.p., 47.
5. Based on the author's personal experience as the logistical planner for the 1st Armored Division Support Command in Germany from 1992-1994.
6. MacDonald, *The Siegfried Line Campaign*, 11–12.
7. Ruppenthal, *Logistical Support*, Vol. I, 520, 522. Ruppenthal notes conflicting loss figures on 522, 130n.
8. MacDonald, *The Siegfried Line Campaign*, 12.
9. *Ibid.*, 34–35; description also based on the author's trips to the area since 1984.
10. *Ibid.*, 14–18.
11. Conversations with veterans and Lanham's daughter, Shirley Lanham McCreary, at the 22d Regiment's October 1997 reunion at Gettysburg, Pa.; other information supplied by Lanham's daughter to the author.
12. Appendix 1 to 22d Infantry Regiment Report of Operations for August 1944; Narrative Report of Activities for August 1944; Enclosure 1 to Strength Report, 29 September 1944. A rifle battalion was authorized 871 soldiers.
13. Daily Operations, 22d Infantry Regiment, 9 September 1944, RG 407, NARA.
14. Carlos Baker, *Ernest Hemingway A Life Story* (New York: Scribner's, 1969), 423.
15. Don A. Warner, Jr., letter to author, n.d., received August 1989.
16. Telephone conversation with Don A. Warner, Jr., 2 November 1996, recounting Ruggles's comments to Warner on 2 October 1996.
17. *V Corps Operations in the ETO 6 January 1942–9 May 1945*, n.p., n.d., 256, hereafter cited as *V Corps Operations*. Maj. Gen. Edward H. Brooks took temporary command on 18 September. Gerow, the former head of the War Department's Operations Division, returned to the States to testify before a Congressional hearing related to Pearl Harbor.
18. MacDonald, *The Siegfried Line Campaign*, 37; Hogan, *Command Post at War*, 147.
19. *V Corps Operations*, 241; 248–49.
20. *Ibid.*, 248, reproduces the corps LOI dated 12 September 1944.
21. 22d Infantry Regiment S-3 Journal entries for 1140 hrs., 11 September; entries for 0736 hrs and later, 12 September 1944.
22. *Ibid.*, entries for 1020, 1025, 1028, 1032, 1245, 1300 hrs., 12 September 1944; 0910 hrs., 13 September 1944.
23. George Wilson, *If You Survive* (New York: Ivy Books, 1987), 82–83.
24. MacDonald, *The Siegfried Line Campaign*, 49.
25. *Ibid.*, 40–41; author's trips to the area, various dates since 1984.

26. *Ibid.*, 50–51; Edgar Christoffel, *Krieg am Westwall 1944–1945* (Trier: Universitäts Buchhandlung, 1989), 102–04.

27. 22d Infantry Regiment S-3 Journal entries for 1000 and 1010 hrs., 14 September 1944.

28. Interview with Capt. Whaley and T/Sgt. Frank B. Garcia, n.p., n.d., 4th Infantry Division CI #33, hereafter cited as Whaley CI; 22d Infantry Regiment Narrative Report for September 1944, dated 14 November 1944.

29. Ernest Hemingway, "War in the Siegfried Line," in William White, *By-Line: Ernest Hemingway* (New York: Simon & Schuster, 1998), 347–48.

30. *Ibid.*, 348–51.

31. *Ibid.*, 351.

32. 22d Infantry S-3 Journal entry for 2025 hrs. 14 September 1944.

33. Whaley Interview.

34. *Ibid.*

35. MacDonald, *The Siegfried Line Campaign*, 52.

36. 22d Infantry S-3 Journal entry for 0810 hrs., 15 September 1944; Narrative Report for Month of September 1944, 8.

37. 22d Infantry S-3 Journal, entry for 0930 hrs., 15 September 1944.

38. *Ibid.*, entry for 0935 hrs., 15 September 1944.

39. *Ibid.*, entry for 1440 hrs., 15 September 1944.

40. *Ibid.*, entry for 1545 hrs., 15 September 1944.

41. *Ibid.*, entries for 1835 and 2200 hrs., 15 September 1944.

42. *Ibid.*, entry for 1245 hrs., 16 September 1945.

43. *Ibid.*, entries for 1045, 1055, 1300, 1345, 1400, 1515 hrs., 16 September 1944.

44. *Ibid.*, entry for 1545 hrs., 16 September 1944.

45. *Ibid.*, entry for 1600 hrs., 16 September 1944.

46. *Ibid.*, entry for 1653 hrs., 16 September 1944.

47. *Ibid.*, entries for 1845 hrs., 16 September 1944 and 0055 hrs., 17 September 1944.

48. 22d Infantry Regiment S-3 Periodic Report No. 60, 16 September 1944.

49. 22d Infantry Regiment S-3 Periodic Report No. 61, 17 September 1944.

50. Statement of Capt. Edward W. Martin, 22d Infantry Combat Interview files, hereafter cited as Martin CI.

51. Entry for September 17 in Report, "Siegfried Line," 2. This report is filed in 22d Infantry Operations files.

52. Martin CI.

53. Entry for September 17 in Report, "Siegfried Line," 3.

54. *Ibid.*, 4; another typed report in the regiment's operations files provides more details on the efforts to withdraw the 1st Battalion. It is based on interviews with Lanham, Blazzard, and Latimer, hereafter cited as 1st Battalion Report. The regiment's S-3 journal does not mention a specific order to withdraw.

55. *Ibid.*; Losses in Action for September 1944.

56. 1st Battalion Report, 6, 7. Latimer's and Lanham's recollections differ considerably.

57. Clifford Henley, diary, copy in author's files provided by Donald A. Warner, entry for 17 September 1944.

58. 22d Infantry S-3 Journal entry for 1035 hrs., 19 September 1944.

59. *Ibid.*, entry for 1315 and 1320 hrs., 18 September 1944; S-3 Periodic Report No. 63, 19 September 1944.

60. MacDonald, *The Siegfried Line Campaign*, 44–45.

61. *Ibid.*, 47–48; 109th Infantry Regiment Unit Reports 13–14, September 1944.

62. MacDonald, *The Siegfried Line Campaign*, 55–65.

63. Chandler, ed., *Eisenhower Papers*, 2124.

CHAPTER 8

1. Kenneth W. Hechler, Combat Interview with members of Company A, 117th Infantry, 30th Infantry Division CI #97, 22 October 1944.
2. Department of the Army, *Rhineland* (Washington, D.C.: GPO, n.d.), 8.
3. Eisenhower, *Papers*, 2215–16.
4. *Administrative History of the Operations of 21 Army Group*, 31; 35–36.
5. MacDonald, *The Siegfried Line Campaign*, 251–53.
6. Eisenhower, *Papers*, 2137.
7. Brown, *Draftee Division*, Appendix 2, 168–75, was one of the first common sense rebuttals to the "mythos of Wehrmacht superiority."
8. MacDonald, *The Siegfried Line Campaign*, 255.
9. Ibid., 99; 257–58.
10. HQ, XIX Corps, *Breaching the Siegfried Line* (Germany 1944), 37, hereafter cited as XIX Corps, *Breaching the Siegfried Line.*
11. Ibid., 38–45.
12. MacDonald, *The Siegfried Line Campaign*, 260.
13. Report of Interview with Brig. General W. H. Harrison, Report No. 27, 30th Infantry Division CI #97.
14. MacDonald, *The Siegfried Line Campaign*, 266–278.
15. *Ibid.*, 279–80; XIX Corps, *Breaching the Siegfried Line*, 21, 47.
16. MacDonald, *The Siegfried Line Campaign*, 283.
17. Weapons quantities for the first week of October are from *First US. Army Report of Operations, 1 August 1944–22 February 1945*, Annex 9, Appendix 4, 30. Full accounting of weapons available for use on a particular day is possible only by individual comparison of each subordinate unit's task organization with its maintenance records.
18. Ruppenthal, *Logistical Support of the Armies*, Vol. II, 248–49; 255–56.
19. *First U.S. Army Report of Operations, 1 August 1944–22 February 1945*, Annex 5, Appendix 1, 63–64.
20. MacDonald, *The Siegfried Line Campaign*, 283–84.
21. First Infantry Division, *Selected Intelligence Reports*, Vol. I, June 1944-November 1944, 6 December 1944, 68–69. D.E. Nash, phone call with the author September 5, 2006.
22. Translation of an order issued by Field Marshal Walther Model, reproduced in Appendix 2 to 1st Infantry Division G-2 PR, 5 October 1944.
23. Biographical information is from Robert W. Baumer and Mark J. Reardon, *American Iliad—The 18th Infantry Regiment in World War II* (Bedford, Pa.: Aberjona Press, 2004), 167. The veteran "Big Red One," named after its shoulder patch with a red numeral '1' superimposed on an olive drab field, had served in North Africa, Sicily, and France. Its service and combat support troops were very experienced, and there remained a sprinkling of 'old soldiers' in the rifle units. Eisenhower had relieved Huebner's predecessor, Maj. Gen. Terry de la Mesa Allen, and his assistant, Brig. Gen. Theodore Roosevelt Jr., partly because they allegedly let troops ransack a rest area in North Africa.
24. Edward W. McGregor, *The Operations of the 1st Battalion, 18th Infantry (1st Infantry Division) in the Vicinity of Crucifix Hill, Northeast of Aachen, Germany, October 1944.* (Ft. Benning, Ga., n.d.) 8, hereafter cited as McGregor, *Operations.*
25. 18th Infantry Regiment, FO #30, 2 October 1944; 1st Infantry Division FO #51, 2 October 1944; 1st Infantry Division Artillery FO #14, 2 October 1944.
26. McGregor, *Operations*, 13; Appendix 4 to Annex 9, First *U.S. Army Report of Operations, 1 August 1944–22 February 1945*, 30.
27. McGregor, *Operations*, 15, and maps attached to the report.
28. *Ibid.*, 11, 18; Infantry regiments often formed so-called "ranger platoons," which were units of hand-picked men to undertake special patrols and other missions.

29. Bobbie E. Brown, *The Operations of Company C, 18th Infantry (1st Inf. Div.) in the Attack on Crucifix Hill, 8 October 1944 (Rhineland Campaign) (Aachen Offensive)*, (Ft. Benning, Ga., 1947), 6–7, hereafter cited as Brown, *Company C*.

30. 18th Infantry Regiment, "Battle of Aachen—18th Infantry Regiment," summary report prepared by First Army Historical Officer from interviews with participants, 2. Copy in the 18th Infantry Regiment operations files for October 1944.

31. *Ibid.*, 2–4.

32. McGregor *Operations*, 22–23; Brown, *Company C*, 8–9.

33. Biographical material supplied by the archives of the 1st Infantry Division Museum (Cantigny) to author. Brown retired from the army as a captain in 1950 and was later employed at the U.S. Military Academy. He died of a self-inflicted gunshot wound in 1971.

34. McGregor, *Operations*, 23–27.

35. Brown, *Company C*, 10–11.

36. McGregor, *Operations*, 17–18; Brown, *Company C*, 12.

37. Brown, *Company C*, 13; McGregor, *Operations*, 28–32.

38. McGregor, *Operations*, 32–35.

39. Brown, *Company C*, 12–14.

40. Brown, *Company C*, 14–15; McGregor, *Operations*, 40–41; Raymond Klawiter, letter to author, n.d. The 2d Battalion, particularly Company G, was hard hit near Verlauternheide. See Baumer and Reardon, *American Iliad*, 287–88, in addition to unit records for details.

41. MacDonald, *The Siegfried Line Campaign*, 288.

42. McGregor, *Operations*, 37–39; 42–44.

43. Battle of Aachen, 18th Infantry Regiment, 10–11.

44. McGregor, *Operations*, 49–50.

45. *Ibid.*, 50–51.

46. MacDonald, *The Siegfried Line Campaign*, 307.

47. 1st Battalion, 18th Infantry Record of Events for October 1944, 4; 3d Battalion, 18th Infantry report dated 24 October 1944. This report was prepared from S-3 journal entries.

48. MacDonald, *The Siegfried Line Campaign*, 289–90.

49. Walter Denkert, MS A-979, *Die 3.Panzer-grenadier Division in der Schlacht von Aachen*, 3–5. The Germans, not mistaken GIs, reported the Tiger tank situation. See also Gerhard Dieckhoff and Erich Borrries, *3. Panzergrenadier Division* (Göttingen, 1960), 349–357.

50. John Baumgardner, *History of the 16th Infantry Regiment*, n.p., n.d., 165–66. This accurate and detailed book relied heavily on official records. Denkert, MS #A-979, 5–10.

51. Baumgardner, *History of the 16th Infantry Regiment*, 166.

52. MacDonald, *The Siegfried Line Campaign*, 291–99.

53. *Ibid.*, 295–300. The platoon leader and 26 of his men were either killed or captured. He was reportedly the officer who threw the boards into the Würm on 2 October.

54. *Ibid.*, 301–03.

55. Heinz Günther Guderian, *From Normandy to the Ruhr With the 116th Panzer Division in World War II* (Bedford, Pa.: Aberjona Press, 2001), 221.

56. MacDonald, *The Siegfried Line Campaign*, 306, 316.

57. Warren B. Eames, Reflections of War, 1990, unpublished typescript in author's possession provided by Warren B. Eames, 150.

58. MacDonald, *The Siegfried Line Campaign*, 314n; War Department General Orders #42, 24 May 1945; War Department General Order #74, 1 September 1945.

CHAPTER 9

1. Capt. John Howe interview with Bruce M. Hostrup, Richard H. Payne, and Raymond E. Fleig, 14 November 1944, hereafter cited as Hostrup CI, 28th Infantry Division CI #77; Raymond E. Fleig, letter to author, 23 March 1992; *First U.S. Army Report of Operations, 1 August 1944–22 February 1945*, Annex 5, Appendix 2, 65–66, details a test to determine the effectiveness of U.S. anti-tank ammunition on German armor. The main source for this chapter is Edward G. Miller, *A Dark and Bloody Ground, the Hürtgen Forest and Roer River Dams 1944–1945* (College Station: Texas A&M University Press, 1995), Chapters 5 and 6. Hereafter cited as Miller, *Dark and Bloody Ground*.

2. The moniker "Death Factory" is from the 4th Infantry Division's report on the battle, December 1944.

3. Collins, *Lightnin' Joe*, 273; Miller, *A Dark and Bloody Ground*, Chapter 3, 36–46.

4. Department of the Army, *Rhineland*, 17.

5. MacDonald, *The Siegfried Line Campaign*, 326–28; Hogan, *A Command Post at War*, 181.

6. Raymond E. Fleig, *707th Tank Battalion in World War II* (Springfield, Ohio, 1991), 25–26, 32, 41. Ray kindly reviewed a draft of this chapter.

7. *Ibid.*, 49–51; 67.

8. War Department, FM 100–5, *Operations*, 15 June 1944, 316–18; Mansoor, *The GI Offensive in Europe*, 161.

9. Miller, *Dark and Bloody Ground*, 54–55.

10. Ripple and his staff had the same doubts as the infantrymen (Ripple interview with author, Vossenack, Germany, September 15, 1994); Miller, *Dark and Bloody Ground*, 50–52; Charles B. MacDonald, *Three Battles: Arnaville, Altuzzo and Schmidt*, The United States Army in World War II (Washington, D.C.: GPO, 1952), 254–56. Hereafter cited as MacDonald, *Three Battles*.

11. MacDonald, *Three Battles*, 253. The division was strongly reinforced with artillery and engineers. Information on the 707th is from 707th Tank Battalion After Action Report for October 1944, dtd. 4 November 1944.

12. Capt. John S. Howe, Interview with James J. Leming, William D. Quarrie, and James J. Ryan, 707th Tank Battalion, 2-3 December 1944. Hereafter cited as Leming CI (CI #77).

13. *Ibid.*

14. *Ibid.*

15. Miller, *Dark and Bloody Ground*, 61.

16. MacDonald, *Three Battles*, 268–71.

17. Hostrup CI; author interview with Richard Ripple, Vossenack, Germany, September 15, 1994.

18. Bruce M. Hostrup letter to author, 26 April 1989.

19. MacDonald, *Three Battles*, 288, 291; author's recurring visits to the battlefield, 1987-2005.

20. Hostrup CI; Hostrup letter to author, 26 April 1989.

21. MacDonald, *Three Battles*, 289.

22. Hostrup CI; Fleig letter to author, September 22, 1991.

23. Hostrup CI.

24. *Ibid.*

25. *Ibid.*; Fleig, letter to author, September 22, 1991.

26. MacDonald, *Three Battles*, 274.

27. Miller, *Dark and Bloody Ground*, 69.

28. William J. Fox, interview with Jack W. Walker, 2 December 1944, CI #75.

29. MacDonald, *Three Battles*, 315; William J. Fox, interview with Edwin M. Howison, Air Liaison Officer to 28th Division, n.d., CI #75.

30. Guderian, *With the 116th Panzer Division*, 242–50; Hostrup CI.
31. Hostrup CI; MacDonald, *Three Battles*, 309.
32. *Ibid.*
33. *Ibid.*
34. 112th Infantry Regiment Unit Reports for the period clearly state the "situation." There is no evidence that anyone on the regimental staff purposely covered up the situation; however, it is apparent that senior officers did not personally verify the reports and that Colonel Peterson's staff also let him down. For example, the 112th Daily Situation Report for 6 November notes an S-3 journal entry claiming that the 2d Battalion was in a critical situation. Yet the division G3 PR #112 (6 November) says that the battalion "received very heavy and concentrated artillery fire" then withdrew to reorganize and later regained its initial positions, which, of course, was not what happened.
35. MacDonald, *Three Battles*, 332–33.
36. *Ibid.*
37. Fleig letter to author, 23 March 1990.
38. Leonard, a 24-year-old graduate of Texas A&M, had already been wounded leading some riflemen against enemy positions. When his TDs did not move as required during the demonstration, he dismounted his M-10, probably intending to lead it into a better fighting position. He remained exposed until a shell fragment took off part of an arm. The Texan removed his belt and wound it tight on the stump. His men helped him a few yards to a temporary collecting point for the wounded, which was little more than a deep crater. The evidence indicates that Leonard, who was too weak to be moved, was still alive when German troops overran the village. His mother received his Medal of Honor in 1945, and a Bundeswehr officer returned Leonard's college class ring, found on the battlefield, to his family in 2001.
39. Hostrup CI.
40. Peterson had already had a long career in the National Guard. The authenticity of the order has since been questioned, and the effect on Cota of Peterson's apparently unauthorized arrival at the rear has been told in detail. However, there is no evidence that Peterson did anything but comply with an order he thought was legitimate. He later received a Silver Star for his service in the battle.
41. Hostrup CI.
42. Miller, *A Dark and Bloody Ground*, 76.
43. MacDonald, *Three Battles*, 386–89.
44. *Ibid.*, 398–99; Fleig letter to author, 23 March 1990.
45. MacDonald, *Three Battles*, 335.
46. John S. Howe, interview with George S. Granger, Carl A. Anderson, and others, 1 December 1944. Hereafter cited as Granger CI.
47. *Ibid.*
48. MacDonald, *Three Battles*, 344–45.
49. Granger CI; Leming CI.
50. Granger CI.
51. *Ibid.*
52. *Ibid.* U.S planes attacked the area that afternoon and hit a few friendly tanks.
53. Granger CI.
54. *Ibid.*
55. *Ibid.*
56. Miller, *A Dark and Bloody Ground*, 80–81
57. MacDonald, *Three Battles*, 414–415; Fleig, *707th Tank Battalion*, 123.
58. HQ, V Corps, Summary of the Operations of the 28th Infantry Division for the Period 2–15 November 1944 [dated 18 November 1944], typed report in V Corps Operations files.

CHAPTER 10

1. Report, "Battle of Lucherberg Germany, December 2 to December 6, 1944," 104th Infantry Division CI #241, 133–34, hereafter cited as "Battle of Lucherberg"; Frederick P. Cooper, interview with Harry Goldberg, James J. Kelly, and Robert H. Jones, 415th Infantry, n.d., CI #241.
2. Omar Bradley, *A General's Life*, 336–40.
3. Hogan, *A Command Post at War*, 181–82.
4. 12th Army Group LOI #10, 21 October 1944, reproduced in 12th *Army Group Report of Operations*, Vol. V, 98–99.
5. MacDonald, *The Siegfried Line Campaign*, 391–92. The divisions were the 104th Infantry and 7th Armored. Another reason for the delay was the benefit to the 12th Army Group of a British attack on the left of the Ninth U.S. Army.
6. Hugh M. Cole, *The Lorraine Campaign*, The United States Army in World War II (Washington, D.C.: GPO, 1950), 318–19; 374–75, mentions the artillery, terrain and weather effects that hampered both sides. See also David N. Spires, *Air Power for Patton's Army* (Washington, D.C.: GPO, 2002), 163, 166–67. Hereafter cited as Spires, *Air Power.*
7. MacDonald, *The Siegfried Line Campaign*, 403.
8. *Ibid.*, 393; The United States Strategic Bombing Survey, The Impact of the Allied Air Effort on German Logistics (Washington, D.C., 2d ed., January 1947), Exhibit II-Z; Exhibit A, Chapter IV; Exhibit IV-G through L.
9. MacDonald, *The Siegfried Line Campaign*, 412–14.
10. Enclosure 5 to VII Corps G-2 PR #173, 9 November 1944.
11. Enclosure 6 to VII Corps G-2 PR #173, 9 November 1944.
12. 104th Infantry Division Artillery Annex (Annex 2 to 104th Inf. Div. After Action Report) for 1–30 November 1944, see entry for 16 November. The division artillery fired only 271 rounds on 16 November; MacDonald, *The Siegfried Line Campaign*, 424–26. Perhaps Allen was acting on the advice of his G-4, who no doubt was concerned with meeting First Army-imposed ammunition allocations.
13. Annex 3 to 104th Infantry Division After Action Report, 1-30 November 1944.
14. MacDonald, *The Siegfried Line Campaign*, 426.
15. *Ibid.*, 427.
16. Annex 5 to 104th Infantry Division After Action Report, 1-30 November 1944.
17. *Ibid.*, 427–28.
18. Fred L. Hadsel, Interview with J. S. Booker, W. M. Tufts, and others, 1st Battalion, 415th Infantry, 9 December 1944.
19. Harold Denny, "Eschweiler Folks Flee to Our Lines," *New York Times*, 22 November 1944, A4.
20. *The Stars and Stripes*, London Edition, Vol. I, No. 122, 23 November 1944, 1.
21. MacDonald, *The Siegfried Line Campaign*, 482.
22. 104th Infantry Division, Directive for Night Attacks, November 1944, 18.
23. *Ibid.*, 16. At 56, Allen was a hard-driving cavalryman who had commanded the 1st Infantry Division in North Africa and Sicily. Bradley did not particularly like him, but his soldiers did, and it is hard, if not impossible, to find a veteran with anything bad to say about him.
24. 104th Infantry Division After Action Report, November 1944, 14 December 1944.
25. MacDonald, *The Siegfried Line Campaign*, 506–10.
26. Annex 5 to 104th Infantry Division After Action Report for November 1944.
27. 415th Infantry Regiment After Action Report, December 1944, n.d., 1.
28. Terrain Study of Lucherberg, Germany, typed report in the 104th Infantry Division CI file, n.d., n.p.; Geschichtsverein der Gemeinde Inden e.V., *Erlebte Geschichte 1939-1947* (Jülich, n.p.: 1981), 73–74.
29. 104th Infantry Division Intelligence Summary, 28 November 1944.

30. 104th Infantry Division G-2 PR #37, 2 December 1944; Fred L. Hadsel, interview with W. H. Buckley, 11 December 1944. Buckley was S-3 of the 3d Battalion.
31. 415th Infantry Regiment, FO #12, 2 December 1944.
32. Fritz Roppelt, *Der Vergangenheit auf der Spur*, (n.p., 1993), 348, 371 Hereafter cited as Roppelt, *Vergangenheit*.
33. Annex 4 to 104th Infantry Division G-2 PR #35, 30 November 1944.
34. Roppelt, *Vergangenheit*, 371, cites the LXXXI Corps artillery command as controlling 180 tubes after the start of the fight for Lucherberg. 104th Division G-2 reports identify the number of firing positions but do not refer to weapons. Roppelt's sources were surviving German archival materials. GIs identified both Panther and some Tiger tanks, and there were heavy tank units in the area.
35. Frederick P. Cooper, interview with members of Company G, 415th Infantry, n.d.
36. *Ibid.*
37. *Ibid.*
38. Frederick P. Cooper, combat interview with Douglas K. Ruch, Company E 415th Infantry, 20 December 1944. The company remained in position as 2d Battalion reserve.
39. Gen. John R. Deane Jr., U.S. Army (Ret.), a member of the 415th at the time, told the author in a 1996 interview that Kelleher "had no fear."
40. Fred L. Hadsel, interview with T. R. Cheatham, Francis Miller, C.F. Shotts, D.C. Fleming, and R.J. Vortz, Company I, 415th Infantry, 11 December 1944. Hereafter cited as Cheatham CI; "Battle of Lucherberg," 111–12.
41. Cheatham CI.
42. "Battle of Lucherberg," 113.
43. Cheatham CI.
44. *Ibid.*, Fred Hadsel, interview with Sgt. Leon Marokus, 13 December 1944. Hereafter cited as Marokus CI.
45. *Ibid.*, "Battle of Lucherberg," 114–15.
46. *Ibid.*, 116–18; Cheatham CI. In a TOT, artillery fire direction center (FDC) personnel computed the precise sequence of firing artillery emplaced at different locations in order for the explosive to hit the target simultaneously.
47. Fred L. Hadsel, interview with T. E. Danowski and John S. Thompson, 13 December 1944. Hereafter cited as Danowski CI; "Battle of Lucherberg," 120.
48. Cheatham CI; Danowski CI.
49. Danowski CI.
50. "Battle of Lucherberg," 131.
51. *Ibid.*, 129–30; 143.
52. Present were: Company I, soon to be relieved; L (Hallahan); one platoon of K; elements of F.
53. "Battle of Lucherberg," 125.
54. Fred L. Hadsel, interview with Bruce G. Keithrow and others, 329th Engineer Battalion, 21 December 1944.
55. Fred L. Hadsel, interview with E. L. Dumler, 329th Engineer Battalion, 22 December 1944; "Battle of Lucherberg," 129, 132.
56. Fred L. Hadsel, interview with R.D. Collins, et. al., Company K, 415th Infantry, 13 December 1944. Hereafter cited as Collins CI.
57. "Battle of Lucherberg," 133.
58. Danowski CI.
59. Fred L. Hadsel and William Henderson, interview with Jim Gibson, Anthony Ferrante and others, 19 December 1944.
60. Collins CI.

61. Fred Hadsel and William Henderson, interview with R.O. Taylor, Shelby Pelfrey, Charles Gary, and others, 19 December 1944.
62. *Ibid.*
63. "Battle of Lucherberg," 139–40.
64. 415th Infantry After Action Report for December 1944, n.d.
65. "Battle of Lucherberg," 142.
66. *Ibid.*, 142–49.
67. 415th Infantry November and December 1944 After Action Reports.
68. Enclosure 10 to VII Corps G-2 PR #177, 29 November 1944.
69. Enclosure 2 to VII Corps G-2 PR #173, 25 November 1944.
70. Enclosure 10 to VII Corps G-2 PR #174, 26 November 1944.
71. Enclosure 5 to VII Corps G-2 PR #174, 26 November 1944.
72. Enclosure 3 to VII Corps G-2 PR #182, 4 December 1944. POW reports filed in the VII Corps operations records for the November-December period make interesting reading and should be the subject of further scholarly research and writing.
73. Carl Wagener, *Report of Chief of Staff, Army Group B*, MS #A965, 13.
74. MacDonald, *The Siegfried Line Campaign*, 582, 593; First Army had an artillery brigade with 240-mm howitzers and 8" guns, but unlike smaller caliber battalions, these had only 6 guns each, not 12.
75. Enclosure 4 to VII Corps G-2 PR, #184, 6 December 1944.
76. MacDonald, *The Siegfried Line Campaign*, 583–93.
77. *Ibid.*, 593–94.
78. MacDonald, *The Siegfried Line Campaign*, 616; 619.

CHAPTER 11
1. Combat interview with 2d Battalion, 11th Infantry, n.p., n.d., All interviews cited in this chapter are in CI #139.
2. Christopher R. Gabel, *The Lorraine Campaign: An Overview, September-December 1944* (Ft. Leavenworth, Kans., 1985), 5–10. Hereafter cited as Gable, *The Lorraine Campaign*.
3. Hugh M. Cole, *The Lorraine Campaign*, The United States Army in World War II (Washington, D.C.: GPO 1950), 257–58. Hereafter cited as Cole, *The Lorraine Campaign*.
4. Martin Blumenson, ed. *The Patton Papers 1940-1945* (Boston: Houghton-Mifflin, 1974), 553.
5. John N. Rickard, *Patton at Bay: The Loraine Campaign, 1944* (Washington, D.C.: Brassey's, 2004), chapter 4, 51–75.
6. Gabel, *The Lorraine Campaign*, 13–18.
7. *Ibid.*, 19–20.
8. Cole, *The Lorraine Campaign*, 127. See also the topographical map (Map XIV) located in the back of that volume.
9. *Ibid.*, 162.
10. *Ibid.*, 261.
11. Spires, *Air Power*, 127.
12. Combat interview with personnel of the 735th Tank Battalion, n.d., n.p., hereafter cited as 735th Tank Battalion CI.
13. XX Corps Memorandum, Fort Driant, dated 21 October 1944. This report was based on an interview with a former French commander of the fort.
14. Headquarters, XX Corps, *History of the XX Corps Artillery* (Miesbach, Germany: W. F. Mayer, n.d.), 23; Cole, *The Lorraine Campaign*, 266, 69.
15. Spires, *Air Power*, 137.
16. Rickard, *Patton at Bay*, 138.

17. *Ibid.*, 141–42.
18. Cole, *The Lorraine Campaign*, 269.
19. *Ibid.*, 269n.
20. Ibid., 270n.
21. 735th Tank Battalion CI..
22. Report, Artillery at Fort Driant, included in CI #39
23. 735th Tank Battalion CI.;
24. Breaching of Fort Driant Defenses by B Company, 11th Infantry. Report in CI #39.
25. *Ibid.* Reeder was wounded by artillery fire a few hours later.
26. *Ibid.*
27. Breaching of Fort Driant Defenses by B Company, 11th Infantry. Report in CI #39.
28. Cole, *The Lorraine Campaign*, 271n.
29. H. A. Morris, Interview with men of Co. E, 11th Infantry.
30. 735th Tank Battalion History, 31 October 1944.
31. *Ibid.*
32. *Ibid.*
33. Cole, *The Lorraine Campaign*, 272.
34. Cole, *The Lorraine Campaign*, 272n.
35. Interview with members of 1st Battalion, 10th Infantry; B Company 7th Engineer Battalion; Company C, 735th Tank Battalion; Company E, 11th Infantry, n.p., n.d. Hereafter cited as 1st Battalion, 10th CI.
36. *Ibid.*
37. *Ibid.*
38. 1st Battalion, 10th CI; Cole, *The Lorraine Campaign*, 274.
39. 1st Battalion, 10th CI; Cole, *The Lorraine Campaign*, 274–75.
40. 11th Infantry Association, *11th Infantry History* (Baton Rouge: Army & Navy, 1945), 24. Capt Richard H. Durst replaced Gerrie after the battle; Lt. Col. Kelly Lemmon, the 2d Battalion commander, retired as a major general.
41. Cole, *The Lorraine Campaign*, 275.
42. Blumenson, ed., *The Patton Papers*, 564.
43. Gabel, *The Lorraine Campaign*, 28–29; Cole, *The Lorraine Campaign*, 546.
44. Spires, *Air Power*, 153–63 provides a welcome discussion of the effects of the weather on availability of air support in the fall of 1944.
45. Cole, *The Lorraine Campaign*, 449n.
46. *Ibid.*, 590–92.
47. *Ibid.*, 592–95.
48. *Ibid.*, 602–04.
49. The primary sources for this section are 4th Armored Division CI #273, a chapter in the 1946 War Department study *Small Unit Actions*, titled "Singling, 6 December 1944," hereafter cited as War Department, *Singling*; and Small Unit Study #8, "Attack on Singling by Elements, 4th Armored Division," prepared by the Historical Section, ETO in 1945. Hereafter cited as Study #8.
50. Cole, *The Lorraine Campaign*, 525.
51. War Department, *Singling*, 177; Study #8.
52. Hanson W. Baldwin, *Tiger Jack* (Fort Collins, Colo.: Old Army Press, 1979), 28–29.
53. Carlo D'Este, Patton: *A Genius for War* (New York: HarperCollins, 1995), 664.
54. A. Harding Ganz, "Patton's Relief of General Wood," *Journal of Military History* 53, No. 3, July 1989, 257–273.
55. Blumenson, ed., *Patton Papers*, 586; Russell F. Weigley, *Eisenhower's Lieutenants*, Book Club ed. (Bloomington: Indiana University Press, 1981), 259–61, hereafter cited as Weigley, *Eisenhower's Lieutenants*. Wood commanded the Armored Force Replacement Training Center at Ft. Knox, and retired in 1946. He served as Chief of the U.S.

Mission to Austria, and UN agencies until 1953. He settled in Reno, Nevada, and died in 1969. He was still highly respected by former subordinates, one of whom, Creighton Abrams, would be chief of staff.

56. Blumenson, ed., *The Patton Papers*, 586.
57. Cole, *The Lorraine Campaign*, 530–33; Study #8, 10–11.
58. War Department, *Singling*, 186–87.
59. Roster of Company B, 51st AIB, filed in CI #273; War Department, Table of Organization 7–27, Armored Infantry Company, 15 September 1943. The full-strength company was authorized 6 officers and 245 enlisted men of all specialties. A platoon was authorized 1 officer and 55 enlisted men, but only 33 of the enlisted men were riflemen; War Department, Table of Organization 17–25, Tank Battalion, 15 September 1943; Table of Organization 17–27, Medium Tank Company,15 September 1943; Table of Organization 7–25, Armored Infantry Battalion, 15 September 1943; Table of Organization 7–27, Armored Infantry Company, 15 September 1943. Cole, 532n, also descries the manpower shortages.
60. Study #8, 5; 12–14; 16.
61. Study #8, p.2, notes that the day was overcast, without rain, and that mud did not play a significant role that day; the confusion over location is noted at pp. 3 and 11.
62. *Ibid.*, 12–13.
63. *Ibid.*, 15–17.
64. *Ibid.*, 18.
65. *Ibid.*, 19–22.
66. *Ibid.*, 24–25.
67. *Ibid.*, 31–32.
68. *Ibid.*, 33–35.
69. *Ibid.*, 36–37.
70. *Ibid.*, 37–39.
71. War Department, *Singling*, 207–10.
72. *Ibid.*, 210–11.
73. War Department, Singling, 210.; Gabel, *The Lorraine Campaign*, 30–31.
74. Cole, *The Lorraine Campaign*, 588n; 589.

CHAPTER 12
1. William C. C. Cavanagh, *Dauntless: A History of the 99th Infantry Division* (Dallas: Taylor Publishing, 1994), 100–104. Hereafter cited as Cavanagh, *Dauntless*.
2. Adolf Hohenstein and Wolfgang Trees, *Hölle im Hurtgenwald* (Aachen: Triangle Verlag, 1986), 229–30.
3. Cavanagh, *Dauntless*, 137.
4. Charles B. MacDonald, *A Time for Trumpets, the Untold Story of the Battle of the Bulge* (New York: William Morrow, 1985), 68. Hereafter cited as MacDonald, *A Time for Trumpets*. The author walked the ground with MacDonald in 1987.
5. Hogan, *A Command Post at War*, 205, 207.
6. MacDonald, *A Time for Trumpets*, 71–72; 77–78.
7. Spires, *Air Power*, 189.
8. Hugh M. Cole, *The Ardennes: Battle of the Bulge*, The United States Army in World War II (Washington, D.C.: GPO, 1965), 63.
9. Hogan, *Command Post at War*, 209, 211.
10. MacDonald, *A Time for Trumpets*, 618–19; U.S. Army Armor School, *The Defense of St. Vith, Belgium, 17–23 December 1944* (Fort Knox: 1948), 9–11. Hereafter cited as Armor School, *St. Vith*.
11. MacDonald, *A Time for Trumpets*, Chapter 8, 160–83, describes the initial fighting in the north. See also William C. C. Cavanagh, *Krinkelt-Rocherath, the Battle for the Twin*

Villages (Norwell, MA: Christopher Publishing, 1986.) for the definitive account of the tactical fight.

12. MacDonald, A Time for Trumpts, 380–81.
13. *Ibid.*, 381.
14. *Ibid.*, 382–88; 395–96.
15. *Ibid.*, 390; 26th Infantry Regiment Association, *Blue Spader Newsletter* 99–1 (March 1999): 1.
16. MacDonald, *A Time for Trumpets*, 327. A few days later, Jones suffered a heart attack and was evacuated, having spent over two decades preparing to lead a division in combat.
17. Armor School, *St. Vith*, 34–36
18. Hogan, *A Command Post at War*, 218–19.
19. William D. Ellis and Thomas J. Cunningham Jr., *Clarke of St. Vith* (Cleveland: Dillon, Liederbach Publishing, 1974), 121. Hereafter cited as Ellis and Cunningham, *Clarke*.
20. MacDonald, *A Time for Trumpets*, 479–81.
21. Ellis and Cunningham, *Clarke*, 128; MacDonald, *A Time for Trumpets*, 482–87.
22. Ruppenthal, *Logistical Support of the Armies*, Vol. II, Table 8, pp. 282–83.
23. Christopher Gabel email to the author, 3 January 2000.
24. Blumenson, ed., *The Patton Papers*, 620.
25. Department of the Army, *Ardennes-Alsace* (Washington, D.C.: GPO, n.d.), 45–47.
26. Interview with William Miley, 19 January 1945, 17th Airborne Division, CI #65. Hereafter cited as Miley CI. All interviews below are from CI #65.
27. John G. Westover, interview with Regimental and Battalion Officers of the 513th Parachute Infantry Regiment, Actions Between 2-13 January 1945, conducted at Flamierge, Belgium, 14-16 January 1945, 2. Hereafter cited as 513th CI.
28. Samuel Calhoun, letter to author, 24 August 1995.
29. Charles B. MacDonald, *The Last Offensive*, The United States Army in World War II (Washington, D.C.: GPO, 1973), 34–35.
30. Miley CI.
31. 513th CI.
32. *Ibid.*
33. *Ibid.*
34. *Ibid.*
35. Blumenson, ed., *The Patton Papers*, 615. A complementary German offensive in the Vosges Mountains of eastern France hit the 6th Army Group (Lt. Gen. Jacob L. Devers) north of Strasbourg and delayed plans to reduce the Colmar Pocket salient. Eisenhower wanted the Seventh U.S. Army (part of the 6th Army Group) to withdraw and shorten its line to create a reserve; however, this would cede northern Alsace, including Strasbourg, to the Germans. The French and senior 6th Army Group commanders objected, and DeGaulle enlisted the support of Churchill in backing the decision to stay put. The successful defense by the Seventh US Army enabled the Allies to avoid a potential political crisis. Part of the defense was composed of the infantry elements of new divisions thrown into combat without their artillery, engineers or support troops.
36. Department of the Army, *Ardennes-Alsace* (Washington, D.C.: GPO, n.d.), 53.
37. Hugh M. Cole, *The Ardennes: Battle of the Bulge*, The United States Army in World War II (Washington, D.C.: GPO, 1965), 660–63.
38. Spires, *Air Power for Patton's Army*, 235–37.
39. Ruppenthal, *Logistical Support*, Vol. II, 270–71.
40. U.S. Forces European Theater General Board Report #58, *Ammunition Supply for Field Artillery*, n.p., 1946, 61–62.
41. U.S. Forces, European Theater General Board Report #94, *Trench Foot*, n.p., 1946, 1–2; 5.

42. Graham A. Cosmas and Albert E. Cowdrey, *The Medical Department: Medical Service in the European Theater of Operations*, The United States Army in World War II (Washington, D.C.: GPO, 1992), 489-94. Production and transportation delays prevented the new 'shoepacs' from reaching the ETO until mid-January 1945, and many troops did not receive them until early spring. Shoepacs had rubber soles and leather uppers, but they were poorly ventilated and caused a new malady called 'shoepac foot.' The 8th Infantry Division ordered troops to turn in their shoepacs. Some troops found the best protection against trench foot was to abandon the boot and simply wear 6-8 pairs of wool socks, or a homemade boot made from a blanket and worn inside the issue overshoes.

43. Ruppenthal, *Logistical Support of the Armies*, Vol. II, 218-221.

44. *Ibid.*, 222-28.

45. Lester Atwell, *Private* (New York: Simon & Schuster, 1962), paperback ed., 228.

46. U.S. Forces European Theater General Board Report #91, *Combat Exhaustion*, n.p. 1946, 1-2.

47. *Ibid.*, 7-8.

48. *Ibid.*, 5; War Department Mobilization Regulation 1-10, *Morale*, 5 March 1943, p. 4, listed loyalty, discipline, self-respect, pride, and esprit, among other factors contributing to high morale in units.

49. U.S. Forces European Theater General Board Report #91, 2-4.

50. Samuel A. Stouffer and others, *The American Soldier: Combat and its Aftermath*, Vol. II (Princeton: Princeton University Press, 1949), 88. Hereafter cited as Stouffer, *Combat*.

51. *Ibid.*, 87.

52. *Ibid.*, 90.

53. Frank Stephens, letter to author, July 15, 1997.

54. Stouffer, *Combat*, 76-77; 174.

55. *Ibid.*, 102-04; 115.

56. *Ibid.*, 118-24.

CHAPTER 13

1. John B. Babcock, "World War II as it Really Was" (Ithaca, N.Y., 1993), unpublished manuscript in the author's files, 61-62.

2. Hogan, *A Command Post at War*, 194.

3. Miller, *A Dark and Bloody Ground*, 180-83. The division had several attachments, including an 18-gun battalion of 105mm self-propelled howitzers, two batteries (8 pieces of 155-mm self-propelled guns); two companies (24 TDs of the 893d Tank Destroyer Battalion); two companies of the 709th Tank Battalion (up to 34 tanks); and twelve 4.2-inch mortars.

4. William M. Baker, interview with Richey V. Graham, Company E, 309th Infantry, 9 June 1945, CI #142.

5. General der Infanterie, a.D Otto Hitzfeld, MS B-101, LXXVII Corps 26 Jan-21 Mar 45, 18-19.

6. Miller, *A Dark and Bloody Ground*, 183-88.

7. Charles B. MacDonald, *The Last Offensive*, 55-67.

8. *Ibid.*, 7-8; Operations of the 78th Infantry Division 30 January-4 February 1945, typed report filed in CI #142, 5-6.

9. Summary of 78th Division Action, typed report in CI #142, 12. Hereafter cited as 78th Summary. Only 740 rounds of artillery were fired on 5 February, though corps and division artillery made use of TOT missions between 6-10 February. As the final operation got underway, U.S. artillery on some nights fired up to 12,000 rounds of "harassing and

interdicting" fire against likely but unobserved targets, where results could span the spectrum of effectiveness from missing a target entirely to neutralizing it.

10. MacDonald, *The Last Offensive*, 72–73; Miller, *A Dark and Bloody Ground*, 191–92. A copy of the schematic of Kesternich is contained in CI #142. Despite the preparations, troops found it very hard to associate the map numbers with nearly destroyed buildings.
11. 78th Summary, 26–27. General Parker sent a letter of thanks to the commander of the 366th Fighter Group.
12. Miller, *A Dark and Bloody Ground*, 192.
13. 311th Infantry Regiment S-3 journal entry for 1352 hrs., 31 January 1945.
14. MacDonald, *The Last Offensive*, 73–76; First U.S. Army LOI, 4 February 1945; HQ 12th Army Group memorandum of staff conference, 1 February 1945.
15. 78th Summary, 32–36.
16. MacDonald, *The Last Offensive*, 71–72.
17. 78th Summary, 9, 30.
18. *Ibid.*, 31–32. Annex 6, Field Artillery Task Organization, to V Corps Field Order #36, 2 February 1945, allotted the following reinforcing artillery to the 78th Division's operation: 60 155-mm howitzers, 12 4.5" guns, and 6 each 8" howitzers.
19. 78th Infantry Division G-3 Journal entries #173 and #174, both at 1640 hrs., 5 February 1945; F.C. Pogue and J.M. Topete, interview with Charles A. McKinney, 19 February 1945, CI #148.
20. 78th Summary, 45–46.
21. *Ibid.*, 50–53; MacDonald, *The Last Offensive*, map on p. 76.
22. F.C. Pogue and J.M. Topete, interview with Maj. Peter J. Newton and others, 3d Bn., 311th Infantry, 16 February 1945; 78th Summary, 66.
23. This description is based on the author's discussions with several veterans of the 78th Division at memorial ceremonies at Kesternich and Schmidt, Germany, June 1993.
24. 78th Summary, 71.
25. The tanks were from the 774th Tank Battalion, and in a kind of justice, the TDs were from the 893d TD Battalion, which had supported the 28th Division's November attack.
26. 78th Summary, 72–74.
27. *Ibid.*, 77–78. Regimental S-3 journals and CIs mention the enemy tanks.
28. McKinney CI.
29. 78th Summary, 80.
30. MacDonald, *The Last Offensive*, 80–81.
31. 78th Summary, 81.
32. Robert J. Bigart, "The Operations of the 1st Battalion, 309th Infantry (78th Infantry Division) in the Attack on the Schwammenauel Dam, Southeast of Schmidt, Germany, 9-10 February 1945," (Ft. Benning, Ga., 1949), 12–13.
33. *Ibid.*, 13–15.
34. *Ibid.*, 15–16.
35. *Ibid.*, 15–18.
36. *Ibid.*
37. 309th Infantry S-3 Journal entry for 0309 hrs., 10 February 1945.
38. *Ibid*, entry for 0309.
39. *Ibid.*, entry for 0500 hrs., 10 February 1945.
40. MacDonald, *The Last Offensive*, 81–83; 83n; 78th Division Historical Association, *Lightning*, 118–120. Parker was a 53-year-old native of Virginia and graduate of The George Washington University. He had three sons in the war: an Army lieutenant, a medical officer, and a naval flight surgeon. Parker's artillery officer, Brig. Gen. Frank Camm, had a son in the 78th. Frank A. Camm graduated with the emergency West

Point class of January 1943. He asked to be assigned to the 78th because his father was assigned to it and he thought the division would see action. The G-3, Lt. Col. Charles McKinney, was a 1935 Princeton graduate who had worked for the Washington *Star* newspaper. Ondrick, the commander of the 309th Infantry, was young for his post, 38 years old. He was a 1932 graduate of West Point and retired as a brigadier general. Robert Schellman graduated from West Point in 1939 and later commanded the 3d Infantry Division. He retired in 1971. Richard Keyes was a graduate of the University of Florida and had worked as a highway surveyor.

41. 78th Infantry Division RO, February 1945; 311th Infantry Regiment RO, February 1945.
42. Karl Püchler, The Operations of LXXIV Army Corps, MS B118, 26 July 1945, 11; 16; 18–23.
43. Ruppenthal, *Logistical Support*, II, 442–52.
44. *Ibid.*, 435–38.

CHAPTER 14
1. 376th Infantry Regiment Historical Committee, *History of the 376th Infantry Regiment Between the Years of 1921-1945* (Wuppertal: Weddingen, 1945), 53–55. Hereafter cited as Historical Committee, *History of the 376th*.
2. Blumenson, ed., *The Patton Papers*, 573.
3. MacDonald, *The Last Offensive*, 116–17.
4. Laurence G. Byrnes, ed., *History of the 94th Infantry Division in World War II* (Washington, D.C.: Infantry Journal Press, 1948), Chapter 8, 38–55. Hereafter cited as Byrne, *94th Division*. This is another good history that supplements the official records.
5. MacDonald, *The Last Offensive*, 117.
6. XX Corps Daily Operations, 1 December 1944-7 May 1945, filed in CI #365, entry for 14 January 1945; Byrne, *94th Division*, 86.
7. Christoffel, *Krieg am Westwall*, 418.
8. Byrnes, *94th Division*, 91.
9. Historical Committee, *History of the 376th*, 65.
10. *Ibid.*, 65–66; XX Corps Daily Operations, entry for 14 January 1945.
11. Byrnes, *94th Division*, 95–98; Historical Committee, *History of the 376th*, 66–68.
12. MacDonald, *The Last Offensive*, 118–19. Even at this late date, Germany still could field some powerful formations. The *"Gespensterdivision,"* or, "Ghost Division," had conducted a fighting withdrawal from the Rhone valley in France against the Seventh U.S. Army in August 1944, and that autumn helped block the Third U.S. Army in Lorraine. By October, the division was again at almost full strength (13,726 men) with a well-equipped panzer regiment, four battalions of panzergrenadiers, and an artillery regiment of three battalions (36 howitzers). See A. Harding Ganz, "The 11th Panzers in the Defense , 1944," *Armor* 103, No. 2 (1994), 27.
13. Walter Schaefer-Kehnert, letters to author, 4 December 1995 and 17 January 1996.
14. Karl Thieme, letter to author, 1 March 1996.
15. Byrnes, *94th Division*, 120–24.
16. Historical Committee, *History of the 376th*, 70–71.
17. *Ibid.*, 71–73; Byrnes, *94th Division*, 125–130.
18. MacDonald, *The Last Offensive*, 121–23.
19. *Ibid.*,123–25; Byrnes, *94th Division*, 161.
20. MacDonald, *The Last Offensive*, 125–26; Spires, *Air Power for Patton's Army*, 249.
21. This section is based on the author's interview with the late Lt. Col. George P. Whitman (U.S. Army, Ret.), Dumfries, Va., June 15, 1996, and George P. Whitman, *Memoirs of a Rifle Company Commander in Patton's Third U.S. Army*, (West Topsham,

Vt.: The Gibby Press, 1993), Chapter 7, pp. 40–57. This book was written from notes made by Whitman shortly after the war, hereafter cited as Whitman, *Memoirs*.

22. Whitman, *Memoirs*, 42, 44.
23. Whitman, *Memoirs*, 45.
24. Historical Committee, *History of the 376th*, 121; 94th Infantry Division, Citation for Silver Star, 14 May 1945.
25. Whitman, *Memoirs*, 46–47.
26. Byrnes, *94th Division*, 225–26.
27. Whitman, *Memoirs*, 49.
28. Byrnes, *94th Division*, 228.
29. O.C. Martin, undated response to author's letter of 16 March 1996.
30. Historical Committee, *History of the 376th*, 122.
31. Blumenson, ed., *The Patton Papers*, 629–30.
32. XX Corps Operational Report, *The Capture of the Saar-Moselle Triangle and the Capture of Trier*, n.p., Germany, 1945, 12–14. Hereafter cited as *XX Corps Report*.
33. MacDonald, *The Last Offensive*, 127–28.
34. *Ibid.*, 129.
35. Harry A. Morris, Combat Interview with Howard Snyder, 18 March 1945, 94th Infantry Division CI #203.
36. Col. Howard Snyder, Memorandum for XX Corps Historical Officer, 5 March 1945, copy in XX Corps CI file.
37. Committee 15, Officer's Advanced Course, The Armored School, "The 10th US Armored Division in the Saar-Moselle Triangle," (Fort Knox, 1949), 74–78.
38. *XX Corps Report*, 15.
39. Monroe Ludden, interview with Maj. Charles R. King, 10 March 1945. King was the 10th Armored Division historian among other duties.
40. Monroe Ludden, interview with officers of the 54th Armored Infantry Battalion, 15 March 1945, 10th Armored Division CI #306.
41. 5th Ranger Battalion S-3 Journal entry for 1333 hrs., 23 February 1945.
42. Typed report, "The Irsch-Zerf Campaign," author's files, provided by the late Lt. Col. Walter N. Mcllwain, U.S. Army, Ret., in 1997. The report was prepared by an anonymous Ranger in early 1945.
43. Michael J. King, *Rangers: Selected Combat Operations in World War II*, (Ft. Leavenworth, Kans.: US Army Combat Studies Institute, 1985), Chapter 1, pp. 5–10. Hereafter cited as King, *Rangers*.
44. William Boyd, letter to author, September 17, 1995.
45. King, *Rangers*, 43. For details on battalion organization, see War Department, Table of Organization 7–85 (Ranger Infantry Battalion); 7–86, (Headquarters and Headquarters Company, Ranger Infantry Battalion), and 7–87 (Ranger Infantry Company), all dated 29 February 1944. The battalion was organized into a headquarters/staff section, six companies of 3 officers and 65 men each, and a headquarters company with 88 enlisted men and 2 officers to provide administrative, mess, supply, communications, and transportation. Each line company had two platoons, each with a headquarters, two assault sections, a machine gun section, and a special weapons section. The battalion had received what is now called a Presidential Unit Citation for its work on OMAHA Beach on D-day (see War Department General Order No. 73, 6 September 1944).
46. Walter N. Mcllwain, letter to author, 6 October 1995. I am indebted to "Mac" for his absolutely invaluable assistance in the preparation of the story of the 5th Ranger Bn. He passed away in 2003.
47. Richard P. Sullivan, letter to author, 7 May 1995. Sullivan was selected to the Ranger Hall of Fame in 1997. Sullivan was a former executive officer of the battalion, and he had earned a Distinguished Service Cross, Silver Star, and Bronze Star in

Normandy.
48. Monroe Ludden, combat interview with Richard P. Sullivan, 9 March 1945, 5th Ranger Battalion CI #336, hereafter cited as Sullivan CI. All interviews of 5th Ranger Battalion personnel for this action are filed in CI #336.
49. Raymond Herlihy, letter to author, received October 28, 1995.
50. Tom Sloboda, letter to author, November 27, 1995.
51. 5th Ranger Battalion S-3 journal entry for 1752 hrs., February 23, 1944.
52. Synopsis of Ranger action filed with CI #336; the information on the footbridge is from Tom Sloboda, letter to author, November 27, 1995.
53. Sullivan CI.
54. Author's trip to the area, February 1994.
55. Commander's names are listed on the summary report in CI #336.
56. Sullivan CI.
57. Monroe Ludden, interview with Bernard M. Pepper, 5 March 1945. Company B was far below strength, and its mission was to handle prisoners. First Lt. Charles Lemmon was the Weapons Platoon leader.
58. Monroe Ludden, interview with George R. Miller, 5 March 1945. Hereafter cited as Miller CI.
59. Sullivan CI.
60. Miller CI; Raymond Herlihy, undated letter to Walter Mcllwain, original in author's collection, received October 28, 1995.
61. Sullivan CI; Pepper CI.
62. Sullivan CI.
63. This account comes from Captain Parker. Sullivan, however, said the Germans abandoned the vehicle without firing.
64. Sullivan CI.
65. Parker CI.
66. Sullivan CI.
67. Miller CI.
68. King, *Rangers*, 50–51.
69. Herlihy letter to author, March 20, 1996.
70. Synopsis of Ranger Action.
71. King, *Rangers*, 51–52; Christoffel, *Krieg am Westwall*, 451–52.
72. Miller CI; Parker CI; Sullivan CI.
73. Monroe Ludden, Interview with Jack. A. Snyder, 9 March 1945.
74. Parker Interview; Synopsis report.
75. Tom Sloboda, letter to author, November 27, 1995.
76. Committee 15, *The 10th US Armored Division in the Saar Moselle Triangle*, 89; Monroe Ludden, Interview with Jack A. Riley, E. M. Lonchar, and Melvin I. Mason, 10th Armored Division, 12, 15 March 1945. Hereafter cited as Riley CI.
77. Riley Interview.
78. *Ibid.*
79. Lou Gombosi, letter to Walter Mcllwain, October 5, 1995. Original given by Mcllwain to the author. Gombosi supplied a photo copy of the *ETO Battle Experiences* report.
80. Bill Boyd, letter to author, received September 3, 1996.
81. Walter Mcllwain, undated letter to author, received approximately October 1995.
82. Riley CI.
83. *Ibid.*
84. Boyd letter to author.
85. 5th Ranger Battalion S-3 Journal entry for 2230 hrs., 26 February 1945.
86. Sullivan CI; Parker CI.
87. XX Corps Reports, 34.

88. Sullivan CI; *XX Corps Report*, 34–35.
89. Snyder CI; Parker CI.
90. Parker CI.
91. Gombosi quoted in Pepper CI.
92. Gombosi letter to Mcllwain, October 5, 1995.
93. XX *Corps Report*, 35.
94. King, *Rangers*, 53–54.
95. *XX Corps Report*, 17; Committee 15, *The 10th Armored Division*, 104–05; MacDonald, *The Last Offensive*, 133–34.
96. Bradley, *A General's Life*, 403–05.

CHAPTER 15
1. Bradley, *A General's Life*, 405–06. The chapter title is from Wagener, MS A-965, 41. This is his description of the impact on Army Group B headquarters of the seizure of the Remagen bridgehead.
2. Maj. W. C. Sylvan quoted in Weigley, *Eisenhower's Lieutenants*, Book Club ed., 916–17.
3. Ambrose, ed., *Eisenhower Papers*, Vol. IV, 2454.
4. Ninth US Army Staff, *Conquer: The Story of Ninth Army* (Washington, D.C.: Infantry Journal Press, 1947), 206, 221. Hereafter cited as Ninth Army Staff, *Conquer*. This book was prepared using official records and it contains useful logistical planning information.
5. Memorandum from G-3 12th Army Group to Chief of Staff, 12th Army Group, 18 October 1944, microfilm reel #13, Item #1337, Combined Arms Research Library, Ft. Leavenworth, Kans.
6. 12th Army Group LOI #16, 3 March 1945, reproduced in *12th Army Group Report of Operations*, Vol. V, G-3 Section, 122–23.
7. MacDonald, *The Last Offensive*, 208.
8. *Ibid.*, 186–88.
9. Weigley, *Eisenhower's Lieutenants*, 904–07.
10. MacDonald, *The Lost Offensive*, 173–74.
11. *Ibid.*, 176–78.
12. *Ibid.*, 191–94.
13. Kenneth W. Hechler, interview with John W. Leonard, 16 March 1945, CI #299. Hereafter cited as Leonard CI.
14. Blumenson, ed., *The Patton Papers*, 637–38. Millikin was a cavalryman, born in 1888 and graduated from the Military Academy in 1910.
15. Hogan, *A Command Post at War*, 253.
16. Weigley, *Eisenhower's Lieutenants*, 919.
17. William C. Sylvan, Diary, entries for 24 and 28 February 1945. Copy in the files of the Combined Arms Research Library, Ft. Leavenworth, Kans.
18. Kenneth Hechler, combat interview with James H. Phillips, Harry C. Mewshaw, Norman B. Edwards, and Thomas J. Sharpe, 11 June 1945, III Corps CI #340. Phillips was the corps chief of staff; Mewshaw was the G-3, and the others were on the G-3 staff. All were in a position to witness first hand the discussions about a bridge. They believed that the seizure of a bridge was on Hodges's mind, but that he did not make it clear to the corps.
19. First U.S. Army G-3 section, Memorandum, Action Taken by First Army Just Prior to and During Seizure of Remagen Bridgehead, prepared in May 1945 to support preparation of a history of the capture of the bridge, copy in CI #340.

20. III Corps Operations Directive 5, dated 2 March 1945, and Operations Directive 6, dated 3 March 1945; III Corps Report of Operations March 1945, p. 11. Hereafter cited as III Corps RO.
21. Kenneth W. Hechler, combat interview with John W. Leonard, 16 March 1945. This is a different interview than that cited above; Kenneth W. Hechler, combat interview with Maj. Gen. John Millikin, 19 March 1945. Millikin recalled that he told Leonard something to the effect that he should use sound military procedure and try to get the bridge intact if the opportunity presented itself.
22. Carl Wagener, Report of the Chief of Staff, A Gp B, MS A-965, Oberussel, German, 4 February 1946, 16–17; 33. Hereafter cited as Wagener, MS A-965.
23. MacDonald, *The Last Offensive*, 209.
24. *Ibid.*, 210–11.
25. *Ibid.*, 209; 213–14.
26. Kenneth W. Hechler, interview with William M. Hoge, 14 March 1944. Hereafter cited as Hoge CI; Leonard CI. He recalled telling Hoge upon hearing of the capture of the bridge that they had "caused a lot of trouble."
27. Robert E. Maxwell, interview with Ben J. Cothran (S-3 of CCB), 14 March 1945. Hereafter cited as Cothran CI.
28. Kenneth W. Hechler, interview with Harold E. Larsen, 10 June 1945; Memorandum, HQ, 16th Armored Field Artillery Battalion to Historical Section, ETO, 16 June 1945, Subject: Ludendorff Bridge, filed with 9th Armored Division CI #300.
29. Kenneth Hechler, interview with Karl Timmermann and Mike Chinchar, 30 April 1945. Hereafter cited as Timmermann CI. Their battalion commander reported that Company A had only one mortar and one light machine gun per platoon.
30. Engeman CI; Cothran CI.
31. Engeman CI; Timmermann CI.
32. George R. Robertson, "Conversations with Gen. William M. Hoge (Ret.)," U.S. Army Military History Institute Senior Officer's Debriefing Program, Carlisle Barracks, Pa., 1974, Section III, 78.
33. Timmermann stated the company met no resistance. Burrows, writing after the war, said that there was some resistance in the center of town. See Emmet J. Burrows, "The Operations of Company A, 27th Armored Infantry Battalion (9th Armored Division) in the Seizure of the Remagen Bridgehead 7-8 March 1945" (Fort Benning, Ga., 1950), 12; 16–17.
34. McMaster CI.
35. Hoge CI.
36. Timmermann CI.
37. MacDonald, *The Last Offensive*, 215–16.
38. Engeman CI.
39. Timmermann CI.
40. *Ibid.* Deevers Interview; Engeman Interview; Harvey E. George, interview with Hugh Mott, John Reynolds, and Eugene Dorland, 9th Armored Engineer Battalion, 14 March 1945. Hereafter cited as Mott CI.
41. Deevers CI.
42. Leonard CI.
43. *Ibid.* Millikin CI.
44. Sylvan diary entry for 7 March 1945.
45. Engeman CI.
46. Headquarters III Corps, AAR, March 1945, 18–19; III Corps Operations Directive #10, 8 March 1945.
47. III Corps AAR, 22.

48. Kenneth Hechler, interview with Donald Russell, 27th Armored Infantry Battalion, 12 June 1945, CI #300.
49. Henry G. Phillips, *Remagen: Springboard to Victory* (Penn Valley, Calif. H. G. Phillips, 1995), 25, 29–30. Hereafter cited as Phillips, *Remagen.*
50. III Corps Operational Directive #10, 8 March 1945.
51. MacDonald, *The Last Offensive,* 220–21.
52. Quoted in Phillips, *Remagen,* 38.
53. MacDonald, *The Last Offensive,* 226–27.
54. Army Ground Forces Observer Report No. 826, Swimming Attacks Against Remagen Bridge, 9 April 1945.
55. See Phillips, *Remagen: Springboard to Victory,* Ch. 7.
56. *Ibid.,* 56–57, 65.
57. Kenneth Hechler, interview with Col. Walter Burnside, 12 June 1945.
58. John S. Howe, interview with Lt. Wilton Wenker, USNR, 27 March 1945; Corrections to Interview memorandum dated 5 April 1945, CI #340.
59. Kenneth W. Hechler, interview with Lt. Col. David E. Pergrin, 22 March 1945, CI #340.
60. First U.S. Army, Report of Rhine River Crossings, May 1945, 3.
61. Memorandum, Headquarters 1159th Engineer Group to Commanding General III Corps, 19 March 1945, Subject: Collapse of the Ludendorff [sic] Bridge; MacDonald, *The Last Offensive,* 230.
62. Sylvan Diary entry for 8 March 1945.
63. *Ibid.,* entry for 9 March 1945.
64. *Ibid.,* entry for 11 March 1945.
65. Hogan, *A Command Post at War,* 251–52.
66. Millikin CI.
67. MacDonald, *The Last Offensive,* 232.
68. Weigley, *Eisenhower's Lieutenants,* 920; MacDonald, *The Last Offensive,* 226; Kenneth W. Hechler, interview with Col. James H. Phillips, Col. Harry Mewshaw, Lt. Col. Norman B. Edwards, and Maj. Thomas J. Sharpe, 11 June 1945.
69. III Corps G-3 Situation Report #307.
70. Sylvan diary entry for 12 March 1945.
71. Kenneth W. Hechler, interview with Lt. Col. Norman B. Edwards, 16 March 1945.
72. Sylvan diary entry for 15 March 1945.
73. Kenneth W. Hechler, interview with Lt. Col. Norman B. Edwards, 14 April 1945.
74. Sylvan diary entry for 17 March 1945. Van Fleet had risen from Colonel to major general in nine months, after Bradley and Eisenhower realized that he was not the same person with a similar name whom they did not deem worthy of high rank.
75. Norman B. Edwards, letter to author, April 23, 1992.
76. Millikin CI.
77. Phillips, et. al., CI.
78. "Sagittarius," *Accident in the Allied Camp,* III Corps CI #340.

CHAPTER 16

1. Department of the Army, *Central Europe* (Washington, D.C.: GPO, n.d.), 3–11; Mac Donald, *The Last Offensive,* maps IX and XII.
2. Ruppenthal, *Logistical Support,* Vol. II, Table 10, 317.
3. Mansoor, *The GI Offensive in Europe,* 233–34; 236.
4. Army Ground Forces, *Statistical Data* (Washington, D.C., 31 August 1945), n.p.

5. Mansoor, *The GI Offensive in Europe*, 252. Information is from *Order of Battle, United States Army in World War II: European Theater of Operations* (Office of the Theater Historian, December 1945).

6. *Ibid.*, 255.

7. William R. Keast, Army Ground Forces Study No. 32, *Major Developments in the Training of Enlisted Replacements* (Washington, D.C., 1946), 1–5; 8–9.

8. ____. Army Ground Forces Study No. 7, *Provision of Enlisted Replacements* (Washington, D.C.,1946), 7.

9. *Ibid.*, 16–22.

10. U.S. Forces, European Theater General Board Report No. 3, *Reinforcement System and Reinforcement Procedures in European Theater of Operations*, n.d., 3; 6–7; 9; 15; 20; 30–31; Appendix 1, p. 4–7;

11. Ruppenthal, *Logistical Support*, Vol. II, 327–34.

12. *Ibid.*, 342–43.

13. Ruppenthal, *Logistical Support*, Vol. II, 442. Both the late-war restrictions and the improved situation are described in the detailed analysis supplied in U.S. Forces European Theater General Board Study No. 61, *Field Artillery Operations*, n.d.

14. U.S. Forces European Theater General Board Report No. 122, *Operation, Organization, Supply and Services of the Transportation Corps in the European Theater of Operations*, n.d., 43–46; 54–57.

15. *Ibid.*, Appendix 1, n.p.

16. Mac Donald, *The Last Offensive*, 297n.

17. *Ibid.*, 352–53; 370–72.

18. Department of the Army, *Central Europe*, 13–21; MacDonald, *The Last Offensive*, 370.

19. U.S. Military Academy, *The War in Western Europe, Part 2 (December 1944-May 1945)*, (Washington, D.C.: GPO, 1949), 153.

20. Department of the Army, *Central Europe*, 23–26.

21. MacDonald, *The Last Offensive*, 415–418. Nürnberg was another story. This ideological, though not physical, seat of Nazi power fell in late April to the Seventh U.S. Army after three days of intense fighting.

22. Ibid., 475. The author's correspondence and conversations with dozens of ETO veterans since 1988 reflect this general line of thinking.

23. Cawthon, *Other Clay*, 172.

24. Chandler, ed., *Eisenhower Papers*, 2696.

25. Office of the Comptroller of the Army, *Army Battle Casualties and Nonbattle Deaths in World War II Final Report, 7 December 1944-31 December 1946*, 54.

26. Overy, *Why the Allies Won*, 2–6.

27. See T.N. Dupuy, *Numbers, Predictions and War* (New York: Bobbs Merrill, 1979). John S. Brown, *Draftee Division*, riddled the argument with holes. See Appendix 2, 168–175.

28. Brown, *Draftee Division*, 174–75.

29. See, for example, Martin Van Creveld, *Fighting Power, German and U.S. Army Performance, 1939-1945* (Westport, CT: Greenwood Press, 1982). Chapter 11 discusses the relative merits of the officer corps of the two armies. The *First U.S. Army Report of Operations, 1 August 1994-22 February 1945*, Annex 1, does, in fact, note that 90 percent of commissioned officer casualties were in the combat arms. However, this should not surprise anyone. Van Creveld, *Supplying War-Logistics from Wallenstein to Patton* (New York: Cambridge University Press, 1977). Chapter 7 gives an overview of ETO logistics but offers supply consumption calculations based on assumptions that would not have been valid in practice.

30. Max Hastings, *Armageddon* (New York: Knopf, 2004), especially 183–87; 510–13.

31. John Ellis, *Brute Force-Allied Strategy and Tactics in the Second World War* (New York: Viking, 1990), 384; 412.

32. Well-meaning historians and soldiers did not realize that Marshall, *Men Against Fire* (Washington, D.C.: Infantry Journal Press, 1947), intended to warn his readers not to adopt without question post–World War II atomic age arguments that technology would supplant the foot soldier. However, scholarship since the late 1980s has revealed that his figures on GI performance were largely fabricated, as were aspects of Marshall's own military career. See Roger J. Spiller, "S.L.A. Marshall and the Ratio of Fire" *RUSI Journal* 133, No. 4, Winter 1988, 63–71; and Frederic Smoler, "The Secret of the Soldiers who Didn't Shoot," *American Heritage* 40, No. 2, March 1989, 37–45, for examples of critical research. According to Spiller, Marshall discounted the impact of terrain on infantry combat; grossly overstated the number of men with whom he spoke, oversimplified the complexities of the battlefield, and misrepresented his World War I service career. On the other hand, his pioneering of group interviews and push to adopt the use of field historians proved beneficial for post-war historians. One must be careful in adopting his conclusions and analysis, though his chronologies are usually dependable, for the reports he supervised or authored himself, such as those of the early airborne operations. See also, F.D.G. Williams, *SLAM, The Influence of S.L.A. Marshall on the United States Army* (Washington, D.C., GPO, 1994).

33. U.S. Strategic Bombing Survey, Military Analysis Division, *The Impact of the Allied Air Effort on German Logistics*, 2d ed., 1947, 30.

34. *Ibid.*, 132, 141–143.

35. Overy, *Why the Allies Won*, 216–17.

36. Kenneth Macksey, *Why the Germans Lose at War* (London: Greenhill Books, 1996) offers a fresh perspective on the myth of overarching German military superiority.

37. This is a theme that appears to be prevalent especially among European writers.

38. Wagener, MS A-964, 6–7.

39. Otto Hitzfeld, "LXVII Corps (26 Jan–21 March 45), MS #B-101, n.p., n.d., 11.

40. War Department, *Logistics in World War II, Final Report of the Army Service Forces* (Washington, D.C.: GPO, 1948) provides details of the scope of global logistics. The manpower numbers are from Randolph Leigh, *48 Million Tons to Eisenhower* (Washington, D.C.: Infantry Journal Press, 1945), 5.

41. Gole, *Road to Rainbow*, Chapters 8–10, provide the most recent scholarly account of the immediate pre-war years.

42. This is reflected in the significant changes in Tables of Organization published in the summer of 1943.

43. Mark. Reardon, electronic mail to author, July 2, 2001.

44. Overy, *Why the Allies Won*, 146.

45. Ruppenthal, Vol. II, Table 8, 282–83.

46. In First Army, for example, the average round per gun per day allocated for 155-mm howitzers between mid-October and mid-November was 10 and 13, respectively. The allocation for the 155-mm gun was only 8 rounds. See *First U.S. Army Report of Operations* for specifics, and Lida Mayo, *The Ordnance Department on Beachhead and Battlefront* for general discussion. Support to the Allies also siphoned resources that might have been available to the combat forces around the world. The Persian Gulf Service Command, for example, which executed much lend-lease support to the Soviets, required the equivalent of two division's worth of soldiers (20,000 men served in Iran alone). A single fuel depot supplied the Soviets with 9 million gallons of gasoline per month. The United States fully equipped eight French divisions and partially outfitted three more. About 27 percent of M10 TD production and nearly 32 percent of 105-mm self-propelled artillery production went to lend-lease and the US Marine Corps. See Thomas H.V. Motter, *The Persian Corridor: Aid to Russia* (Washington, D.C.: GPO, 1952); and Marcel Vigneras, *Rearming the French*

(Washington, D.C.: GPO, 1957); Office of the Chief of Military History, Lend Lease Statistics, 15 December 1952, copy in the author's files and at the US Army Library, The Pentagon.

47. Ruppenthal, *Logistical Support*, Vol. II, 506–07.
48. Christopher Gabel, e-mail to author, January 27, 2000.
49. Arguments relating to tonnage alone mean little since they do not consider weight and cube of the materiel.
50. Hubert Essame, "Normandy Revisited," *Military Review* 43, December 1963, 80. (70–80)
51. Army Ground Forces, *Statistical Data* (Washington, D.C., 31 August 1945), n.p.
52. Overy, *Why the Allies Won*, 317.
53. Ronnie L. Brownlee and William J. Mullin III, *Changing an Army, An Oral History of General William E. DePuy, USA Retired*, Carlisle Barracks, Pa.: U.S. Military History Institute, n.d., 90–91. The publication notes that the comments by DePuy were made during a 1979 interview. DePuy was a staunch critic and put his experiences from World War II, which no doubt left their mark on a young officer with considerable responsibility, to use as the commander of the Army's Training and Doctrine Command. He initiated many of the post-Viet Nam reforms in training for combat.
54. Winston S. Churchill, *The Hinge of Fate* (Boston: Houghton Mifflin, 1950), 387.

APPENDIX B

1. The best source for the development of tank destroyers is Christopher R. Gabel, *Seek, Strike, and Destroy: U.S. Army Tank Destroyer Doctrine in World War II* (Fort Leavenworth, Kans.: Combat Studies Institute, 1985). Hereafter cited as Gabel, *Seek, Strike, and Destroy*. The overall story of interwar armor development is Johnson, *Fast Tanks*. The quote is from p. 219.
2. See Chapter 4, above.
3. Gabel, *Seek, Strike, and Destroy*, 14, 22.
4. Johnson, *Fast Tanks*, Conclusion, 218–29.
5. *Ibid.*, 37–39; 59; 73; 117–121.
6. Green, et. al., *The Ordnance Department: Planning Munitions for War*, The United Army in World War II (Washington, D.C.: GPO, 1955), Chapter VII, particularly pages 189–203, and Chapter X.
7. *Ibid.*, 200–201.
8. Johnson, *Fast Tanks*, 121–24.
9. Mayo, *Beachhead & Battlefront*, 139–40.
10. Johnson, *Fast Tanks*, 148–50.
11. Gabel, *Seek, Strike, and Destroy*, 27–29; 36–38; 67–72.
12. Green, et. al., *The Ordnance Department: Planning Munitions for War*, 296-98, covers the fuels decision. It is important to note, however, that a possibly more significant threat in a burning tank was ammunition. Gasoline fires seem to have received the lion's share of interest.
13. Green, *Planning Munitions for War*, 280–83.
14. *Ibid.*, 284–87.
15. Mayo, *Beachhead and Battlefront*, 330–32.

GLOSSARY

AGCT Army General Classification Test

AGF Army Ground Forces

ASF Army Service Forces

AP armor-piercing ammunition

AT anti-tank

BAR Browning automatic rifle, U.S. .30 caliber weapon

CCA Combat Command A (in U.S. armored divisions)

CCB Combat Command B (in U.S. armored divisions)

CCR Reserve Combat Command (in U.S. armored divisions)

CP command post

G-1 U.S. personnel staff officer at division and higher unit levels

G-2 U.S. intelligence staff officer at division and higher unit levels

G-3 U.S. operations staff officer at division and higher unit levels

G-4 U.S. logistics staff officer at division and higher unit levels

HE high-explosive ammunition

HQ headquarters

Landser German equivalent of "GI"

LD line of departure—start line of an attack (U.S. term)

M-1 standard U.S. semi-automatic rifle

M-3 U.S. medium tank ("Grant") and also designation for a light tank (the "Stuart")

M-4 U.S. medium tank—the "Sherman"

M-5 U.S. light tank

M-10 U.S. tank destroyer

M-26 U.S. heavy tank developed as the T-26 (late war; the "Pershing")

M-29 U.S. light tracked cargo carrier (the "Weasel")

Mk IV German medium tank

Mk V German medium tank—(the "Panther")

Mk VI German "Tiger" tank

MSR   main supply route (U.S. term)

OB-West   German supreme headquarters for the Western Front, used interchangeably as the title of the officer holding the position

OCS   U.S. Officer Candidate School

OP   observation post

S-1   U.S. personnel staff officer at regiment and lower levels

S-2   U.S. intelligence staff officer at regiment and lower levels

S-3   U.S. operations staff officer at regiment and lower levels

S-4   U.S. logistics staff officer at regiment and lower levels

SHAEF   Supreme Headquarters, Allied Expeditionary Forces

SP   self-propelled

TD   tank destroyer

TF   task force (rough U.S. equivalent to German *kampfgruppe*)

XO   Executive officer (U.S.)

BIBLIOGRAPHY

THE FIRST STOP FOR THE RESEARCHER on virtually any aspect of the U.S. Army's participation in World War II is the multivolume set of official histories ("Green Books"), many of which are cited below. Though recent scholarship has added depth to earlier analysis, these books are the basic sources for operational data, locations, dates, and units. They are also the only published source for technical, organizational, planning, mobilization, and logistical information available to researchers outside archival sources. These less than glamorous topics are nonetheless fundamental for a thorough understanding of why the Army conducted its worldwide operations in the manner it did. Historians would do well to make more use of them.

After using the official histories to establish baselines for study, I consulted operational records stored at the National Archives facility at College Park, Maryland. My military service fortunately enabled me to collect copies of many records important to me, but the researcher will find the necessary unit staff journals, combat interviews, after-action reports, and other files in Record Group 407, located at the Modern Military Reference Branch, National Archives II, College Park, Maryland. The researcher looking for more primary source detail on mobilization and training should investigate Record Group 337, Army Ground Forces. However, the applicable official Army histories cited below were sufficient for the purposes of this study. The Combined Arms Research Library at Ft. Leavenworth, Kansas, holds copies of the German interrogation reports (Foreign Military Studies). Unfortunately, many of these interviews were conducted without reference material, and some captured generals used them as a forum to explain away their own shortcomings. Yet they can be valuable to a careful researcher. Both the Pentagon Library and the Center or Military History hold copies of field manuals, Army regulations and tables of organization dating to the early 1930's. CMH and the Pentagon Library maintain copies of the U.S.

Forces, European Theater of Operations General Board special studies on technical aspects of the campaign. These are unclassified but also not widely available. Within the 12th Army Group, the First and Third Armies published valuable and detailed reports of operations. The V Corps report of operations published in Germany in 1945 is very detailed. The VII Corps did not publish a similar work, and one must consult its archival records in RG 407.

Other primary sources include years of correspondence with veterans, many of whom are no longer with us. I have been privileged to know so many, both American and German. Many postwar unit histories have little value to the researcher, but those cited below are reliable if cross-checked with records. Secondary sources listed here are among the most important and reliable available except where described accordingly in the notes. The McCormick Research Center (Cantigny), Wheaton, Illinois, houses an important collection of 1st Infantry Division records. The U.S. Army Military History Institute, Carlisle Barracks, Pennsylvania, holds several important collections of personal papers, copies of senior officer interviews, veteran survey questionnaires, doctrinal publications, and copies of many key German operational records. Armor and Infantry School monographs are stored at the U.S. Army Armor School, Fort Knox, Kentucky, and the Donovan Research Library, Fort Benning, Georgia, respectively.

Books and Published Papers

Atwell, Lester. *Private*. New York: Simon and Schuster, 1962.

Baker, Carlos. *Ernest Hemingway: A Life Story*. New York: Scribner's, 1969.

Baldwin, Hanson W. *Tiger Jack*. Fort Collins, Colo.: Old Army, 1979.

Balkoski, Joseph. *Beyond the Beachhead*. Harrisburg, Pa.: Stackpole, 1989.

Bartov, Omer. *Hitler's Army*. New York: Oxford University Press, 1992.

Baumer, Robert W., and Mark J. Reardon. *American Iliad: The 18th Infantry Regiment in World War II*. Bedford, Pa.: Aberjona, 2004.

Baumgardner, John. History *of the 16th Infantry Regiment*. N.p., n.d.

Blair, Clay. *Ridgway's Paratroopers: The American Airborne in World War II*. New York: Dial, 1985.

Blumenson, Martin. *Breakout and Pursuit*. Washington, D.C.: Government Printing Office [hereafter GPO], 1961.

_____. *Salerno to Cassino*. Washington, D.C.: GPO, 1969.

_____. *The Patton Papers 1940–1945*. Boston: Houghton-Mifflin, 1974.

_____. *The War between the Generals*. New York: Morrow, 1993.

_____. "Kasserine Pass." In *America's First Battles 1776–1965*, edited by Charles E. Heller and William A. Stofft. Lawrence: University Press of Kansas, 1986.

Bradley, Omar N. *A General's Life*. New York: Simon and Schuster, 1983.

Braim, Paul F. *The Test of Battle: The American Expeditionary Force in the Meuse-Argonne Campaign*. Newark: University of Delaware Press, 1987.

Brown, John S. *Draftee Division*. Lexington: University Press of Kentucky, 1986.

Bykofsky, Joseph, and Harold Larson. *The Transportation Corps: Operations Overseas*. Washington, D.C.: GPO, 1957.

Byrnes, Laurence G. *History of the 94th Infantry Division in World War II*. Washington, D.C.: Infantry Journal, 1948.

Carafano, James Jay. *After D-Day: Operation Cobra and the Normandy Breakout*. Boulder, Colo.: Lynne Rienner, 2000.

Carrell, Paul. *Invasion: They're Coming!* New York: Bantam, 1973.

Cavanagh, William C. C. *Dauntless: A History of the 99th Infantry Division*. Dallas: Taylor, 1994.

Cawthon, Charles W. *Other Clay*. Niwot: University Press of Colorado, 1990.

Christoffel, Edgar. *Krieg am Westwall 1944–1945*. Trier: Universitäts Buchhandlung, 1989.

Churchill, Winston S. *The Hinge of Fate*. Boston: Houghton Mifflin, 1950.

Coffman, Edward M. *The Old Army: A Portrait of the American Army in Peacetime 1784–1898*. New York: Oxford University Press, 1986.

_____. *The War to End All Wars: The American Military Experience in World War I*. Lexington: University Press of Kentucky, 1998.

_____. *The Regulars: The American Army 1898–1941*. Cambridge, Mass.: Harvard University Press, 2004.

Colby, John. *War from the Ground Up: The 90th Division in World War II*. Austin, Tex.: Nortex, 1991.

Cole, Hugh M. *The Lorraine Campaign*. Washington, D.C.: GPO, 1950.

_____. *The Ardennes: Battle of the Bulge*. Washington, D.C.: GPO, 1965.

Collins, J. Lawton. *Lightnin' Joe: An Autobiography*. Novato, Calif.: Presidio, 1994.

Cosmas, Graham A. *An Army for Empire*. Columbia: University of Missouri Press, 1971.

—— and Albert E. Cowdrey. *The Medical Department: Medical Service in the European Theater of Operations*. Washington, D.C.: GPO, 1992.

D'Este, Carlo. *Bitter Victory: The Battle for Sicily–1943*. Glasgow: William Collins Sons, 1988.

_____. *Patton: A Genius for War*. New York: HarperCollins, 1995.

Devlin, Gerard M. *Silent Wings*. New York: St. Martin's, 1985.

Dieckhoff, Gerhard, and Erich Borries. *3. Panzergrenadier Division*. Göttingen, n.p., 1960.

Dupuy, T. N. *Numbers, Predictions and War.* New York: Bobbs Merrill, 1979.

Eisenhower, Dwight D. *The Papers of Dwight David Eisenhower.* Vol. 2, *The War Years.* Edited by Alfred D. Chandler Jr. Baltimore: Johns Hopkins University Press, 1971.

11th Infantry Regiment Association. *11th Infantry History.* Baton Rouge, La.: Army and Navy, 1945.

Ellis, John. *Brute Force.* New York: Viking, 1990.

Ellis, William D., and Thomas J. Cunningham, Jr. *Clarke of St. Vith.* Cleveland, Ohio: Lederbach, 1974.

Ellsberg, Edward. *The Far Shore.* New York: Popular Library, 1960.

Fairchild, Byron, and Johnathan Grossman. *The Army and Industrial Manpower.* Washington, D.C.: GPO, 1959.

Fleig, Raymond E. *707th Tank Battalion in World War II.* Springfield, Ohio: N.p. 1991.

Frasier, Harvey R. *The 51st Again.* Shippensburg, Pa.: White Mane, 1992.

Fritz, Stephen G. *Frontsoldaten.* Lexington: University Press of Kentucky, 1995.

Gabel, Christopher R. *The U.S. Army GHQ Maneuvers of 1941.* Washington, D.C.: GPO, 1991.

Garland, Albert N. *Sicily and the Surrender of Italy.* Washington, D.C.: GPO, 1965.

Geschichtsverein der Gemeinde Inden e.V. *Erlebte Geschichte 1939–1947.* Jülich: N.p., 1981.

Gole, Henry G. *The Road to Rainbow: Army Planning for Global War, 1934–1940.* Annapolis, Md.: Naval Institute Press, 2003.

Green, Constance M., Harry C. Thomason, and Peter C. Roots. *The Ordnance Department: Planning Munitions for War.* Washington, D.C.: GPO, 1955.

Griffith, Robert K. Jr. *Men Wanted for the U.S. Army: America's Experience with the All-Volunteer Army between the World Wars.* Westport, Conn.: Greenwood, 1982.

Gropman, Alan L. *Mobilizing U.S. Industry in World War II.* Washington, D.C.: National Defense University Press, 1996.

Guderian, Heinz-G'nther. *From Normandy to the Ruhr with the 116th Panzer Division in World War II.* Bedford, Pa.: Aberjona, 2001.

Harrison, Gordon A. *Cross Channel Attack.* Washington, D.C.: GPO, 1951.

Hastings, Max. *Overlord.* New York: Simon and Schuster, 1984.

———. *Armageddon.* New York: Knopf, 2004.

Hemingway, Ernest. "War in the Siegfried Line." In *By-Line: Ernest Hemingway,* by William White. New York: Simon and Schuster, 1998.

Hoegh, Leo A., and Howard J. Doyle. *Timberwolf Tracks: The History of the 104th Infantry Division, 1942–1945.* Washington, D.C.: Infantry Journal, 1946.

Hogan, David W. Jr. *A Command Post at War: First Army Headquarters in Europe 1943–1945.* Washington, D.C.: GPO, 2000.

Hohenstein, Adolf, and Wolfgang Trees. *Hölle im Hurtgenwald*. Aachen: Triangle Verlag, 1986.

Houston, Donald E. *Hell on Wheels*. San Rafael, Calif.: Presidio, 1977.

Howe, George F. *Northwest Africa: Seizing the Initiative in the West*. Washington, D.C.: GPO, 1957.

Johnson, David E. *Fast Tanks and Heavy Bombers: Innovation in the U.S. Army 1917–1945*. Ithaca, N.Y.: Cornell University Press, 1998.

Kahn, E. J., Jr. *McNair: Educator of an Army*. Washington, D.C.: Infantry Journal, 1946.

Kennett, Lee. *GI*. New York: Scribner's, 1987.

Kirkpatrick, Charles E. *An Unknown Future and a Doubtful Present: Writing the Victory Plan of 1941*. Washington, D.C.: GPO, 1990.

Lewis, Adrian R. *Omaha Beach: A Flawed Victory*. Chapel Hill: University of North Carolina Press, 2001.

Linn, Brian M. *The Philippines War*. College Station: Texas A&M University Press, 2004.

MacDonald, Charles B. *The Siegfried Line Campaign*. Washington, D.C.: GPO, 1963.

———. *The Mighty Endeavor*. New York: Oxford University Press, 1969.

———. *The Last Offensive*. Washington, D.C.: GPO, 1973.

———. *A Time for Trumpets: The Untold Story of the Battle of the Bulge*. New York: Morrow, 1985.

———, and Sidney T. Matthews. *Three Battles: Arnaville, Altuzzo and Schmidt*. Washington, D.C.: GPO, 1952.

Macksey, Kenneth. *Why the Germans Lose at War*. London: Greenhill Books, 1996.

Mansoor, Peter R. *The GI Offensive in Europe*. Lawrence: University Press of Kansas, 1999.

Marshall, George C. *The Papers of George Catlett Marshall*. Vol. 1, *The Soldierly Spirit: December 1880–July 1939*. Edited by Larry I. Bland and Sharon R. Ritenour. Baltimore: Johns Hopkins University Press, 1981.

———. *The Papers of George Catlett Marshall*. Vol. 2, *"We Cannot Delay": July 1, 1939–December 6, 1941*. Edited by Larry I. Bland, Sharon R. Ritenour, and Clarence E. Wunderlin Jr. Baltimore: Johns Hopkins University Press, 1986.

———. *The Papers of George Catlett Marshall*. Vol. 3, *"The Right Man for the Job": December 7, 1941–May 31, 1943*. Edited by Larry I. Bland and Sharon Ritenour Stevens. Baltimore: Johns Hopkins University Press, 1991.

———. *The Papers of George Catlett Marshall*. Vol. 4, *"Aggressive and Determined Leadership": June 1, 1943–December 31, 1944*. Edited by Larry I. Bland and Sharon Ritenour Stevens. Baltimore: Johns Hopkins University Press, 1991.

Matloff, Maurice. "The 90-Division Gamble." In *Command Decisions*, edited by Kent Roberts Greenfield. Washington, D.C., GPO: 1960.

Mayo, Lida. *The Ordnance Department: On Beachhead and Battlefront.* Washington, D.C.: GPO, 1968.

Messerschmidt, Manfred. "German Military Effectiveness between 1919 and 1939." In *Military Effectiveness: The Interwar Period*, edited by Allan R. Millett and Williamson Murray. Boston: Allen and Unwin, 1988.

Miller, Edward G. *A Dark and Bloody Ground: The Hürtgen Forest and Roer River Dams 1944-1945.* College Station: Texas A&M University Press, 1995.

Montgomery, Bernard L. *The Memoirs of Field-Marshal Montgomery.* New York: Signet, 1959.

Mortensen, Daniel R. *A Pattern for Joint Operations: World War II Close Air Support in North Africa.* Washington, D.C.: Office of Air Force History and U.S. Army Center of Military History, 1987.

Motter, Thomas H. V. *The Persian Corridor: Aid to Russia.* Washington, D.C.: GPO, 1952.

Murray, Williamson. *Strategy for Defeat: The Luftwaffe 1939-1945.* Maxwell, Ala.: Air University Press, 1983.

Nenninger, Timothy K. *The Leavenworth Schools and the Old Army.* Westport, Conno.: Greenwood, 1978.

Ninth U.S. Army Staff. *Conquer: The Story of Ninth Army.* Washington, D.C.: Infantry Journal, 1947.

Odom, William O. *After the Trenches: The Transformation of U.S. Army Doctrine 1918-1939.* College Station: Texas A&M University Press, 1999.

Overy, Richard. *War and Economy in the Third Reich.* Oxford, U.K.: Clarendon, 1995.

Palmer, Robert R., et al. *The Procurement and Training of Ground Combat Troops.* Washington, D.C.: GPO, 1948.

Phillips, Henry G. *Remagen: Springboard to Victory.* Penn Valley, Calif.: H. G. Phillips, 1995.

Pogue, Forrest C. *George C. Marshall: Education of a General, 1880-1939.* New York: Viking, 1963.

Prohme, Rupert. *History of the 30th Infantry Regiment in World War II.* Washington, D.C.: Infantry Journal, 1947.

Reardon, Mark J. *Victory at Mortain: Stopping Hitler's Panzer Counteroffensive.* Lawrence: University Press of Kansas, 2002.

Rickard, John N. *Patton at Bay: The Loraine Campaign, 1944.* Washington, D.C.: Brassey's, 2004.

Robey, Duane A. *The Memories of an Infantryman in the I&R Platoon.* N.p.: n.d.

Rommel, Erwin. *The Rommel Papers*. Edited by B. H. Liddell Hart. New York: Da Capo, n.d.

Roppelt, Fritz. *Der Vergangenheit auf der Spur.* N.p. (Germany): N.p., 1993.

Ruppenthal, Roland G. *Logistical Support of the Armies.* Vol. 1. Washington, D.C.: GPO, 1953.

_____. *Logistical Support of the Armies.* Vol. 2. Washington, D.C.: GPO, 1959.

78th Infantry Division Historical Association. *Lightning.* Washington, D.C.: Infantry Journal, 1947.

Smith, R. Elburton *The Army and Economic Mobilization.* Washington, D.C.: GPO, 1985.

Spires, David N. *Air Power for Patton's Army.* Washington, D.C.: GPO, 2002.

Stouffer, Samuel A., Edward A. Schuman, Leland C. DeVinney, Shirley A. Starr, and Robin M. Williams, Jr., eds. *The American Soldier.* Vol. 2, *Combat and Its Aftermath.* Princeton, N.J.: Princeton University Press, 1949.

Thomson, Harry C., and Lida Mayo. *The Ordnance Department: Procurement and Supply.* Washington, D.C.: GPO, 1960.

376th Infantry Regiment Historical Committee. *History of the 376th Infantry Regiment between the Years of 1921–1945.* Wuppertal: Weddingen, 1945.

Truscott, Lucian K. *Command Missions.* Reprint, Novato, Calif.: Presidio, 1990.

Underwood, Jeffery S. *The Wings of Democracy: The Influence of Air Power on the Roosevelt Administration, 1933–1941.* College Station: Texas A&M University Press, 1991.

Van Creveld, Martin. *Supplying War: Logistics from Wallenstein to Patton.* New York: Cambridge University Press, 1977.

_____. *Fighting Power: German and U.S. Army Performance, 1939–1945.* Westport, Conn.: Greenwood, 1982.

Vigneras, Marcel. *Rearming the French.* Washington, D.C.: GPO, 1957.

Walker, Fred L. *From Texas to Rome.* Dallas: Taylor, 1969.

Watson, Mark S. *Chief of Staff: Prewar Plans and Preparations.* Washington, D.C.: GPO, 1950.

Weigley, Russell F. *The History of the United States Army.* Bloomington: Indiana University Press, 1984.

_____. *Eisenhower's Lieutenants: The Campaign of France and Germany 1944–45.* Book Club ed. 2 vols. Bloomington: Indiana University Press, 1981.

White, Charles M. *The Medical Department: Medical Service in the Mediterranean and Minor Theaters.* Washington, D.C.: GPO, 1965.

Whitman, George P. *Memoirs of a Rifle Company Commander in Patton's Third U.S. Army.* West Topsham, Vt.: Gibby, 1993.

Wilson, George B. *If You Survive.* New York: Ivy Books, 1987.

Wilson, John B. *Maneuver and Firepower: The Evolution of Divisions and Separate Brigades.* Washington, D.C.: GPO, 1998.
Wolfe, Martin Green. *Light! A Troop Carrier Squadron's War from Normandy to the Rhine.* Washington, D.C.: Office of Air Force History, 1993.

Journal and Newspaper Articles

Bartov, Omer. "The Conduct of War: Soldiers and the Barbarization of Warfare." *Journal of Modern History* 62 (December 1992 Supplement): 32–45.
Beaumont, Roger. "Wehrmacht Mystique Revisited." *Military Review* 70, no. 2 (1990): 64–75.
Blumenson, Martin. "America's World War II Leaders in Europe: Some Thoughts." *Parameters* 19, no. 4 (1989): 2–13.
Coffman, Edward M. "Conflicts in American Planning: An Aspect of World War I Strategy." *Military Review* 43 (June 1963): 78–90.
Collier, Thomas W. "The Army and the Great Depression." *Parameters* 18, no. 3 (September 1988): 102–108.
Denny, Harold. "Eschweiler Folks Flee to Our Lines." *New York Times,* November 22, 1944.
Essame, Hubert. "Normandy Revisited." *Military Review* 43 (December 1963): 70–80.
"Employment of Tanks and Infantry in Normandy." *Military Review* 24, no. 9 (December 1944): 13–17.
Faulkner, Richard S. "Learning the Hard Way: The Coordination between Infantry Divisions and Separate Tank Battalions during the Breakout from Normandy." *Armor* 99 (July–August 1990): 24–29.
Ganz, A. Harding. "Patton's Relief of General Wood." *Journal of Military History* 53, no. 3 (July 1989): 257–73.
_____. "The 11th Panzers in the Defense, 1944." *Armor* 103, no. 2 (January–February 1994):
Helmer, James B. [Untitled article]. *Glider Tow Line* (Winter 1993–1994): N.p.
Gooderson, Ian. "Heavy and Medium Bombers: How Successful Were They in the Tactical Close Air Support Role during World War II?" *Journal of Strategic Studies* 15, no. 3 (1992): 367–99.
"German Tank Tactics in France." *Military Review* 24, no. 10 (January 1945): 3–5.
"National Affairs." *Time,* 27 May 1940, 19.
"National Defense." *Time,* 18 August 1941, 35–36.
Nenninger, Timothy K. "A Revised Mechanization Policy." *Armor* 78, no. 5 (September–October 1969): 45–49.

Newland, Samuel J. "Blitzkrieg in Retrospect." *Military Review* 84, no. 5 (July–August 2004): 86–88.

Rainey, James W. "The Questionable Training of the AEF in World War I." *Parameters* 22, no. 4 (Winter 1992–1993): 89–103.

Shills, Edward A., and Morris Janowitz. "Cohesion and Disintegration in the Wehrmacht in World War II." *Public Opinion Quarterly* 12, no. 2 (Summer 1948): 280–315.

Sloan, John E. "Experiences with the 36th Division in Italy." *Military Review* 29, no. 10 (January 1945): 15–23.

Smith, Gene. "The Seventeenth Largest Army." *American Heritage* 43, no. 8 (December 1992): 98–107.

Smoler, Frederic. "The Secret of the Soldiers Who Didn't Shoot." *American Heritage* 40, no. 2 (March 1989): 37–45.

Spencer, Henry G. "Baptism in the Hedgerows." *Infantry Journal* 55, no. 4 (1944): 10.

Spiller, Roger J. "S. L. A. Marshall and the Ratio of Fire." *RUSI Journal* 133, no. 4 (Winter 1988): 63–71.

"The People's Army." *Fortune* 24 (August 1941): 97.

"The Hedgerow Country's Tricky and Mean." *Infantry Journal* 55, no. 4 (1944): 15.

The Stars and Stripes. London edition, November 23, 1944.

26th Infantry Regiment Association. *Blue Spader Newsletter* 99-1 (March 1999): 1.

Walker, Fred L. "Experiences with the 36th Division in Italy." *Military Review* 24, no. 10 (January 1945): 15–23.

"Who's in the Army Now?" *Fortune* 12 (September 1935): 39–40.

"Why an Army?" *Fortune* 12 (September 1935): 132–36.

Wyant, Vernon L. Jr. [Untitled article}. *Glider Tow Line* (Winter 1991–92): n.p.

Published Official Government Records, Manuals, and Internal Publications

Foreign Military Studies, U.S. Forces, European Theater:

Badinski, Kurt. "Report on Combat Commitment of 276 ID in Normandy." B-526, 14 April 1947.

Blumentritt, Gunther. "Evaluation of the Armies of 1914–18 and 1939–45." B-293, December 1946.

Denkert, Walter. "Die 3.Panzer-grenadier Division in der Schlacht von Aachen." A-979, n.d., n.p.

Eberbach, Henirich. "Report on the Fighting of Panzergruppe West (Fifth Pz. Army) from 3 July [to] 9 August 1944." B-840, 1 June 1948.

Hitzfeld, Otto. "LXXVII Corps, 26 Jan–21 Mar 45." B-101, 1954.

Köchling, Friederich. "LXXXI Corps Sep 1944–Apr 1945." A-988-997, 12 December 1945.

Püchler, Karl. "The Rhineland–74. Armeekorps—The period from 2 to 27 October 1944 and 16 Dec 1944 to 22 March 1945." B-118, 26 July 1946.

von Zangen, Gustav. "Fifteenth Army Defensive Engagements along the Roer and the Rhine, 22 Nov 44–22 March 45." B-829, 25 April 1948.

Wagener, Carl. "Report of the Chief of Staff, A Gp B." A-964/965, 4 February 1946.

U.S. FORCES EUROPEAN THEATER GENERAL BOARD STUDIES, 1946–1947

No. 1. *Strategy of the Campaign in Western Europe.*

No. 3. *Reinforcement System and Reinforcement Procedures in European Theater of Operations.*

No. 8. *G-1 Reports and Reporting Procedures in European Theater of Operations.*

No. 58. *Ammunition Supply for Field Artillery.*

No. 61. *Field Artillery Operations.*

No. 91. *Combat Exhaustion.*

No. 94. *Trench Foot.*

No. 122. *Operation, Organization, Supply and Services of the Transportation Corps in the European Theater of Operations.*

WAR DEPARTMENT PUBLICATIONS

Annual Report of the Chief of Staff, 1933.

Annual Report of the Chief of Staff, 1934.

Annual Report of the Secretary of War, 1938.

Army Service Forces. *Logistics in World War II: Final Report of the Army Service Forces.* Reprint, Washington, D.C.: GPO, 1993.

Biennial Reports of the Chief of Staff of the United States Army to the Secretary of War 1 July 1939–30 June 1945. Reprint, Washington, D.C.: GPO 1996.

Chief National Guard Bureau. *Annual Report for Fiscal Year 1941.*

Field Manual 7-10. *Rifle Company, Infantry Regiment,* 18 March 1944.

Field Manual 7-20. *Infantry Battalion,* 1 October 1944.

Field Manual 7-30. *Supply and Evacuation. The Infantry Regiment: Service Company and Medical Detachment,* 1 June 1944.

Field Manual 17-40. *Armored Infantry Company,* November 1944.

Field Manual 17-100 (Tentative). *Employment of the Armored Division and Separate Armored Units*, 29 September 1943.

Field Manual 21–50. *Military Courtesy and Discipline*, 15 June 1942.

Field Manual 100–5. *Operations*, 15 June 1944.

Field Manual 100–10. *Administration*, 15 September 1943.

Field Manual 101–10. *Staff Officers' Field Manual: Organization, Technical and Logistical Data*, 10 October 1943.

General Order No. 3, 8 January 1945.

General Order No. 73, 6 September 1944.

General Order No. 42, 24 May 1945.

General Order No. 74, 1 September 1945.

George C. Marshall, Testimony on Military Establishment Appropriation Bill for 1941.

Mobilization Regulation 1. *General Mobilization*, 1 April 1940.

Mobilization Regulation 1–7. *Reception of Selected Service Men*, 1 October 1940 (supplement to Mobilization Regulation 1-9, *Physical Profile Serial*, 30 June 1945).

Mobilization Regulation 1–10. *Morale*, 5 March 1943.

Mobilization Regulation 1–915. *Standards of Physical Examination during Mobilization*, October 1943.

Mobilization Training Plan 7–1, 12 September 1943.

Mobilization Training Plan 17–1, 31 January 1942.

Military Intelligence Division. *The German Squad in Combat*, January 1943.

Military Intelligence Service. Special Series 3, *German Military Training*, 17 September 1942.

OMAHA Beach. Washington, D.C.: GPO, 1946.

Pamphlet 12-8. *The Evaluation, Classification and Assignment of Military Personnel of the United States Army*, 28 July 1944.

Small Unit Actions. Washington, D.C.: GPO, 1946.

Statement of General George C. Marshall in Connection with Retention of Selectees and Reserve Components in the Military Service Beyond One Year, before the Committee on Military Affairs of the United States Senate, July 9, 1941.

Technical Manual 20-205. *Dictionary of United States Army Terms*, 18 January 1944.

Training Regulation 10-5, 10 August 1935.

War Department Special Staff. *Regimental Unit Study 4: Forcing of the Merderet Causeway at La Fiere, France, August 1944*, n.d.

_____. *Regimental Unit Study 5: Preliminary Operations around the La Fiere Bridgehead, Merderet River, Normandy*, n.d.

TABLES OF ORGANIZATION/TABLES OF ORGANIZATION AND EQUIPMENT

No. 6-95. Field Artillery Battalion, 240-mm, Truck-Drawn, 18 August 1943.

No. 7. Infantry Division, 15 July 1943.

No. 7–11. Infantry Regiment, 26 February 1944.

No. 7–15. Infantry Battalion, 26 February 1944.

No. 7–25. Armored Infantry Battalion, 15 September 1943.

No. 7–27. Armored Infantry Company, 15 September 1943.

No. 7–51. Glider Infantry Regiment 5 September 1942, with changes, through 24 May 1944.

No. 7–85. Ranger Infantry Battalion, 29 February 1944.

No. 7–86. Headquarters and Headquarters Company, Ranger Infantry Battalion, 29 February 1944.

No. 7–87. Ranger Infantry Company, 29 February 1944.

No. 17–25. Tank Battalion, 15 September 1943.

No. 17–27. Medium Tank Company, 15 September 1943.

No. 18–25. Tank Destroyer Battalion, 27 January 1943.

DEPARTMENT OF THE ARMY PUBLICATIONS

Kennedy, Robert M. *The German Campaign in Poland 1939*. Washington, D.C.: GPO, 1956.

Kriedberg, Marvin A.. and Merton G. Henry *History of Military Mobilization in the United States Army 1775–1946*. Washington, D.C.: GPO, 1955.

Office of the Comptroller of the Army. *Army Battle Casualties and Nonbattle Deaths in World War II: Final Report, 7 December 1944–31 December 1946.*

The German Campaign in Russia: Planning and Operations (1940–1942). Washington, D.C.: GPO, 1955.

Utah Beach to Cherbourg. Washington, D.C.: GPO, 1947.

WORLD WAR II CAMPAIGN COMMEMORATIVE PAMPHLETS PUBLISHED FOR THE CENTER OF MILITARY HISTORY BY THE GPO BETWEEN 1991 AND 1995

Algeria-French Morocco 8 November 1942–11 November 1942.

Ardennes-Alsace.

Central Europe.

Naples-Foggia.

Normandy.

Northern France.

Rhineland.

Sicily.

OTHER ARMY STAFF AND FIELD COMMAND PUBLISHED DOCUMENTS

Army Industrial College. *The German War Economy.* Washington, D.C.: 29 October 1945.

Brownlee, Ronnie L., and William J. Mullin III. *Changing an Army: An Oral History of General William E. DePuy, USA Retired.* Carlisle Barracks, Pa.: U.S. Army Military History Institute, n.d.

Committee 15, Officer's Advanced Course, The Armored School. *The 10th US Armored Division in the Saar-Moselle Triangle.* Fort Knox, Ky.: 1949.

Conn, Stetson. *Highlights of Mobilization, World War II: 1938–1942.* Washington, D.C.: 10 March 1959. U.S. Army Center of Military History, file 2-3.7AF.B1.

Doubler, Michael D. *Busting the Bocage: American Combined Arms Operations in France, 6 June–31 July 1944.* Fort Leavenworth, Kans.: Combat Studies Institute, 1988.

Gabel, Christopher R. *The Lorraine Campaign: An Overview, September–December 1944.* Fort Leavenworth, Kans.: Combat Studies Institute, 1985.

_____. *Seek, Strike, and Destroy: U.S. Army Tank Destroyer Doctrine in World War II.* Fort Leavenworth, Kans.: Combat Studies Institute, 1985.

Headquarters, Army Ground Forces. *Army Ground Forces Study No. 15: The Desert Training Center and CAMA.* Washington, D.C.: 1946.

Headquarters, Army Ground Forces. *Statistical Data.* Washington, D.C., 31 August 1945.

Headquarters, 12th Army Group. *Report of Operations,* 12 vols. Germany, n.d.

Headquarters, First U.S. Army. *Report of Operations 20 October 1943–1 August 1944.*

_____. *Report of Operations, 1 August 1944–22 February 1945.*

_____. *Report of Rhine River Crossings, May 1945.* Germany, 1945.

Headquarters, V Corps. *V Corps Operations in the ETO 6 January 1942–9 May 1945.*

Headquarters, XX Corps. *History of the XX Corps Artillery.* Germany, 1945.

_____. *Operational Report: The Capture of the Saar-Moselle Triangle and the Capture of Trier.* Germany, 1945.

Historical Section, G-4. Communications Zone, European Theater of Operations. *Outline of Operation Overlord.* Center of Military History file number 8-3.4 AA, v.7.

Historical Section, European Theater of Operations. *Small Unit Study 8: Attack on Singling by Elements, 4th Armored Division*. 1945.

Keast, William R. *Army Ground Forces Study No. 32: Major Developments in the Training of Enlisted Replacements*. Washington, D.C., 1946.

_____. *Army Ground Forces Study No. 7: Provision of Enlisted Replacements*. Washington, D.C., 1946.

King, Michael J. *Rangers: Selected Combat Operations in World War II*. Fort Leavenworth, Kans.: Combat Studies Institute, 1985.

Office of the Theater Historian, European Theater of Operations. *Order of Battle, United States Army in World War II: European Theater of Operations*. December 1945.

Robertson, George R. *Conversations with Gen. William M. Hoge (Ret.)*. U.S. Army Military History Institute Senior Officer's Debriefing Program, Carlisle Barracks, Pa.: 1974.

United States Strategic Bombing Survey. *The Impact of the Allied Air Effort on German Logistics*. 2d ed. Washington, D.C.: January 1947.

U.S. Army Armor School. *The Defense of St. Vith, Belgium, 17–23 December 1944*. Fort Knox, Ky.: 1948.

U.S. Army War College. *Case Study: Operation Overlord*. 5 vols. Carlisle Barracks, Pa.: 1990–1992.

U.S. Military Academy. *The War in Western Europe, Part 2 (December 1944–May 1945)*. Washington, D.C.: GPO, 1949.

MISCELLANEOUS

Records of the Joint Chiefs of Staff, European Theater of Operations, 1942–1945, Microfilm collection, U.S. Army Library, Pentagon.

Public Law 35, 64th Cong., 1st Sess.

Public Law 242, 66th Cong., 2d Sess.

Public Law 783, 76th Cong., 3d Sess.

Headquarters, 21 (British) Army Group. *The Administrative History of the Operations of 21 Army Group on the Continent of Europe 6 June 1944–8 May 1945*. Germany, November 1945.

Interviews

Interview with Gen. John R. Deane Jr. (Ret.), Fort Myer, Va., January 9, 1996.

Interview with Mrs. Shirley L. McCreary, Gettysburg, Pa., October 1997.

Interviews with Col. D. E. Nash, Washington, D.C., 5 May 2005; 5 September 2006.

Interview with Col. Richard Ripple (Ret.), Vossenack, Germany, September 15, 1994.
Interview with Lt. Col. George P. Whitman, (Ret.) Dumfries, Va., June 15, 1996.
Interview with Lt. Gen. Frank A. Camm (Ret.), Arlington, Va., February 1996.

Correspondence

Anderman, Russell.
Boyd, William.
Burd, Neil.
Calhoiun, Samuel.
Clement, Wallace.
Dunfree, Howard
Eames, Warren B.
Edwards, Norman B.
Fleig, Raymond E.
Gabel, Christopher R.
Herlihy, Raymond.
Hostrup, Bruce M.
Hricik, Robert.
Klawiter, Raymond.
McIlwain, Walter.
Martin, O. C.
Miller, Douglas.
Nash, Douglas E.
Schaefer-Kehnert, Walther.
Sloboda, Thomas.
Stephens, Frank.
Sullivan, R. P.
Thayer, Stuart.
Thieme, Karl.
Travelstead, Lee.
Walker, Chester.
Warner, Donald A. Jr.
Whittaker, Arnold.
Wyant, Vernon.
Gombosi, Louis, correspondence with W. N. McIlwain, author's collection.
Herlihy, Raymond, correspondence with W. N. McIlwain, author's collection.
Wilkins, Edmond C., correspondence with Mary E. Wilkins, author's collection.

Unpublished Papers and Manuscripts

Babcock, John B. "World War II as It Really Was." Ithaca, N.Y., 1993.

Bigart, Robert J. "The Operations of the 1st Battalion, 309th Infantry (78th Infantry Division) in the Attack on the Schwammenauel Dam, Southeast of Schmidt, Germany, 9–10 February 1945." Fort Benning, Ga., 1949.

Brown, Bobbie E. "The Operations of Company C, 18th Infantry (1st Inf. Div.) in the Attack on Crucifix Hill, 8 October 1944 (Rhineland Campaign) (Aachen Offensive)." Fort Benning, Ga., 1947.

Brown, John S. *Winning Teams: Mobilization-Related Correlates of Success in American World War II Infantry Divisions.* Master's thesis, U.S. Army Command and General Staff College, 1985.

Burrows, Emmet J. "The Operations of Company A, 27th Armored Infantry Battalion (9th Armored Division) in the Seizure of the Remagen Bridgehead, 7–8 March 1945." Fort Benning, Ga., 1950.

Calhoun, Mark. T. *Defeat at Kasserine: American Armor Doctrine, Training, and Battle Command in Northwest Africa, World War II.* Master's thesis, U.S. Army Command and General Staff College, 2003.

Daubin, Freeland Jr. "The Battle of Happy Valley." U.S. Army Armor School Advanced Officer's Class 1, Fort Knox, Ky., 24 April 1948.

Hazen, David W. *The Role of Field Artillery in the Battle of Kasserine Pass.* Master's thesis, U.S. Army Command and General Staff College, 1963.

Johnson, Richard B. Reminiscences, completed December 1976.

McGregor, Edward W. "The Operations of the 1st Battalion, 18th Infantry (1st Infantry Division) in the Vicinity of Crucifix Hill, Northeast of Aachen, Germany, October 1944." Fort Benning, Ga.

Pierce, Wayne. "Normandy! Let's Go! My First 60 Hrs." Unpublished recollections, 1989.

Rush, Robert S. "Germans Facing the Twenty Second in Hürtgen," 1997.

Orlando Ward Papers, box 1, U.S. Army Military History Institute, Carlisle Barracks, Pa.

Clifford Henley, World War II diary prepared about 1973.

Unpublished Operational Documents from Units in the Field

[The author's collection contains copies of all cited operational documents. However, they are also available in National Archives, Record Group 407. Specific documents footnoted in the text are not cited individually unless necessary for clarification. Combat interviews are listed by number, and many have attached copies of operational records as well. The VII Corps records are particularly complete and contain copies of many First Army and 12th Army Group documents.]

Combat Interview 4, 1st Infantry Division, Battle of Aachen.

Combat Interview 33, 4th Infantry Division, Siegfried Line (Schnee-Eifel Sector).

Combat Interview 39, 5th Infantry Division, Fort Driant Operations.

Combat Interview 65, 17th Airborne Division, Ardennes.

Combat Interview 73, 28th Infantry Division, Kesfeld Area.

Combat Interviews 74–77, 28th Infantry Division, Hurtgen Forest.

Combat Interview 97, 99, 30th Infantry Division, Siegfried Line (Aachen Area).

Combat Interview 142, 148, 78th Infantry Division, Hurtgen Forest, Roer River Dams.

Combat Interview 170, 82d Airborne Division, Normandy.

Combat Interview 203, 94th Infantry Division, Saar-Moselle Triangle.

Combat Interview 241, 104th Infantry Division, Eschweiler-Duren Sector.

Combat Interview 273, 4th Armored Division, Lorraine Campaign.

Combat Interviews 299–300, 9th Armored Division, Roer to Rhine, Remagen.

Combat Interview 306, 10th Armored Division, Saar-Moselle Triangle and Trier.

Combat Interview 336, 5th Ranger Battalion, Action near Zerf.

Combat Interview 340, III Corps, Remagen Bridgehead.

Combat Interview 365, XX Corps, European Operations.

European Theater of Operations. "Notes from Normandy." No. 27, 5 July 1944.

1st Infantry Division. "Selected Intelligence Reports." Vol. I, "June 1944–November 1944." Germany, 6 December 1944.

V Corps. "Summary of the Operations of the 28th Infantry Division for the Period 2–15 November 1944." 18 November 1944.

Memorandum from G-3 12th Army Group to Chief of Staff, 12th Army Group, 18 October 1944.

XIX Corps. "Breaching the Siegfried Line (Germany 1944)."

Records of the G-3, V Corps, September–November 1944.

Records of the G-2, VII Corps, June–December 1944.

Records of the G-3, VII Corps, June–December 1944.

Records of the G-2, 1st Infantry Division, October–December 1944.

Records of the G-3, 1st Infantry Division, October–December 1944.

Records of the S-3, 18th Infantry Regiment, October–December 1944.

Records of the G-3, 4th Infantry Division, May–December 1944.

Records of the S-1, 22d Infantry Regiment, September–December 1944.

Records of the S-3, 22d Infantry Regiment, September–December 1944.

Records of the S-3, 109th Infantry Regiment, September–December 1944.

Records of the S-3, 112th Infantry Regiment, November–December 1944.

Records of the G-3, 82d Airborne Division, May–July 1944.

Records of the G-3, 78th Infantry Division.

Records of the S-3, 309th Infantry Regiment.

Records of the S-3, 310th Infantry Regiment.

Records of the S-3, 311th Infantry Regiment.

Records of the G-3, 104th Infantry Division, November–December 1944.

Records of the S-3, 707th Tank Battalion, October–November 1944.

Records of the S-3, 5th Ranger Battalion, February 1945.

William C. Sylvan. Diary. Combined Arms Research Library.

INDEX